D1607548

Antitrust, the Market, and the State

Walter Adams earned his undergraduate degree from Brooklyn College in 1942, where he was Phi Beta Kappa and Adam Smith Gold Medalist, and his doctorate from Yale University in 1947. Professor of economics at Michigan State University from 1947 until 1992, he also served as president of the University, and was awarded the rank of Distinguished University Professor. He has taught at the Universities of Paris, Lyon, Grenoble and Ancona, the Salzburg and Falkenstein Seminars, and the Industrial College of the Armed Forces. He also has been R.J. Reynolds Professor of Economics at Wake Forest University, and Vernon F. Taylor Distinguished Professor of Economics at Trinity University in San Antonio, Texas. He was appointed to presidential commissions during the Eisenhower, Kennedy, and Johnson administrations, including the Attorney General's Committee to Study the Antitrust Laws (1953–1955), and has served as consultant and expert witness before numerous congressional committees. Past president of the American Association of University Professors, the Midwest Economics Association, and the Association for Social Economics, he holds several honorary degrees, including Doctor of Humane Letters from Brooklyn College.

Antitrust, the Market, and the State

The Contributions of Walter Adams

James W. Brock and Kenneth G. Elzinga
Editors

M.E. Sharpe, Inc.
Armonk, New York
London, England

Library of Congress Cataloging-in-Publication Data

Antitrust, the market, and the state : the contributions of Walter Adams /
edited by James W. Brock and Kenneth G. Elzinga.
p. cm.
Includes bibliographical references.
ISBN 0-87332-854-X.—ISBN 0-87332-855-8 (pbk.)
1. Adams, Walter, 1922–   —Contributions in trade regulation.
2. Trade regulation—United States.
3. Big business—United States.
4. Competition—United States.
5. Antitrust law—United States.
I. Brock, James W.
II. Elzinga, Kenneth G.
HD3612.A32A56   1991
338.8'0973—dc20
90-32017
CIP

Printed in the United States of America

The paper used in this publication meets the minimum requirements
of American National Standard for Information Sciences—
Permanence of Paper for Printed Library Materials, ANSI Z39.48-1984.

MV   10   9   8   7   6   5   4   3   2   1

To Walter Adams

il miglior fabbro

Contents

Foreword

This book collects some choice fruits from a sturdy tree whose roots are firmly implanted in the soil of the late eighteenth century. Or to alter the metaphor, Walter Adams marches behind the banner of two eighteenth-century prophets. One is Adam Smith. Adams's mentor is not the Adam Smith of special interest pleaders, but the Smith who believed passionately in both competition and the need for a compassionate, ethical climate of rules within which competitive market processes could advance the public good. Too few present-day Smithians remember that Adam Smith wrote *The Theory of Moral Sentiments* as well as *The Wealth of Nations*. Adams's other prophet is Publius of the *Federalist Papers,* and in particular, James Madison, who taught that unless both political and economic power remained dispersed, factional interests would "concert and carry into effect schemes of oppression" against the common good.

The essays by Adams in this volume examine the relevance of Smithian and Madisonian doctrine to the American economy of the twentieth century. Adams challenges the popular argument that a wide dispersion of power is no longer feasible because economies of scale require business organizations to be of gargantuan size, or because technological innovation, success in international trade, and economic stability can come only from powerful corporations protected against the gales of domestic and foreign competition. The work reprinted here—for example, on the failure of large steel makers to adopt the basic oxygen process expeditiously; on the apparent absence of socially beneficial efficiencies from petroleum companies' vertical integration; on the inflationary pricing propensities in the auto and steel industries during the late 1950s (that led to serious problems two decades later); and on the inefficiency of major defense contractors—comprise a small but significant fraction of Adams's contribution to our understanding of how the American industrial economy functions. At least as important has been his service as general editor of *The Structure of American Industry*, now available in its eighth edition.

Adams argues that market processes can fail, sometimes badly, when economic power becomes excessively concentrated. Like Publius, he is aware that governmental processes can also fail, especially when they are bombarded by well-organized interest groups. Long before the "public choice" school in economics made its mark, Adams warned that governmental regulatory commissions were susceptible to "capture" by the private entities they regulated. He saw too that such commissions had acquired "an anticompetitive bias, a bureaucratic rigidity, an annoyance with the forces of change." As a remedy, he recommended the promotion of competition "to the maximum extent practicable," including a regulatory presumption *in favor of* competitive entry unless a heavy burden of proof to the contrary was borne. His 1958 *American Economic Review* analysis of the air transport and trucking industries was prophetic of the deregulation that came two decades later.

Although competition has been revived in some traditionally regulated industries, the 1980s witnessed a sharp resurgence of another Adams *bête noire*—governmental protection of domestic industries from foreign competition. My favorite story from that milieu is not in the Adams collection, but it is too laden with Adamsian paradox not to be told. During the early 1980s, U.S. timber and lumber interests sought from the government protection from Canadian lumber imports. Their claim was that the Canadian provincial governments were collecting too little "rent" for the trees sawn into lumber. In this they studiously ignored the teachings of Adam Smith's follower, David Ricardo, on the allocative irrelevance of rent collection. Ignored too was Adam Smith's own observation that, "in many parts of North America the landlord would be much obliged to any body who would carry away the greater part of his large trees." Officials of a U.S. government whose leaders wore Adam Smith neckties rejected Smith's insights and compelled the imposition of restrictions that increased appreciably the cost of lumber used to build shelter for the American public.

Fashions have changed in the economics profession, as in public service. Kudos go now to mathematical virtuosity, not to work that displays an instinct for the factual and philosophical jugular. But being fashionable, Walter Adams has shown repeatedly, is not the same thing as stating the durable truth. Readers young and old can benefit from reading the lessons collected here.

F.M. Scherer
Harvard University
Cambridge, Massachusetts

Preface

I first met Walter Adams in the early 1950s. But before I actually met him in person, I had learned something very important about him. I was a graduate student at the University of Illinois, studying with Horace Gray, one of the senior professors in the Economics Department, and coauthor, with Adams, of *Monopoly in America*. One summer Professor Gray and Mrs. Gray very kindly offered to let my wife and me house-sit for them while they were away from campus. On an evening in late spring, just prior to their leaving Urbana, the Grays invited us over to be sure we were familiar with the house and everything for which we would be responsible. While Mrs. Gray and my wife talked in the kitchen, Professor Gray introduced me to his library. In the course of the evening he talked more candidly and more personally than he typically did on campus. He spoke especially of his concern for the independence of faculty colleagues in economics around the country, particularly those who taught and did research in the areas of monopoly and competition, the regulated industries, and antitrust. He was bothered by corporate behavior that ranged from entertainment and other favorable treatment to the creation of attractive financial opportunities, and what he viewed as the subtle, and sometimes not so subtle, efforts to co-opt those in the discipline who dealt with industry structure, antitrust, the regulatory process, and government's relation to business. After citing in some detail a number of specific examples of individuals and situations he considered anywhere from naive and inappropriate on the one hand, to flagrant and sellouts to special interests on the other, he came to Walter Adams. "Adams is different," he said. "Adams is absolutely incorruptible."

Not too long after that, Professor Gray had occasion to introduce me to his coauthor. He made no further reference to his personal opinion of Adams then or later, but rather left me to affirm for myself the validity of his view of Professor Adams's incorruptibility, as well as his respect for Adams as a scholar and teacher.

Over the years that followed, I came in contact with Adams and his career of antitrust scholarship and activism in many ways. I was assistant counsel to the Senate Antitrust Subcommittee at a time when Adams was a frequent consultant to and expert witness testifying before congressional committees. I have studied his work and used his writings as assigned readings in courses I have taught in economics and law. I was a university president deeply involved in governance issues when he served as national president of the American Association of University Professors. Later, I served as president of Michigan State University, an office Adams had previously held. We are now colleagues in the Economics Department at Michigan State, and I frequently have former students of his in my classes. In each of these relationships, I have had a different view of Walter Adams, seeing his work, his ideas, and his values from a different vantage point. (I sometimes think that the clearest picture one can get of a fellow faculty member comes from knowing well the students he has taught.) What emerges for me, from all these different perspectives and various relationships, is an image of Walter Adams as a man of quintessential integrity, a highly productive scholar, a master teacher, and an activist vitally concerned with all aspects of his discipline and of academia. Above all, a man totally committed to the fight for economic freedom.

Adams's interests, his concerns, and his work are, in the truest sense, interdisciplinary, bringing together considerations of economics, law, and public policy. His primary focus has always been on power—economic power and political power—its aggregation, its abuse, and its potential for harm. Never one to mince words, he directs our attention to the evils of monopoly and the corrupting influences of special interest groups. As he indicated early in his writings, his concern is not with monopoly so much in its narrow, technical, dictionary sense, but rather in a broader sense, denoting an industry situation where a single firm or a small group of firms possesses substantial economic power. Not only is he concerned about the existence of monopoly, he is offended by special privilege and objects particularly to government actions that so often establish, strengthen, or consolidate monopoly power.

In the most straightforward terms, Adams emphasizes the relationships of political and economic power, urges us to confront the problem of how to control them both, and proposes specific means for dealing with the issues at hand. His intellectual and philosophical roots go back to Henry Simons and Adam Smith in economics, and to Thomas Jefferson in politics and the law. Throughout his career he has been concerned with structure—the structure of government and the structure of industry.

Just as "it is the structure of government, not the personal preferences and predilections of those who govern, that is of paramount importance," so, also, for Adams, it is the structure of the economic system—the structure of industry, rather than the personal preferences and predilections of those who wield economic power—that is of paramount importance. What Adams has opposed is the consolidation or concentration of economic power. What he has favored and fought for is the diffusion and distribution of economic power. He is firm in the belief he shares with Henry Simons that "The concentration of power is inherently dangerous and degrading," and that it "militates against good economic performance." Adams concludes that, "in the final analysis, economic power, and the problems it poses, are primarily structural in nature," fundamentally rooted in disproportionate size. He has never been convinced that great size is imperative for the optimal utilization of modern technology or the attainment of efficiency in mass production industries.

Writing of Robert Malthus in *Essays in Biography*, Keynes says:

> If only Malthus, instead of Ricardo, had been the parent stem from which nineteenth-century economics proceeded, what a wiser and richer place the world would be today! We have laboriously to return and force through the obscuring envelopes of our misguided education what should never have ceased to be obvious.

In the same spirit, it is appropriate to say, "If only Adams had been the parent stem from which antitrust policy in the second half of the twentieth century had proceeded!" The world would, indeed, be a wiser and richer place. In addition, U.S. industry would have much less need for restructuring, and would be far better positioned to meet the challenges of international markets and the globalization of production and finance. The welcome and timely publication of this collection of Walter Adams's writings dealing with the economic, legal, and public policy aspects of antitrust affords us the opportunity to reaffirm and reassert what should never have ceased to be obvious concerning the evils of monopoly and the benefits of free competition.

Cecil Mackey
Michigan State University
East Lansing, Michigan

I

Fundamentals

1

Corporate Giantism, Ethics, and the Public Interest

Toward the turn of the century, in that Gilded Age which Walt Whitman called "cankered, crude, superstitious, and rotten," in that era of "flippant people with hearts of rags and souls of chalk," Lincoln Steffens reported on the ethics of city government. He found that everything the cities owned—rights, privileges, franchises, and real property—was subject to sale by the people's elected representatives. Boodling and corruption were widespread, and their source was at the top, not the bottom of society.

In St. Louis, said Steffens, "with few exceptions, no ordinance has been passed wherein valuable privileges or franchises are granted until those interested have paid the legislators the money demanded for action in the particular case. Combines in both branches of the Municipal Assembly are formed by members sufficient in number to control legislation. To one member of this combine is delegated the authority to act for the combine, and to receive and to distribute to each member the money agreed upon as the price of his vote in support of, or opposition to, a pending measure. So long has this practice existed that such members have come to regard the receipt of money for action on pending measures as a legitimate perquisite of a legislator."[1] In Pittsburgh, the machine's idea "was not to corrupt the city government, but to be it; not to hire votes in councils; but to own councilmen."[2] In other cities, the pattern was substantially the same.

Most appalling about this corruption, according to Steffens, was that it involved "not thieves, gamblers, and common women, but influential citizens, capitalists, and great corporations."[3] The big business man, he found, was "buying boodlers in St. Louis, defending grafters in Minneapolis, originating corruption in Pittsburgh, sharing with bosses in Philadelphia, deploring reform in

---

Originally published in the *Review of Social Economy*, vol. 21 (March 1963); reprinted with permission.

Chicago, and beating good government with corruption funds in New York. He is a self-righteous fraud, this big business man," Steffens concluded. "He is the chief source of corruption, and it were a boon if he would neglect politics."[4]

Of course, the big business man was active not only in the government sector of the economy, but also in the private sector. While railroads and gas companies were buying valuable rights-of-way and franchises, free-wheeling, swashbuckling buccaneers were building industrial empires. In tobacco and oil, steel and agricultural machinery, enterprising, visionary architects were constructing trusts, consolidations, and holding companies. In an era of unrestrained, unregulated, rambunctious laissez-faire—when the umpire was trained only to look the other way—it is not surprising that the rules of sportsmanship and fair play were observed mainly in the breach. There were empires to be built, and the robber barons built them by fair means and foul. As the Supreme Court later found, the Tobacco Trust achieved its pre-eminence by such techniques as local price discrimination, fighting brands, bogus independents, exclusive and preclusive dealer arrangements, brand imitation, coupon and premium systems, abstention-from-competition agreements, and the utilization of monopoly profits to eliminate independents.[5] To this and other trusts of the time, the objective of the competitive game was the euthanasia of competitors.

To be sure, there was an ennobling purpose behind this process. From pulpit and rostrum, in the success literature and academic liturgy, contemporary apologists explained how rugged individualism was consistent with the laws of God and nature, the process of natural selection, and the mechanics of deterministic inevitability. In the lexicon of Social Darwinism, the status quo was endowed with sacrosanct qualities, and its maintenance justified in philanthropic terms. According to the gospel of the times, as articulated by Andrew Carnegie, the man of wealth was under obligation "to set an example of modest, unostentatious living, shunning display and extravagance" and after providing for his own needs "to consider all surplus revenues which come to him simply as trust funds, which he is called upon to administer." The man of wealth, said Carnegie, must serve as "the mere agent and trustee for his poorer brethren, bringing to their service his superior wisdom, experience, and ability to administer, doing for them better than they would or could do for themselves."[6] This naturalistic version of the Puritan code of worldly asceticism—this Pauline doctrine of stewardship—found spiritual reinforcement in the observation of Bishop William Lawrence that ". . . in the long run, it is only to the man of morality that wealth comes. . . . Godliness is in league with riches."[7] No wonder that Carnegie presumed to speak, not for an economic class, but for an entire generation.

The Corporate "Soul"

It is both comic and tragic that, in our own day, the apologetic of managerialism is still anchored on this notion of stewardship and conscience as an ameliorator of great power. As most executives, cosmeticized by modern law or business schools, will readily explain, the age of the robber barons is gone. Their carnivorous instinct is civilized by the appearance of a social conscience—that delightful and ethereal fiction which Mr. Berle calls the corporate soul. The modern executive, we are told, is no longer animated by the archaic drive for profits; instead, he is conscious of his multiple responsibilities to the secular trinity of stockholders, workers, and consumers. In a pluralistic society, he quite appropriately has come to be possessed of a "plural" soul. As Morris Sayre, former president of the Corn Products Refining Company, put it: "An active social conscience . . . and individual recognition of social responsibilities will compel us, as individuals, to test every managerial practice, measure every policy by a single yardstick. Not 'what does it mean for me' but rather 'what will this mean to my workers as people, to my customers, to my suppliers, to my stockholders, to the community in which my plant is located, to my government, to the industry of which I am a part, to the economy as a whole?'"[8]

A.A. Berle, Jr., modern high priest of the stewardship principle, argues as follows: if only there were "a keeper of conscience, to whom appeal can be made, by whom inquiry and a fair hearing must be provided, and from whom a humanely fair decision can be had," the present concentration of economic power would not only be tolerable but workable. The corporate conscience could then function in our economy much like the royal or baronial conscience did in feudal times. It was in the 11th century, Mr. Berle reminds us, that Duke Rollo, the Northman, showed "statesmanship enough to see that justice must go with power." He made it a practice, therefore, to go "in person from place to place in Normandy, directly that all who had suffered wrong at the hand of his neighbor, or even from the Duke himself, should cry, 'Ha! Rollo!' whereupon the Duke [had to] listen to his cause, deciding it according to the law of God and good conscience." Under this system, the power of the sovereign and his lords was never disputed, but decisions were based on "conceptions of right, and morality, and justice," as well as on power. "From these even the king was not exempt."[9] Could not the corporate conscience be an equally effective check on the admittedly gargantuan power of collective enterprises, industrial concentrates, and oligarchical holdings?

No detailed recitation of concentration statistics is necessary to brand this view as Kafkaesque fantasy. The doctrine, however generously one may choose to interpret it, still suffers from rather obvious and fatal defects. (1) The corporate soul, at best, is a permissive rather than compulsive control mechanism. It allows for such wide discretion as to accommodate the broadest spectrum of managerial choices. It permits action in the public interest; it does not systematically and predictably compel it. Unlike the invisible hand of Adam Smith or the heavy hand of government, it does not provide an organizing principle for social decision making. It tells no one what society wants done—what goods should be produced, in what quantities, with what techniques, and for whose consumption.

In short, it does not solve the problem of allocating society's resources in accordance with society's preference scales. (2) The corporate soul offers no meaningful and practical *economic* guidelines. What should possessors of great market power like U.S. Steel, General Motors, or du Pont do with it? Labor wants higher wages, fringe benefits, and uninterrupted employment. Customers want fair, low, equitable, non-discriminatory prices and uninterrupted production. Stockholders want incentive-producing, i.e. higher, profits. The White House wants high production, full employment, stable prices, remunerative wages, and healthy profits. The management, in soulful contemplation, is admonished to promote equity, stability, and progress. The result, says Ben W. Lewis, is that "management—as allocator, distributor, stabilizer, trustee, conservator, prophet and chaplain, as well as manager—consults its *conscience*. The diagnosis of the attending psychiatrist will be 'multiple schizophrenia'—the management's personality will not be split, it will be shredded and powdered!"[10] (3) The corporate soul offers no meaningful and practical *ethical* guidelines. In the modern economy which is a highly interdependent network of large bureaucratic organizations, and the diffusion of personal responsibility that goes with it, how are the Ten Commandments to be made a living reality? How is a code of conduct, covering the intensely personal relationship of man with his God, and man's social relationships in groups no larger than a family and an area no wider than a neighborhood—how is such a code to be made a guideline for Organization Man? "Granted," as Tawney observed, "that I should love my neighbor as myself, the questions which, under modern conditions of large-scale organization, remain for solution are, Who precisely *is* my neighbor? and, How exactly am I to make my love for him effective in practice?"[11] (4) The corporate soul is at odds both with the Calvinist and Catholic conceptions of man. In the Calvinist view, original sin has left man totally and hopelessly depraved; he is incapable of goodness, or of influencing to the slightest degree by good works his election or reprobation. He may be saved to virtue but not by virtue. He is an abominable creature in the eyes of God—unworthy of trust, discretion, or authority. In the Catholic view, man inherits Original Sin, and though this guilt may be removed by the sacrament of baptism, he is still left with the *reliquiae peccati* (the remnants of sin). Even baptism, therefore, does not remove man's concupiscence—his disposition to sin.[12] Either view, I think, points to the conclusion that where power is great, temptation strong, incentives enticing, and sanctions feeble, man's predisposition to corruption—to sin, if you please—will assert itself. And this makes it important that such power be under strict and effective control. (5) The corporate soul does not grapple with the question of responsibility and accountability. How and by whom are its possessors anointed? To whom are they accountable? How can they be punished for non-feasance or malfeasance? Put differently, if justice is to depend on someone shouting "Ha! Rollo!," to whom shall the cry be addressed and how is the addressee to be chosen? What if Rollo cannot hear or refuses to hear? How can he be forced to listen? How can he be forced to act? In a democracy, these questions cannot be left unanswered. (6) The corporate soul, finally, is just one of several proposals for dealing with concentrated power. Its efficacy must be measured in comparison with alternative solutions before it is embraced as a safeguard of the public interest.

The Corporate "Soul" in Action

Two recent examples should illustrate the ephemeral nature of the corporate soul as a mechanism for controlling power and safeguarding the public interest.

The "Regulated" Sector

The first, involving the award of Channel 10, Miami, by the Federal Communications Commission, deals with the regulated sector of the economy. It demonstrates that where government is the dispenser of valuable rights, the incentives and proclivities for corruption are as strong today as in the days of Lincoln Steffens. The facts of this case—as revealed by a Congressional Committee, a federal circuit court, and later by the Commission itself[13]—indicate that at least one member of the Commission should have disqualified himself from ruling in the case; that various applicants for Channel 10 "influenced or attempted to influence" a member of the Commission; that these applicants "directly or indirectly secured, aided, confirmed, ratified, or knew of . . . misconduct or improprieties in connection with the proceedings";[14] in short, that the case involved a "corrupt tampering with the adjudicatory process itself."[15] Commissioner Mack, later indicted for bribery for his role in this case, was approached by men who knew him since boyhood, who were credited with having gotten him into a fraternity, and who supported him in past political campaigns. One was a vice president of the Florida Power and Light Company, another an ex-Mayor of Miami who had recommended him for a State regulatory post, another the Chairman of the Florida Railroad and Public Utility Commission, another a lifelong friend who had made interest-free loans to him payable on demand. Two were U.S. Senators who had sponsored Mack for appointment to the F.C.C. Despite the surreptitious efforts of these men "to influence an official charged with the duty of deciding contested issues upon an open record in accord with basic principles of our jurisprudence,"[16] however, Commissioner Mack did not disqualify himself from the proceedings. On the contrary, he ignored these improprieties which "eat at the very heart of our system of government—due process, fair play, open proceedings, unbiased, uninfluenced decision."[17] (How different his conduct from that of Lord Chief Justice Coke who shortly after his appointment to the bench in 1606 told his friends and neighbors: "It is true that I purpose as I must, to take my leave of you all, and to be a stranger to my dearest friends and nearest Allies. I must forget all former friendships, and my most familiar Acquaintance. . . . To keep my conscience clear, I must with equitie and uprightness, justly administer justice unto you all."[18]) No wonder that in the final disposition of the Channel 10 case, it was decided that "all the representations privately made to Mack . . . were grossly improper" and that in adversary proceedings before federal agencies, Commissioners "should be bound by the same legal, ethical, and professional rules as those by which judges are governed. . . . And one of the most constant and immutable of those rules is that communications to a judge designed to influence his judicial action are forbidden in pending proceedings, whether such communications be written or oral, except on notice to all other interested parties, with full opportunity to reply if in writing or to be present if oral."[19]

Unfortunately, the Channel 10 case is not unique—either in the television or other regulated industries.[20] The record is replete with evidence of an accommodation of views between the regulated and their regulators—an accommodation which, in its mildest form, results in subordination of the public interest to private privilege, and, in its most virulent form, in influence peddling and corruption. In the most recent past, the Committee on Legislative Oversight found, federal commissioners have engaged in constant fraternization with individuals and corporations who appear as litigants before their agency. Some have had their room, board, and other expenses paid by the regulated industry while attending industry conventions. Some have made it a practice to permit ex parte, off-the-public-record discussions with litigants in pending cases and allowed reference to the merits of these cases. In short, regulatory commissions have operated in a milieu conducive to the discrimination, restrictionism, protectionism, and privilege creation which have almost become the hallmark of the regulatory process. Impropriety may well be so widespread as to justify the charge that in the regulated industries, "regulatees wind up doing the regulating."

The "Free" Sector

My second example, taken from the private sector of the economy, indicates that here, too, the corporate soul has not yet achieved ubiquity. I refer, of course, to the great electrical conspiracy—involving 20 separate indictments, naming 29 corporate and 59 individual defendants, and resulting in fines of $1,924,500, seven outright jail sentences and several suspended jail sentences. This was the most pervasive and comprehensive conspiracy ever tried under the antitrust laws, and the greatest challenge to industrial image management in recent annals of public relations.[21]

The law in question, the Sherman Act, was clear. It provides that "every contract, combination, or conspiracy . . . in restraint of trade . . . is hereby declared to be illegal." The interpretation of the law was also clear—ever since 1898, when Circuit Judge William Howard Taft announced that any collective action among competitors with respect to prices and terms of sale shall be considered a *per se* violation of the Act.[22] Nor was there any doubt about industry's understanding of this portion of the antitrust statutes. Long before the conspiracy was uncovered, the General Electric Company had made General Policy Directive 20.5 required reading for all its executive and managerial personnel. This directive stated clearly:

"It is the policy of the company to comply strictly in all respects with the antitrust laws. There shall be no exception to this policy nor shall it be compromised or qualified by anyone acting for or on behalf of the company.

"No employee shall enter into any understanding, agreement, plan or scheme, expressed or implied, formal or informal, with any competitor, in regard to prices, terms or conditions of sale, production, distribution, territories, or customers; nor exchange or discuss with a competitor prices, terms or conditions of sale, or any other competitive information; nor engage in any other conduct which in the opinion of the company's counsel violates any of the antitrust laws."

Nevertheless, in spite of the unmistakable clarity of the text of the law, the 60-year history of judicial interpretation, and an official company policy prohibiting violations, the conspiracy took place. It was a brazen, willful, conscious violation by men who, according to the Attorney General, were fully aware of the "wrongful nature of their deeds." These men conspired to fix prices and rig bids to government agencies and private utilities. They allocated markets according to pre-arranged formulas—including an ingenious phase-of-the-moon formula. They had frequent and periodic meetings in hotel rooms and hunting lodges. They telephoned each other at home, used plain envelopes without return addresses, used code numbers and first names in their communications, destroyed written communications upon receipt, etc.—all in an effort to avoid detection of what they knew was a pattern of unlawful conduct. They were not trapped into a random breach of the law; they were not victims of accidental circumstance;[23] many of them, as one Westinghouse official confessed, had been discussing prices with competitors for 25 years prior to the instant indictment.

These men, as one defense counsel told the court, were not "grasping, greedy, cut-throat competitors," but men of quality who devoted "a substantial part of their substance to their communities, to their fellow men." One, a Westinghouse vice president, was described by counsel as "active in his church, a senior warden, member of the Bishop's advisory group, and fund raiser"—a leader in the Community Cancer Society and the Crippled Children's Society. Another, a General Electric vice president, was described to the court as having taken "an active and responsible part in the civic and charitable life of the community. He headed the building drive of the new Jesuit novitiate in Lenox, Mass. He was treasurer of the St. Theresa's Church, member of the board of advisers of the College of St. Rose in Albany." The other defendants had similarly distinguished records of civic and religious virtue. They were mute testimonial to Professor Ross' generalization that "some of the dazzling careers of fraud have behind them long and reassuring records of probity."[24]

Obviously, these defendants did not fit the stereotype of the common criminal. Perhaps, they were merely organization men conforming to the ethical environment of their company and the mores of their industry. Undoubtedly, as Judge Ganey said, "they were torn between conscience and an approved corporate policy, with the rewarding objectives of promotion, comfortable security and large salaries—in short, the organization or company man, the conformist, who goes along with his superiors and finds balm for his conscience in additional comforts and the security of his place in the corporate set-up."[25] If, as the *Wall Street Journal* suggested, conformity required adherence to "a large-scale system of law evasion, they evidently conformed to that, too."[26]

Other explanations were offered for the admittedly unlawful conduct of the defendants. One attorney told the court that his client "knows now what he did was illegal; it was against the law." But, he added, "It was not illegal in the sense that it was criminal; it was criminal only because of this particular conspiracy under the Sherman Act, which makes certain types of business offenses a crime. . . ."[27] Defendants' actions would really have been quite legal and respectable, if only the Sherman Act had not prohibited them! Another conspirator, the president of Allen Bradley, was more aggressive. "No one attending the gatherings," he said, "was so stupid he didn't know [the meetings] were in violation of the law. But it is the only way a business can be run. It is free enterprise."[28] In this view, the antitrust laws were unjust, and constituted government interference with, and harassment of American business. Senator Dirksen could see little wrong with what defendants had done. "There was certainly not very much intrigue that was involved here at all. Here were typical American businessmen sitting down. Everybody was after business and the question was who was going to get it."[29] Mr. Cordiner, Board Chairman of General Electric, condemned the actions of his subordinates, but disclaimed all knowledge of the infractions. To him, the whole matter was one of "*individual* business ethics and morality."[30] Mr. Paxton, president of General Electric, admitted that he had heard occasional references to price fixing activities in the company. But, he told the Kefauver Committee, it was not his "custom to go around gossiping in the General Electric Company"; he did not report what he heard to his superiors because this would have been "tale bearing" and "womanish"—and hence "distasteful" to him.[31] On the whole, the top executives denied all knowledge and involvement, blaming the entire conspiracy on their delinquent subordinates. The latter, in turn, offered what might be called the Eichmann defense; they were merely following orders from on high.[32]

Perhaps, Judge Ganey offered the balanced view. In his opinion the individual defendants knew what they were doing. They may have wrestled with their conscience, but in the end they decided to be good organization men, willing conformists, and brazen mockers of the free enterprise system. Moreover, those in the highest echelons of the corporations involved in the conspiracy—though they were not defendants of record—bore "a grave responsibility." For, said

Judge Ganey, "one would be most naive indeed to believe that these violations of the law, so long persisted in, affecting so large a segment of the industry and finally, involving so many millions upon millions of dollars, were facts unknown to those responsible for the conduct of the corporations. . . ." One would have to be naive indeed to ignore the 39 antitrust proceedings in which General Electric alone had been involved since 1890, or to ignore the fact that 36 of these had occurred since 1941, or to ignore the fact that the company batting average shows a total of 29 convictions, 7 consent decrees, and 3 "adverse findings" by the F.T.C. The protestation of shocked innocence and betrayed virtue was simply not a believable image for General Electric and some of its co-conspirators. In this company and this industry, it would appear, the corporate soul had been anesthetized over a prolonged period of time.

One final comment on the case, and the reverberations left in its wake. Shortly after the convictions were announced by Judge Ganey, the American Management Association decided to call a conference on business ethics. It never took place. In a parallel effort, Luther Hodges, the Secretary of Commerce, assembled a Business Ethics Advisory Council "to help business fashion tools and programs to pursue the search for the highest ethical standards and to encourage businessmen to use them." This effort also came to nought. After some eight months of meetings and memoranda writing, the Council decided not to formulate a "business-wide code of ethics"—leaving the primary moral duty in this regard to boards of directors and top management of each individual enterprise.[33] There was some confusion apparently as to "Rollo's" proper assignment in the organizational structure of modern American industry. Only the Antitrust Division seemed prepared to offer an unmistakably clear guide to individual and corporate conduct: ". . . deliberate or conscious violation of the antitrust laws," said Judge Loevinger, Chief of the Antitrust Division, "is not a mere personal peccadillo or economic eccentricity, but a serious offense against society, which is as immoral as any other act that injures many in order to profit a few. Conspiracy to violate the antitrust laws is economic racketeering which gains no respectability by virtue of the fact that the loot is secured by stealth rather than by force."[34]

Some Guidelines for Public Policy

What, then, are the policy conclusions? What guide lines may be set down for a society transformed by the organizational revolution—where private concentrations of power are pervasive and where Government has become a dispenser of economic rights and privileges? What ethical principles have sufficient efficacy for curbing the power—sought or unsought—of a vast military–industrial complex?[35] How, under these conditions, is the public interest to be vouchsafed from perversion and corruption?

The art of economic statecraft, I submit, consists not only of promoting and encouraging individual ethics, but also—and more importantly—of fashioning an ethical system. The goal is an organizational framework which tends to channel individuals into socially desirable conduct by holding out strong incentives and threatening meaningful sanctions. The objective is a system which harnesses man's virtues and curbs his vices—a system built on the assumption, not of man's perfectibility or depravity, but of his concupiscence. Such a system would diffuse power and circumscribe individual discretion, so that man's proclivities and appetites cannot endanger the public interest.[36] It would guard against anti-social uses of great power by sterilizing it through an institutionalized set of checks and balances.

One such ethical system is the competitive market place. It is not a *bellum omnium contra omnes*. It is not an ecological equilibrium, a state of nature, in which the law of the jungle reigns supreme. Rather, it is a legal, ethical, institutional arrangement—an economic community under covenant—an arena where powerful forces collide, but in accordance with strictly prescribed and socially beneficent rules. In this arena, an individual may seek private gain; his motive may be to benefit neither his neighbor nor his community, but if the rules of the game are properly drawn, the individual seeking his and only his gain should be able to achieve this goal only by serving others as well. In this sense, the market is an organizing principle for coordinating individual activity—a planning mechanism which is autonomous, impartial, and external to human control, manipulation, and perversion. It is a mechanism for harnessing the individual to social ends, while depriving him of power so great that, if abused, it would result in harm to his fellows.[37]

Clearly, the competitive market as thus conceived does not mean laissez-faire. It does not mean individual immunity from social control. On the contrary, it calls for regulations and means for their enforcement. Just as organized football requires a gridiron of given dimensions and teams of prescribed size; just as there are rules against clipping, roughing the kicker, ineligible receivers downfield, and backfield in motion; just as there are referees, umpires, and head linesmen to enforce these rules, so the market must have institutional devices to protect its integrity and assure its efficacy. While the umpire may not dictate to a team whether to call for a line plunge or a forward pass, while he may not interfere with the managerial discretion of the quarterback, he must limit that discretion to permissible bounds. He must confine it to the prescribed general rules—so as to preserve the game and assure the purpose for which it is played. Doubtless, the game might be played under different rules—with no holds barred, for example—but this presumably would not accord with the purpose of the contest. It would not produce the desired results. It might destroy the most valuable prize—the game itself.

The market, then, is built around rules, man-made rules, to serve society's ends. It gives the individual great freedom, but for society's sake more so than for his own. It is, on the one hand, a device for limiting and civilizing individual power and, on the other, a means of cooperation and coordination for interdependent individual activity. While it is designed around the principle of individual freedom, it is as freedom under law. It recognizes, with Adam Smith, that "Those exertions of the natural liberty of a few individuals which might endanger the security of the whole society, are, and ought to be restrained by the laws of all governments; of the most free, as well as of the most despotical."[38] It encourages the individual to walk in the path of righteousness, but it takes no chances.

I would argue, therefore, that the competitive market is both an instrument of economic organization and an expression of ethical precepts. As any man-made institution, however, as any legal covenant, it must be shielded from transgressors. Like a master protects his servant, so must society protect its agent. And this is the function of government, acting in its capacity as arbiter and rule maker.

In addition to this role of rule maker and umpire, however, government in recent years has come to exercise another, perhaps more difficult and delicate role. Rightly or wrongly, by design or by force of circumstance, ours is an era of Big Government, where government's legislative, administrative, and regulatory decisions have more than a neutral impact on the economy. The manner in which it allocates defense contracts, the criteria by which it disposes of surplus property, the goals it sets for the national security stockpile, the standards it employs for distributing tax favors and subsidies—in these and countless other ways, government today has a profound effect on the industrial anatomy of America.[39] And this creates, concomitantly and almost inevitably, the kind of problems to which we have already alluded—the kind of problems which Senator Douglas described so graphically in his book on ethics. "When prices are fixed for an industry," the Senator wrote during the Korean War, "the lobbyists will flock to the National Capital. When the Government determines which firms are to receive steel, aluminum, or copper, expediters and 'fixers' will spring up like the dragon's teeth which Cadmus was reputed to have sown. When the Government decides which firms are to enter an industry, as it now necessarily does in the case of radio, television, and the airlines, it is certain that pressure and influence will be applied by the groups which wish to get the favored positions. When the Government makes loans, there will be concerns which will hire men with influence to obtain them. When it pays subsidies, the ranks of the Government agencies will be permeated by the secret agents of those who are subsidized.

"In short, where economic decisions are made by the people and parties who administer the Government, the decisions will not be on the lofty and abstract grounds which are somewhat naively assumed by many economists who favor pervasive and far-reaching economic controls.... Instead ... the crucial decisions will commonly be made in an atmosphere of pressure, influence, favoritism, improper deals, and corruption."[40]

This is why Jefferson held that the government which governs least, governs best. His plea was not against government, the arbiter, but against government, the instrument of economic privilege, the creator of monopoly, the oppressor of individual liberty. In this new nation, on this virgin continent, he and the Founding Fathers wanted to prevent the revival of the Elizabethan system of privilege creation—a system originally animated by worthy motives and designed for public purposes but eventually abused and corrupted by self-seeking, influence-peddling courtiers. This was the rationale for a government with limited powers, functioning within a comprehensive framework of checks and balances. The fears of 1789, and the safeguards then prescribed, have more than passing historical significance for our own day. To be sure, government cannot whither away. It cannot abdicate the role of active participant in economic life—a role which has been thrust upon it and which it must of necessity accept. It cannot, for example, eschew the maintenance of an adequate (i.e., gigantic) defense establishment or the supervision of industries where competition is incapable of performing its traditional regulatory function. This does not mean, however, that government (as a reluctant participant in the economic game) must throw its weight behind the powerful few, that it must be a shield for vested interests, that it must serve as an instrument of corrupt manipulation and perversion of the public interest. On the contrary, and more than ever, government must follow the central guideline of diffusing economic power to the maximum degree feasible and confining bureaucratic discretion within the narrowest practicable limits.

In concrete terms, this means the total deregulation of those industries where regulation protects the industry from competition rather than the public from monopolistic extortion. In trucking, for example, where competition is both technically and economically workable, where entry in the absence of regulation would be easy, and where economies of scale are virtually non-existent, why not let the market decide who shall transport what commodities over what routes and at what rates? Why not substitute an exogenous, objective, and impartial control mechanism for the rule of a commission whose record is replete with confusion, ignorance, caprice, discrimination, and favoritism? Why not remove the almost irrepressible temptation for influence peddling and corruption in a situation where a government tribunal makes decisions that could better be left to the invisible hand of the market? In such situations, I submit, deregulation would not mean an abdication of governmental responsibility, but its responsible exercise in the public interest.[41]

In other regulated industries—television, for example—total deregulation is obviously impossible. For technical reasons competition is not fully workable. But this does not mean that the present regulatory scheme is a felicitous instrument of social engineering—that power could not be more widely diffused or bureaucratic discretion more narrowly confined. Thus, there is no valid reason for confining television broadcasting to the 12 channels of VHF, when 70 channels could be made available under UHF. There is no reason for permitting a government commission to distribute such valuable bonanzas as television licenses in accordance with so amorphous a standard as "public convenience and necessity," when Congress could easily set up more specific criteria for dispensing government largesse. Could not Congress instruct the Commission to consider competence, diversification of ownership within television, diversification of ownership between competing media of mass communication, promotion of non-profit educational television, etc., as standards for judging rival applications—prior to awarding a given channel to the highest bidder? Would not some such system avoid the more obvious pressures for favoritism and corruption that have been disclosed in the recent F.C.C. scandals?[42]

These illustrations can be multiplied—not only in the regulated industries but also in fields like defense procurement, the allocation of R and D contracts, the creation of a communications satellite industry, government patent policy, etc. They point up the need for social safeguards against individual misconduct, a network of checks and balances structurally built into the economic system, a set of devices which tend to work automatically and autonomously, a framework of rules which tend to minimize individual discretion and the danger of its abuse. If the individual is infused with the conscience of Rollo, well and good; if he is also haunted by the ghost of Senator Sherman, so much the better. But even this is not enough, for in our era of Big Government, perhaps the greatest danger of all is the corruption of the Leviathan himself—the dispenser of privilege and favor, the tempter of concupiscent men as well as soulful corporations. It is important, therefore, to promote a diffusion of economic power, if government is to resist subversion by special interest groups. It is imperative to maintain arm's length relationships between government and economic power blocs. As Mr. Dooley so shrewdly observed: ". . . the only thing to do is to keep politicians and businessmen apart. They seem to have a bad influence on each other. Whenever I see an alderman and a banker walking down the street together, I know the Recording Angel will have to order another bottle of ink."

Notes

1. Lincoln Steffens, *The Shame of our Cities*, p. 22 (1904, reprinted by Hill and Wang, Inc., 1960).

2. Ibid., p. 107.

3. Ibid., p. 74.

4. Ibid., p. 3.

5. *United States* v. *American Tobacco Co. et al.*, 221 U.S. 106 (1911). See also *Standard Oil Co. of New Jersey* v. *United States*, 221 U.S. 1 (1911).

6. Andrew Carnegie, "Wealth," *North American Review*, June 1889, reprinted in Gail Kennedy (ed.), *Democracy and the Gospel of Wealth*, pp. 6–7 (1949). For the spirit of the times, see also Richard Hofstadter, *Social Darwinism in American Thought* (1959).

7. Rt. Rev. William Lawrence, "The Relation of Wealth to Morals," *World's Work*, January 1901, reprinted in Kennedy, op. cit., p. 69.

8. Quoted in Marquis W. Childs and Douglas Cater, *Ethics in a Business Society*, pp. 98–99 (1954). There is no dearth of such statements by big business executives. See, for example, the following books in the McKinsey Foundation Lecture Series published by McGraw-Hill Book Company: Ralph J. Cordiner, *New Frontiers for Professional Managers* (1956); Theodore V. Houser, *Big Business and Human Values* (1957); and Roger

Blough, *Free Man and the Corporation* (1959). One exception is Crawford Greenewalt who finds the image of the "new type" executive unpalatable. "I am afraid," writes Mr. Greenewalt, "I find this notion equally as wearisome as the legend of the toolless plumber. It is presented as though, by some process of sexless eugenics, the bull terriers and bloodhounds of the business past had been cross-bred to produce a race of kindly and socially conscious poodles." *The Uncommon Man,* p. 84 (1959).

9. Adolph A. Berle, Jr., *The Twentieth Century Capitalist Revolution,* pp. 76–77, 62–63 (1954). By the same author, see also *Power without Property* (1959).

10. "Economics by Admonition," *American Economic Review Proceedings,* p. 396, May 1959.

11. R.H. Tawney, *Religion and the Rise of Capitalism,* p. 184 (1926).

12. For a summary of the Calvinist view, see Rod W. Horton and Herbert W. Edwards, *Backgrounds of American Literary Thought,* pp. 7–32 (1952). For a summary of the Catholic view, see Father Theodore M. Hesburgh, C.S.C., *God and the World of Man,* pp. 167–241 (1950). For an incisive comparison of the Catholic position, on the one hand, with Pelagianism and Conservative Protestantism, on the other, see Hesburgh, op. cit., pp. 225–241.

13. Investigation of Regulatory Commissions and Agencies, Hearings before the Special Subcommittee on Legislative Oversight, U.S. House of Representatives, 85th Cong., 2d Sess., Parts 1 and 2, pp. 143 ff (1959); *WKAT, Inc.* v. *F.C.C.,* 258 F2d 418 (D.C. Cir. 1958), 296 F2d 375 (D.C. Cir. 1961); and Decision of Hearing Examiner (on Remand), December 1, 1958, Piker & Fisher, pp. 1003–1022 (1958).

14. Decision of Hearing Examiner, pp. 1005–1015.

15. 296 F2d 375, at 383.

16. Ibid.

17. Ibid.

18. Quoted in Decision of Hearing Examiner, pp. 1010–1011.

19. Ibid., p. 1009.

20. For a discouraging chronicle of corruption and influence peddling in the federal regulatory commissions, see the account of Professor Bernard Schwartz of the New York University Law School, former chief counsel of the Subcommittee on Legislative Oversight, *The Professor and the Commissions* (1959).

21. For a good (journalistic) chronology of the case, see John Herling, *The Great Price Conspiracy* (1962).

22. *United States* v. *Addyston Pipe & Steel Co.,* 85 F. 271 (6th Cir. 1898). See also *United States* v. *Trenton Potteries,* 273 U.S. 392 (1927), and *United States* v. *Socony Vacuum,* 310 U.S. 150 (1940).

23. As the *Wall Street Journal* observed editorially, "Men who make up code words to secretly pass information are not ignorant of what they are doing." December 12, 1960.

24. Edward A. Ross, *Sin and Society* (1907), quoted in Herling, op. cit., p. 288. Another recent (and dramatic) illustration of this proposition is the career of Billie Sol Estes who "has always piously observed the Church of Christ's stern views on such earthly pleasures as drinking, smoking, profanity and promiscuity. He forbade mixed swimming in his pool, unless the bathers were married; whenever the Estes Enterprises Girls' Softball Team was entertained at one of Billie Sol's frequent parties, their escorts were ordered to go play tennis or something while the girls swam. And when the local junior high school had a dance, the Esteses almost always had a lavish party on the same night—in the hope that they could divert the youngsters from the sin of dancing." "A Scandal Hot as a Pistol," *Life Magazine,* June 1, 1962, p. 90D.

25. For the complete text of Judge Ganey's statement, preliminary to sentencing the defendants, see Herling, op. cit., pp. 195–197.

26. "Antitrust and Organization Man," *Wall Street Journal,* January 10, 1961.

27. Quoted in Herling, op. cit., p. 201.

28. "Antitrust and the Organization Man," *Wall Street Journal,* January 10, 1961.

29. Quoted in Herling, op. cit., p. 316.

30. Ralph J. Cordiner, "Business Ethics in a Competitive Enterprise System," January 5, 1960, reprinted in *Administered Prices, Hearings before the Subcommittee on Antitrust and Monopoly,* U.S. Senate, 87th Cong., 1st Sess., Part 27, p. 17117 (1961) (emphasis added).

31. For Paxton's testimony before the Kefauver Committee, see *Administered Prices,* op. cit., Part 28, pp. 17201–17290, esp. pp. 17209, 17227, 17229, 17252 ff.

32. For a cogent analysis of the implications of this case, see Myron W. Watkins, "Electrical Equipment Antitrust Cases—Their Implications for Government and Business," *University of Chicago Law Review,* Autumn 1961.

33. See Herling, op. cit., pp. 300–301, 322–323.

34. "Recent Developments in Antitrust Enforcement," An Address before the American Bar Association, Washington, D.C., April 7, 1961.

35. President Eisenhower underscored the gravity of this problem in his Farewell Address. "This conjunction of an immense military establishment and a large arms industry is new in the American experience," he warned. "We must not fail to comprehend its grave implications. Our toil, resources and livelihood are all involved; so is the very structure of our society. . . . The total influence—economic, political, even spiritual—is felt in every city, every State House, every office of the federal government. . . . We must guard against the acquisition of unwarranted influence, whether sought or unsought, by the military industrial complex."

36. Compare this "diffusion of power" guideline with the "principle of subsidiarity" set forth in *Quadragesimo Anno:* "It is a fundamental principle of social philosophy, fixed and unchangeable, that one should not withdraw from individuals and commit to the community what they can accomplish by their own enterprise and industry. So, too, it is an injustice and at the same time a grave evil and a disturbance of right order, to transfer to the larger and higher collectivity functions which can be performed and provided for by lesser and subordinate bodies. Inasmuch as every social activity should, by its very nature, prove a help to members of the body social, it should never destroy or absorb them." Quoted with approval by Pope John XXIII in *Mater et Magistra,* pp. 23–24 (1961). For a secular enunciation of the "diffusion of power" principle, and its ethical implications, see Lord Acton, *Essays on Freedom and Power* (1955). There is considerable evidence that the present level of power concentration in the United States exceeds both technological and economic imperatives, and that substantial deconcentration could be achieved without loss of economic efficiency. See, e.g., Joe Bain, *Barriers to New Competition* (1956), and Walter Adams (ed.), *The Structure of American Industry* (3d ed., 1961).

37. The foregoing is by no means inconsistent with valid criticisms of *unrestricted* competition. Thus, there can be little doubt about the finding in *Quadragesimo Anno* and *Mater et Magistra* that "unrestricted competition [has] . . . caused a great accumulation of wealth and a corresponding concentration of power in the hands of a few who 'are frequently not the owners, but only the trustees and directors of invested funds, who administer them at their good pleasure.' " Where unrestricted competition has been allowed to go unchecked, it is certainly true that "economic power has been substituted for the free marketplace. Unbridled ambition for domination has replaced desire for gain; the whole economy has become harsh, cruel, and relentless in frightful measure." Where *unrestricted* competition was operative, it is not surprising "that even public authorities were serving the interests of more wealthy men and that concentrations of wealth, to some extent, achieved power over all peoples." *Mater et Magistra,* op. cit., pp. 17–18. It should

be noted, however, that these criticisms are applicable, not to the principle of competition, but its perversion—not to effective and fair competition, but to predatory and *unrestricted* competition. For the prerequisites for effective and fair competition, see Joel B. Dirlam and Alfred E. Kahn, *Fair Competition* (1954).

38. *The Wealth of Nations,* op. cit., volume II, chapter 2.

39. See Walter Adams and Horace M. Gray, *Monopoly in America: The Government as Promoter* (1955).

40. Paul H. Douglas, *Ethics in Government,* p. 33 (1954).

41. See Walter Adams, "The Role of Competition in the Regulated Industries," *American Economic Review Proceedings,* May 1958.

42. See the testimony of Professor Clark Byse of the Harvard Law School in Administrative Process and Ethical Questions, Hearings before the Special Subcommittee on Legislative Oversight, U.S. House of Representatives, 85th Cong., 2d Sess., pp. 166 ff (1958).

2

Economists and Power

Seldom, in modern positive science, has so elaborate a theoretical structure been erected on so narrow and shallow a factual foundation.

— Professor Wassily Leontief, Nobel Laureate and past
president of the American Economic Association

I certainly am thankful to God that I am not an economist. I look back when I was a high school drop-out, I had a sort of a flair for mathematics, and I think now that if I had gone on I might have wound up being an economist. And, to me, this is a kind of sad profession, although it is the one profession where you can gain great eminence without ever being right.

— George Meany, former president of the AFL–CIO

The master economist, wrote John Maynard Keynes, "must possess a rare *combination* of gifts. He must be mathematician, historian, statesman, philosopher—in some degree. He must understand symbols and speak in words. He must contemplate the particular in terms of the general, and touch abstract and concrete in the same flight of thought. He must study the present in the light of the past for the purposes of the future. No part of man's nature or his institutions must lie entirely outside his regard. He must be purposeful and disinterested in a simultaneous mood; as aloof and incorruptible as an artist, yet sometimes as near the earth as a politician." The master economist, Keynes hoped, would belong to that small but brave army of men "who prefer to see the truth imperfectly and obscurely rather than to maintain error, reached indeed with clearness and consistency and by easy logic, but [based] on hypotheses inappropriate to the facts."[1] Believing as he did that the object of studying economics is to help make a better world, and always anxious to influence public policy toward that end,

Originally published as chapter 2 in Walter Adams and James W. Brock, *The Bigness Complex: Industry, Labor and Government in the American Economy* (Pantheon Books, 1986); reprinted with permission.

Keynes advocated the forging of those theoretical tools that were peculiarly useful in the solution of concrete problems.

Judging by some current criticism, there seems to be no oversupply of "master economists"—at least not in the academic world. Like his colleagues in other social sciences, the modern economist, so the critics allege, inhabits "islands of passivity and irrelevance rather than centers of ferment and innovation." He tends his scholarly garden of rare herbs and leafless plants, engaged in "small-scale research backed by large-scale grants."[2] His primary concern seems to be not with the real problems of our time—poverty in the midst of affluence, the degeneration of our inner cities, the growing gap between rich lands and poor lands—but with esoteric model building. A prisoner of self-imposed categories of thought, the academic economist appears to dispense a conventional wisdom and recite an orthodox catechism. He seems to use the most sophisticated techniques to arrive at the most irrelevant conclusions. A professor, some say, teaches what he has been taught, and his students do the same for no better reason than that it was their professor who taught it to them.[3]

It is sobering to note that these criticisms, whatever their validity, are neither novel nor surprising. They always spring up in a time of transition, when the theory developed to explain events of the past no longer seems relevant to the problems of the present. Once a theory is developed and finds public acceptance, it begins to command dogmatic adherence. It becomes progressively more difficult to dislodge; its prestige and authority, its comfortable familiarity, give it an immunity from "internal" reform. Only cataclysmic change, mediated by forces outside the profession, brings about an eventual transformation and reformulation. In the words of Leo Rogin: "As the career of a set of principles is prolonged, adherence to it becomes more uncritical and more precarious—more uncritical, because the original contingence of the theory on a practical issue is lost sight of; more precarious, because the passing of time tends to divest an issue of the rank to which it was originally entitled, or to change the conditions of its practical resolution."[4]

The malaise is neither novel nor unique. At the turn of the century, George J. Stigler reminds us, in the midst of America's most gigantic and unprecedented merger movement, while industrial empires of Brobdingnagian proportions were fashioned by financial magnates and buccaneering promoters, economists (in the academy) were remarkably unruffled and had a ready explanation. Relying on a crude social Darwinism, they parroted the familiar phrases of Herbert Spencer and William Graham Sumner. They could not see the erosive effect of large-scale mergers on the competitive markets that, in theory, they espoused. Says Stigler: "Economists as wise as Taussig, as incisive as Fisher, as fond of competition as Clark and Fetter, insisted upon discussing the movement largely or exclusively in terms of industrial evolution and the economies of scale. They found no difficulty in treating the unregulated corporation as a natural phenomenon, nor were they bothered that the economies of scale should spring forth suddenly and simultaneously in an enormous variety of industries—and yet pass over the minor firms that characteristically persisted and indeed flourished in these industries."[5] Thus, and ironically so, Ida Tarbell, Henry Demarest Lloyd, and the Populist muckrakers did more than the luminaries of the American Economic Association to foster a public understanding of the meaning of competition, and to help forge public policies designed to preserve it.

In 1929, while Herbert Hoover announced (with a naivete pardonable in a politician) that "We shall soon with the help of God be within sight of the day when poverty shall be banished from this nation," so eminent an economist as Irving Fisher echoed these sentiments. He saw us marching along on a "permanently high plateau"—precisely one week to the day before the stock market tumbled over the brink of that plateau. And, even after the Great Depression was in full swing, academic economists still found it difficult to explain the massive unemployment that had befallen the nation. While the indisputable fact of this unemployment "argued more forcefully than any text that something was wrong with the system, the economists wrung their hands and racked their brains and called upon the spirit of Adam Smith, but he could offer neither diagnosis nor remedy. Unemployment—this kind of unemployment—was simply not listed among the possible ills of the system: it was absurd, impossible, unreasonable, and paradoxical."[6] Again, the phenomenon was too new. No adequate theory had yet appeared to explain it, and no "outsiders" had yet begun to experiment with policies to cure it.

Perhaps this lag is inevitable and inherent in the subject matter. Unlike the natural sciences, economics has no ready-made testing ground for the scientific validation and verification of its theories. "The natural sciences," notes Rogin, "articulate the concept of a constant nature, which finds its empirical reference in the uniformities manifested in the heavens and in the materially isolated setting of the laboratories." Economics, by contrast, deals not with the eternal verities of the physical universe but with the changing character of a dynamic social organism. Its only laboratory is the "marketplace" of reality, and the ultimate test for its theories is their correspondence to that reality. In such a subject matter, "where there is no agreed procedure for knocking out errors," the validity of a theory depends on its usefulness as a cognitive instrument, a working hypothesis, and a guide to action.[7]

In our own day, economic theory is again confronted with the specter of irrelevance to public policy. We can boast of an elaborate, sophisticated, highly mathematical box of analytical tools—replete with Pontryagin Principles, Rubizinski Theorems, Disequilibrium Models, Natural-Rate Hypotheses—but we are embarrassingly incapable of dealing with the nagging problems of the real world. Conventional theory—both neoclassical and Keynesian—is in danger of becoming, as Kenneth Boulding warns, the celestial mechanics for a nonexistent universe.

The difficulty may be, in part, methodological. The overemphasis on the mathematical-econometrics approach has resulted in a formidable misallocation of intellectual resources. Economists have tended to ask themselves questions that can be analyzed with their new techniques, rather than finding techniques to deal with the questions they ought to ask. They play games they find amusing, rather than contemplate issues that are crucial and pressing. They quantify what appears to be quantifiable, even though it may not be important, and pass up what should be analyzed even though it may be decisive. As Boulding points out:

> We have been obsessed with macroeconomics, with piddling refinements in mathematical models, and with the monumentally unsuccessful exercise in welfare economics which has preoccupied a whole generation with a dead end, to the almost total neglect of some of the major problems of our day. . . . The whole economics profession, indeed, is an example of that monumental misallocation of intellectual resources which is one of the most striking phenomena of our times.[8]

Technique, it seems, has taken precedence over substance, and economists have not yet learned that algebra and geometry are a complement to, not a substitute for, thought. No wonder, then, that journalists satirize our profession for having embraced a kind of rigor that resembles rigor mortis.[9]

The difficulty with contemporary economics, however, is conceptual as well as methodological. Unlike the political economists who founded our discipline, we largely ignore the power element in economic statecraft; and, lacking a theory of power, we seek to minimize the use of power in matters affecting the production and distribution of wealth. As Kurt Rothschild put it:

> If we look at the main run of economic theory . . . we find that it is characterized by a strange lack of power considerations. More or less homogeneous units—firms and households—move in more or less given technological and market conditions and try to improve their economic lot within the constraints of these conditions. This model has been explored in great detail by modern economic science and very important insights into the working of the market mechanism have been gained. But that people use power to alter the mechanism itself; that uneven power may greatly influence the outcome of market operations; that people may strive for economic power as much as for economic wealth; these facts have been largely neglected.[10]

Thus, the typical microtheorist contemplates a "simplified" world, peopled by rational entrepreneurs, who are owner-managers of single-plant, single-product firms, operating in single markets, and dutifully maximizing short-run profits by following the "time-tested" rule of equating marginal cost and marginal revenue. It is a world in which competition is the norm in both product and factor markets, and monopoly or oligopoly the exception. It is a world in which power per se is unknown, except with reference to particular firms, particular products, and particular markets. It is a world untroubled by conglomerate giants and undisturbed by technological upheavals—an *economic* world, separate and distinct from the world of power politics.

In a similar vein, the typical macroeconomist, although no longer exuding the hubris of the 1960s and no longer claiming to master the art of "fine-tuning" the economy, is still incapable of devising contracyclical stabilization policies to cope with the crucial macro-problems of the day. He may have policy prescriptions to deal effectively with inflation *or* recession, but not with inflation in the midst of recession—or with persistently high unemployment as the price of controlling inflation. Whether monetarist or Keynesian, he seems imprisoned and immobilized by an intractable dilemma: if he recommends restrictive monetary and fiscal policies, this is likely to aggravate recession; if he counsels expansionary measures, this is likely to exacerbate inflation. And so he takes refuge in the comforts of orthodoxy. Protesting the inescapability from the trade-off between the social goal of price stability and the social goal of full employment, he tells us that we can achieve one or the other, but not both simultaneously. And, depending on his ideological preference, he concludes that—at the margin—it is more important to fight inflation with recession, or recession with inflation. He recommends monetary and fiscal stabilization measures *as if* we could realistically assume that the economy approximated a state of "perfect" competition; *as if* we could assume that market power and/or political power were inconsequential phenomena; and *as if* we could assume that structural impediments in the economy were incapable of distorting or neutralizing macro-stabilization measures.

There is, to be sure, an emerging recognition that there is something amiss in such simplistic theorizing. Some twenty years ago, for example, in an incisive article largely ignored by his mainstream colleagues, Paul Samuelson, a Nobel Laureate and past president of the American Economic Association, observed that aggregate demand analysis is only a partial, not a general, guide to understanding macroeconomic phenomena. He pointed out that "there is a good reason to fear that America may, along with other lands, suffer from an institutional problem of cost-push. I mean by this that at levels below those corresponding to reasonably full employment, our institutions of wage bargaining and price setting may be such as to lead to a price and wage creep, a creep which can be lessened by conventional depressing of demand by monetary and fiscal policy measures but only at the cost of creating greater unemployment and excess capacity."[11] Looking ahead to the decade of the 1960s, he estimated that a 3 percent unemployment rate could be obtained at the cost of a 4.5 percent annual inflation rate[12]—a trade-off that a decade later seemed absurdly cheap and eminently tolerable. In the 1970s, economists were wont to assume an "underlying" or "embedded" inflation rate of roughly 10 percent, accompanied by near double-digit unemployment—a somewhat less-than-spectacular triumph of modern economic policy-making.

In 1975, Gottfried Haberler, an avowed monetarist and another past president of the American Economic Association, confessed that "stagflation, the coexist-ence of inflation and recession, is an economic disease which, to my knowledge, has never before existed, at least not as long and as severely as in the 1970s."[13] He noted that in most industrialized countries "stagflation could not have be-come such an intractable problem if our market economy were more competitive than it is, if it were not hamstrung and hobbled by so many restrictions and rigidities, due especially . . . to government intervention designed to keep certain prices and incomes high and by labor unions which have made money wages completely rigid in a downward direction and push them up even in the face of heavy unemployment and slack."[14] Haberler argued that government toleration, protection, and promotion of private monopolies, combined with the restriction-ist pressures of organized vested-interest groups in the private sector, created what the Germans call *Anspruchs-Inflation*—a pernicious type of cost-push or "entitlements" inflation. It creates a persistent upward pressure on the general price level, because "the sum of the shares claimed by the various pressure groups exceeds the available social product" and because the government feels constrained to validate these excessive claims by a constant increase in the money supply. Haberler's conclusion is noteworthy:

> I am afraid that our monetarist friends—Karl Brunner, Milton Friedman, Harry Johnson, and Alan Meltzer, to name only a few of the most prominent ex-perts—delude themselves if they believe that things can be straightened out by monetary policy alone. They are of course absolutely right in stressing that inflation cannot be stopped without an appropriate monetary policy. Tight money is undoubtedly a necessary condition, but it is not a sufficient condition for an economically successful and efficient as well as a politically practicable anti-inflation policy. I agree with William Fellner, Friedrich A. von Hayek, and Friedrich Lutz, who are of the opinion that a tight monetary and fiscal policy must be supplemented by measures designed to make the economy more competitive. In the jargon of economics, macroeconomic measures aim-ing at overall guidance of demand must be accompanied by microeconomic measures designed to promote competition. If we do not succeed in strengthen-ing competition and freeing the market economy at least from its most crip-pling hobbles, the fight against inflation will generate so much unemployment that it will be terminated prematurely.[15]

Similarly, in 1979, Robert Eisner of Northwestern University—an erstwhile stalwart of orthodox Keynesianism who now labels himself a maverick, post-Keynesian free enterpriser—conceded that a simplistic pursuit of macro-stabilization policies cannot cope with stagflation. He urged that the seemingly endemic inflation of the late 1970s and early 1980s be "perceived as the consequence of a world-wide breakdown in competitive forces that could keep prices in line." This breakdown, he pointed out, was largely the result of government policies prom-ulgated in response to the political blandishments of organized vested interests. Said Eisner:

The list is much too long to cite in full: price supports for milk as dairy prices skyrocket; trigger prices to "protect" our steel industry from foreign competition as profits of our steel industry soar; licensing arrangements and route restrictions that drastically curtail competition in the trucking industry, laying the ground for repeated increases in prices and wages while trucks suffer from idle capacity and small trucking firms go out of business; sugar quotas and price supports to maintain and raise sugar prices; acreage restrictions that reduce agricultural supply; import quotas, tariffs, and "orderly marketing agreements" that limit the import of cheaper and frequently better foreign automobiles, television sets, and textiles; and federal, state, and local restrictions in countless occupations and industries that reduce competition and raise prices.[16]

In short, here is a recognition of the fact that the inflation bedeviling the industrialized nations of the West in the 1970s was characteristically of the cost-push variety, fueled by a seemingly uncontrollable price–wage–price spiral, and the result of a power grab by highly organized vested interests for a larger share of a fixed pie or a pie growing more slowly than the combined appetites of the interests that desire to devour it. And equally important, there is recognition here that economic power and political power may be mutually interacting and reinforcing, and that government is more than a neutral bystander and rule maker in an essentially self-regulating economy. These insights, however trenchant, are still isolated and sporadic—*cris de coeur* in the confusing cacophony of economic policy debates. They have not yet become part of mainstream theorizing, and since it is difficult to assess the quantitative significance of the "power" element in economic behavior, the model builders have largely ignored its importance— especially in their macro-forecasts. This, perhaps, explains—certainly in part— the seemingly endemic inaccuracy of recent predictions.

In 1974, for example, three leading popular magazines—*Business Week, Fortune,* and *U.S. News and World Report*—assembled a select group of orthodox economists to predict what the year would bring. With very few exceptions, they said the stock market would rise; it fell by 300 points. They said the inflation rate would decrease; it rose about 12 percent. They said unemployment would peak at 6 percent; it was above 7 percent at year's end, and rising. Above all, they said there would be no recession. These soothsayers were so persuasive that President Gerald Ford, as late as the fall of 1974, embarked on his ill-fated WIN campaign (Whip Inflation Now), urging people to buy less, to retrench on their consumption of durable goods, to save more, etc.—only to be forced to reverse himself 180 degrees by year's end and to face up to a formidable recession.

In 1979, the *Economic Report of the President* stated that "the increase in consumer prices is expected to fall to an annual rate below 7 percent by late in the year." The actual rate was 13.6 percent for the fourth quarter and 15.4 percent for December. Private forecasts were not perceptibly more accurate—

perhaps because, as Arthur Burns ruefully observed in his final days as chairman of the Federal Reserve System, the economy no longer works as it used to work. Despite the sophisticated econometric modeling of the economy—replete with leads and lags and vague references to "supply-side" shocks—the predictive value of economics as a "science" does not inspire confidence. Indeed, a recent poll showed respect for economic forecasters only marginally ahead of stockbrokers and astrologers, and well behind such professions as plumbers and sportscasters.[17]

In this book, we must attempt to avoid the sterile orthodoxy of conventional models—the simplistic abstractions of neoclassicism and Keynesianism, on the one hand, and the radical chic of the New Left, on the other. We must analyze the role of the state in a complex, modern, postindustrial economy and assess the effectiveness of public policy in promoting managerial, allocative, and dynamic efficiency in the economic order. Our approach throughout must be guided by what Paul Samuelson considers the first duty of the economist, "to describe what is out there," because "a valid description without a deeper explanation is worth a thousand times more than a clever explanation of nonexistent facts."[18]

This requires, first and foremost, dispensing with the traditional paradigm in which society's resources are allocated in response to "consumer sovereignty"—individuals or households casting dollar votes in the marketplace to determine what goods shall be produced and in what quantities. It requires dispensing with a paradigm in which the individual firm passively responds to exogenous market forces in an eternal quest to maximize short-run profits in producing particular goods in well-defined, "relevant" markets. It requires dispensing with a paradigm in which individual citizens cast their votes in a free political system to determine the policies of the state in a representative democracy.

Put positively, our approach calls for recognizing the dominant role of the giant corporation in the social decision-making process of what John Kenneth Galbraith calls "The New Industrial State." The giant corporation—as Galbraith notes, with somewhat Pickwickian exaggeration—has achieved substantial control over its environment and considerable immunity from the discipline of exogenous control mechanisms, especially the competitive market. Through separation of ownership from management, it has emancipated itself from the control of stockholders. By reinvestment of profits, it has eliminated the influence of the financier and the capital market. By massive advertising, it has insulated itself from consumer sovereignty. By possession of market power, it has come to dominate both suppliers and customers. By judicious identification with the manipulation of the state, it has achieved autonomy. Whatever it cannot do for itself to assure survival and growth, a compliant government does on its behalf—assuring the maintenance of full employment, eliminating the risk of and subsidizing the investment in research and development, and assuring the supply of scientific and technical skills required by the modern techno-structure. In return for this privileged autonomy, the industrial giant performs society's planning function. This model, despite its exaggeration and its lack of elegant precision (which economists value so dearly), does have descriptive value.[19]

Our approach also calls for revising the traditional view of the giant trade union. Whether we examine the role of the United Automobile Workers (UAW), or the United Steel Workers (USW), or the Communications Workers of America (CWA), these unions do not constitute countervailing power with respect to entrenched corporate interests. In bargaining over wages, hours, fringe benefits, and democracy in the workplace, they may assume an adversarial posture toward corporate management; but, in a larger sense, they represent not countervailing but coalescing power in defending the parochial, short-run interests of their industry. In their Washington lobbying, their demands are indistinguishable from those of their corporate counterparts: "the hand is the hand of Esau, but the voice is the voice of Jacob."

Similarly, it is no longer admissible to view government as an outside force regulating the economy in the same manner as a referee regulates the procedural aspects of an athletic event. The government has become an active participant in the economic game, and in some cases has a symbiotic relationship to the interest groups for which it makes the rules of the game. It, too, can no longer be viewed as a countervailing force whose public policies constitute an independent, autonomous, and incorruptible judgment of what is in the public interest. Nor, incidentally, can it be viewed, with naive simplicity, as "the executive committee of the ruling class." It is far more accurate to view the state as part of a corporate–labor–government complex.

What this means is that we must dispense with paradigms that analyze the economic order in terms of individual actions and individual decisions. We must construct different paradigms that recognize the "organizational revolution" (to use Boulding's term) as a fact of life and try to understand the impact of new structures on economic behavior and ultimately on economic performance. There can no longer be argument over the proposition that, over time, special-interest organizations have gained preeminence in advanced industrial nations and that they now have the power to impede the effective functioning of the economic system—whether they do so through the market or through exercise of their political power to obtain governmental favors and privileges.

In his landmark study, *Capitalism, Socialism and Democracy,* Joseph Schumpeter discounted the significance of the monopoly problem in capitalist society. Monopoly power is dissipated, he believed, not by the static competition adumbrated in economic texts, but by the dynamic competition that comes from "the new commodity, the new technology, the new source of supply, the new type of organization (the large-scale unit of control for instance)—competition which commands a decisive cost or quality advantage and which strikes not at the margins of profits and the outputs of the existing firms but at their foundations and their very lives. This kind of competition is as much more effective than the other as a bombardment is in comparison with forcing a door."[20] This kind of competition, in short, unleashes what Schumpeter called the gales of creative destruction that control monopoly and neutralize the exercise of monopoly power.

Whatever the superficial validity of this theory, it suffers from a fatal defect: those power agglomerations subject to the gales of creative destruction do not willingly submit to their devastating force. They refuse to accept creative destruction as a socially beneficent mechanism for the good and sufficient reason that they themselves are the victims on the altar of the public interest. Not surprisingly, therefore, they try to protect themselves from the Schumpeterian gales by building private storm shelters for themselves where possible and by inducing government to build public storm shelters for them where necessary. They mobilize all the economic and political power at their command to assure survival, growth, and profitability.

That is the essence of the political economy of power.

Notes

1. John Maynard Keynes, *Essays in Biography*, p. 250 (1933).

2. Theodore Roszak, ed., *The Dissenting Academy* (1968). For recent, penetrating critiques of the economics profession, see Robert Lekachman, *Economists at Bay* (1976), and Alfred S. Eichner, *Why Economics Is not Yet a Science* (1983).

3. Joan Robinson, *Economic Philosophy*, p. 81 (1964).

4. Leo Rogin, *The Meaning and Validity of Economic Theory*, p. 4 (1956).

5. George J. Stigler, "Monopoly and Oligopoly by Merger," *American Economic Review Proceedings*, pp. 30–31 (May 1950).

6. Robert L. Heilbroner, *The Worldly Philosophers*, pp. 214, 217, 218 (rev. ed., 1961).

7. Rogin, *Meaning and Validity*, op. cit., pp. 11–12.

8. Kenneth Boulding, "The Economics of Knowledge and the Knowledge of Economics," *American Economic Review Proceedings*, p. 9 (May 1966).

9. This view, although it may be shared by only a minority of economists, is hardly iconoclastic. One notable exception is Professor Wassily Leontief (Nobel Laureate, past president of the American Economics Association, and father of input-output analysis), who writes, "Year after year economic theorists continue to produce scores of mathematical models and to explore in great detail their formal properties; and the econometricians fit algebraic functions of all possible shapes to essentially the same sets of data without being able to advance, in any perceptible way, a systematic understanding of the structure and operations of a real economic system." "Academic Economics," *Science*, July 9, 1982, p. 107. To this assessment, Professor Paul A. Samuelson (Nobel Laureate, past president of the American Economic Association, and mathematical economist extraordinaire) adds this admonition: "The first duty of an economist is to describe what is out there: a valid description without a deeper explanation is worth a thousand times more than a clever explanation of nonexistent facts." "A Brief Post-Keynesian Survey" in Robert Lekachman (ed.), *Keynes' General Theory: Reports of Three Decades*, p. 339 (1964).

10. Kurt Rothschild, *Power in Economics*, p. 7 (1971).

11. Samuelson, "A Brief Post-Keynesian Survey," op. cit., p. 339.

12. Paul A. Samuelson and Robert M. Solow, "Analytical Aspects of Anti-Inflation Policy," *American Economic Review Proceedings*, p. 192 (May 1960).

13. Gottfried Haberler, *The Challenge to the Free Market Economy*, p. 4 (1976). See also Haberler, *Stagflation* (1985).

14. Haberler, *The Challenge,* op. cit., p. 5.

15. Ibid., pp. 17–18.

16. Robert Eisner, "Sacrifices to Fight Inflation," *New York Times,* November 8, 1979. See also Hendrik Houthakker, "A Positive Way to Fight Inflation," *Wall Street Journal,* July 30, 1974.

17. *New York Times,* February 17, 1980.

18. Paul A. Samuelson, "A Brief Post-Keynesian Survey," op. cit., p. 339.

19. John Kenneth Galbraith, *The New Industrial State* (1967).

20. Joseph A. Schumpeter, *Capitalism, Socialism and Democracy,* pp. 82–106 (1943).

II

Selected Industry Studies

3

Big Steel, Invention, and Innovation

The view attributed to Schumpeter, that large firms with substantial market power have both greater incentives and more ample resources for research and innovation, has become part of popular mythology and an article of faith among many economists as well. Ostensibly, Schumpeter felt "that firms had to be protected by some degree of monopoly—to have some room to maneuver . . . " in order to bring about massive innovations. Presumably, he implied "that more concentration would increase innovation and progress."[1]

Though Schumpeter never stated it without careful qualification,[2] this idea has been widely used to explain why some industries, like textiles, are "backward," and others, like petroleum, are not. Galbraith, for example, argues that "a benign Providence . . . has made the modern industry of a few large firms an almost perfect instrument for inducing technical change. It is admirably equipped for financing technical development. Its organization provides strong incentives for undertaking development and for putting it into use. The competition of the competitive model, by contrast, almost completely precludes technical development."[3] In a whimsical vein he adds that "The foreign visitor, brought to the United States to study American production methods and associated marvels, visits the same firms as do the attorneys of the Department of Justice in their search for monopoly."[4]

Similarly, Lilienthal argues that firms that are small and competitive do not have the profits to finance research: "Only large enterprises are able to sink the formidable sums of money required to develop basic new departures."[5] Villard points out that the financing of research is less strategic than the assurance that, after an innovation is introduced, the firm will have a sufficient share of the market to recoup its outlays. And, he holds, only oligopolists in fact can enjoy such assurance.[6]

Originally published with Joel B. Dirlam in the *Quarterly Journal of Economics*, vol. 80 (May 1966); reprinted with permission.

This hypothesis has not remained unchallenged.[7] Moreover, there has been a recent flurry of empirical studies, replete with regression analyses, designed to test the relationship between concentration and innovation.[8] Unfortunately, these studies have yielded inconclusive results.[9] Therefore, an unhurried exploration, in some depth, of a single, revolutionary invention and its introduction into a major oligopolized industry may provide some rewarding insights.

For testing the "Schumpeterian" hypothesis, we have selected the oxygen steelmaking process—the circumstances surrounding its invention, its delayed adoption by the dominant firms in the United States steel industry, and the cost of this delay in terms of the industry's social performance.

I

"In my opinion," Avery C. Adams, chairman of the board and president of Jones & Laughlin, told his stockholders in 1959, "the basic oxygen process represents the only major technological breakthrough at the ingot level in the steel industry since before the turn of the century. With the exception of what we in the industry call trick heats, i.e., one heat made under ideal conditions, the best open-hearth practice today results in a production rate of 39 to 40 tons per hour. Our basic oxygen furnaces have produced at the rate of 106 tons per hour to date this month. On a trick heat basis, we have hit 160 tons per hour." By 1965 this opinion had become virtually unanimous in the industry. Indeed, most steel experts were willing to predict that no new open-hearths would ever again be built in the United States. Nevertheless, Mr. Adams' 1959 pronouncement came some ten years after the potentials of the new process should have been a matter of course to every steelman in the United States.

Despite its revolutionary character, the basic oxygen process employs a relatively simple principle. It refines pig iron into steel by jetting oxygen vertically downward into a molten bath of pig iron. The conversion is accomplished in a pear-shaped vessel that looks something like a cocktail shaker or water carafe—bellied at its central portion and having a restricted mouth. Not only does it produce top-grade, "open-hearth" quality steels more quickly and efficiently than older methods, but it entails lower investment (as well as operation) costs. Finally, and ironically, the process was foreseen by Sir Henry Bessemer almost a century ago.

History of the Invention

Bessemer ushered in the steel age with his principle of pneumatic conversion, patented in 1855.[10] This consisted of passing a "gaseous fluid containing oxygen" through molten pig iron. The Bessemer converter, equipped with an acid refractory lining, was charged with molten pig iron through a top opening. Atmospheric air would then be forced through a number of pipes (tuyeres) in the bottom of the converter and forced upward through the bath of molten metal. No extraneous source of fuel was necessary, because the oxygen in the air blast reacted exothermically with the impurities in the iron which were burned off as a gas or carried off into the slag.

This, the so-called "acid" Bessemer process, could be used only to refine low-phosphorus ores but was not adapted to refining the immense deposits of high-phosphorus ores in Lorraine and Sweden. With a view to using these phosphoric ores, S.G. Thomas invented and patented in 1876 a process which differed from Bessemer's principally in the use of a basic converter lining (dolomite bound with tar) instead of the acid lining employed by Bessemer. It was this Thomas converter (or basic Bessemer process, as it was known in the United States) on which the great development of steelmaking in Europe was based. The Thomas process was uniquely adapted to the use of Europe's large phosphoric ore deposits.

Bessemer recognized that the air blast used in his process posed a major problem. Since air is composed of 80 percent nitrogen and 20 percent oxygen; since nitrogen is bad for steel (making it brittle and less malleable); and since there was no way of preventing the injection of nitrogen into the Bessemer steels through the use of atmospheric air, Bessemer stated as early as 1856: "And here I would observe, that although I have mentioned air and steam because they contain, or are capable of evolving, oxygen at a cheap rate, it will nevertheless be understood that pure oxygen gas or a mixture thereof with air or steam may be used."[11] Indeed, Bessemer not only entertained the possibility of using "pure oxygen gas" in the converter, but also of introducing it through the top instead of the bottom of the vessel.

In spite of Bessemer's insights, early attempts to apply his teachings failed. Two major problems bedeviled steel technology: (1) pure oxygen was not available in commercial quantities and was prohibitively expensive; and (2) an increase in the oxygen content of the air-blast used by Bessemer would reduce the nitrogen content of the refined steel, but would also cause serious damage to the converter's tuyeres and refractory lining. European steelmakers using the Thomas converter faced the additional problem of producing steels with an excessive phosphorus content and hence inferior quality.

In view of these problems, it is not surprising that the basic open-hearth furnace, the so-called Siemens-Martin process, was almost an immediate success after its introduction in 1880. While slower and more expensive than pneumatic methods of steelmaking—requiring about eight hours for a batch of steel as compared with one hour in a Bessemer converter—the open-hearth had two signal advantages. It produced steel almost free of nitrogen, and hence of far greater quality in terms of malleability, and it could use a relatively high percentage of scrap in lieu of pig iron. In the United States, therefore, blessed as it was with plentiful scrap supplies, the Siemens-Martin furnace provided an excellent solution to the quality problems of the Bessemer and Thomas conversion processes. Indeed, by 1909, the open-hearth had outstripped the Bessemer converter as the workhorse of the American steel industry, and by 1953, about 89 percent of the steel produced in the United States was of the basic open-hearth variety.

But pneumatic conversion remained the quickest and cheapest way of refining steel. Hence experiments continued, especially in Europe, to solve the problems of the oxygen supply and the longevity of the refractory lining. One break-through occurred in 1929, when the Gesellschaft fur Linde's Eismaschinen AG in Germany perfected a method (the Linde-Fränkl process) of producing bulk oxygen of 99 percent purity at very low cost. From then on, except for the actual building of the needed oxygen plants, the technical *and economic* problem of an adequate oxygen supply for steelmaking was of no further concern.[12]

The problem of the tuyere and lining longevity, however, was more stubborn and vexing. Attempts to use high purity oxygen in bottom-blown (Bessemer or Thomas) converters resulted in the rapid deterioration of the converter bottom— sometimes within the short time of one heat.[13] Other attempts, i.e., to use oxygen in side-blown converters, encountered similar difficulties.[14] Here the oxygen jet directed at the melt surface caused excessively high temperatures on the side of the vessel facing the oxygen inlet and resulted in serious damage to the refractory lining. Still other attempts, i.e., to use lower concentration of oxygen or oxygen-steam combination[15]—in order to conserve the refractory bottom or the sidewalls of the converter—suffered from the inherent liabilities of the conventional Bessemer method: an excessive nitrogen content of the refined steel and failure to take full advantage of the exothermic role of oxygen as a converter fuel.

The final breakthrough in the development of the oxygen process was based on the work of Schwarz, Miles, and Durrer. In an application filed in 1939 and issued as German Patent No. 735,196, on July 3, 1943, Professor C.V. Schwarz of Berlin–Charlottenburg stated: "The object of the present invention is a method of bringing gases into particularly intimate contact with liquid baths, for instance metal baths, by providing the jet of gas directed onto the surface of the bath with such a high kinetic energy that it is capable of penetrating in the manner of a solid body deep into the bath by the use of extremely high velocities lying preferably above the speed of sound. In this way it is possible, without any additional means, such as for instance a pipe or the like which is subject to rapid wear, to cause the jet of gas to act within the liquid baths so that the reaction takes place extremely rapidly and completely." In this top-blown pure-oxygen process, Schwarz observed, "the danger of rapid wear of the container liner is eliminated since the reaction between oxygen and iron . . . takes place in the center of the steel bath and therefore the walls of the vessel are not substantially attacked."

In Belgian Patent No. 468,316—applied for on October 4, 1946, granted on November 30, 1946, and opened for public inspection on March 1, 1947—John Miles offered some refinements on the art taught by Schwarz. He, too, worked with a top-blown converter and emphasized the importance of keeping the source of the chemical oxidation reactions within the bath "at a good distance from the refractory lining of the furnace."

Finally, Robert Durrer, a Swiss professor who had begun his experimentations at the Institut fur Eisenhüttenkunde of the Technische Hochschule at Berlin–Charlottenburg as early as 1938 and continued them at the Louis von Roll Eisenwerke in Gerlafingen, Switzerland, after the war, succeeded in producing steel with a top-blown, pure-oxygen process in a 2.5 ton experimental converter.[16] On March 21, 1948, as Durrer's associate later reported, he proved that "it is possible to refine pig-iron of varying composition with pure oxygen. There are no difficulties with respect to the durability of the nozzle or the converter lining. . . . The qualities of the steel correspond to those of normal open-hearth steel."[17]

These experiments by Durrer and Hellbrügge provided the last crucial link in the process of technology diffusion, because it was Durrer who transmitted the Schwarz and Miles teaching (and his experimental findings based thereon) to the eventual patentees—the Austrian steel firm VOEST. The sequence of events was as follows: In 1948 VOEST was contemplating an expansion of its steel plants at Linz and was actively considering all available steelmaking processes. Aware of the Durrer–Hellbrügge experiments at Gerlafingen, VOEST dispatched its Works Manager, Dr. Trenkler, to Gerlafingen on May 12, 1949, to inspect the equipment and examine the techniques which had there been employed to produce steel in a top-blown oxygen converter. Encouraged by Trenkler's favorable report, VOEST immediately initiated a test series in a two-ton modified converter which on June 25, 1949, yielded further refinements of the Schwarz–Miles–Durrer art: "first, the blowing of pure oxygen from above onto . . . a highly reactive zone in the upper region of the melt, which zone is spaced from the refractory lining of the vessel. Second, the avoiding of deep penetration of the oxygen jet into the bath [again to avoid damage to the converter lining]. Third, the avoiding of material agitation of the bath by the stirring effect of the oxygen jet. Fourth, the creation of a circulatory movement of the bath, not by mechanical action of the jet, but by the chemical reactions."[18] These refinements of the process solved not only the problem of safeguarding the converter lining, but also the need for dephosphorization through a proper slag composition.

In any event, by mid-August of 1949, VOEST was convinced of the soundness of the process and initiated the final experiments to test the process operationally and practically. These were concluded successfully by November 1950, and a new metallurgy had been born.[19] VOEST then constructed its first L-D plant which went into large-scale, commercial production in 1952.

It is noteworthy that the three major revolutions in steelmaking—the Bessemer, Siemens–Martin (open-hearth), and basic oxygen processes—were not the products of American inventive genius nor the output of giant corporate research laboratories. The oxygen process was developed in continental Europe and perfected by the employees of a nationalized enterprise, in a war-ravaged country, with a total steel ingot capacity of about 1 million tons—by a *firm* that was less than one-third the size of a single *plant* of the United States Steel Corporation.

History of the Innovation

In innovation, as in invention, the giants of the United States steel industry lagged, not led. The first large-scale commercial use of the oxygen process was in an Austrian steel plant (VOEST) in 1952. The first installation of the new process on the North American continent took place in a Canadian plant (DOFASCO) in 1954. The first United States company to obtain a license under the Austrian L-D patents was Kaiser Steel in 1953—at the time, a company with less than 1 percent of United States ingot capacity. The first United States company actually to install the oxygen process was McLouth Steel in 1954—at the time, also a firm with less than 1 percent of United States ingot capacity. The first major steel company to do so was Jones & Laughlin in 1957—to be followed by U.S. Steel and Bethlehem in 1964, and Republic in 1965. In other words, the leaders of the United States steel industry finally decided to innovate this revolutionary process fully fourteen years after an Austrian company of infinitesimal size had done so—successfully.

Instead of adopting the "only major breakthrough at the ingot level since before the turn of the century,"[20] U.S. Steel rested content with a slogan: to call itself a company "where the big idea is *innovation*."[21] John S. Tennant, General Counsel of U.S. Steel, boasted to the Kefauver Committee that "The distinguishing characteristic of the American steel industry is its tremendous productiveness, a quality which other countries have been unable to emulate so far,"[22] and that the U.S. Steel Corporation "is fully aware of, and has continuously studied and tried out, new processes developed both in this country and abroad."[23] As late as November 1957 Mr. Tennant assured the committee that such new processes as oxygen steelmaking (which had been described in glowing terms by engineers appearing before the Committee and in State Department technical dispatches from abroad) required "further development" before they "conceivably could be substituted for, or displace, existing practices."[24] Their "growth potential," he felt, "cannot be forecast."[25]

Was this policy of watchful waiting justified by a paucity of information? Could Big Steel have been expected to know more about the technical feasibility and economic advantages of the oxygen process? Could it reasonably have been expected to gather sufficient evidence sooner than it did, and therefore initiate its move to oxygen at an earlier date? Judged by the available evidence, the answer seems incontrovertibly and emphatically "yes." We say this without probing further to ask why, in view of the long-familiar potential of oxygen conversion, Big Steel had not anticipated the European invention by many years.

(1) Starting in 1952 the steel producers of the world began a ceaseless trek to

the Austrian oxygen installations at Linz and Donawitz. By 1963 some 34,000 had come to observe, inspect, and study the new process in operation.[26] The DOFASCO and McLouth installations were subjected to similar visitations by steel producers, metallurgists, and engineers.

(2) A great mass of technical literature, including literally thousands of articles in engineering and trade journals, started accumulating with the publication of the Austrian invention. As early as 1952 *Stahl und Eisen* devoted almost an entire issue to a steel conference at Leoben, Austria, where some 360 engineers and scientists (60 of them from seven countries outside of Austria) met to discuss the oxygen revolution in steelmaking and to receive first-hand reports from the leading engineers of the Linz–Donawitz plants. These reports dealt with the metallurgical characteristics of oxygen steel, the engineering aspects of operating an L-D converter, and the economic feasibility of the new process.[27] In discussing the Linz–Donawitz experience with investment and operating costs, Kurt Rösner presented detailed data to indicate that (a) the investment cost of an L-D plant was only about half that of an open-hearth plant; (b) if the cost of erecting oxygen facilities were included in the computation, the L-D plant would still cost only about 60 percent as much as an open-hearth plant; (c) operating costs in an L-D plant (exclusive of the cost of raw materials) were 72 percent of those in an open-hearth plant.[28] Rösner's conclusion, that the economic feasibility of the new process appears beyond question, was endorsed by Professor Durrer who observed that the commercial feasibility of L-D refining was firmly established for Austrian (and hence also for United States) low-phosphorus ores, but that additional work had to be done to adapt it to high-phosphorus ores.[29] Ironically enough, Durrer's comment meant that United States producers should have been the first to jump on the L-D bandwagon, whereas the European producers working as they did with high-phosphorus ores could have been excused for a delayed response.

(3) Starting with its 1954 annual report, and regularly thereafter, McLouth expressed its enthusiasm for the oxygen steel process which it had innovated in the United States.[30] In the 1954 Annual Statement, McLouth reported: "However, we are now operating the first Oxygen Steel Process in the United States. It is a revolutionary method of making high quality steel and is reducing our costs."

In the 1955 Annual Statement, McLouth stated: "Our oxygen steelmaking process, which is still the only one of its kind in the United States, has proved outstandingly successful. It has been operating at better than rated capacity."

In the 1958 Annual Statement, McLouth, reviewing its twenty-five years of operation, stated: "The most spectacular phase of the expansion program was the pioneering of the Oxygen Steel Process. . . . The steel industry watched with interest the development of this new steelmaking idea. Today many companies are considering the use of oxygen in conversion."

If these reports by a minuscule steel producer were not required reading for the giants of the industry, the views of Thomas F. Hruby, associate editor of *Steel*, writing in 1955, and endorsing the McLouth reports, should have commanded more serious attention.[31] Discussing the experience of the oxygen innovators in Canada (DOFASCO) and the United States (McLouth), Hruby wrote:

> What about open-hearth practice? Has it reached its peak? Talk to the people who are running the oxygen operations at Dominion Foundries & Steel in Canada and at McLouth Steel in Detroit. Pose the question to the many steelmakers who traveled to Austria for their first look at the process. The answer is an emphatic yes.
>
> At no time in steelmaking history has there been a process that is so right for the present and future economic climate. The key considerations: Low capital investment, a tons-per-hour rate nearly three times the open-hearth record and an operational flexibility that would lend itself to a five-day work week."[32]

DOFASCO, said Hruby, was "completely sold on the transplanted Austrian process," because it was averaging about 1,000 tons per day on a capital investment of $6 million and because this output was "better quality steel than Dominion produced in its open-hearths." As for McLouth, Hruby reported:

> When you're getting 60,000 ingot tons of production from a capital investment of $7 million, it's a pretty good deal. When you find that your ingot costs are down $3 a ton to boot, there's cause for celebration.
>
> But McLouth Steel Corp., Detroit, is too busy making the first oxygen-converter steel in this country to be celebrating. Besides, its management knew pretty well what to expect two years ago when it decided to integrate the Austrian process into its steelmaking operations.[33]

No one, Hruby concluded, could still cling to "the notion that oxygen steelmaking hasn't arrived commercially."[34] The date of Hruby's article was April 1955.

(4) Starting with its annual review issue in January 1954, the authoritative *Iron and Steel Engineer* began to chronicle the accelerating trend toward the oxygen process throughout the world, and to supply "hard" data on the technology of the process, its cost characteristics, and the quality of its product. In January 1955 the journal reported that production rates for oxygen "converters are as much as three times higher per hour than for the conventional open-hearth furnaces, and operating costs, exclusive of metallics and fixed charges, are $3.00 per ton of steel less than similar costs for open-hearth steel. Capital costs are estimated at 50 percent less than a comparably sized open-hearth shop."[35] In March of the same year, the *Iron and Steel Engineer* published an article on the economics of oxygen steelmaking, the data in which are summarized in Table I.

In January 1957 this same journal reported flatly that "The oxygen-blown converter for making steel is now an accepted tool of the steelmaker."[36] After

Table I

Comparative Costs of Oxygen and Open-Hearth Steelmaking

Capital and Operating Costs	500,000-Ton Annual Capacity (Approximately)		1,000,000-Ton Annual Capacity (Approximately)	
	Oxygen Converter	Open-Hearth	Oxygen Converter	Open-Hearth
Capital cost per annual ton	$20.22	$39.61	$12.67	$33.71
Cost of metallics per ton of steel	37.41	36.67	37.41	36.67
Operating cost per ton of steel (exclusive of cost of metallics)	9.37	14.63	8.38	14.25

Source: W. C. Rueckel and J. W. Irwin, "Economic Aspects of the Oxygen Converter," Iron and Steel Engineer, March 1955, p. 62.

offering some additional operating data on McLouth's converter, and announcing oxygen facilities under construction at Kaiser and Jones & Laughlin, it reported a new oxygen process developed in Sweden—the Kaldo or rotary oxygen converter.[37]

In January 1958 this same journal concluded that "The top-blown oxygen converter process is meeting with greater acceptance in the United States and throughout the world," and supported this conclusion with a detailed catalogue of expansions in oxygen steelmaking facilities. It indicated that various rotary oxygen processes were finding favor in France, Germany, and South Africa as well as Sweden.[38]

In January 1959 the Iron and Steel Engineer stated that one of the chief reasons for acceptance of the oxygen converter is "the low capital cost, which has been estimated at $15 a ton, compared with about $40 a ton for added open-hearth capacity."[39]

Finally, in January 1960, after citing an Association of Iron and Steel Engineers estimate of $15 per annual ton of oxygen capacity versus $35 per ton for open-hearth capacity, this same journal offered the "strong conclusion . . . that the United States has probably already seen the last large new open-hearth shop to be built."[40] Indeed, the journal reported the dismantling of "some 175-ton open-hearths" at Jones & Laughlin's Cleveland works to make room for 200-ton oxygen converters.[41] "Oxygen steelmaking techniques," the journal said by way of remarkable understatement, "have had a tremendous impact on future steelmaking plans."[42]

(5) Starting with its annual review of iron and steel technology for 1953, the Economic Commission for Europe corroborated the findings of both American

and foreign trade and engineering journals with respect to the efficacy of oxygen steelmaking. "Undoubtedly the most interesting and extensive recent development in steelmaking has been improvement in quality, by the use of oxygen in basic Thomas converters,"[43] the ECE reported for 1953: "The 'L-D' plant, *including the cost of an oxygen* plant, costs approximately half of the capital cost of an open-hearth plant of the same capacity. . . . It seems clear that this 'L-D' process . . . can produce a high quality of steel with low nitrogen content and at favourable cost."[44]

For the year 1954 the Commission offered the following comparative capital costs for plants with a monthly production capacity of 100,000 tons[45]:

Type of Installation	Total Capital Cost	Tap to Tap Time	Monthly Production
Six 225-ton open-hearth furnaces	$22 million	9 hours	100,000 tons
Five 35-ton L-D oxygen converters (one of which is in reserve)	10 million*	1 hour	100,000 tons

*These capital cost estimates also provide for the necessary tonnage oxygen plant.

The report concluded: "In an existing works, having, say, six or eight open-hearth furnaces, some of which may no longer be up to date, the logical development would appear to be to replace two or three of the older open-hearth furnaces by either conventional or oxygen-blown converters, although this involves considerable alterations in the buildings and layout."[46]

Subsequent ECE reports merely reinforced these findings and chronicled the rapid adoption of the new process both in Europe and elsewhere.[47] In 1959 the Commission stated that "During recent years the share of oxygen converters in new steelmaking capacity has increased tremendously," and predicted that "it seems most likely" that this trend will continue, especially at the expense of open-hearth furnaces.[48]

(6) By mid-1957 steel technology had become a matter of political concern in the United States, and the Kefauver Committee expressed lively doubts about the industry's efficiency and progressiveness. The Committee showed particular interest in the failure of the American industry to emulate the inventive and innovative performance of its European counterparts.

Relying on State Department dispatches, Senator Kefauver challenged the industry to explain its apparent failure.[49] These dispatches—from Vienna, Stockholm, and Luxembourg—added little to what had already appeared in the technical and trade literature. More interesting than their contents was the industry's reaction. Thus U.S. Steel conceded that "some form of oxygen steelmaking will undoubtedly become an important feature in steelmaking in this country," but it declined to say when or to commit itself to introducing this innovation.[50] Indeed,

Table II

Annual L-D Steelmaking Capacity (millions of tons)

Year	United States	World
1953	—	0.5
54	—	0.9
55	0.54	1.9
56	.54	2.0
57	.54	2.7
58	1.35	5.2
59	3.58	9.5
60	4.16	11.5
61	4.65	17.2
62	7.50	24.7

Source: Trial Brief for Plaintiffs, *Kaiser* v. *McLouth*, Civil Action No. 16,900, U.S. District Court (E.D. Mich.), p. 67.

three years later, *Fortune* still pictured the Corporation as confronted by "painfully difficult choices between competing alternatives—for example, whether to spend large sums for cost reduction *now* [1960], in effect committing the company to *present* technology, or to stall for time in order to capitalize on a new and perhaps far superior technology that may be available in a few years."[51] The Kefauver challenge had seemingly done little to stir Big Steel from its lethargy.

Reviewing the history of innovation with respect to oxygen steelmaking, the following conclusions are inescapable. *First,* as Table II indicates, United States steelmakers lagged behind the rest of the world in adopting the L-D process. By September 1963 the United States had some 10,040,000 tons of L-D capacity in place—compared with 46,210,000 tons for the world as a whole.[52] If more than 2.5 million tons of other types of oxygen capacity (Kaldo process and rotary converter) be added to the world total, the United States share would be even smaller. Since the L-D process could not immediately be adapted to most European ores, the contrast is even more striking.

Second, with the exception of Jones & Laughlin, not a single major steel producer in the United States installed an oxygen converter prior to 1962. Two of the Big Three—U.S. Steel and Bethlehem—had no oxygen capacity until 1964, and Republic none until 1965. Yet they, with a much wider age distribution of existing equipment, should have been the first to experiment.

Third, the innovator of oxygen steelmaking in the United States was the twelfth largest steel company (McLouth) in 1954, to be followed by the fourth largest (Jones & Laughlin) in 1957, the ninth largest (Kaiser) in 1958, the nineteenth largest (Acme) in 1959, the tenth largest (Colorado Fuel & Iron) in 1961, the fifth largest (National) in 1962, and by the fifteenth largest (Pittsburgh),

Table III

**Distribution of L-D Oxygen Capacity among
United States Steel Producers, 1963**

U.S. Steel Co.'s Rank in the Industry*	Oxygen Steel Capacity (tons)	Percentage of U.S. Oxygen Steel Capacity	Percentage of Total U.S. Steel Capacity*
1st, 2d, 3d	0	0	52.27
4th, 5th, 6th	6,550,000	50.62	14.76
9th, 10th, 12th, 15th, 19th	6,390,000	49.38	7.06
All companies	12,940,000	100	100

Source: American Iron and Steel Institute, *Iron and Steel Works Directory of the United States and Canada*, 1960; Kaiser Engineers, *L-D Process Newsletter*, Sept. 27, 1963.
*Based on company ingot capacity as of Jan. 1, 1960.

twenty-second largest (Allegheny–Ludlum),[53] and the sixth largest (Armco) in 1963. By the end of 1963 oxygen steelmaking capacity in the United States was distributed as above.

It is also significant that the Swedish Kaldo process, another oxygen steel-making technique, was innovated in the United States by Sharon Steel—a company which accounted for 1.3 percent of total United States steel capacity and ranked thirteenth among ingot producers.

Finally, it is clear that despite Big Steel's decade of rationalization, the technological avalanche of the oxygen converter could not be stopped. Thus, current estimates indicate that by 1975 some 45 percent of United States steel production will come from oxygen vessels and that the open-hearth will be displaced as the workhorse of the steel industry (Table IV).

Moreover, it is ironic that this comprehensive modernization will be taking place during a period of substantial "unused"—or more accurately, economically "unusable"—capacity. Thus, in 1964, the American steel industry was installing oxygen converters at a frenetic pace while using only some 75 percent of existing facilities—and this in a banner year for steel production. Obviously, as the *Wall Street Journal* observed, the increase in ingot capacity came "because of mill efforts to lower costs and not from any lack of raw steel." The industry was mothballing some 7 million tons of open-hearth capacity, reclassifying it as "standby capacity" with the intention of dismantling much of it "before long."[54]

Similarly, the *Iron and Steel Engineer* found it significant that much of the projected new oxygen capacity will in many cases "be used to replace existing

Table IV

Total United States Production of Steel Ingots for 1963 and Forecasts to 1975 (millions of net tons)

Year	Open-Hearth	Bessemer	Oxygen Converter	Electric Furnace	Total
1963	88.8	1.0	8.5	10.9	109.2
1975	54.0	—	61.0	20.0	135.0

Source: Battelle Memorial Institute, "Technical and Economic Analysis of the Impact of Recent Developments in Steelmaking Practices on the Supplying Industries," Oct. 30, 1964, p. X-3.

workable capacity. Companies are being forced to the process in order to compete, and also perhaps in some cases to develop their know-how. *The low capital cost and the savings in operating costs more than overbalance any considerations to continue operating existing equipment."* [55]

In sum, given the steel industry's record of innovation with respect to oxygen steelmaking, it seems reasonable to suggest that Big Steel is neither big because it is progressive nor progressive because it is big.

II

The invention of the oxygen converter, and the history of its innovation, assume particular significance because of the periodic—indeed endemic—complaints by the steel industry about its unreasonably low rates of return and, consequently, its inability properly to finance replacement, expansion, and modernization. While these profit grumbles can be traced back to at least 1939,[56] they have, if anything, been voiced with increasing persistence (and *forte voce*) since then. In 1958, for example, Robert Tyson, Chairman of the Finance Committee of U.S. Steel, argued that steel industry earnings of 13.9 percent on net assets were really subaverage because of a substantial deficiency in recorded depreciation.[57] In the industry's dispute with President Kennedy in 1961, U.S. Steel used profits as a percentage of sales—probably because the President had relied upon a net worth measure.[58] When the 1962 showdown came, U.S. Steel and its fellow oligopolists emphasized the "financial squeeze"[59]; as in 1958, the high cost of "modernization" was not only mentioned, but made a key point in the attempt to justify a price increase.[60] When, in 1964, the steel industry again came into conflict with the White House and the Council of Economic Advisers' guidelines, it once again fell back on an inadequate return on investment to support its price increases.[61]

If the industry added a net of 40 million tons of the "wrong" capacity during the 1950 decade[62]; if the gross addition to capacity during the period amounted to 49 million tons[63]; if the industry could have begun to adopt the oxygen process as early as 1950; if this revolutionary steelmaking process would have provided the industry with substantial savings both in capital investment and operating costs—does it not follow that Big Steel's profit grumbles are in part the result of self-inflicted injury? The rough magnitude of the "improvement" in the industry's level of profits, and the availability of financial resources for replacement and modernization—assuming the industry had followed a policy other than one of suicidal investment—shall now be sketched in rudimentary outline.

According to the theory of replacement economics,[64] a new technique should be substituted for an old one whenever present value of the firm would be greater after the substitution. To make a precise comparison of present values would entail detailed knowledge not only of the immediate outlay on the new process and the cost of capital (to be used as a discount rate), but also of future patterns of operating receipts and expenditures and the net scrap values of presently used and substitute equipment. Obviously, we do not have this information for each steel company. But when there exist operating savings after depreciation from a new process sufficient to cover a reasonable return on the capital required for the new process, it may be assumed that a more precise present value comparison would also show the rationality of substitution. The investment in the old machines is, of course, sunk, and both return on and depreciation of this sunk capital may be disregarded in computations.

Earlier discussion has indicated that the operating savings resulting from use of the oxygen converter may reasonably be taken to be $5 per ton. While a single figure is, of course, subject to qualification, it does not appear that $15 per ton is a serious underestimate of the investment that would have been required in the years 1950–60 to install oxygen converters in United States mills. Unless the cost of capital to steel companies was as high as 33 percent during this period, they could have shown a clear gain by replacing open-hearth with oxygen capacity. Note that this comparison disregards advantages of the BOP process such as superior quality control and lower plant space requirements.

A complete substitution could have been easily achieved by 1961. The industry's cash flow during the years 1950–60 was $14.6 billion. To put in operation 87 million tons of oxygen capacity—the approximate amount necessary to produce the steel made in 1960 by open-hearth facilities—would have required an outlay of no more than $1.3 billion or about 12 percent of the industry's actual capital expenditures of $11 billion. These expenditures included purchase of new and modernization of old open-hearth furnaces.

Assuming the substitution to have been made, we can recompute the rate of return that the basic steel industry could have earned on the equity in 1960. If 87 million tons of steel had been produced by the oxygen process, total operating savings of $432 million could have been realized. After-tax profits would therefore have been $216 million higher. Net worth could have been reduced by as much as $1.7 billion—the difference between the investment required for 87 million tons of open-hearth capacity, and the same amount of oxygen converter capacity. Given an expansion in net profit and a decrease in equity in such magnitudes, the industry's computed return on net worth in 1960 would have been in the neighborhood of 11.6 percent, instead of the 7.6 percent it actually realized—an increase of some 65 percent in profits.[65]

This computation is set forth only for illustrative purposes, but it shows the "ball-park" boundaries wherein a meaningful rate of return for the steel industry may lie. If the assumptions were changed, the magnitude of the difference between actual and potential returns would also be changed. For instance, if the entire open-hearth capacity of 122,000,000 tons had been replaced by oxygen converters, investment and net worth would have dropped by almost $2.5 billion. The computed rate of return would have been still higher.[66] On the other hand, to the extent that the steel companies carried their open-hearth production assets at less than original cost of installation at 1960 prices, the adjusted rate of return would be less.

One further observation might be made regarding the steel industry's persistent complaint that it is earning less than a satisfactory return. Comparisons of return on net worth with averages for manufacturing industry during the years 1947–63 do show a deficiency for steel. The industry, therefore, had additional reason to replace existing plant with less costly production facilities. It would also have been rational for the industry to have reduced its total capital investments, whereas it did just the opposite.

III

Our review of the circumstances of invention, and the pace and sponsorship of innovation, of the most revolutionary cost-saving development in steelmaking since the Siemens–Martin furnace has, we believe, raised serious doubts concerning the *universality* of the "Schumpeter" hypothesis. If the hypothesis is to have general validity, it must be demonstrably applicable to the most important inventions in concentrated, oligopolized industries. But the history of the development of the oxygen process shows just the opposite.

In the first place, the invention was neither sponsored nor supported by large, dominant firms. Nor were these firms leaders in introducing the revolutionary development. Their indifference is explicable either on the grounds of ignorance or delinquency, and the first of these alternatives must be rejected almost summarily. In view of the wide publicity given to the Leoben conference of 1951, the thousands of articles on oxygen and steelmaking in technical and trade journals, and U.S. Steel's assertion that it is aware of every new development in the industry, it is incredible that the engineers of Big Steel were unaware of the Austrian breakthrough.

Second, it was a small firm that first innovated the new process in the United States, and it was other small firms that followed its lead. We submit that this consequence should not be entirely unexpected because it may well be that the structural and behavioral characteristics of oligopolized industries *prevent* the dominant firms from pioneering. Instead, the small firms may be the innovators because, unlike their giant rivals, what they do in the way of cost reductions is unlikely to cause so violent a disturbance of the status quo. Hence, based on the steel industry experience, it seems as reasonable to assume that innovation is sponsored by firms in inverse order of size as it is to assume the contrary. (In fact, we would hazard a guess that inquiry into innovation in other industries might turn up the same conclusion; for instance, the most important breakthrough in petroleum refining techniques since cracking itself—the development of *catalytic* cracking—was innovated by a small, maverick major. Only after Sun Oil had given positive evidence of its commitment to the Houdry process were its billion-dollar giant rivals willing to venture into the area to develop competing processes.)

Third, our assessment of the consequences of the lag in United States adoption of the oxygen process has shown that the steel industry's complaint about inadequate profits and lack of modernization funds have been sadly exaggerated. Had the dominant steel firms seized the initiative, and carried out a genuine modernization program in the 1950s, their earnings would have been substantially higher and their depreciation and replacement requirements appreciably lower—due to much lower operating costs per ton of ingot capacity and lower depreciation and replacement costs on a lower investment base. Until the steel industry restates its accounts to reflect the efficiencies that have been possible for at least the past fifteen years, little credence should be given to its plaintive pleas for higher prices or profits.

Finally, there is another implication to our study of the steel industry's curious inversion of the source of innovation. It has often been assumed that, if homogeneous oligopolies do not compete in price, their leading members compete in innovating—and that the public thereby benefits as much as, if not more than, it would by price competition. Yet the oxygen converter history reveals the steel oligopoly as failing to compete in strategic innovations. What benefits, then, remain for large size in steel?

Notes

1. Richard Caves, *American Industry: Structure, Conduct, Performance,* p. 98 (1964).

2. Schumpeter qualified his hypothesis more carefully than did his disciples. To be sure, he argued that, ". . . largest-scale plans could in many cases not materialize at all if it were not known from the outset that competition will be discouraged by heavy capital requirements or lack of experience, or that means are available to discourage or checkmate it so as to gain the time and space for further developments . . ."; but he also observed that "it is certainly as conceivable that an all-pervading cartel system might

sabotage all progress as it is that it might realize, with smaller social and private costs, all that perfect competition is supposed to realize." *Capitalism, Socialism, and Democracy,* pp. 89, 91 (1942). For a balanced restatement of the Schumpeter hypothesis, see Edward S. Mason, *Economic Concentration and the Monopoly Problem,* pp. 91–101 (1957), and Jesse W. Markham, "Market Structure, Business Conduct, and Innovation," *American Economic Review, Papers and Proceedings,* pp. 323–32 (May 1965).

3. John K. Galbraith, *American Capitalism,* p. 86 (Rev. ed., 1956).

4. Ibid., p. 91.

5. David E. Lilienthal, *Big Business: A New Era,* p. 69 (1953).

6. Henry H. Villard, "Competition, Oligopoly, and Research," *Journal of Political Economy,* p. 483 (Dec. 1958).

7. John Jewkes, David Sawers, and Richard Stillerman, *The Sources of Invention* (1958). Jacob Schmookler, "Bigness, Fewness, and Research," *Journal of Political Economy,* pp. 628–35 (Dec. 1959). And esp. Daniel Hamberg, "Size of Firm, Monopoly, and Economic Growth," *Employment, Growth, and Price Levels, Part 7, Hearings before the Joint Economic Committee,* 86th Cong., 1st Sess., pp. 2337–53 (1959); "Invention in the Industrial Research Laboratory," *Journal of Political Economy,* pp. 95–115 (April 1963); and "Size of Firm, Oligopoly, and Research: The Evidence," *Canadian Journal of Economics and Political Science,* pp. 62–75 (Feb. 1964).

8. Edwin A. Mansfield, for example, has conducted some highly useful statistical research into the relation between size of firm and both the importance and adoption speed of innovations. ("Size of Firm, Market Structure and Innovation," *Journal of Political Economy,* pp. 556–76 [Dec. 1963], and "The Speed of Response of Firms to New Techniques," *Quarterly Journal of Economics,* pp. 290–311 [May 1963].) His conclusions, however, as he would be the first to concede, do not permit assured generalizations with regard to the central hypothesis. For instance, he found some evidence that the length of time a firm waits before using a new technique tends to be inversely related to the size of the innovator ("The Speed of Response of Firms to New Techniques," op. cit.). On the other hand, the steel industry remains an unexplained exception to his conclusion that the larger firms were more likely to innovate than the smaller ("Size of Firm, Market Structure and Innovation, op. cit.). As we see it, the major weakness of the Mansfield approach is that it drowns in aggregate generalization what must be qualitatively evaluated in a careful case-by-case analysis.

9. After a comprehensive review of the recent literature, Jesse Markham concludes that "The difficulty with such regression analyses as these is not so much their statistical as their conceptual inconclusiveness." (Op. cit., p. 331.)

10. British Patent No. 2768 of 1855.

11. British Patent No. 1292 of 1856.

12. By 1948 A.B. Robiette could report that "Developments in the production of cheap oxygen by the Linde–Fränkl and other systems have so reduced the cost of oxygen that it can now be seriously considered both for combustion systems and for the refining of pig iron and the production of steel." "Use of Oxygen for Steelmaking," *The Iron and Coal Trades Review,* May 28, 1948, p. 1103.

13. Between 1936 and 1940, for example, O. Lellep conducted experiments at Oberhausen, Germany, with the use of pure oxygen in a bottom-blown converter. While he succeeded in producing high quality steel at a low cost, he found no way of preserving the service life of the converter bottom, and hence failed to come up with a commercially feasible process. "Versuche zur Stahlherstellung im Herdofen und Konverter unter Benutzung von konzentriertem Sauerstoff, ausgeführt in der Gutehoffnungshütte A.-G., Oberhausen, in der Zeitperiode von 1936 bis 1940," published in Mexico City in 1941; cited in *Stahl und Eisen,* Vol. 71 (Dec. 20, 1951), p. 1442.

By 1945 the Russians had built a special converter plant at their Kuznetsk Steel Works to study the production of Bessemer steel by use of an oxygen-enriched or pure-oxygen blast in a bottom-blown converter. They too failed to develop a method for preserving the service life of the tuyere when using 100 percent concentration of oxygen. See the article by V.V. Konjakov in *Engineer's Digest,* Nov. 1947, p. 522, cited in *Iron Age,* Feb. 19, 1948, p. 70.

The Germans conducted successful experiments in bottom-blown converters by use of 64 percent pure oxygen at Haspe and 73 percent pure oxygen at Oberhausen (*Stahl und Eisen,* Vol. 70 [Apr. 13, 1950], pp. 303–21 and Vol. 71 [Nov. 8, 1951], pp. 1189–99), but failed in further efforts to increase the oxygen concentration in the blast without excessive wear and tear of the converter bottom.

14. As early as 1904 Herman A. Brassert described a side-blown converter using "dry air," oxygen, or oxygen-enriched air. He suggested that a suitable number of tuyeres be positioned around the converter vessel above the metal line "So as to direct the air issuing from them downwardly onto the surface of the metal in the bath whereby a whirling or rotary motion will be given to the metal." (U.S. Patent No. 1,032,653, applied for on November 11, 1904, and issued on July 16, 1912.) Notable among the experiments and pilot projects subsequently undertaken were those of Jones & Laughlin (started in 1942) and Carnegie–Illinois (started in 1946). By 1949 both companies had concluded that their side-blown converter (turbo-hearth) process was "fundamentally sound" and that it could be made to yield low-nitrogen, low-phosphorus steels in commercial quantities, if certain operating problems were solved and the equipment design modified. See E.C. Bain (vice-president, Carnegie–Illinois) and H.W. Graham (vice-president, Jones & Laughlin), "The Turbo-Hearth—A New Steelmaking Technique," *Iron Age,* Apr. 21, 1949, pp. 62–65. For a discussion of other side-blown converter experiments, see *Stahl und Eisen,* Vol. 62 (Sept. 3, 1942), pp. 749–56 and Vol. 64 (June 1, 1944), pp. 349–58. Both of these volumes of *Stahl und Eisen* were reproduced and distributed to scientific centers in the United States during World War II by the Alien Property Custodian.

15. Extensive experiments with oxygen-steam combinations were conducted by Coheur, Marbais, Daubersy et al. at the Belgian Centre National de Recherches Metallurgiques in Liège. For accounts of these experiments, see *Stahl und Eisen,* Vol. 70 (Oct. 26, 1950), pp. 1015–17, (Nov. 9, 1950), pp. 1077–79, and Revue Universelle de Mines, Vol. 93 (1950), pp. 104–8, 401–2, 402–7, 408–17, 418–23 and 423–30.

16. R. Durrer, "Sauerstoff-Frischen in Gerlafingen," *von Roll Werkzeitung,* Vol. 19 (May 1948), pp. 73–74.

17. H. Hellbrügge, "Die Umwandlung von Roheisen in Stahl in Konverter bei Verwendung von reinem Sauerstoff," *Stahl und Eisen,* Vol. 70 (Dec. 21, 1950), p. 1211 (freely translated from the original German).

18. Testimony of Dr. Hauttmann, one of the co-inventors of record, in *Kaiser v. McLouth,* Civil Action No. 16,900, U.S. District Court (E.D. Mich.), 1964, Record p. 2754.

19. The Austrians refer to the process as L-D which either stands for Linz–Dusenverfahren or for Linz–Donawitz (the location of the patentee's steel plants). In the United States, it is variously referred to as the Oxygen Converter Process, Basic Oxygen Furnace Process, BOP, or OSM.

20. Statement by Avery Adams of James & Laughlin, quoted in *Forbes,* Jan. 1, 1960, p. 95.

21. Advertisement, *Wall Street Journal,* Jan. 13, 1965, p. 13 (emphasis in original).

22. Hearings of the Subcommittee on Antitrust and Monopoly, Administered Prices: Steel, Part 3, 85th Cong., 1st Sess., p. 1059 (1958) (hereinafter cited as Kefauver Hearings).

23. Ibid., p. 1060.

24. Ibid., p. 1057.

25. Ibid., p. 1058. Not even the trade journals had the charity to accept (or at least ignore) this stance of self-congratulatory catatonia. *Forbes* called it a "sad fact" that "despite the 49 million tons of new capacity the U.S. industry had added in the Fifties, its over-all operations were slack and inefficient, its technology retarded, its plant antiquated and inefficient." (Jan. 1, 1963, p. 31.) After 1957, *Forbes* pointed out, "the U.S. industry discovered to its astonishment that European and Japanese producers were ahead not only in labor costs but in production efficiency as well." (Ibid.) It was not before 1962, however, and then "at whatever cost," that the "U.S. steel industry seemed determined to create a national steel plant as modern and efficient as those of its foreign competitors." (Ibid.) During the fifties, according to *Business Week*, the industry was seemingly gripped by technological indecision. So the industry leaders did "what steel has done in similar situations for years. They're withholding major investments while they watch very closely the operating results—and problems—of the pioneers." (Nov. 26, 1955, pp. 58–64.)

26. Trial Brief for Plaintiffs, *Kaiser* v. *McLouth*, Civil Action No. 16,900, U.S. District Court (E.D. Mich.), p. 65.

27. The proceedings of the Leoben conference, held in December 1951, were printed in *Stahl und Eisen*, Vol. 72 (Aug. 14, 1952), pp. 989–1024.

28. Ibid., p. 997 ff. Rösner points out, inter alia, that labor costs in the L-D process are only half those in the open-hearth process.

29. Ibid., p. 1019.

30. McLouth, Annual Reports for years cited.

31. "Oxygen Steelmaking Arrives," *Steel*, April 4, 1955, pp. 80–83. The same issue of *Steel* contains an article, "What Happens in the Oxygen Vessel," giving operational details on the process based on DOFASCO's experience.

32. Ibid., p. 80.

33. Ibid.

34. Ibid.

35. Ibid., p. 125. A $3 saving in processing cost of L-D vs. OH steel was reported in *Iron Age*, Feb. 6, 1958, pp. 55–58, and a $3–$12 saving in conversion costs was reported in *Iron Age*, Sept. 24, 1959, pp. 67–68.

36. Ibid., p. 137.

37. Ibid., p. 141.

38. Ibid., p. 165.

39. Ibid., p. 33. This estimate was based on the experience at Jones & Laughlin, and was previously reported in *Iron Age*, Dec. 12, 1957, p. 87.

40. Ibid., p. 67. The estimate presented at the Association of Iron and Steel Engineers meetings was previously cited in *Steel*, Vol. 144 (Apr. 27, 1959), p. 61.

41. Ibid., p. 68.

42. Ibid., p. 43.

43. United Nations, Economic Commission for Europe, *Some Important Developments during 1953 in Iron and Steel Technology* (Geneva: January 7, 1954), p. 10.

44. Ibid., pp. 13, 15 (emphasis supplied).

45. United Nations, Economic Commission for Europe, *Recent Advances in Steel Technology and Market Development*, 1954 (Geneva: February 22, 1955), p. 31.

46. Ibid., p. 30.

47. United Nations, Economic Commission for Europe, *Advances in Steel Technology in 1955* (Geneva, 1956), and *Advances in Steel Technology in 1956* (Geneva, 1958). The latter contained an article by I.P. Bardin, member of the Soviet Academy, stating that "In the USSR experience obtained in the use of oxygen in top-blown converters (at the

Novo-Tulsk, Enakiev and Petrovsky Works) has shown that steel produced by this method has nearly the same physical and mechanical properties as open-hearth steel." (Op. cit., p. 13.) Bardin also reported that "The cost of installing a converter shop *with oxygen-producing equipment* is considerably lower than that of building an open-hearth shop of the same capacity. Operational costs with the converter process are also somewhat lower." (Ibid., emphasis supplied.)

48. United Nations, Economic Commission for Europe, *Long-term Trends and Problems of the European Steel Industry* (Geneva, 1959), p. 104, and *Comparison of Steelmaking Processes* (New York, 1962), esp. pp. 77–83.

49. See Kefauver Hearings, op. cit., pp. 1365 ff. and passim.

50. Ibid., pp. 1057–60.

51. Charles E. Silberman, "Steel: It's a Brand-New Industry," *Fortune*, p. 124 (Dec. 1960) (emphasis supplied).

52. Kaiser Engineers, *L-D Process Newsletter,* Sept. 27, 1963, pp. 3–6. The lag of the United States behind other major steel producers is all the more remarkable, because the L-D process developed by the Austrians was immediately applicable to conversion to our low-phosphorus ores. Major European steelmakers by contrast, had to wait until 1957 before the L-D process was modified sufficiently (by the addition of lime powders in the LD-AC, OLP, and LD-Pompey processes) to be suitable for processing high-phosphorus ores constituting their primary supply. Once this adaptation was made, these countries moved to install the latest technology. So did Japan. See *Comparison of Steel-making Processes,* op. cit., esp. pp. 78–82.

53. Allegheny–Ludlum's installation was experimental only.

54. Jan. 4, 1965, p. 4. The *Wall Street Journal* also reported new oxygen capacity of 10.2 million tons, projected by U.S. Steel, Republic, Inland, and Wheeling, commenting that "Mills generally put in the new furnaces to cut costs rather than expand capacity. Oxygen furnaces turn out a batch of steel in 40 minutes, compared with six hours for even the fastest open-hearth furnaces. Capital expense per ton of capacity is lower, too, running around $12 to $15 compared with $30 to $35 for an open-hearth." January 7, 1965, p. 1.

55. Jan. 1963, p. 171 (emphasis supplied). Precisely how much open-hearth capacity —even if equipped with oxygen lances—is obsolete is a closely guarded industry secret.

56. See Kaplan, Dirlam, Lanzillotti, *Pricing in Big Business,* p. 169 (1958).

57. *Steel and Inflation: Fact vs. Fiction,* Public Relations Dept., U.S. Steel Corp., p. 37 (1958).

58. See "Dear Mr. President . . . ," pp. 2, 7, and also speeches by Senators Gore and Kefauver, *Congressional Record,* Aug. 15, 1961.

59. See "The Steel Price Rise: A Matter of Necessity," a statement by Leslie B. Worthington, President of U.S. Steel, April 10, 1962, p. 3, and "In the Public Interest" remarks by R.M. Blough, Annual Meeting of Stockholders, U.S. Steel, May 7, 1962. Blough stressed the rise in costs, the decrease in profit margins as a percent of sales, and the rising costs of replacement and "modernization."

60. See R.M. Blough, "My Side of the Story," *Look,* Jan. 29, 1963, p. 21. There he states that the proposed "very small increase would have made it possible for U.S. Steel to invest in modern plants and equipment . . . and eventually allow us to compete more effectively with foreign steel imports."

61. See statements quoted in *New York Times,* Section III, Nov. 1, 1964, pp. 1 and 12. Mr. Block of Inland Steel said that "The clear fact is that we do not make a satisfactory return on the vast sums of money invested in the industry." C.M. Beeghly, chairman of Jones & Laughlin, asked for a "competitive return on investment."

62. *Business Week,* Nov. 16, 1963, pp. 144–46.

63. *Forbes,* Jan. 1, 1963, p. 31. Drawing on capacity data of the American Iron &

Steel Institute, the Office of Business Economics, Department of Commerce, places the net increase at 48.6 million tons. Joint Economic Committee, Steel Prices, Unit Costs, Profits, and Foreign Competition, 88th Cong., 1st Sess., p. 193 (1962). The Bureau of Labor Statistics Background Statistics, brought up to April 1963, Table 2a, also indicates a 48 million ton increase in capacity—with identical figures taken from the AISI.

64. Cf. Morris A. Copeland, *Our Free Enterprise Economy*, pp. 181–209 (1965). While his illustrations are simplified, Copeland presents the fundamental elements of capital cost, timing of expenditures and receipts, and their discount to present value, clearly and forcefully.

65. According to financial data for firms accounting for 93 percent of basic steel production in 1960, stockholders' equity was shown as $10.2 billion, and net income at $767 million. With the adjustments noted above, income and equity would have been $983 million and $8.5 billion, respectively. *The Iron Age Annual Review Number*, Jan. 1962.

66. Substantial asset write-downs would necessitate readjustment of surplus and perhaps even capital accounts of some firms; but this would not alter the currently realized rate of return.

4

Vertical Divestiture of the Petroleum Majors: An Affirmative Case

I. Introduction

On September 30, 1940, the Department of Justice filed a massive antitrust case against twenty-two major oil companies, 379 of their subsidiaries and affiliates, and the American Petroleum Institute (which Clarence Darrow had described in 1934 as "the switch board for the controlling companies").[1] The Department articulated the rationale for filing this comprehensive structural case, which came to be known as the *Mother Hubbard* case, as follows:

> This proceeding is being instituted under the Department's policy of taking up in a single investigation or proceeding all of the restraints which affect the distribution of a product from the raw material to the consumer. Only in this way can economic results be achieved. Piecemeal prosecutions against segments of an industry are both costly and inconclusive. They do not raise the fundamental issues which the Court should decide, and therefore do not clarify the law. They allow restraints of trade to flourish in one segment of the industry while they are being prosecuted in another.
>
> In the past 10 years, the Department has been flooded with complaints from independents and consumers against various practices in the oil industry. These complaints have resulted in a series of piecemeal prosecutions in all of which the Government has been successful. Yet in spite of the success of these prosecutions, the complaints continue, prices are still inflexible, independent enterprise is still under a handicap, because the cases applied only to segments rather than to the entire structure of the industry.
>
> For this reason the present action is brought. It will eventually present to the Supreme Court of the United States for final decision all of the issues with respect to the reasonableness of the present vast combinations in the production, transportation, refining, and distribution of petroleum products.[2]

Originally published in the *Vanderbilt Law Review,* vol. 30 (November 1977); reprinted with permission.

The complaint as originally drafted asked that the twenty-two principal defendants be ordered to divest their transportation and marketing facilities. With the outbreak of war in Europe and the United States' imminent involvement in the conflict, however, the Attorney General agreed to delete the request for structural relief from the complaint.[3] Like so many other cases of great pitch and moment, the *Mother Hubbard* case eventually was settled by a pusilanimous consent decree.[4]

On July 18, 1973, the Federal Trade Commission issued a complaint against the eight largest domestic oil companies.[5] The complaint in *In re Exxon Corp.* charged the companies with maintaining and reinforcing "a noncompetitive market structure" in the refining industry on the East and Gulf coasts through their control of crude oil and crude transportation. In language reminiscent of the *Mother Hubbard* case, the Commission stated the rationale for its action as follows:

> The history of the Federal Trade Commission's activity in the petroleum industry has been characterized by a case-by-case attack on specific anticompetitive marketing practices. This approach has, in general, been of limited success in controlling wasteful marketing practices, dealer coercion, and the lack of competition in the petroleum industry. Despite the staff's success in bringing and winning cases before the Commission and in the courts, as well as obtaining compliance orders, the petroleum industry over the last 50 years has managed to circumvent the orders in many cases by subtle changes in policy or practices. . . .
>
> The reason for the limited success of the early petroleum cases is not to be found in the cases or remedies themselves. The staff did a thorough job in researching, developing and prosecuting the individual cases. The remedies applied in each case were directed at the particular abuse. But the practice-by-practice approach to antitrust attack, which sought to correct specific anticompetitive conduct at the marketing level, did not adequately address the industry's vertically integrated structure or its multi-level behavior. The major oil companies operate on four levels—crude production, refining, transportation, and marketing. To fashion a remedy for one level without considering the performance of a company, or the industry, at the other levels, ignores the market power associated with vertical integration and limited competition.[6]

As in *Mother Hubbard*, the antitrust authorities recognized that an industry's noncompetitive structure militates toward noncompetitive behavior and results in noncompetitive performance. They recognized that, if the goals of the antitrust laws are to be attained, there is no alternative to structural reorganization of the horizontally and vertically integrated oil oligopoly.

More important than this latest antitrust action against the petroleum industry, however, is the growing awareness in Congress—precipitated in part by the Arab oil embargo of October 1973 and by the subsequent rise in petroleum prices and oil company profits—that the oil industry for all intents and purposes is operating a worldwide cartel that is not subject to effective regulation by the government, to the discipline of a competitive marketplace, or to systematic compulsion to promote the public interest. Policy makers grow increasingly aware that structural reform of the industry is imperative and that such reform probably will have to be achieved by legislation rather than by litigation. Accordingly, several divestiture bills were introduced in the Ninety-fourth Congress, some providing for functional vertical divestiture within the petroleum industry, others for horizontal divestiture to prevent the leading oil companies from dominating alternate sources of energy.[7] One of these bills, S. 2387, was reported out favorably by the Senate Judiciary Committee on June 15, 1976, but no floor action was taken. Nevertheless, S. 2387 was attached as a vertical divestiture amendment to the natural gas deregulation bill, but was defeated by the narrow margin of only nine votes, forty-five to fifty-four.[8] Divestiture had become one of the central issues in congressional debates during the energy crisis.

This article will examine: first, the concentration of economic power in the oil industry; second, the manner in which vertical integration reinforces the horizontal control exercised by the major oil companies; third, the extent to which prevailing patterns of vertical integration are based on efficiency considerations; and, finally, whether vertical divestiture is a feasible remedy.

II. The Concentrated Power of Big Oil

Spokesmen for the oil industry claim that it includes some 10,000 producers and that the concentration ratios, especially in crude oil, are far lower than in other major industries, notably the automobile, aluminum, computer, and aircraft industries.[9] Commenting on this line of argument, John W. Wilson has observed:

> Despite its size, conventional concentration ratio measurements indicate that oil is not particularly concentrated in comparison with other major industries. . . . [W]hile the concentration ratios for the top four or top eight crude oil producers have increased substantially in the last twenty years, the industry still seems to compare favorably with other leading manufacturing industries, such as automobiles, copper, computers, and aluminum. Thus, argue the industry's defenders, right-thinking rational men should direct their antitrust interests toward more critical targets like breakfast cereals and beer, and leave oil alone.[10]

At first blush, the oil industry's argument seems persuasive (see Table 1), but, in fact, it is misleading for a number of reasons.

First, concentration has been increasing steadily since the mid-1950's, so that by 1974 the eight largest companies controlled almost as large a share of crude oil production as did the twenty largest in 1955. This trend is explained in part by the massive mergers during the period, especially mergers between the very largest companies. In 1965, for example, Union Oil (assets of 916.5 million

Table 1

Concentration in Crude Production

	1955	1965	1974
Top 4	21.2%	27.9%	31.1%
Top 8	35.9	44.6	54.0
Top 20	55.7	63.0	76.9

Source: Energy Action Committee, *Divestiture Factbook* 15 (1976).

dollars) acquired Pure Oil (assets of 766.1 million dollars). In 1966, Atlantic Refining (assets of 960.4 million dollars) acquired Richfield (assets of 499.6 million dollars), and in 1968, Sun Oil (assets of 1,598.5 million dollars) acquired Sunray DX (assets of 749.0 million dollars). In 1969, Atlantic Richfield (assets of 2,450.9 million dollars) acquired Sinclair (assets of 1,851.3 million dollars). As a result, the twenty majors of 1955 have become the sixteen majors of today. Moreover, as Professor Walter Measday points out,

> concentration in reserve ownership is even more important, particularly for the future, than concentration in current production. And the largest companies control most of the proved reserves. The Federal Trade Commission staff found that in 1970 our sixteen major companies controlled 77 percent of the net proved oil reserves in the United States and Canada. The producer has effective control, however, over all of the oil he lifts including the shares for royalty owners and other nonworking interest holders. In terms of gross reserves, the sixteen majors may control more than 90 percent of existing proved reserves.[11]

Second, the major oil companies are not the run-of-the-mill corporate giants dominating *Fortune's* list of the 500 largest industrial corporations. Rather, they are multinationals whose domains extend from Alaska to Kuwait, from Indonesia to Venezuela. Indeed, the sun never sets on their far-flung empires. Table 2 compares the control over crude production exercised in the United States, the Middle East, the OPEC countries, and the Free World by the seven largest majors, the so-called Seven Sisters.[12] The percentage control exercised by *all* the majors, of course, is even higher than that of the Seven Sisters. That these companies may no longer *own* their erstwhile properties in the OPEC countries is, as shall be demonstrated, of secondary importance. In practice, they still *control* the disposition of the lion's share of the free world's crude oil production.

Third, the major oil companies are intertwined with one another through a seamless web of interlocking control.[13] They do not function as independent or competitive units but as cooperative entities at every strategic point in the

Table 2

The Seven Sisters' Shares of World Crude Oil Production (1972)

Company	Production in U.S. (Thou. b/d)	% of total U.S. production	Production in Middle East[2] & Libya (Thou. b/d)	% of total M.E.[2] & Libya production	Production in all OPEC (Thou. b/d)	% of total OPEC production	Production[1] worldwide (excluding E. Europe & China) (Thou. b/d)	% of world production (excluding E. Europe & China)
	(1)	(2)	(3)	(4)	(5)	(6)	(7)	(8)
Exxon	1,114	9.9	2,527	12.9	4,050	15.2	6,145	14.7
Texaco	916	8.1	2,155	11.0	2,674	10.0	4,021	9.6
Socal	528	4.7	2,155	11.0	2,614	9.8	3,323	7.9
Gulf	651	5.8	1,887	9.7	2,409	9.0	3,404	8.1
Mobil	457	4.1	1,178	6.0	1,477	5.5	2,399	5.7
BP	—	—	3,903	20.0	4,506	16.9	4,659	11.1
Shell	726	6.5	1,372	7.0	2,877	10.8	5,416	12.9
Total	4,392	39.1	14,165	77.6	20,607	77.1	29,367	70.0

[1] Taken from company annual reports.
[2] Excludes Bahrain.

Source: Multinational Corporations and United States Foreign Policy: Hearings before the Senate Subcomm. on Multinational Corporations of the Senate Comm. on Foreign Relations, Part 4, 93d Cong., 2d Sess. 68 (1974).

industry's integrated structure. They are meshed with one another like strands of spaghetti in a symbiotic relationship almost inevitably precluding any genuinely competitive behavior. John W. Wilson, the former chief of the Federal Power Commission's Division of Economic Studies, has explained the significance of bringing "horizontally and vertically juxtaposed firms into close working relationships with each other" as follows:

> They *must* work together to further their joint interests. Consequently, each becomes familiar with the others and with each other's operations. Men in such close working relationships learn to consider one another's interests. This process of learning to live together is, of course, quite laudable in certain social and political contexts. The success of our Nation's international relations, for example, depends greatly upon this process. But it is, most assuredly, not the kind of institutional setting within which a free market economy can be expected to function efficiently. Real economic competition is made of tougher stuff. . . . In order to function both efficiently and in the public interest, free markets must be competitive. This means that the participants must be structurally and behaviorally independent of each other. That precondition, quite apparently does not apply to the petroleum industry.[14]

The claim, therefore, that the petroleum industry fits the structural model of effective competition is pure fiction.

Joint ventures are one manifestation of this symbiotic relationship. A joint venture establishes a community of interest among the parents and a mechanism for avoiding competition between them. The mechanism provides an opportunity for foreclosing nonpartners from access to supplies and/or from access to markets and serves as a forum in which ostensible competitors can meet to exchange information and coordinate plans with apparent impunity.[15] Most important, perhaps, the device, at least in the oil industry, thus far has remained immune from antitrust attack. Table 3 indicates how the major oil companies use joint ventures, now with one partner and then with another, in a seemingly infinite set of permutations and combinations in bidding for federal offshore lease sales. Thus, Amerada Hess submitted no independent and 168 joint bids during the period; Getty, no independent and 281 joint bids; Phillips, no independent and 169 joint bids; and Union, no independent and 245 joint bids.

According to Professor Walter Mead, this amounts to bid rigging:

> In any given sale, it is obvious that when four firms . . . each able to bid independently, combine to submit a single bid, three interested, potential bidders have been eliminated; i.e., the combination has restrained trade. This situation does not differ materially from one of explicit collusion in which four firms meet in advance of a given sale and decide who among them should bid (which three should refrain from bidding) for specific leases and, instead of competing among themselves, attempt to rotate the winning bids. The principal difference is that explicit collusion is illegal.[16]

Table 3

Joint Bidding in Federal Offshore Lease Sales (1970–72)

Company	Number of independent bids	Bidding partners	Number of joint bids with each
Amerada-Hess	0	Signal	50
		Louisiana Land	51
		Marathon	51
		Texas Eastern	16
Amoco	6	Texas Eastern	117
		Union	96
		CNG	79
		Transco	15
		Shell	14
Atlantic-Richfield	12	Cities	106
		Getty	73
		Continental	114
Chevron	79	Mobil	25
		Murphy	17
		General American	17
		Pennzoil	12
		Pelto	13
		Superior	9
		Gulf	7
		Burmah	4
		Mesa	4
Cities Service	7	Atlantic	106
		Getty	100
		Continental	163
		Tenneco	3
Continental	27	Atlantic	114
		Cities	163
		Getty	102
		Tenneco	5
Exxon	80		
Getty	0	Atlantic	73
		Cities	100
		Continental	102
		Placid	4
		Superior	2
Gulf	17	Mobil	17
		Pennzoil	8
		Standard Oil of California (Chevron)	7
Marathon	24	Signal	65
		Louisiana Land	69
		Amerada	51
		Texas Eastern	29
Mobil	8	Pennzoil	30
		Standard Oil of California (Chevron)	25
		Mesa	16
		Burmah	13
		Gulf	17
		Ashland	2
Phillips	0	Skelly (Getty)	69
		Allied Chemicals	66
		American Petrofina	34
Shell	59	Transco	47
		CNG	15
		Standard Oil of Indiana (Amoco)	14
		Florida Gas	17
Sun	115	Pennzoil	2
Texaco	15	Tenneco	32
Union	0	Amoco	96
		Texas Eastern	96
		Texas Gas	48
		Florida Gas	5

Source: The National Gas Industry: Hearings before the Senate Subcomm. on Antitrust and Monopoly of the Senate Comm. on the Judiciary, Part 1, 93d Cong., 1st Sess. 481 (1973).

Table 4

Joint Ventures in the Oil Pipeline Industry

Pipeline company and co-owners	Percent held by each	Pipeline company and co-owners	Percent held by each
Badger Pipeline Co. (assets = $12,400,000):		Texaco	17
Atlantic–Richfield	34	Clark	11
Cities Service	32	Marathon	10
Texaco	22	Cities Service	8
Union Oil	12	Shell	7
Dixie Pipeline Co. (assets = $46,400,000):		Platte Pipeline Co. (assets = $33,000,000):	
Amoco	12.1	Continental	20
Atlantic–Richfield	7.4	Marathon	25
Cities Service	5.0	Union Oil	15
Continental	4.1	Atlantic–Richfield	25
Exxon	11.1	Gulf	15
Mobil	5.0	West Shore Pipeline Co. (assets = $17,600,000):	
Phillips	14.5	Shell	20
Shell	5.5	Amoco	16.5
Texaco	5.0	Mobil	14
Gulf	18.2	Texaco	9
Transco	3.6	Marathon	9
Allied Chemical	8.6	Clark	8
Laurel Pipeline Co. (assets = $35,900,000):		Cities Service	8
Gulf	49.1	Continental	6.5
Texaco	33.9	Union Oil	5.5
Sohio	17.0	Exxon	3.5
Colonial Pipeline Co. (assets = $480,200,000):		Wyco Pipeline Co. (assets = $14,100,000):	
Amoco	14.3	Amoco	40
Atlantic–Richfield	1.6	Texaco	40
Cities Service	14.0	Mobil	20
Continental	7.5	Yellowstone Pipeline Co. (assets = $16,000,000):	
Phillips	7.1	Continental	40
Texaco	14.3	Exxon	40
Gulf	16.8	Husky	6
Sohio	9.0	Union Oil	14
Mobil	11.5	West Texas Gulf Pipeline Co. (assets = $19,800,000):	
Union Oil	4.0	Gulf	57.7
Plantation Pipeline Co. (assets = $176,100,000):		Cities Service	11.4
Exxon	48.8	Sun	12.6
Shell	24.0	Union Oil	9.0
Refiners Oil Corp	27.1	Sohio	9.2
Four Corners Pipeline Co. (assets = $20,900,000):		Chicap Pipeline Co. (assets = $25,600,000):	
Shell	25	Union Oil	43.4
Chevron	25	Clark	33.2
Gulf	20	Amoco	23.4
Continental	10	Cook Inlet Pipeline Co.:	
Atlantic–Richfield	10	Atlantic–Richfield	20
Superior	10	Marathon	30
Olympic Pipeline Co. (assets = $30,700,000):		Union Oil	30
Shell	43.5	Mobil	20
Mobil	29.5	Texas-New Mexico Pipeline Co. (assets = $30,500,000):	
Texaco	27.0	Texaco	45
Wolverine Pipeline Co. (assets = $21,800,000):		Atlantic–Richfield	35
Union Oil	26	Cities Service	10
Mobil	21	Getty	10

Source: *The Natural Gas Industry: Hearings before the Senate Subcomm. on Antitrust and Monopoly of the Senate Comm. on the Judiciary, Part 1*, 93d Cong., 1st Sess. 485 (1973).

Table 5

Selected International Joint Ventures of Petroleum Companies

Petroleum Company (1971 crude production)	Co-owners	Percent Held by Each
Arabian American Oil Co. (1.45 bil. bbls.)	Texaco	30.00
	Exxon	30.00
	Chevron	30.00
	Mobil	10.00
Iranian Oil Participants, Inc. (1.3 bil. bbls.)	Mobil	7.00
	Exxon	7.00
	Chevron	7.00
	Texaco	7.00
	Gulf	7.00
	B. P.	40.00
	Shell	14.00
	Atlantic	1.67
	Signal	.83
	Getty	.83
Iraq Petroleum Co.	B. P.	23.750
	Shell	23.750
	Exxon	11.875
	Mobil	11.875
Kuwait Oil Co., Ltd. (1.27 bil. bbls.)	Gulf	50.00
	B. P.	50.00

Source: Horizontal Integration of the Energy Industry: Hearings Before the Subcomm. on Energy of the Joint Economic Comm., 94th Cong., 1st Sess. 112 (1975).

Indeed, explicit collusion has been illegal per se since bid rigging was condemned in 1898 by *United States* v. *Addyston Pipe & Steel Co.*[17]

The major oil companies also use joint ventures in their control of interstate pipelines (see Table 4). Outside of the United States, the pattern is similar. In 1952, according to one report, "every important pipeline in existence or even proposed [was] controlled by the seven principal international oil companies, individually or jointly."[18] The significance of this joint control over pipelines as a vertical integration lever will be discussed below.

Table 5 is a selected list of joint ventures by the major oil companies outside of the United States. A more comprehensive listing of these ventures and an analysis of their anticompetitive impact is found in the Federal Trade Commission's landmark *Report on the International Petroleum Cartel.*[19]

In all, according to one estimate, joint ventures among the major oil companies provide approximately 12,000 occasions each year for ostensible competitors, the joint venture parents, to meet and discuss their common problems and means for resolving them.[20] The devices are the cement for binding together a loose-knit cartel into a cozy system of mutual interdependence.

Fourth, as Table 6 demonstrates, the major oil companies are further bound together by a network of indirect interlocks. With the exception of Gulf and Socal, as John Blair has observed,

> all of the eight largest oil companies were interlocked in 1972 through large commercial banks with at least one member of the top group. Exxon had four such interlocks—with Mobil, Standard (Ind.), Texaco, and ARCO. Mobil had three (with Exxon, Shell, and Texaco), as did Standard of Indiana (with Exxon, Texaco, and ARCO), as well as Texaco (with Exxon, Mobil, and Standard of Indiana). ARCO was interlocked with Exxon, and Standard (Ind.), and Shell with Mobil.[21]

At the very least, Blair concluded, "meeting together presents directors of competing companies with potential conflicts of interest."[22]

Fifth, the extensive use of exchange agreements among the major oil companies not only has cemented their horizontal fraternity, but has given them a powerful weapon against their vertically nonintegrated competitors. For years the United States has gone without a meaningful crude oil market. Most crude oil is bought and sold under exchange agreements by which the buyer of x barrels of crude oil for his refinery at a particular location agrees to deliver an equivalent amount to the seller at another location. Walter Measday has pointed out that such exchange agreements "replace a competitive market with a network of bilateral or multilateral barter transactions from which nonintegrated firms can be easily excluded as first purchasers of crude and which, by their very nature, must be less efficient allocators of resources than open markets would be."[23]

Sixth, oil companies, discontent with their control over only the oil and natural gas industries, have expanded, largely by merger and acquisition, into other energy industries. They have acquired coal, uranium, geothermal, and tar sands reserves to protect their oil and gas empires from interfuel competition (see Table 7). In 1965, one oil company (Gulf) engaged in coal operations and produced less than two percent of the industry's output. Ten years later, eight oil companies produced more than twenty percent of the industry's output, and eleven of the sixteen majors controlled more than forty percent or more of all privately held coal reserves. Companies like Phillips, Mobil, Shell, Atlantic Richfield (ARCO), and Sun Oil are all in the multibillion-ton coal-reserve class without ever having mined a single ton of coal. The biggest risk they face in becoming major producers, as Senator Kennedy has pointed out, "is that coal may become technologically obsolete before they could exhaust their reserves."[24]

Table 6

Indirect Interlocking Directorates among Major Oil Companies through Commercial Banks (1972)

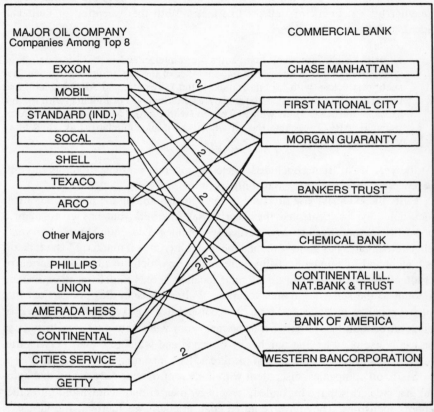

Source: J. Blair, *The Control of Oil*, p. 145 (1976).

The same takeover pattern occurred in the uranium industry. In 1967, two oil companies engaged in uranoso-uranic oxide (U_3O_8) milling operations with less than twenty-eight percent of the industry's output. In 1972 Exxon and Continental Oil entered the industry, giving oil companies thirty-eight percent of the milling capacity. By 1977 Atlantic Richfield (ARCO) had acquired Anaconda, the third largest uranium producer, and Standard Oil of Ohio also had entered the field. As a result, oil companies now control from fifty to fifty-five percent of the uranium industry's reserves.[25]

Table 7

Energy Reserves of Top Thirty Oil Companies in Trillions of BTU's

Company	1975 Net Domestic Crude OIL/NGL	1975 Net Domestic NATURAL GAS	1975 COAL	1975 URANIUM
1. Exxon	23,374.0	23,198.7	199,332.0	7,525.0
2. Texaco	16,344.0	15,872.0	47,460.0	—
3. Shell	10,782.2	7,101.4	23,730.0	—
4. Standard of Indiana	13,003.6	10,936.3	—	—
5. Gulf	7,424.0	6,736.9	61,698.0	34,400.0
6. Standard of California	10,248.6	7,341.1	—	1,290.0
7. Atlantic–Richfield	13,166.0	12,820.5	52,206.0	—
8. Mobil	5,800.0	7,782.4	59,325.0	—
9. Getty	9,488.8	3,449.9	—	8,600.0
10. Sun	5,115.6	4,198.4	53,890.8	—
11. Union	3,543.8	7,354.4	—	—
12. Phillips	4,036.8	5,462.0	47,460.0	5,375.0
13. Continental	3,010.2	3,212.3	316,795.5	10,750.0
14. Cities Service	4,332.6	4,710.4	—	—
15. Marathon	4,634.2	2,345.0	—	—
16. Amerada Hess	3,132.0	1,536.0	—	—
17. Tenneco	1,258.6	3,843.1	40,341.0	—
18. Louisiana Land & Exploration	1,084.6	1,353.7	—	—
19. Pennzoil	852.6	1,923.1	—	—
20. Superior	1,160.0	3,481.6	—	—
21. Union Pacific	684.4	809.0	237,300.0	2,150.0
22. Sante Fe	765.6	81.2	8,780.1	—
23. R. J. Reynolds	N/A	N/A	—	—
24. International Paper	580.0	362.5	—	—
25. Kerr–McGee	342.2	840.7	66,444.0	62,350.0
26. Standard of Ohio	26,332.0	6,425.6	18,984.0	2,150.0
27. General American	585.8	630.8	—	—
28. Ashland	365.4	1,010.7	21,357.0	—
29. American Petrofina	324.8	192.5	—	—
30. Diamond Shamrock	713.4	1,126.4	—	—

Source: "Horizontal" Oil Company Divestiture and Separation Proposals, Exhibit IV-D. (Report to the American Petroleum Institute, Oct. 15, 1976).

The impact of these incursions by the major oil companies into the domain of substitute fuels is not difficult to conjecture. After all, no man can be expected to compete with himself, nor can any man be expected to serve two masters and be equally loyal to each. As Walter Measday has observed:

> Would Continental Oil encourage price and market competition between [its subsidiary] Consolidation Coal and its traditional oil operations? Would Union Oil push geothermal development in an area where it might cut into the market

for Union's fuel oil? The question extends to the exploitation of successful R
& D. According to Senator Bartlett (R., Oklahoma), 49 of 52 patents relating
to coal gasification or liquefaction issued from 1964 to 1974 went to oil companies. Let us make the highly unlikely assumption that an oil company with extensive foreign investments were to achieve a technological breakthrough which
could make the United States self-sufficient in energy. Would Exxon enjoy telling
Sheik Yamani or would Occidental inform Col. Qadaffi that no more Saudi
Arabian or Libyan oil would be lifted for the U.S. market? Or would there be some
temptation to delay exploitation of the technology until "it's really needed"?[26]

Such considerations lend force to current congressional attempts to protect interfuel competition by prohibiting the oil companies from further expansion into
rival branches of the energy industry.[27]

Finally, the government historically has done for the oil companies what they
could not do for themselves without clear violations of the antitrust laws. Under
the guise of conservation and national defense, the Bureau of Mines has set
national output quotas, the states have authorized prorationing schemes, and
Congress has approved the Interstate Oil Compact and has legislated tariff protection and import quotas. In addition, the federal government has subsidized the
multinational giants with special tax offsets and both the domestic and the multinational producers with magnanimous depletion allowances. In war and peace
and in times of crisis, real or imagined, the government has favored the industry
with antitrust exemptions. The State Department, according to one analyst, has
been the industry's law firm, the Interior Department its Washington office.[28] No
wonder that the industry is sometimes depicted as a government-sanctioned,
government-protected, government-subsidized cartel operating a finely tuned
scheme to restrict output and maintain prices on a worldwide scale.[29]

In summary, introduction of the "moderate" concentration ratios recorded in
Table 1 as proof that the oil industry is competitive in structure is disingenuous
indeed. These ratios, as has been demonstrated, seriously understate the pervasive horizontal control exercised by the petroleum giants and, when simplisti-
cally accepted at face value, conceal the worldwide dominance of these giants
over energy reserves.

III. The Reinforcement of Shared Monopoly
Power through Vertical Integration

Vertical integration by corporate giants is the capstone of control in the petroleum industry. As the mechanism for harnessing and transmitting market power
through the successive stages of production, refining, and marketing, vertical
integration constitutes the primary barrier to new competition. Specialized firms
at any one stage of the industry must live at the sufferance of the integrated
majors—vulnerable to the constant threat of price squeezes, the denial of supply,

and the foreclosure from markets. The very fact of vertical integration, therefore, militates against workable competition in the petroleum industry and relegates competition to the interstices and fringes of the marketplace.

For example, the combined effect of vertical integration and the depletion allowance encouraged the integrated companies to report their profits at the crude oil stage rather than at the refining or marketing stage. The majors accomplished this objective by posting a high price on crude oil, which they then sold to their own refineries as well as to independents. For the vertically integrated companies, the high price for crude was simply a bookkeeping transaction. Its effect was to increase profits on crude, to reduce tax payments, and, in spite of lower profits at the refining stage, to increase total profits for the integrated concern. For the independent refiner, by contrast, the increase in crude prices meant a decrease in both refining profits and total profits; nonintegrated, he could not recoup the narrowed margins in refining at some other stage of operations.[30]

To illustrate, assuming a 27.5 percent depletion allowance, an integrated concern that could supply seventy-seven percent of its refinery needs with its own crude oil production stood to gain from an increase in crude prices even if the increase was not passed on at the refining stage. If the integrated company had a self-sufficiency ratio in excess of 38.5 percent, it stood to gain even if it passed on only half of the crude oil price increase.[31] In other words, an integrated company could decide to operate its refineries at zero or subnormal profits and thus discipline, squeeze, or bankrupt the nonintegrated refiners who are both its customers for crude and its competitors in the sale of refined products. (Incidentally, fifteen of the top seventeen refiners in the United States have a crude oil self-sufficiency ratio in excess of 38.5 percent.[32])

As the Federal Trade Commission concluded in its recent petroleum report, "The vertical integration system contained all the elements essential to a squeeze on refining profits and could be overcome only if the potential refining entrant could enter the industry on a vertically integrated basis."[33] By thus raising the cost of entry at the refining stage, vertical integration in and of itself becomes a formidable entry barrier that few newcomers can afford to hurdle. The system is also a barrier to established, independent refiners, many of whom eventually give up the battle for survival and sell out to their integrated rivals. (Incidentally, acquisitions of independent refiners accounted for 40.7 percent of the increase in refining capacity among the top twenty oil companies between 1959 and 1969.[34])

The control of pipelines by the vertically integrated majors poses a similar problem. A pipeline rate set well above the competitive cost of transporting crude oil, for example, imposes no burden on the majors who own the pipeline. For them, the high price is simply a bookkeeping transaction involving a transfer of funds from the refinery operation to the pipeline operation. To the nonintegrated refiner, however, an excessive pipeline charge is a real cost increase that he cannot recoup elsewhere and that places him at a competitive disadvantage vis-à-vis his integrated competitors.

The implications of the integrated majors' control over pipelines has been explained by Beverly Moore as follows:

> Almost every one of the major pipeline systems constructed since World War II is jointly owned by the few companies which dominate the marketing areas which the pipelines serve. From the standpoint of the owners, the arrangement is perfectly natural.
>
> If a few companies wish to exploit a market by constructing a joint venture pipeline to it, they will have little interest in inviting all their actual and potential competitors to come along with them. Likewise, the owners will have an incentive to lay the line so that it or its feeder spurs will pass in close proximity to their own refineries and marketing terminals, but not to those of their nonowner competitors. The owners will have an incentive to provide input and output facilities, storage tanks, and synchronization geared to their own operations, but again not to those of their nonowner competitors.
>
> The result is that, while joint venture pipelines are theoretically common carriers, equally accessible to all, access can be substantially more expensive for nonowners than for owners.
>
> This initial disadvantage is widened by the fact that the nonowner must pay the full rate or tariff while the owner actually pays only the pipeline cost, recouping the difference through the pipeline company's dividend payments to him. The rate-cost differential which measures this further degree of discrimination is commonly as high as 20 to 30 percent.[35]

The integrated majors also can use their control of pipelines as an entry barrier if they choose to exclude or limit flows of crude oil to the independents. According to the Federal Trade Commission's 1973 report:

> This can be done by (1) requiring shipments of minimum size, (2) granting independents irregular shipping dates, (3) limiting available storage at the pipeline terminal, (4) imposing unreasonable product standards upon independent customers of pipelines, and (5) employing other harassing or delaying tactics.[36]

The companies controlling the pipelines control, to a large extent, the oil moving through those lines and determine the allocation of that oil among non-integrated refiners. In addition, as Interstate Commerce Commission statistics for 1973 indicate, ninety-two percent of the crude going into reporting lines was owned individually or jointly by the sixteen majors.[37] Thus, through control of crude oil supplies or through ownership of pipelines, vertical integration gives the majors dominating the petroleum industry the power to mollify, discipline, coerce, and exclude their nonintegrated rivals. It empowers them to determine the conditions for entry and the rules for survival in the petroleum industry.

The consequences of vertical integration by the major oil companies are particularly striking in the international sphere. The ability of OPEC to limit output and to maintain or raise its revenue levels rests upon its ability to proration cutbacks satisfactorily among its member countries. OPEC, in other words, needs an agency to perform for it the same function as the Texas Railroad Commission traditionally performed for the domestic industry. To the extent that OPEC can rely upon the integrated oil companies to serve as its prorationing and marketing agent or, in other words, to the extent that it can rely upon these companies to exercise coalescing rather than countervailing power, it can assure the viability of its worldwide control over oil prices. That the companies more or less willingly have lent themselves to the attainment of that objective was made clear by the Church Committee:

> First, access to crude oil is the necessary precondition for an oil company to stay in business. In a supply-limited situation a refiner without secure access to crude is faced with the high probability of being unable to operate. Second, the price at which OPEC sells oil to companies other than the traditional concessionaries has, up to this time at least, been somewhat higher than the cost of similar oil to the established majors. One reason for this differential has been that the established companies have continued to lift some part of the oil produced within their concessions at tax paid cost, i.e., the cost of production, plus royalties plus taxes rather than at the higher buyback price. Finally, certain tax advantages which reduce the real cost of oil accrue to a company from its ownership of equity oil in a foreign producer country. Thus, for example, a company which lifts part of its foreign oil at tax paid cost may presently credit the income tax portion of that cost against its U.S. tax liability on other foreign income.
>
> Multinational oil corporations are currently engaged in a series of negotiations designed to ensure their exclusive right to "buyback" oil—oil which has become the property of the producer countries by virtue of the various participation "agreements," and which those countries now wish to sell back to the previous company concession holders. The four Aramco shareholders—Exxon, Texaco, Socal and Mobil—by joint negotiations seek to establish a special relationship with Saudi Arabia which would give them preferential access to the Saudi crude oil supply at a discount off the going market price, even should that country acquire 100 percent of Aramco.
>
> The multinational oil companies, on the other hand, provide the OPEC with important advantages. As vertically-integrated corporations, the major oil companies guarantee OPEC members an assured outlet for their production in world markets. The primary concern of the established major oil companies is to maintain their world market shares and their favored position of receiving oil from OPEC nations at costs slightly lower than other companies. To maintain this favored status, the international companies help proration production cutbacks among the OPEC members. Their ability to do this derives from the existence of their diversified production base in OPEC countries.[38]

The importance to the OPEC countries of maintaining common interests with the integrated majors was not lost on the prime movers in the cartel. Said Sheik Zaki Yamani, Saudi Arabia's Minister of Petroleum:

> . . . Nationalization of the upstream (production) operations would inevitably deprive the majors of any further interest in maintaining crude-oil price levels. They would then become mere offtakers buying the crude oil from the producing countries and moving it to their markets in Europe, Japan and the rest of the world. In other words, their present integrated profit structure, whereby the bulk of their profits are concentrated in the producing end, would be totally transformed. With the elimination of their present profit margin of, say, 40 cents a barrel from production operations, the majors would have to make this up by shifting their profit focus downstream to their refining and product-marketing operations. Consequently, their interest would be identical with that of the consumers—namely, to buy crude oil at the cheapest possible price.[39]

In other words, by avoiding nationalization of the integrated majors' crude oil properties, and instead entering into participation agreements with them, the companies would be given an incentive to identify with OPEC interests rather than with the interests of consuming countries. In the words of Sir Eric Drake, the companies would not only be the tax collectors for the producers[40]; they now would be much closer partners, serving also as OPEC's prorationing and marketing mechanism. In effect, as Professor M.A. Adelman has stated, they would be the "agents of a foreign power."[41]

The Church Committee summed up the symbiotic relationship between OPEC and the integrated majors in the following fashion:

> Thus the current changeover from the concession system to exclusive long term, large-volume supply contracts does not alter the interest that the international oil companies have in helping OPEC carry out its production and pricing policies. So long as the individual OPEC countries have assured outlets for their oil through exclusive joint arrangements with the major oil companies, the divisions within OPEC are unlikely to manifest themselves in lower oil prices, even in the face of a worldwide surplus of crude oil productive capacity estimated at over eight million barrels per day. There are, thus, parallel interests between OPEC and the major oil companies in which the companies ensure their access to the crude but at the price imposed by OPEC regardless of a theoretical crude oil surplus.[42]

In short, the very logic of vertical integration has permitted the Seven Sisters and the lesser international majors to enjoy a tenuous co-habitation arrangement, if not an indissoluble marriage with the OPEC producers.

The implications for consumer interests have been clearly spelled out by Walter Measday:

> So long as they can control the marketing of OPEC oil, the integrated majors have little reason to oppose OPEC price increases. They can pass such increases through into the prices of their own products secure in the knowledge that competitors, who are also their customers, are not getting oil any cheaper. They may, indeed, enjoy positive benefits from OPEC price increases through the enhanced values of the reserves which they still possess.

The Prudhoe Bay field alone provides an example here. Each one-dollar increase in the value of a reserve barrel raises the North Slope assets of Exxon, Atlantic Richfield and Sohio/BP by a minimum of $10 billion and probably much more—the improvement in asset values is none the less real because it is off-balance sheet. A good case can be made that had it not been for the Arabs, the North Slope would have been a financial disaster, given the escalation in pipeline construction costs. As it is, a recent estimate forecasts profits in the range of $2.00 a barrel for production delivered from this area. Similarly, North Sea oil has been made profitable only through OPEC actions. There is, in short, no great divergence—now that OPEC ownership in its own reserves has been accepted—between the interests of the international majors and the interests of OPEC member nations.[43]

All that has happened since 1973 is the replacement of Seven Sisters private cartel by a cartel of OPEC governments working hand-in-glove with a consortium of vertically integrated international oil giants.

IV. Vertical Integration and Efficiency

In appearances before Congress and in releases to the media, industry spokesmen are fond of picturing the vertical integration of major oil companies as a finely tuned machine assuring a smooth and continuous flow of materials from the crude fields to service stations. Tampering with that machine, they claim, would make coordination and planning of supply more difficult, would result in wasteful duplication, would increase overhead costs, and generally would entail sizable losses of efficiency. Vertical divestiture, they say, would saddle consumers with higher costs for heating fuel and gasoline.[44]

Little hard-core evidence supports these claims. Indeed, the evidence *produced by the integrated majors themselves* points in the opposite direction. First, there is no such thing as a continuous flow from a major's crude field to its own refinery and through its own marketing organization into its own branded gas pumps. As was noted above, the major companies systematically exchange purchases and sales agreements. An indeterminate and probably modest proportion of a major's oil moves in a continuous flow through its own vertical system. Exxon admitted as much in testimony before the Senate Antitrust and Monopoly Subcommittee in 1975:

> It is not possible to trace Exxon-owned feedstocks to each refinery. Exxon's crude production is often commingled with purchased crude, part of the commingled stream sold to others, and some Exxon crude is sold outright. For example, during 1974, Exxon's net crude plus condensate production was 701 [million barrels per day]. We purchased 868 [million barrels per day] from others (including royalty oil), and we sold 780 [million barrels per day] to others.[45]

In other words, Exxon operates a crude oil business, supplied in part from its own wells and in part by outside firms, and distributed in part to Exxon's refineries and in part to other refiners.

Second, the majors repeatedly argue, when the argument suits their purpose, that the functional components of their vertical organization operate quite independently from one another. Thus, Exxon told the South Carolina Tax Commission:

> Each of these functions is managed and accounted for on a functional operating basis. Each is a segment of [Exxon's] total corporate enterprise, but each has its own accounting, budgeting and forecasting, its own management and staff, its own profit center, its own investment center, its own physical facilities, etc. The profit or loss of each function is separately and accurately computed.[46]

Similarly, before the Wisconsin Tax Appeals Commission, Exxon argued:

> [N]one of [Exxon's] functional departments are integral parts of a unitary business composed of all functions combined; rather it [Exxon] will show that each function is independent and not unitary to, or an integral part of, any other function.[47]

Apparently oblivious of the industry's claim that divestiture would result in the wasteful multiplication of company headquarters, one of Exxon's senior vice presidents explained the organization of his company's production, refining, and marketing departments to the Wisconsin Commission as follows:

> [E]ach of the operating departments had its own separate management responsible for the proper conduct of that operation. Each of these management managers had a technical staff to provide all the supporting technical service that he needed to operate his particular operation. He also had the administrative staff when necessary to assist him. Each of these departments had its own separate and distinct field organization which conducted the operations in the field.
>
> . . . [W]hen all these elements are taken together the entire organization of each of these separate functional segments is designed to permit them to operate independently and separate from each other segment . . . [T]hey were on a self-sufficient basis, except . . . the availability of some of the Coordination and Service Departments which was provided at the corporate level. These departments were free to consult with those staff departments, if they felt it was necessary.[48]

Equally revealing is the testimony of Dr. Ezra Solomon, a former member of the President's Council of Economic Advisors, appearing on behalf of Exxon before the Wisconsin Commission. Dr. Solomon gave the following answers in response to questioning by Exxon's counsel:

Q. Do you have an opinion . . . as to whether Humble [i.e., Exxon] was a unitary company?

A. No, by my definition. If it is integrated, it is by definition not unitary.

Q. And on the same basis do you have an opinion as to whether the functional operations of the Humble Exploration and Production Department, the Refining Department and the Marketing Department were carried on as separate businesses?

A. Yes, there are three separate unitary businesses, and if I remember right, there were even more, but these are the major important stages that a vertically integrated company combines.

Q. Each stage, E and P, Refining and Marketing, you would say were separate businesses?

A. Yes.

Q. On the same basis do you have an opinion as to whether or not the Wisconsin Marketing operations were an integral part of the Humble E and P function?

A. No, they are not.

Q. Did you find any economic dependence between the Wisconsin operation and the E and P Department?

A. No, none whatever. It appears that Humble's E and P Department was a functioning unit even before there were any Wisconsin operations.

. . . .

[Dr. Solomon] A. Could Humble's E and P Department sever its relationship with the Wisconsin operation without affecting the Wisconsin operation?

[Mr. Ragatz] Q. Right.

A. Yes, I imagine it could.

Q. And could the Wisconsin Marketing operations have been severed without damage to the E and P function?

A. Yes, the Wisconsin Marketing end of it didn't exist for a while, and after it existed, it could have been severed without affecting the E and P viability.

Q. Now, on the same basis as I previously asked, do you have an opinion as to whether the Wisconsin Marketing operations were during the years in issue an integral part of the Humble Refining Department?

A. They were not.

Q. Was there any economic dependence in that relationship?

A. Not that one could see from the record at all. The Refining Department was a unitary business that could have functioned with or without the Wisconsin Marketing.

Q. And so there was no—or the Department could have been feasibly economically severed without damaging the Wisconsin Marketing operations?

A. You could have a Wisconsin Marketing operation without having a Refining Department.

Q. Then in other words, there was an ample supply of products without obtaining them from Humble Refining?

A. That's correct.

Q. Could the Wisconsin Marketing operations have been feasibly economically severed without damaging Humble's Refining Department operations?

A. Yes.

Q. And going back to the E and P Department for a minute, I take it that in the market there would be an ample demand for crude oil without the Humble Refining Department being in the picture so that Humble's E and P Department could have disposed of its crude oil produced?

A. Yes. Many companies exist as crude oil producers.

Q. And as to the Refining Department, there was an ample supply of crude oil in the market so that the Refining Department was not economically dependent upon Humble's E and P Department?

A. Not in the sense that I am using the word here.

Q. And the two departments could have been economically severed on a feasible basis?

A. The very fact that refineries exist as independent refineries and producers exist as independent producers and on a fairly large scale suggests that this can be done.[49]

Later, after counsel for the State of Wisconsin had finished his cross-examination, Exxon's counsel resumed his questioning of Dr. Solomon:

Q. Professor Solomon, on cross-examination you were asked questions that seemed to be driving at a dependent relationship between separate functions of an integrated oil company. Would you comment on the concept of dependence in terms of demand and supply in the market itself as to whether or not everybody in business has some dependency on market conditions and distinguish that from an economic dependency in terms of the concept of unitary?

A. Well, in the case of a unitary business, the degree of dependence between the subcomponents that comprise that unit are very strong. They are essential, they are necessary. You could not feasibly run it in today's economy, or whatever economy we are talking about, without all of those components.

In the case of a vertically-integrated company, the presence of business or unitary businesses within the vertical combination, the dependence is not as strong at all. It is quite a bit weaker. There is, obviously, some advantage for each unitary business belonging in a family of businesses. Size alone does provide some help. That degree of dependence is sort of trivial compared to the interdependence within each unit itself.

Q. In the market could you say that the dependence for a refinery would be that there be a supply of crude in the general market itself and that there not be a dependence between ownership of a producing function and a refining function?

A. Well, the common ownership of the two functions is not all that important in terms of the demand and supply of the flow of product, either crude or the products that come out of them. There is a well-established market for crude petroleum. It has a daily quotation. A refinery can buy there, a crude producer can sell there. Likewise, at the refined end there is a clear cut market for petroleum products in which a lot of people engage and in which there are daily quotations so that the degree of dependence is not that great at all.

Q. In other words the refinery can get crude from market sources that have no ownership relationship to the refinery and, in turn, can sell its product to the market sources that have no ownership relationship to the refinery?

A. Quite. The total demand and supply for crude is balanced. It really doesn't matter where you get it. It's the same kind of thing and you get it at the same price anyway.[50]

"Truth," it seems, depends upon the forum in which the majors happen to be testifying. In one case, vertical integration is indispensable for efficiency and cost minimization; in another, it does not seem to make much difference.

Professor M.A. Adelman, who, incidentally, does not support vertical divestiture, has made perhaps the most forthright judgment of the industry's efficiency argument:

> The industry's contention, that vertical integration helps efficiency, is unfounded. Common ownership of these activities, by one company, neither saves money nor costs any. (There are bound to be some exceptions to the rule; relatively, they are unimportant.) Most companies became integrated long ago for reasons that are now history. They have stayed integrated because there is no reason to change.[51]

In addition, interposing genuine markets between successive stages of the oil industry would not impair efficient operations. Given past experience, however, such markets certainly would enhance competition by lowering the entry barriers to newcomers at all levels of the industry.

V. The Feasibility of Divestiture

After extensive hearings on S. 2387, the Senate Subcommittee on Antitrust and Monopoly concluded that divestiture of the vertically integrated petroleum majors is not only desirable, but feasible.[52] Divestiture is technically feasible because, as has been noted already, the majors operate their departments as functionally separate units. Several companies, including Gulf, Sun, and Continental, already have restructured their organizations to place production activities within wholly owned subsidiaries that are separate from other functional subsidiaries. Other companies have a similar functional separation in their organizations, although they operate through separate divisions rather than through distinct subsidiaries. In other words, they already have accomplished *technical* divestiture as a result of internal management decisions. As counsel for Exxon told the Wisconsin Tax Appeal Commission:

> The evidence will show that Humble [Exxon] was organized on a functionally independent basis, and that its separate functions were operated as separate businesses in competition with other oil companies having similar functions and other companies which only operated in the business activity of a particular function.
>
> We intend to develop through the evidence the functional independence of the various departments.[53]

As for the *financial* feasibility of divestiture, courts are fully equipped to handle the remedy's problems—problems no less routine than those arising from bankruptcies and voluntary spinoffs in cases of corporate reorganizations. As one expert in the field told the Subcommittee,

> All of the activity which I have described in general terms should provide us with a measure of comfort, in that we are not without the requisite legal, accounting and financial expertise to accomplish complex corporate transactions of substantial magnitude without making economic tidal waves and without transcending the constitutional limitations of due process and on deprivation of property rights. These have been accomplished in the main, without denigrating the rights of shareholders, debtholders, or other creditors and where the rights of shareholders, debtholders or creditors have been affected, our judicial system has adequately dealt with these situations.[54]

Experience with the Public Utility Holding Company Act of 1935 indicates that massive divestiture can take place without crippling the reorganized industry, damaging the efficiency of its operations, or riding roughshod over the interests of stockholders or creditors.[55]

Rearranging stockholder equities would be the simplest problem. If past practice is followed, the petroleum majors would be reorganized into functional subsidiaries whose stock would either be sold off or, more likely, distributed to existing stockholders with the proviso, of course, that the interests controlling the company before divestiture would not control more than one of the functionally separate successor companies. Management of the corporate debt, issued with the backing of the full faith and credit of a corporate entity that is to be altered substantially by divestiture, would pose a stickier problem. Debt under covenants of this type clearly might have to be refinanced. If securities issued in the past at a relatively low rate of interest must be refinanced at a time when interest rates are higher, the major concern would be the effect on the embedded cost of a company's debt. As Walter Measday points out, however, such problems are not insoluble:

> An example of one such solution is the recent divestiture of Northwest Pipeline by El Paso, which affected 26 series of El Paso's long-term debt. By court order, each of these series was replaced by an El Paso issue and a Northwest issue bearing the same maturities as the original series but with a 1/8 percent higher interest rate "to sweeten the deal." The ratio between the two companies' debt is the proportion between the taxable basis of properties retained by El Paso and those transferred to Northwest. In other words, an investor in El Paso 5's issued in 1962 and maturing in 1982 now holds El Paso 5–1/8's and Northwest 5–1/8's, still maturing in 1982. The increase in interest rate is minor compared to the inflation in rates since 1962, while the value of the securities to investors has been enhanced.[56]

Such problems, although obviously not devoid of complexity, clearly are soluble without prejudice to investor interests.

Moreover, companies threatened with divestiture would not likely find the raising of needed funds in the capital market an impossible task. For example, Georgia Pacific, which was the subject of an FTC divestiture action, was able to raise nearly 500 million dollars in debt on favorable terms in the short period between the announcement of the FTC's complaint and the spinoff of Louisiana–Pacific pursuant to a voluntary consent settlement.[57] Similarly, in the six years between the filing of the FTC's complaint against Kennecott, in which the government sought divestiture of Peabody Coal, the company raised at least 700 million dollars on terms at least as favorable as those available to most other large corporations. Indeed, six months after the Supreme Court denied certiorari in the case, Kennecott obtained a revolving credit of 250 million dollars—at the prime rate for two years and thereafter at one-fourth above the prime rate until the last two years of the loan, during which an interest charge one-half above the prime rate was to be in effect.[58] The investment community apparently views the "uncertainties" of divestiture with considerably more equanimity than many other risks to which its business clients may be subject.[59]

A vertical divestiture action against the petroleum majors should be an even less than average cause for concern. Contrary to the industry's dire forebodings about "disintegration" and "dismemberment"—implying that the majors would be broken down to the size of the neighborhood gasoline station—the successor companies still would be corporate entities of impressive size and power. In the words of the Senate Subcommittee:

> Exxon was the largest U.S. manufacturing company, in terms of 1974 assets, on the Fortune "500" list. Divested, Exxon's manufacturing—refining, chemicals, etc.—and marketing assets would have totaled about $15.8 billion, surpassed only by General Motors—$20.5 billion. Exxon's producing operations —$10.5 billion in assets—would have been in sixth place—behind General Motors, Exxon manufacturing and marketing, Ford, IBM, and, by a narrow margin, I.T.&T. Exxon Pipe Line Co., with assets of $709 million, would have been nearly within the top 200 companies.
>
> Marathon Oil, smallest of the majors in assets, ranked No. 77 on this basis among U.S. companies in 1974. The surviving producing operation—$883 million in assets—would still have been among the top 200 companies, as would refining and marketing—$751 million. Even Marathon Pipe Line Co.'s assets—$102 million—were within the range spanned by the 500 largest companies.[60]

If the successor companies resulting from divestiture of the petroleum giants were to find survival difficult or if they were to find raising capital impossible in spite of sound management, the 99.8 percent of United States manufacturing firms that are smaller than those successors must abandon hope.

In its report on S. 2387, the Senate Judiciary Committee recommended that the eighteen vertically integrated petroleum giants be reorganized into separate producing and refining–marketing companies and that all pipelines be reconstituted as independent common carriers having no interest in the crude oil and products being transported through them.[61] The Committee assured the Senate that the proposed divestiture could be accomplished:

Without the loss of managerial and operating efficiencies;
Without inhibiting needed capital investments;
Without injuring investors in the companies;
Without inhibiting the timely growth of energy supplies.[62]

The Committee expressed the confidence that implementation of its divestiture proposal would:

Allow the development of free markets in crude and products;
Bring about increased efficiencies in the industry;
Deliver products and services at the best prices to consumers;
Protect the independent refiners and marketers from extinction without requiring Governmental intervention;
Remove the Government from various phases of the industry's operation;
Put pressure on the operation of the OPEC cartel;
Forestall the nationalization of the oil industry.[63]

In the light of available evidence, these contentions seem eminently reasonable, especially because the policy alternatives to divestiture—the status quo, governmental regulation, or nationalization—clearly are deficient in protecting the public interest.

Notes

1. A. Sampson, *The Seven Sisters*, p. 202 (1975).
2. *Consent Decree Program of the Department of Justice: Hearings before the Subcomm. on Antitrust of the House Comm. on the Judiciary*, 85th Cong., 1st Sess., pp. 123–24 (1957), quoted in *Senate Comm. on the Judiciary, Petroleum Industry Competition Act of 1976*, S. Rep. No. 1005, 94th Cong., 2d Sess., p. 105 (1976) [hereinafter cited as *Petroleum Industry Competition Act Report*]. This report makes a cogently reasoned case, replete with documentary references, in favor of vertical divestiture.
3. Prior to filing the case, Attorney General Robert H. Jackson submitted the complaint to the Council of National Defense. The Council in turn referred it to its Oil Industry Advisory Commission, nine of whose eleven members were connected with either Jersey Standard (Exxon) or Shell. Both of these companies, of course, were parties to the case and it came as no surprise that the advisory commission found that divestiture of transportation and marketing would adversely affect the defense effort. Any effort at using the antitrust laws to restructure the industry would, in their words, "becloud relationships between the Government and Industry." Attorney General Jackson acquiesced in the Commission's report and deleted the request for structural relief from the complaint.

Petroleum Industry Competition Act Report, op. cit., p. 105.

4. For the deplorable record of antitrust versus the petroleum industry and some of the reasons for it, see *Market Performance and Competition in the Petroleum Industry: Hearings before the Senate Comm. on Interior and Insular Affairs, Part 1,* 93d Cong., 1st Sess., pp. 370–98 (1973) (testimony of Mark J. Green). See also *Petroleum Industry Competition Act Report,* op. cit., pp. 95–124.

5. *In re Exxon Corp.,* 83 F.T.C. 233 (1973).

6. Staff of Senate Permanent Subcomm. on Investigations of the Senate Comm. on Government Operations, 93d Cong., 1st Sess., *Investigation of the Petroleum Industry,* pp. 4–5 (Comm. Print 1973) [hereinafter cited as *Investigation of the Petroleum Industry*].

7. E.g., S.739, S.745, S.756, S.1137, S.1138, and S.2387, 94th Cong., 1st Sess. (1975), dealing with vertical divestiture, and S.489, 94th Cong., 1st Sess. (1975), dealing with horizontal divestiture.

8. J. Blair, *The Control of Oil,* p. 382 (1976).

9. See, e.g., Ritchie, "Petroleum Dismemberment," *Vanderbilt Law Review,* pp. 1137–42 (1976). See also *The Petroleum Industry: Hearings before the Senate Subcomm. on Antitrust and Monopoly of the Senate Comm. on the Judiciary, Part 3,* 94th Cong., 1st Sess., pp. 1849–1917, 2102–29, 2217–49 (1975) [hereinafter cited as *Vertical Integration Hearings*].

10. J. Wilson, "Market Structure and Interfirm Integration in the Petroleum Industry," *Journal of Economic Issues,* p. 324 (1975).

11. Measday, "The Petroleum Industry," in Walter Adams ed., *The Structure of American Industry,* p. 136 (5th ed., 1977). For concentration in refining, see Blair, op. cit., pp. 131–36.

12. See also Blair, op. cit., pp. 25–76.

13. Ibid., pp. 136–51; S. Ruttenberg, *The American Oil Industry: A Failure of Anti-Trust Policy,* pp. 41–118 (1973).

14. *The Natural Gas Industry: Hearings Before the Senate Subcomm. on Antitrust and Monopoly of the Senate Comm. on the Judiciary, Part 1,* 93d Cong., 1st Sess., p. 499 (1973). The Wilson evidence on joint ventures, interties, and interlocks deserves detailed attention. Id., pp. 478–97.

15. A classic example is the Cal-Tex group of companies through which Texaco and Standard of California jointly have operated many of their foreign assets for the past 40 years.

16. Mead, "The Competitive Significance of Joint Ventures," *Antitrust Bulletin,* p. 839 (1967).

17. 85 F. 271 (6th Cir. 1898).

18. *FTC Report on the International Petroleum Cartel,* pp. 27–28 (Comm. Print 1952).

19. Ibid., pp. 37–193.

20. S. Ruttenberg, op. cit., p. 61.

21. Blair, op. cit., pp. 144–46.

22. Ibid., p. 147.

23. Measday, "Feasibility of Petroleum Industry Divestiture," p. 8 (paper presented to Stanford University Institute for Energy Studies, Sept. 1976) (on file at the *Vanderbilt Law Review*).

24. Letter from Senator Kennedy to the Senate Judiciary Committee (Aug. 27, 1977) (on file at the *Vanderbilt Law Review*) (asking for support of his amendment to the Coal Conversion Bill [S.977], which would bar future acquisition of competing coal and uranium resources by major oil companies).

25. Ibid. A recent compilation by the Federal Energy Administration of nonpetroleum holdings by oil companies revealed the following:

Chart 1. **Number of NonPetroleum Holdings of Oil Companies**

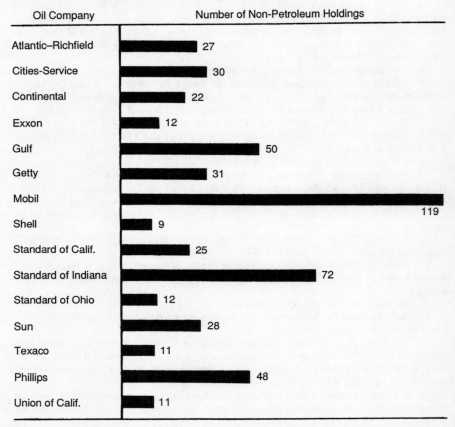

Oil Company	Number of Non-Petroleum Holdings
Atlantic–Richfield	27
Cities-Service	30
Continental	22
Exxon	12
Gulf	50
Getty	31
Mobil	119
Shell	9
Standard of Calif.	25
Standard of Indiana	72
Standard of Ohio	12
Sun	28
Texaco	11
Phillips	48
Union of Calif.	11

Source: FEA, *The Petroleum Industry, A Report on Corporate and Industry Structure* (1975).

26. Measday, op. cit., p. 13. These questions are not entirely rhetorical. The oil giants have a track record in the suppression of competing fuels. Jersey Standard's (Exxon) handling of the hydrogenation patents, acquired pursuant to a cartel agreement with I.G. Farben of Germany, is a case in point:

> To Standard, these agreements promised, first, ownership and control, outside Germany, of IG's hydrogenation processes and any future IG processes for making synthetically products having similar uses to those of the customary petroleum refinery products, from whatever raw material they might be derived; and, second, a junior partnership with IG, outside Germany, in the manufacture of new chemical products derived from petroleum or natural gas. . . .
> Standard's use of its exclusive rights to IG's processes in the oil industry shows clearly that its main object in acquiring them was to strengthen its control over the oil industry. For the purpose, the IG agreements performed a dual function—defensive and offensive. Acquisition of the hydrogenation rights eliminated the most serious threat

". . . which has ever faced the company since the dissolution," according to Frank Howard, the Standard official who played a leading role in the negotiations with IG. Once these rights were safely acquired, Standard and Shell showed little disposition to use them, or to encourage others to use them, in actual productive operations. Their acquisition forestalled the threat to the oil industry of liquid fuels and lubricants from coal. . . .

Standard and Shell did little to encourage widespread synthetic production of liquid fuels and lubricants from coal. They had acquired these processes primarily to protect their own vast interests in petroleum. Standard summarized its policy as follows:

I.H.P. [International Hydrogenation Patents Company] should keep in close touch with developments in all countries where it has patents, and should be fully informed with regard to the interest being shown in hydrogenation and the prospect of its introduction. . . . It should not, however, attempt to stir up interest in countries where none exists. If the Management decides that in any country the interest in hydrogenation is serious, or that developments in such country are likely to affect I.H.P.'s position adversely, then I.H.P. should discuss the matter actively with the interested parties, and attempt to persuade them that its process should be used. . . .

If coal, tar, etc., hydrogenation be feasible from an economic standpoint, or if it is to be promoted for nationalistic reasons or because of some peculiar local conditions, it is better for us as oil companies to have an interest in the development, obtain therefrom such benefits as we can, and assure the distribution of the products in question through our existing marketing facilities. [G. Stocking & M. Watkins, Cartels in Action, pp. 491–93 (1946) (footnotes omitted).]

27. See, e.g., Interfuel Competition: Hearings Before the Senate Subcomm. on Antitrust and Monopoly of the Senate Comm. on the Judiciary, 94th Cong., 1st Sess. (1975); Horizontal Integration of the Energy Industry: Hearings before the Subcomm. on Energy of the Joint Economic Comm., 94th Cong., 1st Sess. (1975) [hereinafter cited as Horizontal Integration Hearings].

28. See R. Engler, The Brotherhood of Oil: Energy Policy and the Public Interest (1977); R. Engler, The Politics of Oil: A Study of Private Power and Democratic Directions (1961). The erstwhile description of the political influence of oil—according to which "the Standard has done everything with the Pennsylvania legislature except to refine it"—may no longer be apt, but the omnipresence of oil in the corridors of political power is unshaken. Respectable men with bulging briefcases still penetrate the portals of government. As Sampson reports, the oil companies contributed generously to the Republican Party, and President Nixon's fundraisers, Maurice Stans and Herbert Kalmbach, leaned heavily on them to help finance the notorious 1972 campaign. Four of the sisters contributed substantially, mostly through individuals. Officials of Exxon gave $217,747 led by the chairman, Ken Jamieson ($2,500), the president Jim Garvin ($3,200) and the head of their Greek affiliate, Thomas Pappas ("the Greek bearing gifts") ($101,672); while the Rockefeller family gave $268,000. Socal gave $163,000, led by their chairman, Otto Miller ($50,000) and including $12,000 from John McCone. Mobil gave only $4,300, and Texaco (whether through caution or meanness) apparently gave nothing. By far the biggest contributor was Gulf whose offerings included a million dollars given clandestinely by Richard Mellon Scaife, a major Gulf shareholder with his own political ambitions; and at least $100,000 which was produced through the Bahamas subsidiary of Gulf by the chief lobbyist of the company, Claude Wild. The eventual discovery of these illegal gifts, and of others, was to bring back all the old public suspicions of the corruptions of oil money.

The global scope of the oil money, however, was not to emerge until 1975, when the Securities and Exchange Commission began investigating political contributions. In April 1975 Gulf was eventually compelled to admit, in their 1975 proxy statement, that between

Chart 2. **U.S. Taxes Paid by the American Sisters**

	1972		1962–1971	
Company	Net income before taxes ($ billions)	% paid in U.S. taxes	Net income before taxes ($ billions)	% paid in U.S. taxes
Exxon	3.700	6.5	19.653	7.3
Texaco	1.376	1.7	8.702	2.6
Mobil	1.344	1.3	6.388	6.1
Gulf	1.009	1.2	7.856	4.7
Socal	0.941	2.05	5.186	2.7

Source: Multinational Corporations and United States Foreign Policy: Hearings before the Senate Subcomm. on Multinational Corporations of the Senate Comm. on Foreign Relations, Part 4, 93d Cong., 2d Sess. 104 (1974), quoted in Sampson, supra note 1, at 205.

1960 and 1973 "approximately $10.3 million of corporate funds were used in the United States and abroad for such purposes, some of which may be considered unlawful." Soon a succession of countries—Venezuela, Bolivia, Peru, Ecuador—demanded to know whether their politicians had been bribed, and Peru even expropriated Gulf's properties. Eventually the chairman of Gulf, Robert Dorsey, had to confess to having paid bribes of $4 million from 1966 onwards to the ruling party in South Korea; and to having given another $350,000, together with a helicopter, to the late General Barrientos in Bolivia. The limelight then shifted to Exxon, whose chairman, Ken Jamieson, had to admit in May 1975 that his company had made political contributions in Canada and Italy; and a new uproar ensued. Sampson, op. cit., pp. 206–07. One indication that such efforts are not in vain is the generous tax treatment Congress has accorded the oil industry over the years (see Chart 2).

29. See, e.g., *Horizontal Integration Hearings, op. cit., p. 108; Investigation of the Petroleum Industry,* op. cit., p. 27.

30. *Investigation of the Petroleum Industry, op. cit.,* pp. 12–31.

31. M. De Chazeau & A. Kahn, *Integration and Competition in the Petroleum Industry,* pp. 221–22 (1959). See also Kahn, "The Depletion Allowance in the Context of Cartelization," *American Economic Review,* pp. 286–314 (1964).

32. *Investigation of the Petroleum Industry,* op. cit., p. 20.

33. Ibid., p. 26.

34. *Market Performance and Competition in the Petroleum Industry: Hearings before the Senate Comm. on Interior and Insular Affairs, Part 1,* 93d Cong., 1st Sess., p. 1664 (1973).

35. *Anticompetitive Impact of Oil Company Ownership of Petroleum Products Pipelines: Hearings before the House Subcomm. on Special Small Business Problems of the House Select Comm. on Small Business,* 92d Cong., 2d Sess., p. 129 (1972). The argument that pipelines are common carriers regulated by a government agency is hardly convincing when one examines the profits data (see Chart 3).

36. *Investigation of the Petroleum Industry,* op. cit., p. 26.

37. ICC, *Transport Statistics in the United States, Pipelines, Part 6,* pp. 8–11 (1973).

38. Senate Comm. on Foreign Relations, 93d Cong., 2d Sess., *Report on Multinational Oil Corporations and U.S. Foreign Policy,* p. 10 (1975) [hereinafter cited as *Multinational Oil Corporations*].

Chart 3. **Pipelines: Average Annual Return on Paid-In Investment, 1968–72**

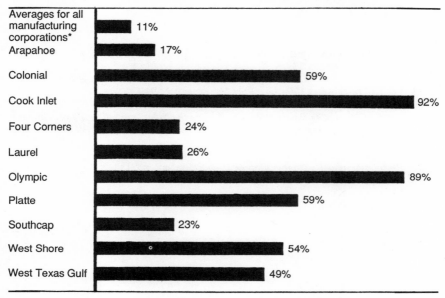

Averages for all manufacturing corporations*	11%
Arapahoe	17%
Colonial	59%
Cook Inlet	92%
Four Corners	24%
Laurel	26%
Olympic	89%
Platte	59%
Southcap	23%
West Shore	54%
West Texas Gulf	49%

*FTC, *Quarterly Financial Report for Manufacturing Corporations* (1968–72).
Source: ICC, *Transport Statistics in the United States Pipelines, Part 6* (1968–72).

39. Ibid., p. 11.
40. Sampson, op. cit., p. 236.
41. Ibid. As Adelman put it to the Senate Committee on Foreign Relations, "The cartel governments use the multinational companies to maintain prices, limit production, and divide markets. This connection, I submit, is the most strategic element in the world oil market." *Multinational Corporations and United States Foreign Policy: Hearings before the Senate Subcomm. on Multinational Corporations of the Senate Comm. on Foreign Relations, Part 2*, 94th Cong., 1st Sess., p. 3 (1975).
42. *Multinational Oil Corporations,* op. cit., p. 11.
43. Measday, op. cit., p. 11.
44. See, e.g., *Vertical Integration Hearings, Part 1*, op. cit., p. 131 (testimony of Frank Ikard).
45. *The Industrial Reorganization Act: Hearings on the Energy Industry before the Senate Subcomm. on Antitrust and Monopoly of the Senate Comm. on the Judiciary, Part 9*, 94th Cong., 1st Sess., p. 529 (1975). Professor Adelman underscored this point in his assessment of the logic of vertical integration in petroleum:

> The industry's job, of arranging an immense flow of sticky combustible liquids, is made no easier or harder by common ownership of the segments. A company that on paper is balanced and produces "enough" crude for its own use actually has to dispose of much of most of it to others. Oil is where you find it, scattered in thousands of fields all over the country or the world. It often doesn't pay to bring it home.

Petroleum Industry Competition Act Report, op. cit., p. 125.

46. *Vertical Integration Hearings, Part 2*, op. cit., p. 1174.

47. Ibid., pp. 1229–30.

48. Ibid., pp. 1285, 1293.

49. Ibid., pp. 1739–42.

50. Ibid., pp. 1750–52.

51. *Washington Post*, April 30, 1976, § D, at 9, quoted in *Petroleum Industry Competition Act Report*, op. cit., p. 139.

52. *Petroleum Industry Competition Act Report*, op. cit., pp. 147–50.

53. *Vertical Integration Hearings, Part 2*, op. cit., pp. 1219–20.

54. Ibid., Part 3, p. 2049.

55. *Study of Monopoly Power, Hearings before the Subcomm. on Study of Monopoly Power, House Comm. on the Judiciary,* 81st Cong., 1st Sess., pp. 1339–53, 1460–69 (1949).

56. Measday, op. cit., pp. 21–22.

57. *Petroleum Industry Competition Act Report*, op. cit., pp. 134–35.

58. Ibid., pp. 133–34.

59. Measday, op. cit., p. 22.

60. *Petroleum Industry Competition Act Report*, op. cit., pp. 132–33.

61. Ibid., p. 5.

62. Ibid., p. 6.

63. Ibid.

5

The Role of Competition in the Regulated Industries

Ideally, competition and regulation are opposite sides of the same coin. In theory, both are directed at the same objectives: efficient use of resources and protection of the consumer against exploitation. The means to these ends, however, are different. To be effective, competition requires rivalry among many sellers and freedom of entry into markets. It envisions a regulatory scheme in which the operation of autonomous market forces obviates the need for detailed government supervision. This is the philosophy embodied in the Sherman Act of 1890.

Regulation, as originally conceived, was to be both a supplement to and substitute for competition. It was to be applied in those industries where the cost of entry was so great or the duplication of facilities so wasteful that some degree of monopoly was considered unavoidable. Here the visible hand of public regulation was to replace the invisible hand of Adam Smith in order to protect consumers against extortionate charges, restriction of output, deterioration of service, and unfair discrimination. This was the rationale of the Interstate Commerce Act of 1887.

In many respects, the Sherman Act and the Interstate Commerce Act were generically different. One was cast in terms of negative prohibitions on certain types of conduct. The other was aimed at detailed and direct supervision of individual firms. One sought to protect the public by preserving competition, the other by regulating monopoly. Nevertheless, both hoped to protect the public against the aggressions of private interests rather than to shield these interests from the bargaining power of the public. Both relied on competition wherever its operation was functionally feasible and economically beneficent. Thus, Congress did not exempt railroads from the antitrust laws. On the contrary, Congress insisted

Originally published in the *American Economic Review,* vol. 48 (May 1958); reprinted with permission.

on the direct regulation of individual railroads as well as on competition between them. As long as railroads "stood in the very gateway of commerce taking toll from all who pass," the Sherman Act was strictly enforced against railroad combinations and conspiracies.

This regulatory policy, however, was first eroded and then extended. The regulatees themselves came to recognize that the better part of wisdom was not to abolish regulation but to utilize it. Gradually the public utility concept was transformed from consumer-oriented to industry-oriented regulation. By a process so brilliantly analyzed by Horace Gray, "the policy of state-created, state-protected monopoly became firmly established over a significant portion of the economy and became the keystone of modern public utility regulation. Henceforth, the public utility status was to be the haven of refuge for all aspiring monopolists who found it too difficult, too costly, or too precarious to secure and maintain monopoly by private action alone. Their future prosperity would be assured if only they could induce government to grant them monopoly power and to protect them against interlopers, provided always, of course, that government did not exact too high a price for its favors in the form of restrictive regulation."

Once this "new mercantilism" had taken root, it was extended to important segments of the economy. Between 1934 and 1940, Congress subjected radio, television, motor carriers, water carriers, freight forwarders, air carriers, and natural gas transporters to the certification requirements of independent regulatory commissions. To mitigate the debilitating effects of depression, the role of competition was substantially curtailed. New commissions were created, and "public convenience and necessity" became the shibboleth of the day.

It is significant, nevertheless, that in these regulatory statutes Congress did not sanction the abandonment of competition. The standards set up to guide administrative action may have been indefinite—"public interest" and "public convenience and necessity" may lack precise meaning—but, as the Supreme Court has squarely held, there can be "no doubt that competition is a relevant factor in weighing the public interest." In the transportation industry, said the Court, Congress has not made the antitrust laws "wholly inapplicable" nor has it authorized the regulatory agency "to ignore their policy." In short, Congress provided for the regulation of competition, not for its elimination by administrative fiat. Yet this is precisely the task which some commissions—not by intent, perhaps, but in effect—seem to have undertaken.

It is my contention that the experiments in public regulation during the last two decades have been singularly unsuccessful and that the creation of a fourth branch of government has, in many cases, resulted in undue restriction of entry, encouragement of mergers and consolidations, sanction for anticompetitive rate and service agreements, erosion of interindustry competition, and suppression of unregulated competition. Since this creeping paralysis infests most regulated industries, the following analysis of transportation is only illustrative of a more general and pervasive challenge.

I. Trucking

Entry Restrictions

Under the Motor Carrier Act, the ICC was empowered to regulate entry into the trucking industry through the licensing of common and contract carriers. Carriers which had conducted regular operations for three years prior to 1935 were to receive "grandfather" certificates or permits. Private and agricultural haulers were to be exempt.

In carrying out this mandate, the Commission imposes an almost insurmountable burden on applicants for new operating authority, extension of existing authority, and alternate route privileges. According to a recent report of the Senate Small Business Committee, the Commission tends to ignore shipper needs and to show an inordinate concern for the protection of established carriers. In its restrictive view of public convenience and necessity, the Commission often loses sight of the congressional directive to promote efficient, economical, and flexible transportation service for the public.

Shipper need, the Commission admits, is to be measured in physical rather than economic terms; i.e., as long as existing carriers are physically capable of performing a particular service, prospective competitors are to be denied entry—even if their service is cheaper, better, and more efficient. In its decisions, the Commission emphasizes repeatedly that where existing carriers have expended their energy and resources in developing facilities to handle all available traffic and where their service is adequate, they are entitled to protection against the establishment of a new, competitive operation. This is what might be called the "going-concern" theory of regulation, a reluctance to subject existing firms—especially large firms—to competitive pressure. The test throughout is the physical adequacy of existing service, not the promotion of better and cheaper service.

The economic results of such regulation are not only restrictive but, at times, absurd. A carrier operating between New York and Montreal must operate via Reading, Pennsylvania, a detour of some 200 miles. A carrier between the Pacific Northwest and Salt Lake City may haul commodities eastbound, but not westbound—and so on, *ad nauseam*. According to James C. Nelson's study, 40 per cent of the specialized carriers were allowed to carry only one commodity; seven in ten regular route common carriers possessed less than full authority to serve intermediate points; more than one-third of the regulated intercity truckers had return haul limitations, and about one-tenth had no backhaul authority at all. That these regulations result in empty mileage, deadhead runs, higher unit costs, inefficiency, and wastefulness is too obvious for further comment.

But, more fundamentally, why are any entry restrictions necessary, if the objective of regulation is to protect the public? The trucking industry does not fit the public utility, natural monopoly model, and does not require one or a limited number of large firms to achieve cost minimization. In trucking there are no substantial economies of scale. According to the New England Governor's Committee, for example, the coefficients of rank correlation between carrier size (as measured by gross revenues) and cost per vehicle-mile, ton-mile, or average haul in miles were so low as to indicate—at least for carriers operating in and out of New England—that size of firm bears little relation to operating cost. Efficiency in trucking seems primarily related to effective route utilization rather than size. This means that large firms have no inherent economic advantages over small firms and that existing firms have no insurmountable leads over new firms. It means that entry, in the absence of restrictions, would be brisk and the number of competitors large. It also means that by increasing competitive pressures, entry could work toward better route utilization and hence greater operating efficiency.

In an industry of this sort, entry restrictions tend merely to preserve the capitalized expectations of established carriers—carriers who maintain, on the one hand, that they are efficient and provide superior service and who demand, on the other, government protection from interlopers and competitors. In the final analysis, however, these restrictions do not assure the adjustment of capacity to demand, because the Commission, unlike its British counterpart, limits the number of firms rather than the number of trucks in operation. Entry control does not prevent established carriers from creating and, in the absence of rate competition, from perpetuating excess capacity. Without competition, moreover, there are no effective pressures to compel either efficient use of existing capacity or elimination of the excess capacity which tends to develop in a cartelized, monopolistically competitive industry. Thus, ironically enough, regulation may breed the very evils it was supposed to eradicate.

Mergers

Under the Motor Carrier Act, mergers and acquisitions require prior approval by the Interstate Commerce Commission. Approval is contingent on a finding that the proposed combination "will be in the public interest," in which case the participating parties are expressly relieved from the operation of the antitrust laws.

In a recent study for the Senate Small Business Committee, Professor Hendry and I found an increase in the number and size of trucking mergers as well as increasing concentration in important segments of the trucking industry. Also notable was the upturn in aggregate concentration. Thus, in 1947, the largest 2,097 carriers (constituting 9.99 per cent of all carriers) earned 67.92 per cent of the industry's revenues. By 1954, the largest 853 carriers (constituting 4.7 per cent of all carriers) earned almost the same share of revenues; viz., 62.3 per cent. In other words, by 1954, the 853 largest controlled only a slightly smaller share of the industry (5.6 per cent less) than the 2,097 largest carriers (a 60 per cent larger number) had seven years earlier. This increase in concentration was accompanied by the net disappearance of some 2,800 carriers, or more than 10 per cent of the industry's population, in the brief span of seven years.

The rationalization of this trend seems to rest on a vague and vacillating merger policy which shows little consistency in approach or decision. What is embraced in one opinion as a natural and inevitable result of the economic facts of life is rejected in a second as not shown to be in the public interest. Where the fears of competitors are airily waved aside in one instance, the probable plight of competitors is of great importance in another. The Commission approves some acquisitions (usually by large carriers) because nothing has been adduced to show that they are contrary to the public interest. It rejects other acquisitions (usually by small carriers) because they are not shown to be consistent with the public interest. The first standard represents an effective rear-guard action by the Commission against protests; the second standard puts the full burden of proof on the applicant, with the necessary volume and quality of proof somehow always just beyond his reach.

Most disturbing, perhaps, about these decisions is the Commission's failure to indicate the specific public benefits to be derived from particular combinations. To be sure, the Commission goes through its ritualistic legalisms and turgid incantations, but it seldom makes an affirmative, economically meaningful showing that a given merger will result in lower rates or better service. More important, it seldom considers the possibility of achieving the statute's regulatory objectives by alternative, less restrictive techniques, such as granting extensions or admitting new carriers. Some years ago, for example, the Commission approved the combination of seven large eastern motor carriers into Associated Transport, Inc., which, as a result of the consolidation, became the largest trucking company in the country. The merger not only eliminated competition between the participating carriers over roughly one-third of their routes but also made Associated the only carrier to provide single-line, through-service from Florida to the Northeast. Despite the protests of the Agriculture and Justice Departments, the Commission insisted that this large-scale diminution of competition would result in improved transportation service, greater efficiency of operation, and substantial operating economies. Apparently the Commission ignored the alternative of permitting some of the companies in the area to extend their operations and offer an integrated through-service—thus giving the public all the alleged benefits of the merger, plus competition on the long haul, and without sacrifice of the competitive mileage. The Commission eschewed this alternative, much to its subsequent embarrassment. Today, Associated is still the nation's largest trucker, but its recurrent deficits lend force to the suspicion that there may be more effective, and less anticompetitive, ways of promoting the public interest than by merger.

Nevertheless, the Commission seems to proceed on the assumption—so candidly stated by Chairman Clarke—that "there hasn't been enough concentration" and that "we need more concentration than has occurred if we are going to have a healthy, vigorous motor carrier industry." The Commission seems untroubled by the fact that this is nothing but an unproved assertion and that available evidence points in the opposite direction, indicating that carrier size per se has little or no relation to efficiency, profitability, or better service. If it did, why has Congress not empowered the Commission to do more than merely authorize mergers initiated by private parties? Why has the Commission not asked for, and received, the power to compel mergers in the public interest?

In the final analysis, the Commission's anticompetitive merger policy creates problems primarily because entry into the industry is restricted. Were entry free, "rarely, if ever, would a consolidation raise important antitrust problems." Competition, as the Brownell Committee observed, would then serve as "an adequate safeguard against private regulation of the market by would-be monopolists." But entry into trucking is not free, and competition is not allowed to perform its regulatory role. This makes it doubly important to ascertain whether mergers and concentration are, in fact, the most efficacious means of promoting the public interest.

Rate Bureaus

The Reed–Bulwinkle Act empowered the ICC to approve rate-making agreements which are in furtherance of the national transportation policy and accord to "each party the free and unrestrained right to take independent action." Commission approval immunizes such agreements from antitrust coverage.

Generally speaking, the Commission favors and encourages collective action in rate matters, regarding such action as a necessary part of the rate-making process. To guard against what it calls cutthroat competition, the Commission sees "no alternative to procedures calling for . . . initial joint consideration of rate changes." Throughout, it emphasizes "the need for as much stability of rates as is practicable," in the belief that rate stability is more important than rate competition. But the Commission does not dismiss rate competition entirely. It still sees some value in competition from other modes of transportation.

This position might seem plausible, were it not for the manner in which the ICC exercises its maximum–minimum rate powers. As the Brownell Committee observed, the Commission utilizes its minimum rate power "both to protect the railroads from motor carrier competition as well as to safeguard the motor carrier industry from 'destructive' competition within its own ranks. Indeed, from the inception of motor carrier regulation to the present day, the power to fix minimum rates has been more significant than the authority to fix maximum charges." Under the circumstances, intermode competition can hardly contain the upward pressure on the entire rate structure. It cannot neutralize the combined impact of minimum rate fixing by government and private rate fixing by trade associations.

But what about the built-in checks and balances—the right of independent action as a safeguard against arbitrary and exorbitant charges, collusively arrived at? The record shows that, in practice, this right is little more than a sterile gesture. To the rate bureaus, it represents a minor annoyance which cannot break down the self-imposed restraints "born of history, habit, and strong mutual self-interest." To the Commission, it represents no more than an element of flexibility, a safety valve, to take care of special situations which must not be allowed to undermine general adherence to the idol of rate stability. In other words, independent action is not to be encouraged, but tolerated—tolerated so long as it falls short of promoting genuine rate competition.

That the right of independent action is more formal than real is repeatedly demonstrated in the cases. In the Southern Motor Carriers case, for example, the record showed substantial interference with managerial discretion and individual initiative in the rate-making process. The general manager of the conference announced his determination "that every member . . . should have exactly the same level of freight rates." The conference filed several suspension proceedings against the independently announced rates of its own members—no doubt to encourage independent action, free from coercion or fear of retaliation. The conference utilized meetings to facilitate the submission of identical Section 22 bids to the government. Finally, the conference used its power as a trade association to boycott recalcitrant outsiders who refused to go along with its rate policies. Yet the Commission, after insisting on some purely formal safeguards in the written agreement, approved the conference charter. The Commission held that rate bureaus have a right to protest the independent action of their members, that such protests in no way prevent or discourage independent action, nor work any hardship on bureau members. In short, the Commission once again sacrificed substance for form. It looked at provisions in the charter rather than practices in the market place.

Ultimately, rate bureau regulation raises two major issues. First, does the Reed-Bulwinkle Act afford adequate protection to the public interest? Second, if so, does the Commission possess the wisdom to determine, as Congress intended, "whether the advantages to the public interest, through furtherance of the national transportation policy, are such as to outweigh the disadvantages to the public interest . . . guarded against by the antitrust laws." Obviously, carriers must be permitted a degree of collaboration in setting joint rates and through rates. "No one," as Wendell Berge concedes, "would gainsay this right. Common sense dictates it, the Interstate Commerce Act provides for it, and the Sherman Act does not forbid it." But when does collaboration become collusion and coercion, and how much of it must be tolerated in order to promote the public interest?

Intermode Competition

The Interstate Commerce Act directs the Commission not to authorize the acquisition of a motor carrier by a railroad or its subsidiary except upon finding that the transaction will be consistent with the public interest, will enable the railroad to use motor vehicle service to public advantage in its rail operations, and will not unduly restrain competition. This—as well as federal legislation affecting air carriers, freight forwarders, and inland waterways—reflects a historic opposition to common control over competing media of transportation.

Since the early days of the Motor Carrier Act, the Commission has respected this Congressional policy. Starting with the Barker case of 1936, the Commission consistently rejected the notion that "the way to maintain for the future healthful competition between rail and truck service is to give the railroads free opportunity to go into the kind of truck service which is strictly competitive with, rather than auxiliary to, their rail operations." The Commission always insisted that motor carrier service furnished by a railroad "be confined to service auxiliary and supplementary to . . . its rail service and in territory parallel and adjacent to its rail lines." Given the difficulty of promoting competition among railroads, the policy objective was to preserve as much competition with other means of transportation as possible.

Two recent decisions, however, may foreshadow a reversal of Commission policy. In the Pacific Motor Trucking case, the Commission permitted a subsidiary of the Southern Pacific to acquire one of the largest independent motor carriers on the West Coast and a formidable competitor of both the railroad and its trucking subsidiary. The hearing examiner, after concluding that the transaction was a "concerted plan to restrain competition" and that its "primary objective" was the elimination of a powerful competitor, recommended denial of the application. But the Commission approved the merger without requiring, as is customary, the selection of key points which are break-bulk and consolidation points on the parent railroad. It shrugged off its responsibility to restrict the railroad's trucking operations to bona fide auxiliary and supplementary service. In short, the Commission not only sanctioned a substantial diminution of competition but also a significant erosion of intermode rivalry.

Similarly, in the Rock Island case, the Commission authorized a railroad subsidiary to conduct unrestricted motor operations across the breadth of the state of Iowa. Here again the Commission departed from the well-established precedent that railroads should be prohibited from initiating new or acquiring existing motor carrier operations which are not supplemental or auxiliary in character.

The issue here is fundamental. The railroads have persistently demanded the right to engage in unrestricted motor operations. Congress has consistently rebuffed them. Yet the Commission seems now prepared to effectuate through administrative adjudication what powerful pressure groups have failed to achieve through legislation. On the one hand, the Commission justifies drastic departures from intramode competition. On the other hand, the Commission approves the gradual erosion and undermining of intermode competition as well. If this trend continues, the integration (as distinct from co-ordination) of rail-truck service will become a reality—without legislative sanction and without an affirmative demonstration of the public benefits to be derived from eliminating this major source of competition in a regulation-riddled, restriction-infested industry.

Unregulated Competition

Under the Motor Carrier Act, agricultural haulers, as well as private carriers, were freed from the entry, rate, and route restrictions of the ICC. Section 203(b)(6) exempted motor vehicles carrying ordinary livestock, fish, or agricultural commodities (not including manufactured products thereof), if such vehicles did not carry other property for compensation. Attacked almost from its inception by the regulated carriers and the Commission, the exemption has had a profound competitive impact on both rail and motor carriers and has been a live laboratory for testing the viability of competition in the trucking industry.

No comprehensive comparison of exempt and regulated rates is available, primarily because rates on exempt commodities do not have to be filed with the Commission. Individual studies, however, indicate that the impact of exempt carriers has been substantial. One USDA study, for example, concluded that the rates on agricultural commodities "charged by railways and by regulated motor carriers generally have been reduced by the competition of exempt and otherwise unregulated motor carriers below a level which they would otherwise attain." Another study showed that on Florida citrus, the railroads in 1950 were forced to reduce their rates to several Midwestern cities in order to recoup their traffic losses to exempt haulers. Again, because of traffic losses, the railroads in 1950 reduced the rate on Virginia apples to southern destinations by 22 per cent—with the result that during the next two years the rail unloads of Virginia apples in southern cities increased by 159 per cent whereas the rail unloads in northern cities showed no significant change. In short, given the high cross-elasticity of demand for transportation, railroads and certificated motor carriers have felt the profound impact of exempt competition.

This impact is, perhaps, best measured by the extent to which unregulated carriers have increased their relative share of the market. Between 1949 and 1955, according to the ICC, nonregulated truck ton-miles increased 92 per cent, compared to 18.1 per cent for railroads and 56.8 for regulated trucks. Even more notable is the growing importance of truck transportation of commodities moving under the agricultural exemption. In 1939, for example, 0.5 per cent of the oranges shipped into Chicago came by truck; in 1955, 28 per cent. On cattle, the analogous percentages are 49 and 92; on hogs, 46 and 94; and on shell eggs, 60 and 99. With respect to apple shipments from the Appalachian belt, the preponderant volume in 1952 was handled by for-hire trucks operating under the agricultural exemption and by private carriers, also exempt from ICC regulation. This distribution of market shares appears to reflect significant differences in rates, speed, and quality of service.

Though the shipper benefits from the agricultural exemption have consistently been defended by all the farm organizations, by the Secretary of Agriculture and the Attorney General (under Roosevelt, Truman, and Eisenhower), and by Congress, the ICC never gave up the fight. Its persistent attempts to eliminate or emasculate the exemption are marked by both determination and futility.

First, the Commission announced the "poisoned vehicle" doctrine which held that if a vehicle was ever used to transport nonexempt goods, it automatically lost the benefit of the exemption. This interpretation, which sought to make the vehicle rather than the commodity the test for the exemption, was struck down by the courts.

Second, the Commission announced the "channels of commerce" theory which held that the exemption covers only the first haul from farm to market. This too was struck down by the courts.

Third, the Commission announced a number of restrictive commodity interpretations. Contrary to expert testimony of the Agriculture Department, the Commission held that redried tobacco leaf, dressed poultry, shelled nuts, nursery stock, flowers and bulbs, and frozen fruits and vegetables are not agricultural but manufactured goods. In all these cases, the courts have reversed the Commission—often with overtones of ridicule. One judge pointed out that "a chicken which has been killed and dressed is still a chicken." Another observed that "after shelling, a nut is still a nut." Substantial identity, according to the Supreme Court, is the relevant test: "where the commodity retains a continuing substantial identity through the processing stage we cannot say that it has been 'manufactured' within the meaning of Section 203(b)(6)."

Fourth, defeated in its frontal assaults, the Commission launched a flank attack. It decreed that all trucks leased by a common carrier must be leased for at least thirty days. This would have nullified the exemption for agricultural haulers who use single-trip or backhaul leases to achieve full utilization of equipment and consequent economy of operation. But this stratagem also failed, when Congress specifically exempted agricultural haulers from this crippling regulation.

In general, the Commission has been consistently defeated in both its judicial and legislative efforts to curtail the exemption. As Judge Graven concluded in the Kroblin case:

> There are two features that stand out most predominantly in the voluminous legislative history relating to amendments made or proposed to Section 203(b)(6). One feature is that every amendment that Congress has made to it has broadened and liberalized its provisions in favor of exemption and the other feature is that although often importuned to do so, Congress has uniformly and steadfastly refused or rejected amendments which would either directly or indirectly have denied the benefits of the exemptions.

The explanation for this is probably twofold. First, performance under the agricultural exemption has demonstrated that shipper and carrier interests can both be served through a competitive industry organization. The shipper benefits from lower rates, speedier and more flexible service, while the carrier retains his managerial discretion and competitive opportunity. Second, and more important, perhaps, the exemption has remained inviolate because the political strength of the farmer effectively neutralized the bureaucratic rapacity of the Commission. Here, indeed, is countervailing power at its best.

Summary

Motor carrier regulation, after twenty-five years of ICC administration, can boast of one major achievement. It has created a government-approved freight cartel—with entry restricted, mergers encouraged, rate fixing tolerated, and outside competition harassed. It has proceeded on the untenable assumption that competition in trucking is unworkable and, hence, against the public interest.

This anticompetitive policy rests on bizarre rationalizations. Entry restriction is tolerated, because the Commission protects shippers against unreasonable rates. Private rate fixing is allowed, because intermode competition guards against exploitation. Intermode competition is curtailed, on the one hand, to protect each mode and preserve its "inherent advantages"; it is eroded, on the other, to permit rail-truck integration in the public interest. Mergers are sanctioned to promote efficiency, but exempt carriers are harassed precisely because their operations are too efficient, their rates too low, and their service too good. The only constant in this equation is a paranoid, bureaucratic fear of competition and its effects on established carriers.

There is, to be sure, some current agitation for more competition. The Cabinet Committee on Transportation, for example, has urged a greater reliance on competitive rate making and a curtailment of the Commission's rate regulation powers. But this is not a fundamental policy reorientation. In essence, the Committee proposes to allow railroads to use cost-of-service pricing on commodities where the demand elasticity is high and intermode competition strong, and to use value-of-service pricing on other commodities—thus shifting more of the overhead burden to commodities primarily dependent on rail service. This means more discrimination, not more competition. Strangely enough, the Weeks Committee advocates competitive rate making, but is silent on collusive, Reed–Bulwinkle rate fixing. It eulogizes competition, but favors tighter controls over private and exempt motor carriers. It speaks of competition, but, in the same breath, stresses the need for protecting common carriers in the interest of national defense.

This position is neither consistent nor sound. If we are to stifle unregulated competition to protect common carriers and prevent traffic dilution, where is this process to stop? Should we also restrict common carrier trucks to increase the load factor of railroads, and curtail private automobile travel to assure fuller

utilization of bus line capacity? What evidence is there that competition cannot
—as in other industries—eliminate excess capacity and prevent the dilution of
traffic for existing carriers? Moreover, is an inherently competitive industry like
trucking incapable of serving the national defense? Would Mr. Weeks, in the
interest of national defense, urge government regulation of the steel industry,
where there is less evidence that competitive forces are strong enough to promote the public interest? Finally, if common carriers are to provide stand-by
capacity for national defense or to engage in uneconomic operations, should we
pay for this by suppressing more efficient competitors or through outright subsidization?

Perhaps the root of the problem is political rather than economic. Once a
commission is given power to dispense private privilege, it is almost compelled
to validate the financial values predicated on such privilege and does so by
suppressing competition wherever possible. The only escape from this dilemma
is to abolish the power of privilege and, where economically and technologically
feasible, to place greater reliance on the regulatory machinery of competition.

II. Air Transport

Entry

Like the trucking industry, air transport is not a natural monopoly. It does not
require a heavy investment in rights of way, airports, weather stations, etc. The
individual airplane is the basic unit of efficiency, and there are no marked economies of scale. Competition, therefore, is technologically possible and economically feasible. But the amount of competition and its role in the industry depend
primarily on the entry policy of the Civil Aeronautics Board. The Congressional
mandate, though more precise than in the Motor Carrier Act, requires only that
the Board consider "competition to the extent necessary to assure the sound
development of an air transportation system."

Until very recently, the Board's certification policy was unduly restrictive and
protective. Despite a 4,000 per cent increase in demand between 1938 and 1956,
not a single new passenger trunkline carrier was allowed to enter the industry. As
Ross Rizley, a former CAB chairman, told the Celler Committee:

> In every instance thus far in which the Board has found that additional and
> competing passenger truckline services on high-density segments are required
> by the public convenience and necessity it has concluded that the objectives of
> the act would be better served by the award of the route to a carrier already
> holding certificate authority than to a new company.

According to Mr. Rizley, this restrictive entry policy reflects an "undue shift
of emphasis from public convenience and necessity to the seeking and protection

of private carrier rights." As a result, eighteen years after regulation was instituted, the grandfather carriers still earn roughly 90 per cent of all commercial revenues in the industry.

Most questionable was the Board's policy toward the irregular or nonscheduled airlines. These carriers were denied entry because the Board feared the probable diversion of traffic from established carriers, the effect of such diversion on existing load factors, and the consequent subsidy drain on the federal treasury. But these fears were unfounded. As the Senate Small Business Committee concluded in 1953:

> . . . irregular airlines have not caused a diversion of traffic from the certified carriers. While there is duplication of routes between the irregular and certificated carriers there is relatively little duplication of markets. The introduction of hundreds of thousands of lower income bracket travelers to aviation should be attributed to the irregulars. Their pioneering, which has been along economic rather than geographic lines, has shattered the concept of the fixed, limited market for civil aviation. As a result, the question is no longer what portion of a fixed pie any company will get, but rather how much the entire pie can grow.

Clearly, the Board failed to appreciate the dual role which non-scheduled competition played in the industry. On the one hand, the nonskeds provided a yardstick for measuring the possibilities of profitable, unsubsidized service. By exerting competitive pressures on the certificated carriers, the nonskeds proved a valuable adjunct to conventional regulatory controls. On the other hand, and probably more important, the nonskeds provided promotional competition. They innovated low-cost coach service and thus tapped formerly untapped markets. Far from diverting traffic from the certificated carriers, the nonskeds created traffic which formerly did not exist. As the Celler Committee points out, the "skimming of the cream" complaint against the nonskeds "does not have substance." The best indication that the certificated airlines have not been hurt by "diversion" is that, with minor exceptions, they no longer require government subsidy.

It is significant that the Board, under the leadership of Ross Rizley, modified its unduly restrictive entry policy. Starting in 1955, the Board began to give additional routes to the have-nots of the certificated industry. It also elevated the nonskeds to the status of supplemental carriers, permitting them ten flights per month in the same direction between any single pair of cities. The Board conceded that its past efforts to restrict regular operations by the nonskeds in order to protect the certificated lines had "outlived its usefulness." In short, the Board recanted but only after many nonskeds and their competitive potential had been eliminated. It took a step toward more effective competition. But before this goal is reached, the Board will have to assure more balanced route structures and greater participation by small carriers in major traffic markets.

Rate Conferences

Just a word about rate conferences. Though Sections 412 and 414 of the Civil Aeronautics Act are closely comparable to the Reed–Bulwinkle Act, the CAB has been far more sympathetic to competitive rate making than the ICC. In the Air Freight Tariff case, for example, the Board refused to permit compulsory advance notice of rate changes or group discussion of "local" rates charged by a single carrier. It refused to sanction "the establishment of rate levels by agreement rather than by competitive forces." Upholding "the concept of individual rate making in the air transport field," the Board insisted that "this spur to competition should not be cast aside in the absence of compelling reasons for doing so."

The Board's record on international rate conferences, however, is less impressive. The Board approved the IATA agreement despite its condemnation of IATA as a "monopolistic price-fixing cartel" which serves "the private interests of the international carriers . . . , is contrary to the philosophy of the antitrust laws, and is opposed to the protection of the basic rights of the traveling and shipping public." The Board advised Congress that "no proper concept of governmental responsibility can justify leaving the ultimate determination of a fair and reasonable international rate structure wholly in the hands of an all-embracing international cartel." Yet, by approving the IATA agreement and refusing to withdraw its antitrust immunity, the Board has done just that.

As a result, international air fares are outrageously high and bear little relation to operating costs. Transatlantic fares, for example, are more than double the corresponding domestic rates: a New York–London round trip, first class, costs $720 compared to a New York–Los Angeles round-trip fare of only $301.90. The respective coach fares of $522 and $198 are even more divergent. A further result of IATA's rate fixing is the substitution of service competition for price competition. But this service competition tends merely to divert traffic from one carrier to another without at the same time enlarging the over-all market. Costs are raised through increased sales efforts, overexpansion of schedules, and the operation of more luxurious equipment than the traffic justifies. These higher costs eat into profit margins and benefit neither the consumer nor the investor. Unlike price reductions, such competition does not expand the total size of the market in which all carriers share.

To be sure, the Board has asked Congress for the same power over international fares as it has in the domestic field. This power the Board should have. But even without it, the Board can still choose an open rate situation. Lacking authority over specific rates, it can still reject a collusive rate fixing machinery. To do so would not precipitate certain chaos. On the contrary, competitive rate reductions may well stimulate the same phenomenal increase in international travel which coach competition triggered in the domestic market.

III. Ocean Shipping

Entry

The regulatory restrictions in ocean shipping are somewhat analogous to those in trucking and airlines. While the Federal Maritime Board does not control entry directly through certificates of convenience and necessity, it limits entry through the operating differential subsidy. The Board determines, for example, which routes are "essential for the promotion, development, expansion, and maintenance of the foreign commerce of the United States" and how much subsidy a particular carrier shall get in order to meet foreign flag competition. Where more than one American line applies for subsidy on a given route, the Maritime Board must deal with the same type of issues as arise in certification proceedings before the ICC and CAB.

Rate Conferences

The right of shipping conferences to engage in collusive rate fixing has long been recognized by law. What is at issue, however, is whether these conferences—unlike their rail, truck, and air counterparts—may also coerce outsiders through an exclusive patronage dual rate system which imposes a penalty rate against shippers patronizing nonconference vessels. Counsel for the Maritime Board has frankly conceded that this contract system, if effective, "will result in a complete monopoly in the sense that all cargo moving in a trade where the system is used will move in ships of conference carriers." The Board has justified the system on the grounds that "something more than voluntary shipper co-operation" is necessary if the conferences are to operate effectively. The courts, however, in the Isbrandtsen case (1956), have held that the coercion and discrimination inherent in exclusive patronage contracts are not authorized by statute. This raises the basic policy question: whether the conference system per se is sufficiently desirable to justify coercive measures which would ultimately drive independents out of business or into the conferences. The issue, in short, is rate fixing by compulsory cartels.

IV. Conclusion

Summarizing, then, public regulation involves the application of two fundamental policies. One is purely regulatory in nature. Its aim is to assure the public of adequate service at reasonable rates in industries with "natural" monopoly characteristics. Its orientation is static, negative, and protective. The other policy involves primary reliance on competition. The yardstick device is used, not only as a measure of industry performance, but also as a spur to increased efficiency, rate reductions, and service improvements. Promotional competition is used to foster developmental pioneering and over-all growth of the industry. Throughout, the emphasis is on progressive performance—achieved through the maintenance of competitive opportunities and the promise of competitive rewards. Thus competition serves as a useful adjunct to regulation and promotes the attainment of goals that are seemingly unattainable by administrative fiat.

Unfortunately, this regulatory role of competition has never been fully appreciated by the high priests of administrative expertise. Even in the absence of misfeasance, venality, or irregularity, they have generally succumbed to the institutional infirmities of the regulatory process. The cost and delay of processing applications, the harassment by powerful protestants, the slavish adherence to legal technicalities, the pharisaical devotion to a case-by-case approach, the petulant defense of the *status quo*—all these have militated against the competitive entrepreneur and the dynamic innovator. Commissions have proved peculiarly sensitive and susceptible to organized pressures: witness, for example, the integrated opposition of railroads, railroad labor, giant motor carriers, and a slightly tainted teamsters union to a more competitive trucking industry. Commissions have shown a congenital distaste for dealing with large numbers of firms. They have dreaded the necessity of facing up to the realities of today rather than clinging to the outmoded regulatory concepts of the eighties or thirties. In short, commissions have acquired an anticompetitive bias, a bureaucratic rigidity, an annoyance with the forces of change. In an era of unparalleled technological advances, they have tried to freeze an anachronistic grandfather pattern and to suppress whatever dynamic forces threaten to disturb that pattern.

What, then, are the policy implications? First, with respect to such inherently competitive industries as trucking, gradual but total deregulation seems desirable. Second, in industries where some economic regulation is considered necessary, Congress should specifically direct the administrative agency "to promote competition to the maximum extent practicable" and "to grant no exemptions from the antitrust laws unless the regulatory need therefore is clear." Third, Congress should make the approval of entry applications mandatory, except where a commission can affirmatively show that such approval would be prejudicial to the public interest. In other words, the presumption should be in favor of competition and the burden of proof, in case of denial, should be on the commission, not the applicant. Fourth, Congress should specifically prohibit private rate fixing. If rate fixing is necessary to prevent destructive competition and to protect the public interest, this task should be assigned to a duly constituted public body, not delegated to private interests. Never should governmental entry restrictions be coupled with private rate fixing. Finally, where appropriate, competition should be encouraged from whatever source it may spring. The integrity of interindustry or intermode competition should be preserved from erosion by merger or internal expansion. And where, as in electric or atomic power, the autonomous forces of competition may be inadequate, we should place increasing reliance on institutional competition; i.e., competition from federal, state, municipal, and cooperative bodies. Such competition, as experience shows, benefits not only the consumer but also the private segment of the industry which is subject to its pressure.

Oliver Wendell Holmes once said that we need education in the obvious more than investigation of the abstruse. May I suggest, however, that education in the obvious is not enough. What we need most of all is the courage to act on it.

6

The Reality of Administered Prices

In 1610 a Padua professor rejected Galileo's discovery of the Jupiter satellites.

We know—

he said—

> that there are seven planets and only seven, because there are seven openings in the human head to let in the light and air: two eyes, two ears, two nostrils, and a mouth. And the seven metals and various other examples also show that there have to be seven. Besides, the stars are invisible to the naked eye; therefore they do not influence human events; therefore they are useless; therefore they do not exist. (Quod erat demonstrandum)[1]

In a manner somewhat reminiscent of the Padua savant, Professor George J. Stigler has recently challenged the administered price heresy.[2] He exposes the wicked witchcraft of Gardiner C. Means, in an effort to exorcise the spell of a devious doctrine over gullible Senators and naive economists. He warns that a heresy which had ostensibly been stamped out two decades ago is still among us, and that its progenitors are still spreading the erroneous belief "that there is an important phenomenon called administered prices, and that if such prices existed they would have something to do with inflation."[3] Stigler's argument runs essentially as follows: (1) administered prices are difficult to define; (2) such prices, if they exist at all, are characterized by inflexibility; (3) but this inflexibility is inherent only in quoted (fictitious) prices, not transaction (actual) prices; (4) since actual prices must therefore be flexible, "administered" prices can really be "a gross statistical illusion"[4]—the product of "bizarre statistical play"[5]; and (5) since "administered" prices are an illusion, they do not exist and could not possibly be responsible for inflation.

Originally published with Robert F. Lanzillotti in *Administered Prices: A Compendium on Public Policy,* U.S. Congress, Report of the Senate Subcommittee on Antitrust and Monopoly, 88th Cong., 1st sess. 1963.

It is the conclusion of this paper that Stigler is in error, that prices which are administered manifest a type of behavior which is conspicuously different from the behavior of market-determined prices, that most of the responsibility for the price inflation of the middle and latter fifties is centered in the administered-price industries; and that they pose a problem for which there is at present no adequate public policy.

I. Quoted versus Transaction Prices

First, take the matter of quoted versus transaction prices. Long ago, Walton H. Hamilton observed that the "quoted price wears an air of pecuniary exactitude," but that its exposure to the play of market forces makes it "a base, an approximation, a hypothesis, or an unreality." Noting that price is only one of the bargaining terms between buyers and sellers, he warned that the "distinction between flexible and inflexible prices must be accepted with critical scrutiny; the stability of a price that seems to stand against the buffets of a disorganized market may conceal breakdowns in other terms of the bargain."[6] In short, the pecuniary magnitude of the quoted price must be understood within its natural habitat.

It is no longer a novelty, therefore, to suggest, as Professor Stigler has, that in some industries, for some commodities, and at some times, list prices are a fiction. We know that in gasoline marketing the quoted tank-wagon price does not reflect the sizable allowances granted during price wars. In crude oil, the posted price conceals the discounts granted in some years, and the premiums charged in others. Periods of excess demand for steel create grey markets. The manufacturer's suggested retail price for automobiles is translated into a market price by trade-in allowances or under-the-counter premiums. The imposition of Government rent controls on housing does not equate roofs and ceilings. Additionally, there are constant pressures to accommodate the quoted price— especially if it is set at artificially high or low levels—to the more realistic free-market price.

In questioning the universal applicability of list or quoted prices, therefore, Stigler is only repeating a truism; but it is a truism which does not disprove the price doctrines of Means and others. Quoted prices, and their inflexibility in some industries, are still of major significance—for a number of reasons. First, in many industries, quoted prices are the foundation of the price structure—the point of departure for bargaining over premiums and discounts, the takeoff point for price revisions.[7] It is the price structure and the manner in which it is constructed that constitute a major concern of public policy.[8]

Second, price structures normally provide for various discounts from list, which are made available to different classes of buyers. The numerous Robinson–Patman Act cases are illustrative of special transitional prices, some of which evidently are what Professor Stigler's data reflect. But no one would seriously argue that the pressure of offlist pricing, either in conformance with or in violation of Robinson–Patman destroys the meaning of list prices.[9] What is really significant is the structure of prices and how it changes over time. The mere fact that some sales are made at discount prices is not relevant to the points at issue.

Third, if transaction prices are always an understood and invariate discount below quoted prices, then changes in the latter are fully representative of changes in transaction prices. Thus, if circuit breakers usually sell at 20 percent off book list, the movement of the quoted price is an accurate reflection of changes in the transaction price.

Fourth, if Stigler is correct about the illusion of quoted prices, why in the spring of 1962 did United States Steel not simply raise its transaction prices to the level of its quoted prices? Why did Roger Blough, who is certainly conversant with the facts of life in the steel industry, insist on raising a fictitious price? Did he not know that a simple revision of transaction prices would have served his purpose and also saved him from detection by the BLS (and its henchmen)? In short, given Stigler's model, Mr. Blough was either a fool or a provocateur, hankering for a joust with the President of the United States. Both these interpretations of Mr. Blough's behavior tax credulity.

Fifth, Stigler himself has recognized the competitive significance of alternative price structures and the quoted prices on which they are built. In developing his theory of delivered pricing, for example, Stigler relied on a comparison of quoted prices for empirical verification of this theory.[10] He contrasted the behavior of quoted steel prices under the f.o.b. mill system (1898–99) with quoted prices under the basing point system (1939–40) "as to both frequency of price changes . . . and the stability of differences between prices at different production centers." While acknowledging the "uncertainty of the significance of quoted prices," he was not deterred by this uncertainty from concluding that f.o.b. prices were more flexible than basing point prices; that they were so flexible, in fact, "as to make collusion impracticable"; that therefore adoption of the f.o.b. system in lieu of the basing point system would trigger "more frequent outbreaks of price competition"—over and above the price shading that normally occurred in industries like steel and cement. In short, Stigler used a comparison of quoted prices to show that one price system promoted price flexibility and price competition "beyond the reach of colluding oligopolists," whereas another was conducive to price stability and price administration.[11] He showed—eloquently and persuasively—that the structure of an industry's quoted prices and the methods by which these are set, has a crucial impact on the amount of price competition which is possible and probable under the circumstances. In doing so, Stigler has provided empirical support for the "administered" price doctrine he now attacks.

Furthermore, contrary to Stigler's contentions, the quoted prices collected by the BLS from sellers are not necessarily less realistic than the transaction prices collected under rather special circumstances from buyers. Certainly, the buyer

Table 1

Comparison of Steel Prices in Three Markets, 1898–99, 1939–40

Market	1898–99, steel billets (f.o.b. pricing)	1939–40, steel bars (basing point pricing)
Pittsburgh:		
Possible price changes	51	103
Price changes	27	1
Philadelphia:		
Possible price changes	51	103
Price changes	38	1
Chicago:		
Possible price changes	48	103
Price changes	21	1
Pittsburgh–Philadelphia differential:		
Possible changes in differential	51	103
Changes in differential	30	0
Pittsburgh–Chicago differential:		
Possible changes in differential	48	103
Changes in differential	34	0

Source: George J. Stigler, ''A Theory of Delivered Price Systems,'' *American Economic Review*, December 1949, p. 1152.

prices reported in the McAllister and Flueck studies, initiated and carried out under Stigler's direction[12] and now quoted with approval by Stigler, do not justify the sweeping conclusion that the "BLS greatly underestimated the frequency of prices changes, and—it may be added—the amplitude of prices changes."[13] Nor do these studies support the claim that the rigidity observed in some BLS prices series constitutes "bizarre statistical play" or "a gross statistical illusion."

A. The McAllister Study

The relevant portion of the McAllister study, it should be noted, contrasts BLS wholesale price quotations with prices "collected from large companies which regularly bought items in large quantities."[14] It shows that over a 3-year period, company buying prices for some items were more flexible than BLS seller prices—the former showing 236 changes and the latter only 127. These findings, while deserving some weight, are far from conclusive. McAllister does not state which companies he sampled; how many he sampled; how representative they were; nor does he give any indication of why he selected the 43 products investigated. They seem to have been selected by McAllister's informants rather than by McAllister himself—a whimsical sampling technique, one might say.

In fact, McAllister's study raises almost as many questions as it answers. For example, were the discount prices available generally or only to certain large buyers? Were the discounts confined to a limited group of the industry's products? Were they available from all sellers or only particular sellers? Were the discount-granting sellers in a position to undermine the industry's price structure, or were they marginal competitors controlling a small percentage of industry capacity? In short, were the buyer prices reported to McAllister the rule or the exception—an isolated instance of price discrimination or a pervasive deviation from the established price structure?

Relevant in this connection is the BLS's own experience with the collection of buyers' prices. In 1942, the Bureau prepared a series of such prices for eight selected steel mill products. The series covered six time periods and was based on data collected from a sample of representative purchasers of this class of steel. Significantly enough, the Bureau found "that for relatively short periods, because of stresses and strains in the economy, invoice prices varied from the published lists (the prices at which steel mill products are quoted), but the situation soon became adjusted and invoice prices and published lists were comparable."[15] In this instance, at least, the collection of buyers' prices established only temporary deviation from the quoted price structure. Indeed, the study was more significant for revealing the "striking stability in average delivered prices despite violent changes in steel production" than for proving the deceptive character of quoted prices.[16]

B. The Flueck Study

The Flueck study cited by Stigler is also subject to serious reservations. Flueck also used buyers' prices—the bids on Government purchase orders—to show that there were 310 out of 319 possible price changes, whereas the BLS recorded only 191. Again, Stigler regards this as persuasive evidence that the BLS seriously underestimates the frequency of price changes. But here, too, as in the case of McAllister's findings, the real question is whether the data are truly representative of industrial product markets or simply a segment of such markets. After all, the bid prices on Government contracts are "for purchases by special classes of purchasers, for quantities which are not typical of the usual transaction, or for variations of the commodity built specifically to the purchasers' designs and differing from the standard generally sold."[17] In effect, Stigler should have noted that Government bid prices are for a small part of the market and that prices to other buyers are not necessarily at the same level, nor do they change at the same rate or by the same amount. Clearly, the evidence presented by Flueck deserves some weight, but it can hardly be stretched to support Stigler's sweeping conclusions. One can accept the Flueck (and McAllister) findings and retain confidence in the BLS index without inconsistency.[18] One can concede that list prices do not always or adequately reflect shortrun price movements without embracing Stigler's refreshing but unqualified skepticism.

Finally, the BLS series of quoted prices may suffer from a degree of unreality, but is this unreality confined only to products in concentrated industries? Is there a systematic bias in the BLS index which would conceal price concessions in steel and aluminum while revealing such concessions in ladies' dresses and ponderosa pine box board? Are the deviations from list prices relatively greater in industries of high than of low concentration? If they are, Stigler offers no documentation on that score, and overlooks pertinent literature on the subject.[19] Yet this is a crucial link in his chain of proof—the thrust of which is to invalidate the BLS index as an accurate reflection of price flexibility in different industries.

II. Unexplained Pricing Phenomena

None of these criticisms of the integrity of the BLS index really comes to grips with pricing curiosities such as occurred in steel in 1957, 1958, and 1962, and in new automobiles after 1955. How can Stigler explain these phenomena?

How can he explain the fact that the steel price index since World War II "continued its virtually unbroken rise even when demand and production declined (as they did in 1949, 1954, and 1957)"; that the index "also continued its climb when unit labor costs declined (as they did in 1950 and 1955)"; that "no matter what the change in cost or demand, steel prices since 1947 have moved steadily and regularly in only one direction, upward'"?[20]

How can he explain the fact that prices were raised in 1957, that the price increase substantially exceeded the cost increase, and that the higher prices were subsequently maintained in the face of declining demand, with operations at less than 60 percent of capacity, and a general recession?

How can he explain the fact that the industry in the spring of 1962 again attempted to raise prices, with operations still lagging at less than 50 percent of capacity, and in the face of severe foreign competition?

How can he explain the fact that industry leaders attempted to justify these price increases not only on the basis of a cost push, but also on the basis of a need to raise capital for plant replacement and plant expansion?

Would Stigler really have us ignore these (actual and proposed) price increases, because they represented only a change in quoted prices?

Does he assume that the steel industry is simply going through a periodic ritual—staged for the entertainment of its stockholders and, perhaps, for the malevolent amusement it derives from the reactions of the Kefauver committee?

If quoted prices are as meaningless as Stigler asserts, does he suggest that not only President Kennedy, the Council of Economic Advisers, and the academic critics of steel pricing policy, but also Roger Blough, other steel executives, and countless businessmen (who simultaneously condemned and applauded United States Steel) are playing a pointless game?

On the other hand, can it be that Stigler has carried a good argument a bit far—that he has tried to apply a theoretical model to a situation beyond its reach?

Similarly, with respect to automobiles, how could prices have been raised steadily after 1955, in the face of declining domestic demand, falling U.S. exports, rising imports, and persistent underutilization of capacity? If demand shifts were the cause for these price increases, were they a species of demand unrelated to auto sales? Or, were the price increases purely fictitious? Or were they due to rising unit costs—not only wage costs, but also nonmarginal costs like white-collar, noncash depreciation, and other overhead costs?[21] Or, as in the case of steel, perhaps the simplistic model offered by Professor Stigler is not adequate to explain the observed phenomena?

The answer to these questions, we submit, is to be found in an analysis of the price-making process in specific industries. The critical problem is whether and to what extent this pricing mechanism is demonstrably related to the inflation under study. The challenge, both for analytical and policy purposes, is to find a model that fits the facts.

A. Inflation in the Midst of Recession

To begin with, let us understand inflation proper. In a perfectly competitive economy, where nobody has any power over a price, inflation can occur only when there is an excess of demand, and depression only when there is a general deficiency of demand. In such an economy, inflation can be cured by eliminating the excess demand through restrictionist monetary-fiscal policies; depression can be cured by stimulating deficient demand through expansionary monetary-fiscal policies. Accordingly, price stability can be achieved by regulating the aggregate level of demand on a contracyclical basis.

This does not hold true, of course, in an economy where some sellers possess significant market power and the ability to exercise considerable pricing discretion. In such an economy, the aggregate demand which assures full employment and capacity operations is not necessarily identical with the aggregate demand which assures price stability. In such an economy, as Fellner says, "part of the effective demand needed for full use without inflation will be used up for wage and price increases at an underemployment level of output."[22] Or, as Lerner puts it, the "level of demand that divides prosperity from depression is not the same as that which divides inflation from deflation." Where market power is pervasive, "it may take a long and severe depression to overcome the reluctance to reduce wages and prices" and a "considerable depression even to overcome the propensity to raise them."[23] Price stability and full employment may be twin goals impossible of attainment when sellers of products and factors have significant market power.

Samuelson and Solow have suggested—tentatively, to be sure—that an unemployment rate of 5½ percent may be required to achieve price stability.[24] (Lerner has put the figure as high as 7 percent.[25]) At an unemployment level less than that the economy may suffer from recession and inflation at the same time.

Moreover, attempts to control the inflation by restricting aggregate demand tend to aggravate the recession, while attempts to cure the recession tend to aggravate the inflation, thus confronting the policy maker with apparently impossible choices.

Indeed, in the postwar years, this policy dilemma was underscored by the course of events. There were four distinct slumps in business activity: 1948–49, 1953–54, 1957–58, and 1960–61. The first was ended by the outbreak of the Korean war and the appearance of classic, demand–pull pressures. The others, however, ended with recoveries which did not represent a return to full employment. Each successive recovery was more anemic than its predecessor; each brought with it a succeedingly higher unemployment rate; each seemed to be choked off by a renewed—and perhaps, premature—effort to control inflation. From 1953 to 1958, average wholesale prices were rising, while unemployment fluctuated between 2.9 and 6.8 percent. From 1958 to 1961, average wholesale prices were relatively stable, but unemployment never dipped below 5.5 percent, and leading industries were operating far below rated capacity. No wonder, then, that Alvin Hansen expressed the doubt "that we can achieve both a satisfactory level of employment and price stability without major improvements in our anti-inflation weapons."[26]

B. Traditional Hypotheses

Various explanations have been offered for the peculiar price behavior and the persistent increase of steel prices in particular. One such explanation, advanced by John K. Galbraith, may be termed the "unliquidated monopoly gains" theory.

With inflation—

says Galbraith—

the demand curves of the firm and industry are moving persistently to the right. Under these circumstances there will normally be an incomplete adaptation of oligopoly prices. Prices will not be at profit-maximizing levels in any given situation, for the situation is continually changing, while the adaptation is by deliberate and discrete steps. This means that at any given time there will ordinarily be a quantum of what may be called unliquidated monopoly gains in the inflationary context. The shift in demand calls for a price increase for maximization; since the adaptation is currently incomplete, prices can at any time be raised and profits thereby enhanced. Absolute generality cannot be claimed for this proposition. There is an obvious, although I think outside, possibility that although adaptation is by discrete steps there will be anticipatory adaptation at each move.[27]

In other words, Galbraith seems to embrace some form of friction-ridden, profits-maximization hypothesis.

Another explanation, the "imperfect knowledge" theory, has been offered by M.A. Adelman.[28] "Other things being equal," he says, "a group of rational monopolists would not keep raising the price year after year; they would rather set the price at the monopoly level in the first place." But knowledge is imperfect, and this forces the intelligent monopolist to grope forward slowly once he enters the discretionary zone between the competitive and monopoly equilibrium. Where the industry demand curve is not well defined, and industry-labor cooperation somewhat imperfect, the pursuit of monopoly equilibrium becomes difficult and protracted. An industry like steel, "limited by the antitrust laws to a somewhat awkward and inefficient 'fall-in-and-be-counted' kind of collusion, has to be sure of the ground at each step." It must go through its annual ritual of raising prices, "and so long as the market did not react unfavorably, the next year would see a repetition."[29] This theory, like that of Galbraith, is based on the conventional profit-maximizing assumption.[30] The firm under oligopoly strives for maximum return, but either does not attempt to get all it can in one fell swoop (Galbraith), or it does not know precisely how much it can get at any given time, and therefore spreads the maximizing process out over a period of time (Adelman).

Such simple assumptions that demand and oligopolistic optimization suffice to explain price behavior in steel are far from adequate. The unanswered questions are: (a) How do United States Steel and other steel producers arrive at a reckoning of a "justifiable" price; (b) what does the corporation regard as a "fair" return; and (c) how does it conceive of capacity—how much of the excess is high cost, how much will be junked in the next 5 years?

The third explanation, offered by George Stigler, is that of traditional theory which denies any connection between monopoly prices and inflation. "A monopolist," says Stigler, "sets a profit-maximizing price for given demand-and-cost conditions. If inflation leads to a rise in either demand or costs, a new and usually higher price will be set. The price will usually be above the competitive level at any given time, but its pattern over time will not be other than passively responsive to monetary conditions."[31] In this formulation, monopoly prices cannot possibly lead to persistent price increases, unless the monopolist is irrational with respect to profit maximization, the degree of monopoly is increasing, or the monopolists are not able to "recognize a trend and adjust to it either currently or by anticipation."[32] The monopolist, no less than a firm under perfect competition, adjusts to changing cost and/or demand conditions. He responds to inflationary stimuli external to the firm; he adapts to inflation; he does not create it.

Notwithstanding their respective beliefs about the relation between pricing behavior and inflation, Galbraith, Adelman, and Stigler are all toying with the same tautology, viz.: if prices are changed, it must be in order to maximize profits. How do we know that profits are being maximized? Because prices are changed. Specifically, why were steel prices raised in 1958 and 1962? Because demand had increased. How do we know that demand had increased? Because prices were raised.

Whatever the reason may have been, it is quite clear that steel prices rose persistently between 1953 and 1958 and that these increases could not be explained only by changes in cost and/or demand conditions. Whether such behavior can be termed rational or not is beside the point; whether it is in accord with traditional profit maximizing assumptions is also irrelevant at this point.

Let us examine Professor Stigler's position in detail. He states that according to traditional economic theory "oligopoly and monopoly prices have no special relevance to inflation."[33] Following the orthodox view, he reasons that if inflation leads to either a rise in demand or costs, a new price will be set usually "above the competitive level at any given time, but its pattern will not be other than passively responsive to monetary conditions." To attack this traditional position, Stigler contends one must either argue (a) that "monopolists and oligopolists want higher prices per se, rather than maximum profits" (which he considers a "peculiar theory of motivation for entrepreneurs"); (b) that the important industries are becoming concentrated and acting more monopolistically (which he suspected would be refuted by the 1958 census); or (c) that oligopolists' prices lag behind the prices that would maximize profits (which seems "implausible" and "really not directed to the problem of inflation").[34]

With respect to (a), it is not necessary to argue that monopolists want higher prices per se in order to demonstrate that their price behavior has a definite inflationary impact under certain circumstances; nor, as we shall show, is it necessary to argue that monopolists and oligopolists want maximum (Stiglerian) profits per se. On (b), Stigler's suspicion that the 1958 census will offer a refutation that the economy is becoming more concentrated, is itself refuted by those very statistics. To disregard the new concentration data and argue alternatively that even so the Judiciary Committee's hearings "should have been directed toward newly concentrated industries, not such old standbys as steel, automobiles, and drugs," is merely to beg the question: It is at least a debatable point that if durable goods manufacturers faced more competition in the 1955–58 period, we certainly should not have had the continuous price rises that prevailed. Finally, what seems implausible to Stigler—(c) that oligopolists' prices would lag behind profit maximizing prices—was well-documented empirically during the grey markets in automobiles and steel following World War II.

It is no answer to the market power thesis to quibble over whether Gardiner Means' definition is good or not; everyone who has studied the problem knows what administered prices are, in contrast to market-determined or market-governed prices.[35] The central question is whether, under the impact of given cost and demand changes, market-determined prices behave differently from market-determining prices; whether market-determined prices behave consistent with, and market-determining prices perversely to changing demand conditions[36]; and whether the phenomenon of discretionary power may be related to observed fluctuations in economic activity. The phenomenon underlying these questions cannot be dismissed with the breezy observation that it couldn't possibly occur.

Stigler's contribution to the administered-price controversy thus is interesting, ingenious, and, we regret to say, irrelevant. He does not explain, indeed he never recognizes, (1) how the economy can simultaneously suffer from inflation and recession, a condition which has puzzled most of the economic fraternity; (2) why "competitive" (market-determined) prices move in sympathy with cyclical changes in demand, while "administered" (market-determining) prices seem to move in a perverse manner; or (3) whether there is a possible connection between these phenomena. These are the problems which cannot be ignored, nor defined out of existence.

C. Target Return Pricing and Inflation

The adequacy of traditional theoretical tools to handle the analysis of price behavior over time is brought into serious question by the observations of Lerner, Galbraith, and Fellner. The standard short-run explanations of price and output behavior are singularly unhelpful in explaining price movements in the administered markets. Where institutionalized pricing formulas (such as target-rate-of-return pricing) are used, combined with price leadership, the tendency is to produce identical price revisions for all rival oligopolists, without disturbance to accustomed profits margins or traditional market shares. Price changes of this type hardly conform to the automatic market-clearing reaction to demand–supply forces envisaged by marginal price theory. More significantly, price changes based upon pricing formulas and pricing institutions do not conform to the traditional profit-maximizing calculus.

In the circumstances, revised pricing hypotheses are called for. If we are to give operational meaning and predictability to oligopoly analysis, it would seem necessary to eschew strict marginalism and take account of the price-making formulas actually used by decision makers in oligopolistic industries.[37] Instead of approaching pricing via cost and demand estimates and then selecting the profits-maximizing price for these conditions, it is commonplace for price setters to begin with a target-rate-of-return on investment that is considered satisfactory and is consistent with estimates of entry threats, antitrust threats, union threats, as well as intraindustry threats to equilibrium and interfirm togetherness.[38] The calculus from this point is to work backward to determine prices that will yield this target rate of profits over a period which will include both good times and bad, in the range of capacity utilization that is consistent with engineering design, total industry capacity, and traditional market-share relationships. The major steps involved in target pricing are:

(1) Determination of a target rate of return on investment (or stockholders' equity, plus long-term debt). The particular target rate is a longrun objective, over periods of economic fluctuations, not a single year. The rate should be low enough effectively to discourage or limit entry, especially if entry barriers are not formidable.

(2) Determination of rate of utilization of plant at "standard volume," usually the average rate of operations over the cycle—e.g., 75 or 80 percent.

(3) Determination of "standard costs" at "standard volume" rate of operation. Costs utilized for pricing are not the actual costs incurred at actual output rates, but the estimated, or "standard" unit costs at standard volume.

(4) Determination of the margin to be added to standard costs, at standard volume, to produce the desired target rate of return on investment. This margin yields a target price. The particular margins added to standard costs may be altered if standard volume is revised, if standard costs are revised, or if management decides to revise its target rate of return.

The point here is that once we discard (a) the assumption of traditional theory that firms can and normally will experiment with continuously changing prices, as well as (b) the assumption of shortrun profits maximization, we create a serious vacuum in our theoretical apparatus. The evidence of price behavior in concentrated oligopoly makes it clear that price administrators do not seek to maximize profits (in Stigler's sense) in the short run. The tendency to adopt target pricing is rational behavior for price administrators but it cannot be derived from traditional theories of monopoly or oligopoly which rely upon the conventional marginal calculus.

The latter yields no meaningful predictions regarding the exercise of monopoly pricing power, other than to suggest that it may (a) dampen, (b) aggravate, or (c) have negligible effects on cyclical movement upward or downward.[39] The target-rate-of-return thesis, however, permits us to be more precise in predicting not only actual behavior, but also the impact of such pricing on economic stability.

The Demand-Pull Case

Consider now the case of overall demand-pull theory of inflation, either the purely monetary variant or the Keynesian or income-expenditure theories. Given a powerful demand-pull, concomitant with such booms as 1946–48, how would the target-rate-of-return pricing operate and what would be its effects? Since output and sales would be running ahead of standard volume rate, profits would be likely to exceed the longrun target-rate-of-return on investment. The concentration of sellers on their longrun target-rates-of-return, and longrun market shares, means that the rise in volume will greatly increase the shortrun profit margin over all costs, including overhead factor; but, the markup itself will not be revised unless the change in current demand is interpreted by price administrators as altering previously determined estimates of the longer term demand prospects of the particular firm or the industry generally.

An increase in demand, generated by an increase in money supply, which induces an upward revision in the long-term prospects might lead to a reduction in the markup on standard costs to produce the desired target rate of return. This seemingly was the case during the period of grey markets in automobiles and steel following World War II. The fact that (a) used car prices were higher than new car prices, (b) grey market steel sold above quoted prices, and (c) "bonuses" were paid to retailers of consumer durables verified the "oligopolistic lag" or non-profits-minimizing behavior Stigler finds so implausible.[40] Paradoxical under traditional marginal price theory, this behavior follows quite logically from the target-rate-of-return theory. Significantly, prices of the firms following the target return approach will be reacting perversely to the pressures of industry demand, with the additional effect of tending to distort the structure of relative prices in the economy.

The Cost-Push Case

In the case of cost- or wage-push inflation, the target-rate-of-return approach will produce not a dampening, but accentuating inflationary tendency. Since the formula for target pricing bases prices on elements of direct cost that tend to affect all rival sellers in common, an increase in direct costs (say, wage costs) will result in standard markups applied to the rising wage costs[41] despite a rate of operations lagging below standard volume.

Rising costs obviously pose a dilemma for the firm. Under the marginalist approach, the firm should disregard fixed-cost elements in pricing, since these costs are fixed, and rational behavior calls for the marginal cost calculus. Traditional theory and Professor Stigler argue this case persuasively, and we are convinced of its validity in the world of pure competition. "Blind," "misguided," "unschooled" businessmen,[42] however, display a concern for overhead costs in pricing that suggests less than due respect for the marginalist approach. For example, on February 20, 1958, the retiring president of the American Paper & Pulp Association stated that "the Nation's papermakers will be forced to raise prices if operations continue to lag."[43] Steel executives and others have made similar statements.

As a result of Professor Schultze's work, we now have data showing that overhead salary costs and depreciation accounted for the very large proportion (62 percent) of the increase in total unit cost between 1947 and 1957.[44] Moreover, "the rate of increase in overhead unit costs accelerated significantly after 1955." According to Schultze, this was not the result of an acceleration in the technological shift to overhead costs, but of the failure of output to continue to rise after late 1955.[45] The fact that fixed costs were found to have accounted for the bulk of the rise in total costs, of course, does not offer conclusive evidence that they were responsible for the inflationary rise between 1955 and 1957. Indeed, this is not critical to our arguments concerning target pricing and oligopolistic inflation.

The crucial question is whether the variations in fixed costs, working through target pricing or similar full-cost pricing policies, operated in a manner not predictable under orthodox pricing theory—since fixed costs are not supposed to have an impact on pricing decisions. In the orthodox sense, of course, all pricing is short run. But the pricing decisions envisioned by orthodox theory are seldom made. Why should a firm with market power consider either shortrun marginal cost or shortrun marginal revenue? Indeed, it is questionable whether any significant operational meaning can be attached to "maximizing profits in the long run."[46]

Under target return pricing, the markup is designed to cover fixed costs plus the desired target at standard volume—with both fixed and variable costs figured at standard volume. While an increase in output will not normally lead to a price rise, in this case we are dealing not with a decline in output, but with its failure to rise at the same rate as capacity and overhead. As Schultze observes, "In a situation characterized not by declining sales and output, but by stable or slowly rising output, it is not at all unlikely that these higher costs formed the basis for price increases" of the 1955–57 period.[47]

Such attempts to finance plant expansion and to cover a target rate of return on investment at rates of output falling progressively short of optimum are tantamount to a reduction in the standard volume on which prices are based. Professor Schultze has provided us with the essential framework in which the aggressive influence of target pricing can be traced. At the microlevel, the experience of industries characterized by target pricing, price leadership, and price followership is especially illuminating. For example, during this period, steel profit margins were rising.[48] More than that, the margins were apparently increasing without necessarily producing increased profits for target-price leaders.

The case of United States Steel, cited by Professor Stigler, offers an excellent illustration of the manner in which cost-push works under target-return pricing. A comparison of the 1954–56 and 1957–58 periods shows that the corporation widened the gap between rising unit costs and prices, while operating at a median capacity of 87 percent in the first period and 74 percent in the second.[49] Here is a good illustration of the paradoxical case of increased profits per ton, reflecting higher markups, with no significant change in total profits.

The Profits Paradox

This leads us to a related point. In criticizing the Kefauver committee, Professor Stigler observes that it is not enough to show that administered prices during the last decade increased more than enough to compensate for increases in costs. It would also have to be shown that they produced monopoly profits. "But," he adds, "even a showing of monopoly profits would not prove that oligopoly prices were the source of a new kind of inflation: what was needed was a demonstration that profits were rising over time"[50]—a fact which in Stigler's opinion the committee never successfully proved.

Here again, Stigler's point is not germane to the issue. Whether steel profits rise or fall during inflation depends on the behavior of steel costs relative to steel prices. These costs (including wages) may very well rise faster than prices, thus squeezing profits. But does this prove anything about the impact of steel prices in inflation? Certainly not. Steel may be likened to the man who cries "Fire" in a crowded theater and runs for the exit. The crowd panics and follows him. Later the man denies responsibility for the panic, because he is no longer at the head of the crowd.

Similarly, a cost-push, fueled by target-rate-of-return pricing, can produce inflation without necessarily producing increased profits for the price administrators. It is perfectly conceivable, for example, that steel and automobile profits may have declined during the period in question—not because administered prices had a neutral effect on inflation, but because such prices helped induce an inflation during which costs rose faster than the prices themselves.

Since public authorities are extremely sensitive to threats of inflation, as reflected in autonomous wage–price increases, such rises will induce them to follow restrictive monetary policies that curtail aggregate demand. This, in turn, may induce a perversity by corporations in their pricing since the firms must now think in terms of a lower rate of utilization than would normally be considered under target-rate-of-return procedures. This means higher markups. Labor unions will view the higher markups in such a way that they increase their eagerness to push wage rates up, even though their power may not be changed.

Under the circumstances, it is fully consistent in a cost-push situation, such as described, to have the following set of circumstances: (a) rate of utilization of plant decreased; (b) increased unit costs due to decreased utilization and wage-push; (c) higher markups on unit costs due to both decreased utilization and wage-push; and (d) unchanged total profits despite wider markups.

Conclusion

Professor Stigler's disquisition, in spite of its empirical gloss, is essentially an apologetic for abstraction—a neglect of physiological empiricism. His analysis is based on the proposition that the conventional wisdom, derived from traditional assumptions, ought to explain reality; that the facts of economic life must be made to fit the procrustean bed of orthodoxy; and that any conflict between theory and fact should always be resolved in favor of theory. A phenomenon must never be allowed to embarrass a theory; its only function is to validate a theory.

Be that as it may, it is disheartening even for inflation buffs to engage Professor Stigler in a skirmish of the last war. The administered price inflation of the 1950's is now history—overshadowed by a lagging growth rate, persistent unemployment, and a gnawing underutilization of capacity. These are the problems deserving the attention of industrial organization specialists in the decade of the 1960's. Moreover, it is ironic to dispute matters of diagnosis when there is agreement on the cure to be prescribed. We share Professor Stigler's policy orientation. We, too, believe in the kind of industry structure which will be conducive to competitive behavior and promotive of competitive performance.

We agree that the crux of the problem is the degree of industrial concentration, and regard administered prices as no more than a symptom of the disease. We also agree on the need for structural surgery under the Sherman and Celler–Kefauver Acts.

Nevertheless, we cannot agree with Professor Stigler that the "entire performance of the Kefauver committee over the past 4 years has been a highly unsatisfactory one." This conclusion is not warranted by the facts, nor documented with more than Stigler's gratuitous innuendos. The committee, we submit, did not engage in an aimless "fishing expedition." It did not conduct a witch hunt on the Potomac. The "digression" into stock options was not "vulgar," nor was it irrelevant to the matters at issue. The cost analyses by the staff were not "desultory" given the persistent refusal by corporate witnesses to supply the necessary facts and figures. The committee was painstaking and patient in compiling the kind of information that both economists and policymakers need, and without which they would be dabbling with elegant chimeras and academic abstractions—condemned to a hopeless and incurable catatonia.

Notes

1. Quoted in Frank H. Knight, *Intelligence and Democratic Action*, p. 57 (1960).
2. "Administered Prices and Oligopolistic Inflation," *The Journal of Business*, pp. 1–13 (1962) (hereafter cited as "Administered Prices").
3. Ibid., p. 13.
4. Ibid., p. 4.
5. Ibid., p. 2.
6. Walter Hamilton, *Price and Price Policies*, pp. 531–535 (1938). See also Willard L. Thorp and Walter F. Crowder, "The Structure of Industry," T.N.E.C. Monograph No. 27, (1941); Alfred C. Neal, *Industrial Concentration and Price Inflexibility* (1942); and Robert F. Lanzillotti, "Competitive Price Leadership," *Review of Economics and Statistics*, pp. 55–64 (1957). For a comprehensive review of the literature on this subject, see John M. Blair, "Means, Thorp, and Neal on Price Inflexibility," *Review of Economics and Statistics*, pp. 427–435 (1956).
7. Joel B. Dirlam and Alfred E. Kahn, "Leadership and Conflict in the Pricing of Gasoline," *Yale Law Journal*, pp. 818–855 (1952).
8. In antitrust law, it is the quoted price which is of decisive significance. Thus, a gentleman's agreement is not immunized by the fact that 60 percent of the conspirators are gentlemen, 30 percent just act like gentlemen, and 10 percent neither are nor act like gentlemen. A cartel is not beatified by the fact that it is under constant pressure from unethical insiders and interloping outsiders. A price-fixing arrangement is not saved by the fact that it does not work. Indeed, conspiracies and monopolies are seldom insulated from competition at the margin; yet they are contrary to public policy because peripheral competition is not enough to undermine a whole price structure. Independents may nibble away at that structure; they may threaten a collusive or monopolistic equilibrium; but they are rarely in a position to subvert it altogether. That is why an industry's price structure—whatever the occasional deviations from it—has crucial antitrust significance.
9. It is curious that Messrs. Blough and Homer took great pains—not always patiently —to explain to the Kefauver committee why steel prices had to be identical. ("Under the

Robinson-Patman Act," Mr. Homer said, "we are required to quote the same price to everyone on the same product. . . . [W]e are permitted to quote a competitive delivered price, but we cannot quote under that without affecting, under the Robinson–Patman Act, the f.o.b. mill prices back at our base plant.") If Stigler is right, and price concessions beyond "meeting the equally low price of a competitor in good faith" are indeed widespread, the Blough–Homer testimony must be construed as a clever camouflage for Robinson–Patman Act violations. *Hearings before the Subcommittee on Antitrust and Monopoly,* U.S. Senate, "Administered Prices," pt. 2, Steel, 85th Cong., 1st sess., pp. 310, 312, 617 ff (1957).

10. "A Theory of Delivered Price Systems," *American Economic Review,* pp. 1143–1159 (1949).

11. Ibid., pp. 1152, 1157 ff.

12. *The Price Statistics of the Federal Government,* National Bureau of Economic Research, No. 73, 1961, p. 16.

13. Stigler, "Administered Prices," op. cit., p. 7.

14. Harry E. McAllister, "Statistical Factors Affecting the Stability of the Wholesale and Consumers' Price Indexes," *The Price Statistics of the Federal Government,* op. cit., pp. 393–394.

15. *Hearings before the Subcommittee on Economic Statistics of the Joint Economic Committee,* "Government Price Statistics," pt. 2, 87th Cong., 1st sess., p. 602 (1961).

16. George W. Stocking, "Basing Point Pricing and Regional Development," p. 119 (quoted in Blair, op. cit., p. 429).

17. "Government Price Statistics," pt. 2, op. cit., p. 602.

18. Do not the lower bid prices to the Government underscore the importance which sellers attach to maintaining the integrity of their quoted prices on the bulk of their sales in the regular market?

19. "For the purpose of analyzing the relationship between concentration and price rigidity the BLS series are invalidated only if it is assumed that during a downswing secret discounts become relatively more important in products of high than products of low concentration. Neither Thorp nor the other critics of Means ever explicitly made this assumption, nor, incidentally, did Means ever call upon them to do so." Blair, op. cit., p. 429. Richard B. Heflebower is prepared to make the assumption, but offers nothing to substantiate it. "Do Administered Prices Involve an Antitrust Problem?" *Northwestern University Law Review,* pp. 190–191 (1962).

20. *Report of the Committee on the Judiciary,* U.S. Senate, "Administered Prices, Steel," Rept. No. 1387, 85th Cong., 1st sess., p. 129 (1958).

21. See *Report of the Subcommittee on Antitrust and Monopoly,* U.S. Senate, "Administered Prices, Automobiles," 85th Cong., 2d sess., pp. 115–124 (1958); see also John M. Blair, "Administered Prices: A Phenomenon in Search of a Theory," *American Economic Review Proceedings,* pp. 439–441 (1959).

22. Statement of William J. Fellner, *Hearings before Joint Economic Committee,* "Employment, Growth, and Price Levels," pt. 7, 86th Cong., 1st sess., p. 2334 (1959).

23. Statement of Abba P. Lerner, ibid., p. 2264.

24. Cited in Alvin H. Hansen, *Economic Issues of the 1960's,* p. 4 (1960).

25. Lerner, op. cit., p. 2264.

26. Hansen, op. cit., p. 4.

27. *Hearings before the Subcommittee on Antitrust and Monopoly,* U.S. Senate, "Administered Prices," pt. 1, 85th cong., 1st sess., p. 65 (1957).

28. "Steel, Administered Prices and Inflation," *Quarterly Journal of Economics,* pp. 16–40 (1961). In fairness to Adelman (and Galbraith), it should be observed that their theories were advanced prior to the events of April 1962.

29. Ibid., pp. 24, 28 ff.

30. Incidentally, it also assumes that quoted prices are a valid index of price levels and pricing behavior.

31. Stigler, "Administered Prices," op. cit., p. 8.

32. Ibid., p. 8.

33. Ibid., p. 8. In support of this view, Stigler cites an unpublished study by Richard Selden and Horace J. DePodwin which showed little association between concentration of production and the amplitude of price increases during the 1950's. In this connection, it is noteworthy that a model showing the association between changes in target-rate-of-return pricing, changes in break-even points, changes in union bargaining power, and changes in the price level is about to be investigated by Hubertus von und zu Swickenstein and Boris Przmysl-Watson. Their analysis of price changes from 1953 to 1959, based upon a three-stage model, will no doubt show: (1) a high correlation (r = 0.7) between increases in prices and rate of decline in break-even points, and (2) a somewhat less significant correlation between the rate of increase in the general price level and the rate of adoption of target-rate-of-return pricing (thus, incidentally, disproving Gibrat's law). An early version of their estimating equation takes the following form:

$$\Delta P = a + b_1 \Delta TR + b_2 \Delta\left(\frac{F_{TR}}{F}\right) + b_3 UBP + b_4 \Delta BEP,$$

Where

TR   = target rate of return,

$\frac{F_{TR}}{F}$ = proportion of total output accounted by firms using target rate of return,

UBP = union bargaining power index,

BEP = break-even point.

34. Ibid., p. 8.

35. In challenging Means' definition of administered prices, Stigler observes: "For example, a university changes tuition fees only once a year, but transactions take place only once a year so supply-and-demand conditions effectively change only once a year at most" (op. cit., p. 4). Is Professor Stigler saying that a university which changes its tuition once a year, or once every 5 years, is an example of a firm effectively balancing supply and demand? Or is the quoted tuition merely a fiction, while the real tuition (transaction fee) carefully equilibrates short-run market conditions?

36. Many observers have been puzzled by the peculiar perversity of steel prices. Prof. Richard B. Heflebower, for example, is unable to explain why, in 1958, administered prices in steel were raised "even though the industry was operating at 55 percent of capacity" and even though it suffered from "comparable unemployment." Nor is he able to explain why, in 1962, "In the face of this demand situation—foreign competition, excess capacity, and some price weakness—the list prices of steel were increased in April by the largest seller and followed promptly by most other producers." Heflebower, op. cit., pp. 203, 204.

37. See R.J. Hall and C.J. Hitch, "Price Theory and Business Behavior," *Oxford Economic Papers*, II, 1939, pp. 12–45; P.W.S. Andrews, *Manufacturing Business* (1939); National Bureau of Economic Research, *Cost Behavior and Price Policy* (1943); K.W. Rothschild, "Price Theory and Oligopoly," *Economic Journal*, pp. 299–320 (1947); R.A. Gordon, "Short Period Price Determination in Theory and Practice," *American Economic Review*, pp. 265–88 (1948); Alfred Oxenfeldt, *Industrial Pricing and Market Practices* (1951); Sir Roy Harrod, *Economic Essays* (1952); Jean Pierre de Bodt, *La Formation des*

and R.F. Lanzillotti, *Pricing in Big Business* (1958); B. Fog, *Industrial Pricing Policies* (1960); Neil W. Chamberlain, *The Firm: Micro-Economic Planning and Action* (1962).

38. Cf. Robert F. Lanzillotti, "Pricing Objectives in Large Companies," *American Economic Review,* December 1958, and "Comments" by Morris A. Adelman and Alfred E. Kahn, and "Reply," ibid., December 1959. There are, to be sure, institutional–frictional factors that impede the workings of the traditional theoretical model. Given (1) oligopoly uncertainty, (2) the costs of continuous price changes, (3) liquidity considerations, (4) taxes, (5) the amount of management time to evaluate alternative prices, (6) the impact on customers who vastly prefer stable prices, and (7) the impact of such changes on production and inventory problems, oligopolists either do not feel free to, nor inclined to experiment continuously with alternative sets of prices. Also, even if sellers could estimate present and future sales at various alternative prices, it is quite conceivable that the difference in total profits based upon a policy of lower prices and higher sales volume would not be significant. It is the combination of all these considerations that underlies the concept of the "zone of price indifference," or price discretion. But, even if all these frictions and institutional factors did not exist, and even if the zone of price indifference had never been developed, target-rate-of-return pricing could not be dismissed as implausible, irrational, or unsophisticated.

39. Stigler contends that the Kefauver hearings shed no light on "the question of why, on certain occasions in recent years, the steel industry raised prices while operating at relatively low outputs. . . ." His own explanation is political, not economic, viz, that "The presence of congressional investigations such as this is a very strong reason for the steel industry to raise quoted prices whenever a suitable occasion (cost increase) occurs" (op. cit., p. 11)—the very quoted prices which he claims are meaningless.

40. In this connection the view of corporate conscience and corporate responsibility as explanations for restraint in pricing, or oligopoly price lags, may have been misinterpreted by various observers. The target-pricing concept does not require any such rationale of the corporate soul or public conscience. As General Motors President Harlow Curtice observed in response to the suggestion that some of the high profits of 1955 might have been passed on to buyers in the form of lower prices, "They [our car prices] are as low as they can be and still produce the indicated return on net worth at standard volume. We can never be sure whether we are going to exceed the standard volume or whether the marketplace will be such that we will sell less than the standard volume." (Emphasis added.) U.S. Senate, Subcommittee on Antitrust and Monopoly of the Committee on the Judiciary, *A Study of the Antitrust Laws,* hearings, 84th Cong., 1st sess., p. 3609 (1956).

41. Prof. James S. Dusenberry, for example, finds that "the more highly concentrated industries contribute to inflation . . . not so much through raising their profit margins but through being in a position where it is fairly easy for them to give wage increases and pass them on into prices." "Employment, Growth, and Price Levels," pt. 7, op. cit., p. 2333.

42. I.e., those businessmen who want to raise prices because of changes in what seem to them to be significant costs. While perhaps they should ignore the cost of replacing existing capital and the actual cost of raising new capital—and should rely, instead, on a simultaneous determination of price, new investment, net anticipated cash flows, and internal rate of return—they do not.

43. Blair, "Administered Prices," op. cit., p. 441.

44. Charles L. Schultze, "Recent Inflation in the United States," "Study of Employment, Growth, and Price Levels," Study Paper No. 1, Joint Economic Committee, 86th Cong., 1st sess., p. 83 (1959).

45. Ibid., p. 88.

46. In commenting on longrun profit maximization, Fog observes that the concept "seems to be a way of avoiding the problems [rather] than a way of solving them" (op.

cit., p. 28). And, if refuge is sought in psychic human income, P.J.D. Wiles' statement is pertinent: "To say that a man maximizes his psychic profit is to say that he does what he pleases, or wishes, or likes" (op. cit., p. 174).

47. Schultze, op. cit., p. 91.

48. For a comparison of the relationship between United States Steel's operating rate and (a) net profits per ton and (b) rate of return on net worth, 1954–56 and 1957–58, see *Congressional Record,* June 30, 1959, p. 111165.

49. Ibid.

50. Stigler, "Administered Prices," op. cit., p. 11.

7

The Military–Industrial Complex:
A Market Structure Analysis

Some 200 years ago, Adam Smith reported on a disastrous experiment in mercantilist statecraft. The great trading companies, he found, had been organized to conduct Great Britain's commerce in "remote and barbarous nations," and to maintain forts and garrisons for its protection. Chosen instruments to effectuate a public purpose, they were often given exclusive privileges and either had the right to exclude private adventurers ("interlopers") altogether, or to tax them in return for providing military and civil defense. These companies, Smith found, "have very seldom succeeded without an exclusive privilege: and frequently have not succeeded with one. Without an exclusive privilege, they have commonly mismanaged the trade. With an exclusive privilege, they have both mismanaged and confined it."

So widespread were the folly and negligence of their functionaries that the companies eventually fell victim to bankruptcy and could not even maintain the forts and garrisons which had been the prime purpose and pretext of their formation. By 1773, the Crown was petitioned to bail out the East India Company which could no longer meet its financial or military obligations. By that year, Smith reports,

> their debts, instead of being reduced, were augmented by an arrear to the treasury in the payment of the [franchise levy of] four hundred thousand pounds, by another to the custom-house for duties unpaid, by a large debt to the bank for money borrowed, and by a fourth for bills drawn upon them from India, and wantonly accepted, to the amount of upwards of twelve hundred thousand pounds. The distress which these accumulated claims brought upon them, obliged them not only to reduce all at once their dividend to six percent, but to throw themselves upon the mercy of government, and to supplicate, first, a release from the further payment of the stipulated four hundred thou-

Originally published with William J. Adams in the *American Economic Review*, vol. 62 (May 1972); reprinted with permission.

sand pounds a-year; and, secondly, a loan of fourteen hundred thousand, to save them from immediate bankruptcy. The great increase of their fortune had, it seems, only served to furnish their servants with a pretext for greater profusion, and a cover for greater malversation, than in proportion even to that increase of fortune. The conduct of their servants in India, and the general state of their affairs both in India and in Europe, became the subject of a parliamentary inquiry.

Today's aerospace giants and purveyors of munitions are simply reincarnations of the old trading companies. And their performance is hardly more reassuring. Congressional investigations abound with evidence to show: (1) that cost overruns have been enormous[1]; (2) that product quality has fallen short of original promise and contract requirements[2]; and (3) that profits have in some instances been astronomical.[3] Yet, despite their desultory performance, the defense contractors seem to be safely sheltered in the womb of government with their umbilical cord tied to the U.S. Treasury.

The prodigious documentation of deficient performance, however, has not been matched by equivalent efforts to explore analytically the reasons for such performance and the implications for public policy. We should like to address ourselves, therefore, to the following questions: (1) What is the explanation of the poor performance in defense industries? Here we shall suggest that the answer lies in the structure of relevant markets. (2) What are the determinants of these market structures? Here we shall suggest that the answer lies, to a substantial degree, in government intervention and privilege creation. (3) What are the implications for public policy? Here we shall evaluate some structural remedies which might correct observed performance deficiencies.

Throughout, we shall ask the reader to keep in mind that the military–industrial complex is only one illustration of the more general phenomenon of government intervention in the economy creating and reinforcing market imperfections.[4]

I. Market Structure as a Determinant of Poor Performance

Let us begin, then, with the question of why performance is so bad in defense industries. The most fashionable answer is that the military bureaucracy and its industrial suppliers form a natural coalition of interests. Both, it is suggested, benefit from a military focus to government expenditure. Hence, each can be expected to support the other for mutual advantage. This is the origin of the term "military–industrial complex," the usage of which is not difficult to justify. One need only consider the pressure on Congress to bail out Lockheed,[5] or the apparent right of the Department of Defense (DOD) to use PL 85–804 to maintain any firm it deems essential to national defense.[6]

Nevertheless, similarity of interest does not imply identity of interest. While both groups might agree on the desirability of a large and growing defense budget and even engage in occasional collusion, it does not follow that both would want to forsake their adversary posture as buyers and sellers. To the extent that DOD believes in the importance of its mission, it will want to procure the biggest bang for its buck. It should then have a clear preference for obtaining any given bundle of defense services at least cost. Its suppliers, on the other hand, given their market power, are not compelled to *prefer* least cost methods of production. Thus, the coalition-of-interest explanation does not tell us why government fails to use its monopsony power in military procurement in a manner designed to promote technological efficiency.

Another answer, current in somewhat different circles, is that government is by its very nature insensitive to costs, secure in the knowledge that higher costs can always be covered by increased taxes. This explanation of price insensitivity may apply to the defense sector, but there is little evidence of Congressional reluctance to cut civilian expenditures whenever it feels the price is not right. Thus, general condemnations of the government as an irrational consumer seem suspect.

The question, therefore, remains. Why does the government use its monopsony power so sparingly in the realm of defense spending? The best answer, we suggest, emanates from a structural analysis of defense procurement markets. Let us explain why.

Consider a market which is perfect on both sides. The price mechanism would elicit all relevant information on tastes and technology simply from the self-interested behavior of all economic agents. If the buyer's side were characterized by monopsony, but the seller's side continued to be perfect, all relevant information on technology would still be revealed. Through the process of competition among sellers, the buyer would know exactly what the real (private) opportunity costs of producing the commodity in question were and hence the precise extent of technological efficiency in each potential supplier. His choice among suppliers would not, therefore, be difficult to make. Equilibrium price would reflect cost, even though it would fail to reflect consumer preferences.

Now consider a market comprised of the monopsonist and an oligopolistic configuration of sellers. Here there is no guarantee that market operation will reveal the technological information the monopsonist needs in order to buy rationally, even if such information exists. Collusion among sellers, whether tacit or overt, could prevent technology and cost information from being revealed by equilibrium market prices. Despite his monopsony power, then, the buyer could not be sure he is procuring at least cost. For the market no longer supplies a benchmark for cost performance. The monopsonist could, of course, hire scientific experts to tell him what his product ought, in theory, to cost. Such experts could not tell him, however, how much it actually costs or whether ongoing firms would use their market power to destroy any potential entrant who would produce and sell at what the experts ascertain to be least cost. The market power of the monopsonist can thus be practically neutralized by a strong oligopolistic group of sellers obscuring technological efficiencies.

It is this combination of monopsony and oligopoly which characterizes defense procurement markets. The existence of monopsony is obvious. The existence of oligopoly—arising from high concentration, high barriers to entry, and high product differentiation on the seller's side, and leading to market power among ongoing sellers—may require some elaboration.

Without delving into a detailed examination of defense market structure, suffice it to say that the best empirical indicator of structural economic power among sellers would be the presence of economic profit and/or the presence of technological inefficiency. The existence of economic profit is a matter of some debate, although we believe it has been well documented.[7] The existence of technological inefficiency, though, should be beyond doubt. It explains the inability of even large defense contractors to enter successfully civilian industries where markets are unsheltered.[8] It even explains some of the cost overruns which appear to be against the best interest of defense contractors: in a learning-by-doing framework, firms rarely compelled to exert themselves will find it quite difficult systematically to uncover best-practice technique (given the state of technology), even where information on the subject would benefit the firm.[9] As Adam Smith already had observed, monopoly power weakens its beneficiaries as much as it strengthens them.[10]

In sum, the best explanation of poor performance in the military–industrial complex is the uncertainty emanating from inadequate technological information and the monopsony–oligopoly configuration it promotes. It is these structural elements of current defense markets which explain the apparent willingness of government to bet on the supplier-horses it has, regardless of the cost and regardless of the chance of winning. Why these structural elements exist must, therefore, be understood before it is possible to appraise public policy options.

II. Some Determinants of Market Structure

Whenever ongoing sellers face price-insensitive demand, permitting them to survive regardless of their performance, they may be said to operate in sheltered markets. Sheltered markets occur, of course, for many reasons. Some are "natural" in the sense that they would appear even under a regime of laissez faire. (Bain, for example, has noted industries where economies of scale relative to market size are responsible for the barriers to entry which render demand for the products of ongoing firms price-insensitive.) But sheltered markets can also occur for artificial as well as natural reasons. In these cases, it is not so much the rock formation of technology as the house built by government which shelters producers from Schumpeterian gales. In such cases, government policy rather than technology bears the responsibility for existing market structures and hence for existing economic power.

To what extent are the shelters in military procurement markets natural, and to what extent are they artificial? This is the key question, of course, for government policy. As Caves has suggested, current public policy can be appraised only by comparison with feasible rather than ideal alternatives.[11] This requires a sorting out of the net effects "nature" and policy have on the market structures which conduce to poor performance. Only then is it possible to ascertain the scope government has for mending some violations in the Pareto conditions without creating others. We turn, therefore, to the following cursory examination of the natural and policy-induced components of defense industry structures.

The natural determinants of market structure are obvious. The product in question, a major weapons system, has not yet been produced. Its technical attributes, its performance reliability, its ultimate costs are largely a matter of conjecture. Technological uncertainty is omnipresent and pervasive. Under the circumstances, the government finds it difficult to choose a contractor simply on the basis of price. Even more important, it must consider the impact of awarding a particular contract on the overall capability of the whole industry to meet future government needs. Interdependence of project choices compounds the difficulties imposed by uncertainty.[12]

The presence of these natural elements of market structure, however, does not imply the absence of artificial structural forces. After all, it is the government which ultimately determines who shall enter and survive in the defense industry. Thus, the major aerospace firms depend on the government for as much as 95 percent of their business. They typically operate in government-built plants, use government-owned machinery, receive government-furnished working capital, obtain patents on government-financed research and development, and enjoy government-guaranteed profits. Incompetence, extravagance, or mismanagement are no threat to their survival. If adversity strikes, whether in their military or civilian operations, these companies can count on government bailouts. As courtiers of DOD, NASA, and AEC, they function in a world of socialized risks and private profit.

As a monopsonist, moreover, the government has wide latitude in its choice of purchasing practices, and these have a profound structural impact. Thus, government can decide how many contractors to subsidize in drawing up preliminary plans for a new weapons system and whether to continue subsidizing them well into the engineering development phase. It can decide whether to commit itself to a single contractor on the basis of paper studies, plans, and proposals emanating from the design competition (the "lying and buying" process) or to delay that choice until several contractors have produced and demonstrated actual prototypes. It is free to assume overall responsibility for an entire weapons system and to engage in direct contracting for subsystems and hard goods characterized by lesser degrees of uncertainty. It can also "break out" the simplest parts of a weapons system for competitive bidding early in the production program, and gradually extend that effort to include fairly complicated components and subassemblies. It can decide that prevailing levels of secrecy are not required in the interest of national defense and hence merely serve to heighten entry barriers by raising the cost of information to potential suppliers. Finally, in TVA fashion, it can create and maintain some in-house capability for providing yardstick competition for private contractors, both in R and D on new weapons systems and in their production.

This catalog of options open to the government is suggestive rather than exhaustive.[13] It is sufficient to indicate that the present structure of procurement markets is fraught with artificial as well as natural attributes and that it is therefore subject to transformation by a change in policy. While there are no alternatives to monopsony, there are alternatives to oligopoly: there are no inherent imperatives which explain the fact that in fiscal 1968, 57.9 percent of the defense contracts were let after negotiation with only a single source, and that an additional 30.6 percent were awarded on the basis of only peripheral, ritualistic negotiations with alternative sources.[14]

The dynamic of current contracting procedures thus reinforces rather than reduces natural uncertainty in defense markets. In no small measure, it is because the government concentrates its defense spending in a few firms that it appears *obliged* to do so. If the government backed more suppliers, it would receive more information on technology. The resulting reduction in uncertainty would vitiate the prevailing logic which has the government awarding contracts to firms less because they offer it a good deal than because their capabilities must ostensibly be preserved for the future. It would greatly shrink the number of situations in which, as Galbraith points out, "the interest of the [Armed] Services in sustaining a source of supply will be no less than that of the firm in question in being sustained."[15] We are not arguing that, by spending more on defense, the government could reduce uncertainty by increasing the information at its disposal. That argument is too true to be interesting. Rather, we are suggesting that by spending more early on in a project, to back multiple sources of ideas, the government could save money on the project as a whole by ultimately obtaining product designs and production plans involving substantially lower costs. More formally put, while it might appear wasteful to back multiple sources of supply, expected net returns are likely to be higher, even given a fixed budget constraint. In an uncertain world, the alleged wastes of competition are really its virtues, because competition provides society with an inimitable laboratory for discovering what is possible.

This hypothesis can be verified empirically. Since the government publishes information on the time profile of defense project costs, it is possible to calculate the net gains that could accrue from redistributing a given defense budget toward the earlier stages of the product. As note 12 suggests, the temporal redistribution required to insure significant increases in potential sources of supply need not be great.

The alternative approach of concentrated contracts serves simply to validate existing market structure irrespective of natural imperatives. It diverts the government from rational choice on the basis of quality, price, and delivery, toward preserving existing contractors for precautionary reasons. It makes the government, willing or not, an agent of protectionism and an instrument of the status quo.

We have shown, then, that not all observed imperfections in defense markets are natural. Precise quantification of the relative roles of nature and government, however, must await further study. In such study, international evidence could be of major help. To the extent that structures of defense markets vary across countries, it would be possible both to infer that the structure of defense industries is not primarily natural and to correlate any cross-national variations in performance with those differences in structure. Since there is no guarantee that military procurement policy varies as much as it might across countries, the international evidence can only provide a lower bound on the degree to which the structure of defense markets is artificial. Our conjecture is that even this lower bound will prove much higher than many people suspect.

III. Conclusion

We have suggested that poor performance in American defense industries is caused by existing market structures. We have further suggested that existing structures are not strictly determined by the nature of relevant technologies. It remains to discuss the direction public policy should take in altering existing market structures. The industrial organization framework continues to be useful in this regard.

Nationalization is the most obvious direction for reform. Consider, however, its impact on market structure. Nationalization of defense firms would increase rather than decrease existing market power and thus compound the uncertainty currently characterizing military research, development, and production. By substituting monopoly for oligopoly, it would reduce further the number of organizations grappling with given design and production problems, thus entailing at least two perverse economic effects. First, the nationalized firm would be even less likely than the present oligopoly to find the best solution,[16] thus affecting technological efficiency. Second, it would be less likely to use the best solution actually found—given the absence of competitive pressures. This distorts the marginal rate of transformation perceived by those who must choose between defense and other goods and hence affects allocative efficiency. In short, nationalization does not alter current market structure in such fashion as to mitigate poor performance. The virus of bureaucracy is equally deadly to public and private monopoly. We pass over the metaeconomic problems of concentrating political and economic power in the hands of those who gave us Vietnam.

A second approach to improved performance is direct regulation of defense suppliers, as by a government agency independent of the Pentagon. Market structure analysis is no more charitable to this solution than it is to nationalization. For permission to regulate its suppliers confers few powers on the monopsonist he does not already possess. If he does not have the relevant information to determine whether or not to buy from a firm, the monopsonist will not have the relevant information to determine how to regulate it. Experience teaches, moreover, that even where regulatory bodies have clear conceptions of correct conduct, they have seldom been able to induce powerful firms to comply with their prescriptions. At best, regulation has been able to enjoin bad practices without being able to require good ones. Regulation simply does not change the balance of structural power.

Neither nationalization nor direct regulation withstands the test for public policy provided by market structure analysis. Is there anything government can do? Our interpretation of current market structure in defense industries suggests not simply an affirmative but a specific answer. To the extent current market structures are artificial, a reorientation of the procurement process away from concentration of contracts in a few firms would reduce entry barriers on the supply side. It would thus reduce market power and its abuse—economic and political—by ongoing firms. To the extent current market structures are natural, the only options available to public policy involve redistribution of risk sharing between the government and its suppliers. Contracts, more sophisticated in their specification of who bears risk when, may help to reduce risk even below natural levels. They may also serve to distribute more equitably the risk actually encountered. Apart from devising such contracts, Congress and the people can cope with natural uncertainty only by limiting the defense establishment to the minimum size consistent with true national security. This will not reduce the market power of ongoing firms. But it will reduce the perverse effects of that power on both the economy and society.

Notes

The Editors wish it known that the original references have been incorporated into the notes.

1. As of June 1971, according to Senator Proxmire, cost overruns on some 45 major weapons systems amounted to $35.2 billion compared to $28.2 billion on the same systems a year earlier. In the words of Robert H. Charles, erstwhile Assistant Secretary of the Air Force, "The procurement of our major weapons systems has in the past been characterized by enormous cost overruns—several hundred percent—and by technical performance that did not come up to promise."

U.S. Congress, Joint Economic Committee, Subcommittee on Economy in Government, *The Economics of Military Procurement*, p. 3 (May 1969). See also U.S. Congress, Senate Committee on Banking, Housing and Urban Affairs, *Emergency Loan Guarantee Legislation*, parts 1 and 2, 1971; Seymour Melman, *The War Economy of the United States* (1971); and William Proxmire, *Report From Wasteland* (1970).

2. Thus, in his study of 13 major aircraft and missile programs initiated since 1955 (at a total cost of $40 billion), Richard A. Stubbing found that "less than 40 percent produced

systems with acceptable electronic performance. Two of the programs were canceled after total program costs of $2 billion were paid. Two programs costing $10 billion were phased out after 3 years for low reliability. Five programs costing $13 billion give poor performance; that is, their electronics reliability is less than 75 percent of initial [contract] specifications."

Joint Economic Committee, *Economics of Military Procurement,* op. cit., p. 3; see also Melman, op. cit., pp. 106–110.

The resulting waste, according to Senator Proxmire, is staggering. "Altogether," he reports, "the services spent a grand total of $4.1 billion on twenty-eight systems abandoned before deployment and $18.9 billion on fifteen more abandoned after deployment." Proxmire, op. cit., p. 6.

3. In one case, the Tax Court found that North American, while allowed an 8 percent markup on costs, actually earned 612 percent and 802 percent returns on its investment in two successive years. *North American Aviation* v. *Renegotiation Board* (1962). See also Richard Kaufman, *The War Profiteers* (1970); Proxmire, op. cit.; and Joint Economic Committee, *Economics of Military Procurement,* op. cit.

4. See Walter Adams, "The Military–Industrial Complex and the New Industrial State," *American Economic Review,* pp. 652–65 (May 1968).

5. See Senate Committee on Banking, op. cit.

6. According to a GAO official's interpretation, dated January 25, 1971, the authority granted in PL 85–804 and its implementing Executive Order amounts to this:

1. The Department of Defense or any of ten other executive departments may designate any company "essential to the national defense." [Note that the company receives the designation "essential," not the company's products nor the instant contract.]

2. Firms designated "essential," may then be given contracts, modifications to contracts and funds with or without consideration.

3. Determinations of essentiality and subsequent contracts or grants do not require justification, and are not subject to challenge [i.e., the GAO cannot "look behind" such decisions]. Senate Committee on Banking, op. cit., p. 469.

If this interpretation is correct, it would seem to validate a growing impression that Elizabethan grants of privilege are not an outmoded instrument of statecraft—that government promotion of private socialism is alive and well, and that it flourishes on the banks of the Potomac.

7. See Kaufman, op. cit.

8. Melman, op. cit., pp. 197ff.

9. Examples abound to illustrate the proposition that firms operating in sheltered markets, especially where they are protected from competition by a benevolent government agency, tend to pursue the quiet life. Steeped in the conventional wisdom and the comfort of accustomed practice, they abhor experimental change—even where it may redound to their private advantage. As late as 1949, for example, the major airlines persisted in the notion that coach service would undermine the financial stability of the industry. The demand for air travel, they said (and the CAB agreed), was fixed; coach service would divert traffic from first class; it would reduce the industry's overall fare structure to the coach level; it would precipitate sizable losses and make the industry dependent on government subsidies. This myth was shattered through the competition of the nonscheduled carriers, which demonstrated that the demand for air travel was not inelastic, and that coach fares meant greater profits and unparalleled expansion rather than losses and financial distress. "It was their pioneering," said a Senate committee, "which shattered the concept of the fixed market for civil aviation. As a result, the question is no

longer what portion of a fixed pie any company will get, but rather how much the entire pie can grow." U.S. Congress, Senate Small Business Committee, *Report on Role of Irregular Airlines in United States Transportation Industry*, Report No. 540 (1951). Similarly, it was the yardstick competition of the Tennessee Valley Authority which proved that the demand for electric power was far more elastic than an overly cautious industry, operating in a noncompetitive milieu and with government sanction, ever dared to imagine. It was this competition which demonstrated *ex post* the profitability of a market strategy which a somnolent monopoly refused to believe was possible *ex ante*.

10. There is, as Alfred Marshall so aptly put it, "the danger that in the trade which had got a bounty or in other trades which hope to get one, people would divert their energies from managing their own business to managing those persons who control the bounties." Marshall, *Principles of Economics*, p. 473 (8th ed., 1936).

11. By "practical alternatives" we mean *feasible* alternatives given the state of technology. The concept could be broadened without difficulty to require political feasibility as well, just as Samuelson has done regarding the utility possibility frontier.

12. The fixed cost of research and development on major weapons systems is often alleged to constitute an "inherently" high proportion of total cost, thus militating toward "natural" monopoly in the defense industry. Like most generalizations, this claim is both exaggerated and empirically unverified. It may apply to one-of-a-kind articles like space vehicles and aircraft carriers. However, in the case of weapons systems where the development process requires substantial innovations, where R and D is followed by production in some quantity, and where the ratio of development to total cost is therefore more moderate, a competitive acquisitions strategy would seem to be not only feasible but sensible.

Moreover, even where R and D appears to constitute a substantial percentage of total costs, this may be due to X-inefficiency more so than to natural economies of scale. According to a Rand Corporation study, for example, Avions Marcel Dassault in France was able to complete the design and prototype production of the Mirage III fighter plane with fourteen engineers and seventy shop fabricators—at a time when its military project staff ranged from a minimum of five to a maximum of twenty employees. U.S. Congress, Senate Judiciary Committee, *Competition in Defense Procurement—1969*, p. 28 (1969).

In sum, austere development which calls for testable hardware made largely on "soft" tooling, coupled with competition among several firms working on rival designs through the prototype stage, is certainly a feasible acquisitions strategy. Far from increasing fixed costs, it may well enhance technological efficiency, reduce costly design errors, avoid subsequent cost overruns, and thus improve the deplorable performance which characterizes the present weapons acquisitions process.

13. See Frederic M. Scherer, "The Aerospace Industry," in Walter Adams (ed.), *The Structure of American Industry* (4th ed., 1971).

14. Joint Economic Committee, *Economics of Military Procurement*, op. cit., p. 15.

15. Ibid.

16. Some might argue that the government could set many groups to work on the same project to approximate the results of competition among firms. To the extent this is practically feasible, decisions are effectively made at a level more disaggregate than the government, which implies there is no advantage to nationalization in the first place. Since the same opportunity for intra-agent competition in decision making is available to ordinary firms, however, and since ongoing oligopolists do not employ it, we find it unlikely that a government bureaucracy would engage successfully in such decentralizing activity. Thus, decentralized nationalization is no improvement, with respect to efficiency, over decentralized markets, and is unlikely, in any case, to occur.

III

Selected Policy Studies

8

Looking Backward: Some Medieval Precedents

Free enterprise is an ambiguous concept. It might mean, as with the Manchester liberals, a fighting belief in the virtue of competition; or it might mean, as with present-day conservatives, a fighting belief in the vice of government intervention. Both meanings can be traced to the prophet of modern capitalism; both can be found in *The Wealth of Nations*, the bible of laissez faire.

It is true, of course, that Adam Smith opposed government interference in the economic life of a nation; but, contrary to current folklore, he did not oppose *all* such interference. What he rejected was government action which exploits the people rather than protects the nation. "Those exertions of the natural liberty of a few individuals," he wrote, "which might endanger the security of the whole society, are, and ought to be restrained by the laws of all governments; of the most free, as well as of the most despotical."[1] As long as government action benefits the community at large, Smith was not too concerned with the incidental losses to a few individuals. Injustice, in his view, was committed only when the fortunes of a small group were advanced at the expense of the general public.[2]

What Smith opposed was business manipulation of the state. What he attacked—in his quiet, dispassionate, scientific, yet forceful way—was the alliance of government and business. What he tried to demonstrate was the deleterious effect of monopoly on the economic growth of the nation and the material well-being of its citizens. While he doubted that government could prevent "people of the same trade from sometimes assembling together," he felt it "ought to do nothing to facilitate such assemblies; much less to render them necessary."[3] Government ought to promote, not restrict, the liberty of its subjects. It ought to be concerned with the welfare of the many, rather than the few. It ought never become the mask for economic privilege.

This was the core of Smith's philosophy—the system of "natural" liberty. This was the base of Jefferson's republicanism. This was the root of Jacksonian democracy. It represented a distrust of government and a plea for restricted governmental powers—a protest against the abuses of tyrants. Experience had indicated that government was an instrument of privilege, a creator of monopoly, an oppressor of individual liberty. Hence it seemed logical to conclude that the government which governs least governs best.

The Medieval Monopoly System

Smith and his contemporaries protested against the prevailing theory that trade and industry should be regulated by the government acting through the instrumentality of the medieval guilds and the great trading companies. The guilds, first formed in the eleventh century, had obtained royal charters giving them the sole right to regulate and supervise trade within the town. Like the national monopolies chartered in a later age, the guilds held meetings and elections, drafted bylaws and prescribed oaths, made rules to bind the members together, and levied assessments for common expenses. They appointed searchers and overseers, and settled their own disputes. This was an elaborate system of industrial self-government behind which lay the enforcement powers of the Privy Council and the Star Chamber.[4]

Just as the guilds controlled and regulated trade within the towns, so the great trading companies—created by royal charter—dominated foreign trade. Beginning late in the fourteenth century, groups of Englishmen trading abroad were given the right of self-government and the privilege of local jurisdiction. They were allowed to issue reasonable ordinances (*pro meliore gubernatione*) if made in proper form and with common consent. In an age when the supervision of production, the regulation of employment, and the exclusion of competition were accepted traditions, the exclusive rights granted to these companies appeared to be an efficient and expedient instrument for controlling foreign trade.

The system of monopoly charters was a deliberate policy of the Crown, and was looked upon as an organizational force in a planned economy. Whether the royal grants were designed to regulate a company of merchants, to encourage a joint-stock undertaking, to organize an industry or profession, the charters laid great stress on the need of "good government." And good government, it was thought, was best attained by granting an exclusive privilege to select individuals or to corporations. These became the chosen instruments for effectuating the Crown's commercial policy. They became the agency for confining individual activity within "proper" limits and subjecting it to group control. To them was delegated, in effect, the royal power to regulate trade and industry in the national interest.

The motives behind this monopoly policy were not as venal and corrupt as some writers have implied. England, during the Middle Ages, was an industrially backward nation. She wanted to attract and protect foreigners who had anything to teach. As early as 1331, therefore, a certain John Kempe "received a patent of protection for himself, his men, servants, apprentices, goods and chattels, that he might instruct and inform all who were willing to learn; a promise was added of similar protection to other men of that mystery, dyers and fullers, willing to come hither from overseas and remain for the same purpose."[5] Such grants were no more than passports; they merely licensed experiment and encouraged innovation. They offered rewards and privileges to newcomers and innovators to protect them against the jealously guarded, exclusive rights of the guilds, which at that time dominated the English town economy. Far from granting monopoly rights, these early grants of privilege were no more than letters of royal protection.[6] Moreover, they differed from later grants in that the Crown retained control of the privileged industry.

Under Elizabeth, however, the nature of the royal grant changed. Instead of offering mere protection, it bestowed monopoly. Instead of keeping the privileged industry under the control of the Crown, it delegated police powers to the monopolist, allowing him to carry out forcible searches for contraband goods manufactured in violation of his exclusive rights. Instead of granting a group privilege, it was given to favored individuals. Under the new system, the patentee applied for the grant and, having received it, was free to act under the powers conferred by it.[7]

Even so, the monopoly licenses were granted—in theory at least—only where some social benefit could be demonstrated and where the interests of the public were safeguarded. Thus many of the early Elizabethan monopoly grants were made in return for the introduction of new manufacturing processes, formerly unknown in England. While giving the innovator a monopoly, these grants usually stipulated that the privilege be of limited duration; that the new process be put to work within a specified time; that prices be not extortionate; and that established manufacture by older methods be free from interference. These stipulations were to protect the public interest; they were designed to make monopolies part of an honest and unobjectionable economic policy.[8]

Under Elizabeth fifty-five grants of monopoly privilege were awarded, twenty-one of which were issued to aliens or naturalized subjects. Theoretically, they were designed to attract foreign workmen and foreign skills; stimulate invention and innovation; expand international trade; and regulate domestic commerce by insuring the maintenance of quality and supply. They at least *pretended* to serve and protect the interests of the public. Thus "Raleigh's patent purported to be designed to avoid the engrossing of inn licenses in towns, and to prevent the sale in unfit premises of 'such corrupt, mingled, and unwholesome wines as were unmeet for the health of our people.' Drake's vinegar patent was to remedy unwholesome and quickly putrefying liquor, with its attendant dangers of infection and diseases in great cities and towns. Smith's grant was to restore the good effect of statutes which had 'by negligence and corruption of bad informers been of long time neglected,' so that leather had become worse and dearer. It was intended that Cornwallis should remedy abuses of gambling, and, in licensing houses for dice, cards, tables, bowls, tennis play and cockfighting should exact recognisances against fraudulent play, betting and the demoralisation of apprentices. Bellingham's office was to arrest the decay in the quality of cordage and oakum, and the danger to shipping, the Navy and the Commonwealth."[9] Wilkes had the sole right to manufacture salt in certain districts but he was to supply the public in adequate quantities and not to raise prices. Others had exclusive licenses to export wool cloth, cast iron, or beer, or the sole right to import Irish linen yarn, starch, or playing cards—ostensibly for the benefit of the realm.

The validity of these monopoly grants was recognized by the medieval judges, wherever they could be shown to be clearly in the interest of the realm. As early as the reign of Edward III, "et issint *nota* que artificers ou sciences queux sont pur le publike bien, sont graundement favore en le lay etc. Et auxy le Roy come chiefe guardain del common wele ad power et auctority per son prerogative, de graunter mult des privileges par le pretence d'un publike bien, comment que (*prima facie*) il apiert merement encontre comen droit."[10] Where, however, a contract or special privilege imposed restraints on trade unknown to the common law, the judges condemned it as contrary to public policy and invalid. To be sure, "many of the privileges which had been conferred on the boroughs by royal charter often operated to restrain trade; but these grants were hallowed by time and recognized by the law; moreover they were intimately bound up with the jurisdictional and governmental privileges of the boroughs, and were therefore regarded as standing on a different footing."[11]

Whatever the purpose of the monopoly system, its execution under the Tudors and Stuarts was abused and corrupted. Prices were raised and quality deteriorated. Trade was artificially restrained rather than expanded. Interlopers were prosecuted. The search and seizure privilege was misused. Statute law was, in many cases, dispensed with. Extortion was commonplace. According to one conservative observer, the Crown sometimes granted monopolies "for purely mercenary reasons, attempting to obtain either a case payment or a share of the profits from the grant or dispensation. In the hands of the corrupt courtiers, the system of monopolies, designed originally to foster new arts, tended to become degraded into a system of plunder, for the holders of the monopolies in some cases knew nothing of the arts and acted in the widest spirit of exploitation and extortion. In some cases the monopolies were sold to companies of merchants, who enhanced the price to the utmost ability of the purchaser. In practice, commercial operations were hampered by a number of the grants; and although many which had previously been given to foreign merchants were rescinded and bestowed upon English merchants, the tendency was towards a concentration of power in corporate hands, until free competition was practically destroyed, and almost all commodities were in the hands of a favored few, who fixed prices, terms and conditions, on such bases as would return them the greatest profit. Of necessity the general body of the citizenry suffered."[12]

The popular outcry generated by these abuses reached crescendo proportions during the latter years of Elizabeth's reign. It precipitated a series of political and legal battles which eventuated in the Statute of Monopolies (1624) and the Bill of Rights (1689). During these turbulent years, the granting of monopolies became a matter of parliamentary discretion instead of an exercise of royal prerogative; jurisdiction in monopoly cases was transferred from the Privy Council and the Star Chamber to the common law courts; and the common right of Englishmen freely to engage in a trade of their own choosing was, subject to exceptions made in the national interest, officially reaffirmed.

The Legal Battle against Monopoly

In the legal battle against monopoly, the first skirmish was fought in *Davenant* v. *Hurdis* (The Merchant Tailors' Case), decided in 1599. The case arose under a bylaw passed by the London tailors' guild which required every member who sent cloth to be finished by outside labor to have an equal amount of such work done by members of his own guild. This bylaw was intended to prevent competition from the rival clothworkers' guild, which at the time was a serious challenge to the status of the tailors. In questioning the validity of the bylaw, plaintiff argued that it was unreasonable and contrary to law. A guild ordinance, he argued, which confines half of the cloth dressing work to guild members, might eventually be extended to cover the entire trade—with the result that there would be no cloth dressing except at the guild's pleasure and the further result that all other clothworkers would be unemployed and live on relief. Plaintiff concluded that any bylaw which, if extended, would establish a monopoly was against common law and void. The judges upheld this view, and decided unanimously that "a rule of such nature as to bring all trade or traffic into the hands of one company, or one person, and to exclude all others, is illegal."[13] The decision made it clear that an ordinance creating a monopoly was void at common law, even though the ordinance was issued under a charter, the terms of which had been confirmed by Parliament. It remained only for the courts to hold that a monopoly created directly by royal grant was equally void.

This was done in *Darcy* v. *Allen*, the famous Case of Monopolies decided in 1602. Elizabeth—in order to encourage the exercise of husbandry among her subjects—had granted one Darcy exclusive rights to buy, sell, and import playing cards into the realm. No other person was to make or offer for sale such playing cards upon pain of royal displeasure and "of such fine and imprisonment as offenders in the case of voluntary contempt deserve."[14] When Allen, without license from the Queen or permission of plaintiff, caused to be made eighty gross of playing cards and imported another hundred gross—none of which were marked with the plaintiff's officially approved seal—he was sued for infringe-ment and damages. In his defense it was argued that as a citizen of London and a member of the society of Haberdashers he was free to buy, sell, and merchandise all things merchantable within the realm. The plea was that all royal grants "procured contrary to the usual and settled liberty of the subject are void and those also which tend to their grievance and oppression."[15]

The judges ruled that Darcy's monopoly was contrary to common law for these reasons:

> (1) All trades, as well mechanical as others, which prevent idleness and exer-cise men and youth in labor for the maintenance of themselves and families, and for the increase of their substance, to serve the Queen when occasion shall require, are profitable for the commonwealth and therefore the grant to the plaintiff to have the sole right of making them was against the common law and the benefit and liberty of the subject. . . .
> (2) The sole trade of any mechanical artifice or any other monopoly is not only a damage and prejudice to those that exercise the same trade, but also to all other subjects, for the end of all these monopolies is for the private gain of the patentees; and therefore there are three inseparable incidents to every mo-nopoly against the commonwealth:
> (a) That the price of the same commodity will be raised. . . .
> (b) That after the monopoly is granted, the commodity is not as good and merchantable as it was before. . . .
> (c) It tends to the impoverishment of divers artificers and others, who before, by the labor of their hands in their act or trade had maintained them-selves and their families, who will now of necessity be restrained to live in idleness and beggary.[16]

To soften this blow to the royal prerogative, the judges pointed out that the Queen was deceived into making the grant; that she intended it to be in the public interest but that, in reality, it would be used for private gain and to the prejudice of the public. Nevertheless, the decision stood as a clear precedent that a monop-oly created by royal charter was actionable at common law and, if found contrary to law, could be declared void.

One aspect of the case is especially noteworthy—the reaffirmation of the common-law right possessed by members of the community to carry on any trade or business in such manner as they thought best in their own interest. This right was part of Magna Carta, which declared that all merchant strangers in the realm should be able to buy and sell their goods by the old and rightful customs. It was embodied in successive statutes of Edward III and Richard II, which provided that "All merchants may buy and sell within the realm without distur-bance, notwithstanding any Statutes, Ordinances, Charters, Judgments, Allow-ances, Customs and Usage made or suffered to the contrary, which Charters and Franchises, if any there be, they shall be utterly repealed and admitted as a thing made, used or granted against the common Profit and [for] the Oppression of the

People."[17] These statutes were designed to confirm Magna Carta and thus enable merchants to indulge in general trade without risk of interfering with some other trader's exclusive privilege. They constitute an earlier limitation on the royal prerogative to grant monopolies.

To the extent that the liberty of the subject to engage in trade was a right, it connoted an obligation on others not to interfere with it. Monopolies, since they restricted economic liberty, were a derogation from this right.[18] Hence, by implication at least, the Crown could not grant monopolies unless there was some just cause for doing so. It could not interfere with the "common right" (i.e., economic freedom) of the citizen. Of course, economic freedom did not mean the same thing in medieval England that it does today. It meant only "freedom from arbitrary restraints not recognized by the law; but this was quite consistent with considerable restrictions of that freedom whenever it was desirable in the interests of the state that it should be restricted."[19] And such restrictions were both numerous and broad. Thus monopolies could be granted to guilds and boroughs for the sake of insuring "good government" of trade and industry. They could be granted as a reward for the opening of trade with new countries, the exercise of inventive ingenuity, or the discovery and introduction of new techniques. These were looked upon as valid methods of promoting the public interest, and hence as justifiable grounds for interfering with the liberty of the subject.

In practice, to be sure, English sovereigns "claimed and exercised the much wider prerogative . . . of granting all types of monopolies, some beneficial, some detrimental, some granted as royal favor, others as means of increasing the royal revenue"[20]; but their power to do so legally was doubtful. In theory, the sovereign could not interfere with the economic liberty of the subject of granting a monopoly unless the grant was in the national interest. In all cases, there had to be some consideration flowing to the public. Any legal doubts on this score were resolved, with a note of finality, by *Darcy* v. *Allen*. After 1602 monopolies were prima facie void under the common law.

The Political Battle against Monopoly

This legal victory did not precipitate the demise of private and corporate monopolies. Though very much weakened by 1602, the monopoly system was still too widespread and too firmly entrenched to be destroyed by common-law remedies applied in specific cases. It had to be curtailed by political action and, in the end, to be destroyed by legislation.

Periodic outbursts of popular resentment brought concessions from the Crown. In 1597 Elizabeth promised to leave the alleged monopolies "to abide the trial and true touchstone of the law, hoping her subjects would not take away her prerogative, which is the chiefest flower in her garden and the principal and head pearl in her crown and diadem."[21] Attack on the prerogative per se or sympathy with infringers, however, would still be regarded as contempt of the

Queen. In 1601, to quell a parliamentary uprising, Elizabeth, with a royal sense of the occasion, undertook to reform some of the monopolistic abuses. While still threatening punishment to those who seditiously or contemptuously questioned her prerogative, she proclaimed that many monopolies were granted upon false and untrue suggestions of benefit to the realm and had subsequently been notoriously abused. Some of the grants were declared void. As to the others, Her Majesty's subjects were left free to take their ordinary remedy by the laws of the realm "any matter or thing in any of the said grants to the contrary notwithstanding."[22]

In 1603 James I, Elizabeth's successor, suspended all monopoly grants and charters, all licenses to dispense with the penal laws, all grants to corporations of arts or mysteries, and all grants for enlarging trade, until they could be examined by the King and his Council. In characterizing the Elizabethan grants, James's proclamation stated: "Though they had and might have foundation in princely prerogative, yet either by too large extending thereof, or for the most part in respect that they were of such nature as could hardly be put in use without hindrance to multitudes of people, or else committed to inferior persons, who in the execution thereof did so exceedingly abuse the same, as they became intolerable,"[23] these grants were in need of re-examination.

In 1610, James issued another proclamation (The Book of Bounty) which declared that monopolies were against the laws of the realm. It expressly commanded that no subject presume to move the King to grant one. Despite the high-sounding phrases of this declaration and the similarity of its language to the judgment in *Darcy* v. *Allen*, James continued to use his prerogative practically unchecked by parliamentary supervision. But Parliament was fast becoming conscious of its political power, and its antimonopoly agitation caused the King to issue another proclamation (1621) in which numerous monopoly privileges were revoked. Even so, the storm could not be stilled and in 1624 the Statute of Monopolies was passed.

A milestone in antimonopoly legislation, the Statute declared void "all monopolies and all commissions, grants, licenses, charters, and letters patent heretofore made or granted to any person or persons, bodies politick or corporate whatsoever, of or for the sole buying, selling, making, working, or using of anything, or of any other monopolies."[24] It provided further that "all monopolies ought to be and shall be forever hereafter examined, heard, tried and determined by and according to the common laws of this realm and not otherwise."[25] It exempted from its provisions letters patent and grants of privilege made for a period of fourteen years, on the condition that such grants "be not contrary to the law, nor mischievous to the state, by raising prices of commodities at home, or hurt trade, or generally inconvenient.[26] But then, in almost direct contravention of its earlier provisions, the Statute exempted grants to cities, boroughs, and towns, as well as "any corporations, companies or fellowships of any trade, occupation, or mystery, or ... any companies or societies of merchants within this Realm, erected for the maintenance, enlargement, or ordering of any trade of merchandise."[27]

The law was, therefore, little more than a statutory declaration of the then prevailing common-law view of monopoly. Its net effect was to assure the transfer of jurisdiction in monopoly cases from the Privy Council and the Star Chamber to the courts of common law; to transmute monopoly from a creature of the Crown to a creature of Parliament; to discourage the arbitrary granting of monopolies—especially to private persons. When the Bill of Rights (1689) prohibited the Crown from dispensing with the law (through *non obstante* actions), the royal prerogative to grant monopolies in evasion or defiance of the statute was finally abrogated, and parliamentary control over monopolies assured.

The Statute of Monopolies altered, rather than ended, the national grievance. While attacking monopolies, it left loopholes through which corporations could safely pass. While imposing limitations on the royal prerogative, it symbolized a willingness to have monopolies—provided Parliament alone granted them. Thus "only a few years after Darcy's monopoly of playing cards was judged void at common law, the same monopoly was given, under authority of the Statute of Monopolies, to the Company of Card Makers."[28] Government was still creating monopolies. The source of monopoly grants, however, shifted from the Crown to Parliament which, in this as well as other fields, was in the process of establishing its political supremacy.[29]

Throughout the seventeenth, and for the better part of the eighteenth century, cities, boroughs, guilds, corporations, and trading companies continued to exercise their monopolistic restrictions; and the common law continued, by and large, to protect their customary monopoly privileges. There were, to be sure, periodic flare-ups of antimonopoly feeling. In 1640 the Long Parliament declared many monopolies void, and the House of Commons decided that no monopolizer should thenceforth be allowed to sit in the House. A year later the Commons actually expelled the holders of monopolies in sea coal, tobacco, bone lace, and soap, and declared their seats vacant. But monopoly proved both resilient and resurgent, and the monopoly system was destroyed only with the disintegration of mercantilism and the rise of economic liberalism. It withered under the impact of powerful economic forces, and the new doctrines of Adam Smith which gave them a raison d'être.

The Doctrine of Economic Freedom

In attacking the foundations of mercantilism, Adam Smith advocated economic freedom as the soundest principle for organizing society. The pretense, he wrote, that monopoly charters for corporations "are necessary for the better government of the trade, is without foundation. The real and effectual discipline which is exercised over a workman, is not that of his corporation, but that of his customers."[30] Competition, not regulation, is the key to economic welfare. Government interference with the individual's choice of occupation or trade "is a manifest encroachment upon the just liberty both of the workman, and of those who might be disposed to employ him. As it hinders the one from working at what he thinks proper, so it hinders the others from employing whom they think proper. To judge whether he is fit to be employed, may surely be trusted to the discretion of the employers whose interest it so much concerns. The affected anxiety of the law-giver lest they should employ an improper person, is evidently as impertinent as it is oppressive."[31]

The exclusive privilege of an incorporated trade necessarily restrains competition and restricts the trade to a smaller number than might otherwise be disposed to enter it. The state, by granting monopoly privileges, prevents resources from flowing into those channels where—in the judgment of consumers—they can contribute most to economic welfare. Governmentally created monopolies, while benefiting the trades, the crafts, and the mysteries, victimize the public by restraining that free competition which results in a reduction of prices and a normalization of profits. Industrial self-government by traders and artificers is oppressive to the public, because it is "the manifest interest of every particular class of them to prevent the market from being overstocked, as they commonly express it, with their own particular species of industry; which is in reality to keep it always understocked."[32] The state, by granting monopoly charters with the attendant rights of industrial self-government, thus promotes artificial scarcity to the prejudice of the consuming public.

If monopoly control over domestic commerce was indefensible, so were the grants of privilege to the great international trading companies. These companies, wrote Smith, "though they may, perhaps, have been useful for the first introduction of some branches of commerce, by making, at their own expense, an experiment which the state might not think it prudent to make, have in the long-run proved, universally, either burdensome or useless, and have either mismanaged or confined the trade."[33] To be called useless, indeed, was the highest eulogy which could ever justly be bestowed on these companies.

The great trading companies tried to keep their rate of profit as high as possible by keeping the market, both for the goods which they exported and those which they imported, constantly understocked; by restraining competition; and by discouraging the entry of newcomers into the trade. Without a monopoly grant from the state, such companies seldom succeeded, and frequently they did not succeed with one. "Without an exclusive privilege they have commonly mismanaged the trade. With an exclusive privilege they have both mismanaged and confined it."[34] Thus the Royal African Company found itself unable to withstand the unlicensed competition of private adventurers whom they called interlopers and whom they persecuted as such. Yet despite a 10 percent tax imposed on all the trade carried on by private adventurers—a tax which the company was to spend on the maintenance of forts and garrisons—the Royal African Company found itself unable to meet competition. It proved itself incapable of maintaining the forts and garrisons which had been the sole purpose and pretext for its exclusive privileges. Eventually the company failed, as had its predecessors in the African trade. It failed despite its monopoly charter and the privileges granted under it.

Smith opposed governmental grants of monopoly to an individual or trading company primarily because "all the other subjects of the state are taxed very absurdly in two different ways; first, by high price of goods, which, in the case of free trade, they could buy much cheaper; and, secondly, by their total exclusion from a branch of business, which it might be both convenient and profitable for many of them to carry on."[35] These burdens on the public, according to Smith, served no useful purpose other than "to enable the company to support the negligence, profusion, and malversation of their own servants, whose disorderly conduct seldom allows the dividend of the company to exceed the ordinary rate of profit in trades which are altogether free, and very frequently makes it fall even a good deal short of that rate. Without monopoly, however, a joint-stock company, it would appear from experience, cannot long carry on any branch of foreign trade."[36] It cannot survive whenever private adventurers are allowed to engage in any sort of open and fair competition with it.

Smith's policy recommendation was clear: eliminate the mercantilist restrictions on free enterprise, and stop the government's promotion of monopoly and creation of special privilege. Encourage the kind of competition which protects the consumer against exploitation and provides opportunity for new men, new firms, and new ideas. Then, with the state performing its rightful role of umpire, the economic system will tend to assure liberty for the individual and well-being for the masses.

Unfortunately, Smith's language lent itself not only to an attack on government when it promoted monopoly, but also to an attack on government when it sought to enhance the general welfare. "In the end," says Professor Schlesinger, "business altogether captured the phrases of *laissez faire* and used them more or less ruthlessly in defense of monopoly."[37] Big business, in order to protect itself from competition, opposed any governmental action which would preserve, restore, or promote competition. Instead of fighting for competition, big business concentrated its efforts on securing domination over, or subservience by, the government to obtain its monopolistic ends. Ironically enough, therefore, the laissez-faire slogans developed by Adam Smith to destroy monopoly have today become its bulwark.

Notes

1. Adam Smith, *The Wealth of Nations* (Modern Library edition), Vol. II, Chapter 2.
2. Eli Ginzburg, *The House of Adam Smith*, p. 90 (1934).
3. Smith, op. cit., p. 128.
4. Our discussion here will be confined to England, although analogous developments also took place on the Continent.

5. Cecil T. Carr, *Select Charters of Trading Companies,* p. lvi (1913).

6. In a sense, these early grants promoted competition and operated in derogation of trading privileges previously granted to the craft guilds. Hence, these grants were carefully drafted to give "full power and authority . . . any law, statute, Act of Parliament, Proclamation, restraint or any other matter, cause, or thing whatsoever . . . to the contrary notwithstanding." Harold G. Fox, *Monopolies and Patents,* p. 42 (1947).

7. W. S. Holdsworth, *A History of English Law,* Vol. IV, p. 346 (1937).

8. See Fox, op. cit., p. 27; Carr, op. cit., pp. lviii–lix.

9. Carr, op. cit., p. lxiii.

10. Year Book of Edward III, quoted in Holdsworth, op. cit., p. 344.

11. Holdsworth, op. cit., p. 344.

12. Fox, op. cit., p. 70. See also Walton Hamilton, *Patents and Free Enterprise* (T.N.E.C. Monograph No. 31, 1941), pp. 1–23. According to Hamilton, these grants of privilege served "a score of public uses and twice as many royal whims" (p. 7). Almost inevitably, "the royal favor begets the royal favorite and becomes an incentive to curb the royal favor" (p. 6).

13. Quoted in William L. Letwin, "The English Common Law Concerning Monopolies," *University of Chicago Law Review,* p. 362 (1954).

14. Quoted in Fox, op. cit., p. 318.

15. Quoted in ibid., p. 320.

16. Quoted in ibid., pp. 324–25.

17. Quoted in ibid., p. 59.

18. Cp. *Attorney General of Australia* v. *Adelaide Steamship Co. Ltd.,* 1913, A.C. 781 at 793.

19. Holdsworth, op. cit., p. 350.

20. Fox, op. cit., p. 57.

21. Quoted in Carr, op. cit., p. lxv.

22. Ibid. The House of Commons debates in 1601 had raised questions not only as to the power of the Crown to grant patents and dispensations, as well as privileges to trading companies, but also questions as to the nature of the royal prerogative and its relation to the law. " 'Two great things,' said Cecil, 'had been drawn in question: first the Prince's power; secondly the freedom of Englishmen.' And it was inevitable that these questions should be raised. Those aggrieved by these patents had long thought, and thought with some justice, that the common law did not warrant these infringements of liberty to trade, from which the public not only drew no advantage, but were actually damaged." Holdsworth, op. cit., p. 348.

23. Quoted in Fox, op. cit., p. 94.

24. For the text of The Statute of Monopolies 21 Jac.I, c.3 (1623), see Louis B. Schwartz, *Free Enterprise and Economic Organization,* pp. 217–18 (1952).

25. Ibid.

26. Ibid.

27. Ibid.

28. Letwin, op. cit., p. 367.

29. In the United States grants of privilege were, at the beginning, issued by the state legislatures and by Congress. Thus private railroad construction was, in the early days, encouraged by many forms of public assistance, including corporate charters which frequently conferred tax exemption, broad rights of eminent domain, monopoly, commercial banking (credit creation) privileges, and even lottery rights for raising funds. (Cf. G.R. Taylor, *The Transportation Revolution,* pp. 88–90.) Later, such privileges as patents, licenses, franchises, and certificates of public convenience and necessity were mostly spawned by administrative tribunals operating under extremely lax and unduly broad

legislative mandates. This shift brought in its wake the same political pressures, the same clamor for privilege, the same difficulty with defining the public interest as Parliament had experienced two hundred years earlier. However, it raised the added problem of executive responsibility, since the latter-day grants of privilege in America were issued largely by appointed rather than elected officials.

30. Smith, op. cit., p. 129.
31. Ibid., p. 122.
32. Ibid., p. 124.
33. Ibid., p. 691.
34. Ibid., p. 700.
35. Ibid., p. 712.
36. Ibid.
37. Arthur M. Schlesinger, Jr., *The Age of Jackson*, p. 317 (1945).

9

Is Bigness a Crime?

In recent years, the Department of Justice has attempted to revitalize the long-dormant Section 2 of the Sherman Act by placing an increased emphasis on dissolution, divorcement, and divestiture cases. The theory underlying this program is that the problem of concentrated economic power in certain industries can, within the framework of the antitrust laws, be dealt with in only one way—through dissolution, i.e., trust busting in the literal sense.

This approach to the monopoly problem has—quite inevitably, perhaps—elicited the charge by some business men that the Government is attacking bigness *per se*; that the Government is trying to make "a sin of efficiency, a crime of success, a felony of size, and a corpse of private enterprise."

From a public policy point of view, this controversy raises three fundamental questions. *First*, does the law, as presently interpreted by the courts, in fact make bigness a crime? *Second*, if so, is there any economic justification for such a law? *Third*, if an attack on bigness *per se* is unwise, along what lines should our present antitrust statutes be revised? These are the questions to be discussed in this paper.

Bigness and the Law

Turning first to the legal aspects of the problems, we find that Section 2 of the Sherman Act categorically declares:

"Every person who shall monopolize, or attempt to monopolize, or combine or conspire with any other person or persons, to monopolize any part of the trade or commerce among the several States, or with foreign nations, shall be deemed guilty of a misdemeanor, and, on conviction thereof, shall be punished. . . ."[1] While this provision seems clear in its prohibition of monopoly and *attempts to create a monopoly*, it was not long before the courts formulated a new standard which for many years made Section 2 practically unenforceable. The new stan-

---

Originally published in *Land Economics,* vol. 27 (November 1951); reprinted with permission.

dard was the "rule of reason," announced in the Standard Oil and American Tobacco cases of 1911, which held that not *every* combination was to be considered unlawful but only *unreasonable* combinations—i.e., combinations motivated by unlawful purposes or combinations employing predatory practices.[2]

This "rule of reason" was applied with devastating effectiveness in the United States Steel case of 1920. Here the Court ruled that even though the Corporation had attempted to monopolize the steel industry, the Sherman Act was not violated since the attempt failed.[3] Moreover, since the Corporation had not used the predatory practices previously employed by the oil and tobacco trusts—since it had always abided by the golden rule of live-and-let-live—it was a "reasonable" combination within the meaning of the Sherman Act. Said the court: ". . . the law does not make mere size an offense or the existence of unexerted power an offense."[4] While U.S. Steel was big, it had never deviated from a policy of "friendly" competition. Hence, in the eyes of the Court, it was a "good" trust.[5]

This ruling was firmly nailed down by the International Harvester case[6] of 1927, and Section 2 of the Sherman Act became for all intents and purposes a dead letter. It was not until 1945, when Judge Learned Hand's celebrated opinion was handed down in the Aluminum case, that renewed force and vigor were injected into the anti-monopoly provisions of the Act. "In the Aluminum case Judge Hand finally interred and reversed the old dictum that size is not an offense under the Sherman Act. Size, he concluded, was not only evidence of violation, or a potential offense, as in Justice Cardozo's conciliatory formula of the Swift case: it was the essence of the offense. Size, meaning market control, was what competition and monopoly were about. All other aspects of the case were subordinated to the central and decisive fact that the Aluminum Company of America, many years after its patents had expired, made and then fabricated or sold over 90 percent of the virgin aluminum used in the United States. Its arrangements with foreign companies for dividing the world markets were further evidence of monopolizing. That it had engaged in deplorable tactics to prevent other companies from entering the field helped compound the offense. But the case was proved, in Judge Hand's view, by showing the company's market power. It made over 90 percent of virgin aluminum and therefore had monopoly power."[7]

The reasoning of the opinion is unmistakable. Our antitrust laws, according to Judge Hand, were not designed to condone *good* trusts or condemn *bad* trusts, but to forbid *all* trusts. The antitrust laws had as their basic philosophy and principal purpose "to perpetuate and preserve, for its own sake and in spite of possible cost, an organization of industry in small units which can effectively compete with each other."[8] Hence the existence of predominant market control was considered sufficient to prove a violation of the Sherman Act. No specific evidence of "intent" was needed, nor was the Government required to show the use of predatory or illegal practices. Contrary to the U.S. Steel and International Harvester dicta, mere size and the existence of unexerted power could—under specified conditions—be ruled a violation of the Sherman Act.

The doctrine of the Aluminum case was given the approval of the Supreme Court in the American Tobacco decision of 1946. There the court found it to be unnecessary that unequivocal expressions of the intent to monopolize be shown or a premeditated and calculated plan to obtain a monopoly be demonstrated. Said the Court: "It is not the form of the combination or the particular means used but the result to be obtained that the statute condemns. . . . The . . . material consideration in determining whether a monopoly exists is not that prices are raised and that competition actually is excluded but that power exists to raise prices or to exclude competition when it is desired to do so."[9] With this decision the *legal* issue of bigness was settled. The highest court of the land had accepted the proposition that grave injury to competition can result from size and power, standing by themselves, and that monopoly means predominant size within an industry regardless of the methods by which such size was achieved.[10]

The Economics of Bigness

At this juncture, the battle over bigness was shifted in part from the legal to the economic and political arena. In the court of public opinion, some businessmen began to argue that little can or should be done about size; that we should not—as a matter of sound public policy—oppose size as such but content ourselves with controlling its abuses by enforcing the antitrust laws against monopolistic *practices*. These men contend that some concerns are big merely because they are efficient; that such concerns are big because consumers want them to be big; in short, that bigness is the result of a "passive" adjustment to the technological and economic dictates of the twentieth century market place.[11] This view—sometimes referred to as the "abuse" theory of size—is economically unrealistic and practically unenforceable for the following reasons.

In the first place, experience would seem to indicate that a mere attack on monopolistic *practices* cannot, in most instances, succeed in curbing monopoly and fostering competition—especially in industries which evidence basic structural deviations from the competitive norm. While numerous illustrations could be cited in support of this claim, let us examine only one—the case involving the United Shoe Machinery Company. In 1922 the courts perpetually enjoined the company's use of the tying contract,[12] and it was thought then that the primary means for lessening competition and creating monopoly in the industry had thus been eliminated. This was not the case, however, for the company merely substituted other provisions in its leasing contracts to achieve the same unlawful ends.[13] Moreover, it used its overwhelming financial power to crush independent competitors whenever and wherever they appeared. In addition, the company infringed on the patents of numerous small competitors and then distributed machines covered by those patents at disastrously low prices so as to drive their rightful owners out of the industry. The new result was that 25 years after the

1922 decree, the Department of Justice was impelled to file a dissolution suit against United States Shoe Machinery Corporation.[14] This, it was decided, was the only way of restoring competition in the shoe machinery industry.

The United Shoe Machinery and similar cases would tend to show that drastic surgery, painful though it may be, is often the only means of restoring competition. There are few industries in which monopolistic power can be neutralized by eradicating a single "critical" restraint; for, if all the possible highways of restraint are blocked, the monopolist will simply travel "cross-country." Moreover, a decree which attempts to block every single highway of restraint—assuming the Antitrust Division had the omniscience to fashion such a decree—would require constant and careful surveillance; the kind of policing job the Antitrust Division is not prepared, and should not be forced, to undertake. The competitive system is designed to minimize, to the greatest extent feasible, the administrative regulation and supervision of private industry by the government. Hence, the ideal type of decree is one which is basically self-enforcing. A dissolution, divorcement, or divestiture judgment has the great virtue of meeting that requirement, for it creates the type of structural arrangement in an industry which obviates the necessity for direct interference and control.

The second weakness of the "abuse" theory of size is that it is hopelessly unrealistic from an economic point of view; for, once a firm has attained a dominant position in the market place, it no longer has to engage in predatory practices to achieve its monopolistic ends. Its mere existence will be sufficient warning to smaller competitors that non-cooperation is tantamount to suicide. As Justice Brandeis so brilliantly expressed it: "restraint of trade may be exerted upon rivals; upon buyers or upon sellers; upon employers or upon employed. Restraint may be exerted through force or fraud or agreement. It may be exerted through moral or through legal obligations; through fear or through hope. It may exist, although it is not manifested in any overt act, and even though there is no intent to restrain. Words of advice, seemingly innocent and perhaps benevolent, may restrain, when uttered under circumstances that make advice equivalent to command. For the essence of restraint is power; and power may arise merely out of position. Whenever a dominant position has been attained, restraint necessarily arises."[15]

Or, as Thomas Nixon Carver put it: "The larger the corporation, the greater is its power, either for good or for evil, and that makes it especially important that its power be under control. If I may use a homely illustration, I will take the common house cat, whose diminutive size makes her a safe inmate of our household in spite of her playful disposition and her liking for animal food. If, without the slightest change of character or disposition, she were suddenly enlarged to the dimensions of a tiger, we should at least want her to be muzzled and to have her claws trimmed, whereas if she were to assume the dimensions of a mastadon, I doubt if any of us would want to live in the same house with her. And it would be useless to argue that her nature had not changed, that she was just as amiable as ever, and no more carnivorous than she always had been. Nor would it convince us to be told that her productivity had increased and that she could now catch more mice in a minute than she formerly could in a week. We should be afraid lest, in a playful mood, she might set a paw upon us, to the detriment of our epidermis, or that in her large-scale mouse-catching she might not always discriminate between us and the mice."[16]

Thirdly, it would appear impossible to attain the objectives of the Sherman Act if only predatory behavior is prohibited while monopoly as such goes unchallenged. The reason is obvious. Section 1 of the Act forbids conspiracy in restraint of trade; Section 2 enjoins monopoly and attempts to monopolize. If Section 2 were repealed or allowed to die for lack of enforcement, corporations could achieve by combinations, mergers, holding companies, etc., a more complete control over price and output than they could ever hope to realize under the most elaborate forms of conspiracy. Hence, if we believe that group control over prices, effectuated through concerted action is economically undesirable, logic and realism require us to oppose similar control achieved through the combination of independent firms into corporate aggregations of Brobdingnagian proportions.[17]

Finally, we must bear in mind that the "abuse" theory of size is based on the rather dubious assumption that bigness is the guarantor of efficiency in a mass production economy. While there has been considerable discussion on the relative efficiency of small, medium-sized and large firms,[18] the most we can say in support of bigness *per se* is that the findings are inconclusive. As one conservative student of the subject points out: "No published cost studies have made the adjustments necessary to eliminate variables other than size, and the results are open to the same objection whether they show one size or another to be more profitable. As a generalization from the inadequate data available, it may be said that there is little evidence to support the conclusion that the largest enterprises are relatively inefficient. Nor, on the other hand, has it been proved that they have a superiority on a cost basis."[19] Thus, if the giant size of firms in some of our mass production industries is to be justified, it will have to be done on grounds other than the results of the efficiency studies available to date.

From our discussion so far, then, we may conclude that in the eyes of the law bigness is a crime—bigness being defined as the power to raise prices and the power to exclude competitors whenever it is desired to do so. We may also say that it is unrealistic, from an economic point of view, to attempt enforcement of the antitrust laws only against monopolistic practices while leaving untouched the giant combinations which can—with or without the resort to unlawful practices—achieve their monopolistic ends. With these considerations in mind, let us now turn to a discussion of public policy.

Bigness and Public Policy

While public policy must necessarily take into account social, political, ethical and psychological as well as economic objectives, the economist can nevertheless inquire: "Assuming that efficiency is the goal of economic organization, what kind of antitrust policy—if any—is likely to be most effective in promoting this goal? How can competition be preserved and encouraged without simultaneously penalizing efficiency? How can an attack on bigness be reconciled with the maintenance of an efficient organization for production and distribution? Finally, granting that the optimum size of firms is large in many industries, *how* big must a concern be to be efficient?"

I have attempted to answer the above questions by drafting a proposal for a new antitrust law which was submitted to the House Judiciary Committee December 1, 1949.[20] The proposed law, which would deal with non-financial corporations only, has a double purpose: to preserve, wherever feasible, a competitive structure of industry while at the same time providing safeguards against an interference with business efficiency. In cases where these basic goals come into conflict, the proposed law would forsake competition and choose efficiency as the objective of public policy. The basic purpose of the new law would be not to make bigness *per se* a crime, but rather to eliminate such bigness as is not based on efficiency in production and distribution.

Specifically the bill provides that corporations which control 10 percent or more of a commodity's supply (or corporations with assets totalling more than $25,000,000) must register with the Securities & Exchange Commission. These corporations must then file pertinent data so that the commission can determine—in a case-by-case approach and in accordance with specific standards[21] set forth in the bill—whether the corporate structure of a given firm, its position in the industry, or its business policies and practices have a detrimental effect on the interests of investors, consumers, or the general public. If they do, the Commission can, after opportunity for hearing, order the dissolution of such a firm or "the divestiture thereby or divorcement therefrom of any property, assets, securities or other holdings which are not reasonably incidental, or economically necessary or appropriate to its efficient functioning ... or which tend to hinder, obstruct, impede or render difficult the maintenance or achievement of effective competition in one or more lines of commerce."[22]

This simply means that, if the Commission were to discover that the du Pont control over General Motors and U.S. Rubber was not economically necessary or appropriate to the efficient functioning of a chemical firm, or that such control was motivated primarily by a desire for monopoly, the Commission might order du Pont to rid itself of the GM and U.S. Rubber holdings. Similarly, if the Commission were to find that General Motors was indeed an efficient producer of automobiles but that its manufacture of diesel locomotives, refrigerators, electric appliances, etc., merely represented an attempt to aggrandize the firm's size and economic power, the company might be forced to confine its operations to the automobile field. Finally, if the Commission were to find that a firm like U.S. Steel could operate as efficiently but less monopolistically at one-third its present size, an order to that effect could be issued.[23]

Here then is the central provision of the proposed law: it permits an administrative authority, subject to judicial review, to order a giant firm to "unmerge," wherever the effect of such an order is likely to stimulate competition and/or increase efficiency. But the bill goes further. It leans over backward to afford companies protection against wanton and arbitrary atomization. This protection is provided in the form of escape clauses under which an industrial giant can avoid dissolution or divestment orders by the Commission, if it can demonstrate that its present size is necessary for the attainment of efficiency or that its business performance in the past has materially benefited the general public. Contributions to the public interest can be established simply by showing that the company in question has participated in technological progress, passed on savings in cost to consumers, provided enough plant capacity to fill consumer needs and actually used such capacity fully, earned a normal rate of profit as compared to competitive industries, and has benefited consumers by price reductions as well as by advertising competition.[24] When a company, judged by these standards, can show that the manner of its past performance has been in the public interest, it escapes dissolution or divestment—regardless of its monopolistic position in the economy.

Note that the burden of proof as far as business performance and efficiency are concerned is on the corporation. For once the existence of the corporation has been shown to be incompatible with the maintenance or establishment of competition, the corporation—in order to escape dissolution, divorcement and divestiture—must rebut the prima facie case set forth by the Commission. There are those who feel concern about this method of procedure, thinking that it is a departure from our traditional presumption of innocence until proven guilty, a presumption which applies in cases involving criminal procedure. There seems to be little cause for alarm on this score, however, since it is well-established procedure under civil law that the burden of proof shifts from party to party in accordance with the changing weight of the evidence. Thus the Commission puts into the record evidence which proves that the operation and policies of a firm are injurious to competition and promotive of monopoly. Having done this, it may rest its case and it is for the respondent to come forward with his proof of efficiency and business performance in the public interest as a rebuttal maneuver. The Commission is, therefore, under no obligation to prove the negative of the conditional (escape) clause. The clause is there for use of the respondent if he has the facts necessary of proof. Were the entire burden of proof on the Commission, this would require an extension of the agency's investigatory powers to a degree which would be burdensome to both the respondent and the Commission.[25]

The main advantages of the proposed bill are threefold: *First*, it is not a general dissolution decree against all industrial giants. It is not a death sentence for big business merely on the grounds that it is big. Instead, the bill provides for a careful, selective, case-by-case approach to cope with such concentrated economic power as is conducive neither to a maintenance of efficiency nor to the encouragement of competition. *Secondly*, the bill proposes to benefit not only consumers and the general public but corporate investors as well. It does so simply by requiring that no business be so big that its component parts could function more efficiently as separate units than as parts of the whole.[26] *Thirdly*, the bill implements dissolution proceedings by more sophisticated techniques than the hammer-and-tongs method available under the Sherman Act. Whereas the Sherman Act equips the Justice Department with a blunt axe, this bill provides the enforcement agency with a set of fine surgical instruments. By contrast with the Sherman Act, it sets up clearer and more concrete standards for judging unlawful behavior in the market place,[27] thus eliminating some of the confusion and uncertainty concerning the antitrust laws from which the business community now suffers. *Finally*, while the proposed bill is by no means a panacea for our monopoly problems, while it should not preclude attempts to aid the small businessman, to reform the patent laws, to cope with interlocking financial control, etc., it ought, nevertheless, to constitute the core around which an enlightened, rejuvenated, and modernized antitrust program is formulated.

In conclusion, two observations are in order: (1) If we are to retain the basic philosophy of the antitrust laws, if we are to make the preservation of free competitive enterprise the goal of social and economic policy, then, *"quite apart from what we decide to do about it, the problem of antitrust is the problem of size.* Expeditions into the tangled jungles of antitrust will bring results only if we keep the scent and follow the main trail—only if we realize that, whether we destroy it, capture it or just take pictures of it, the real bag is bigness, and that the rest are nothing but small game and battered decoys."[28] (2) If, however, we decide to add the standard of efficiency to the traditional criterion of competition as the objective of public policy, our antitrust laws will have to be revised so as to provide that bigness is a crime only when monopolistic concerns cannot justify their size on grounds of superior efficiency. If we undertake such revision of the antitrust laws, let us recognize that it implies a willingness to reverse our traditional opposition to concentrated power in any form—a willingness to incur a calculated risk in the sphere of social and political philosophy. On the other hand, let us also recognize that, if we do nothing, if we fail to enforce the antitrust laws in their present form and simultaneously refuse to amend and modify them as here proposed, in short, if "neither business nor Government makes any moves whatever in the direction of breaking down industry into smaller, more compact, more mobile, and better earning units; if bigness is allowed to remain as the standard concept of the economy; then the American businessman, and the American politico, and in short all American citizens, must prepare themselves for a different order of things; an order in which the powers of Government are not limited; in which the right to risk-and-profit is not clear; and in which the making, the selling, and even the buying of the products of the biggest show in history are all mysteriously directed from above."[29]

Notes

1. 26 Stat. 209; 15 U.S.C. 2; Public No. 190, 51st Cong. (1890).
2. See *United States* v. *Standard Oil Company of New Jersey*, 221 U.S. 1 (1911) and *United States* v. *American Tobacco Company*, 221 U.S. 106 (1911). While both companies were broken up—in spite of the "rule of reason"—neither case can be cited as a good example of what a dissolution policy can accomplish. See E. Jones, *The Trust Problem in the United States*, pp. 123–63, 452–74 (1922); H.R. Seager and C.A. Gulick, *Trust and Corporation Problems*, pp. 149–95 (1929); W.H.S. Stevens, *Industrial Combinations and Trusts*, pp. 440–61, 472–516 (1913); R. Cox, *Competition in the American Tobacco Industry* (1933); and G.E. Hale, "Trust Dissolution: 'Atomizing Business Units of Monopolistic Size'," *Columbia Law Review*, pp. 617–20, 628–31 (April 1940).
3. It is interesting to note that this application of the "rule of reason" stands in contrast to the standard used in *United States* v. *United Shoe Machinery Company*, 247 U.S. 32 (1918). In the latter case the Court held that a combination which controlled 95 percent of the output in its industry was lawful, since the combination was formed for the purpose of attaining greater efficiency rather than with the intent to monopolize. Thus, in the Shoe Machinery case the Court emphasized the "intent" standard, whereas in the Steel case, the question of intent was completely subordinated to the issue of whether the intent to monopolize had in fact been realized.
4. *United States* v. *United States Steel Corporation*, 251 U.S. 417 (1920).
5. In criticizing the "rule of reason" as it was applied in the United States Steel and other cases, Professor Milton Handler points out: "The proponents of any combination always profess the most exalted motives. Since their hearts and minds cannot be searched by the Courts, the Government, in the absence of admissions, must rely on the objective facts for contradiction. To infer intent from extrinsic circumstances is to add another link to the chain of proof and to open the door to metaphysical distinctions, evasions, and further uncertainty. The antitrust laws should be concerned not with a state of mind but with economic realities. It is the existence of monopoly, and not the reasons which prompted those responsible for its creation, which calls for corrective action. . . . Monopoly is reprehensible in a political democracy whether or not accompanied by evil purpose or improper conduct. There is no reason why monopoly and predatory behavior should not be both outlawed, whether they occur separately or in combination . . . and it is inferable from the authorities as a whole that both are equally inhibited by the statute. The distinction between good and bad trusts belongs to that outmoded era when the antitrust laws were regarded as a moral pronouncement rather than a charter of economic freedom." "A Study of the Construction and Enforcement of the Antitrust Laws," T.N.E.C. Monograph No. 38, pp. 78–9 (1941).
6. *United States* v. *International Harvester Company*, 274 U.S. 693 (1927).
7. Eugene V. Rostow, *A National Policy for the Oil Industry*, pp. 126–7 (1948).
8. *United States* v. *Aluminum Company of America*, 148 F. (2d) 416 (C.C.A. 2d, 1945).
9. *American Tobacco Company et al.* v. *United States*, 328 U.S. 781, 811 (1946).
10. In this connection, it should be noted that—in spite of the "liberal" interpretation of Section 2 recently announced in the Aluminum and American Tobacco cases—the government has made little progress along the dissolution, divorcement, and divestiture front. In sharp contrast to the many *legal* triumphs, the government has generally failed to obtain meaningful economic relief. Remedial action approved by the courts has, in most instances, failed to lessen concentration and restore effective competition. As an examination of the record indicates, firms found guilty of possessing *and* exercising monopoly power have—with the notable exception of the motion picture companies (*United States*

v. *Paramount Pictures, Inc.,* 334 U.S. 131; 1948)—escaped dissolution, divorcement, and divestiture. See W. Adams, "The Aluminum Case: Legal Victory—Economic Defeat," *American Economic Review,* December 1951.

11. The late Charles A. Beard lent support to this point of view when he wrote: "As to myself, my conviction is clear and positive. After reading tons of trust-busting literature, briefs of lawyers in trust cases and judicial decisions and thousands of pages of testimony and recommendations, after listening to any number of anti-trust speeches by honest men and demagogues, after suffering from the frightful din and racket of more than fifty years, after reading statistical studies, such as John Moody's and Berle's and Means' I have come to the conclusion that ours is now and in the nature of things destined to be a great continental, technological society and the trust busters, however honest and honorable, are just whistling in the wind." ("The Antitrust Racket," *The New Republic,* September 1938, p. 184.)

12. *United States* v. *United Shoe Machinery Corp.,* 258 U.S. 451 (1922).

13. The following provisions replaced the tying clauses which the courts had outlawed in 1922: "That the lessee shall use the machine for not less than a term of five or ten years, . . . that the lease may be canceled during said term only by United; and that, thereafter, the lessee shall continue to use the machine indefinitely subject to the right of United or the lessee to terminate the lease upon 60 days' notice.

"That the lessee of each unit charge machine shall use the machine each month upon a stipulated minimum number of pairs of shoes, and shall pay to United a stipulated sum of money at the conclusion of each month during which the machine is not used upon said minimum number of pairs of shoes.

"That the lessee of each unit charge machine shall use the machine to its full capacity upon all shoes made by the lessee upon which the machine is capable of being used.

"That upon termination of the lease the lessee shall surrender the machine to United in good order and condition, shall reimburse United for the cost of all broken or missing parts, and *shall pay to United a stipulated sum of money varying according to the machine leased from about 20% to 85% of the value of the machine.*" (Emphasis supplied.)

14. *United States* v. *United Shoe Machinery Corporation,* Civil 7198; filed December 15, 1947.

15. Dissenting Opinion in *United States* v. *American Column & Lumber Co.,* 257 U.S. 337 (1921). Mr. Justice Murphy emphasized the same point when he wrote: "Domination may spring as readily from subtle or unexercised power as from arbitrary imposition or command. To conclude otherwise is to ignore the realities of intercorporate relationships." *North American Company* v. *Securities Exchange Commission,* 327 U.S. 686 (1945).

16. *Essays in Social Justice,* op. cit., p. 332.

17. In this connection it is noteworthy that monopoly and predatory behavior usually go hand in hand. As a matter of fact, no industrial giant has ever been found guilty of violating Section 2 of the Sherman Act without a showing by the Government that the firm possessed *and* exercised monopoly power. Moreover, as Professor Edward H. Levi observes: "The truth is, of course, that in most monopoly cases, if the court has a mind to do so, it can find abuses." "The Antitrust Laws and Monopoly," *University of Chicago Law Review,* p. 158 (1947).

18. See "Relative Efficiency of Large, Medium-Sized, and Small Business," T.N.E.C. Monograph No. 13 (1941); John M. Blair, "The Relation between Size and Efficiency of Business," *Review of Economic Statistics,* August 1942; S. R. Dennison, "The Problem of Bigness," *The Cambridge Journal,* November 1947; John M. Blair, "Does Large-Scale Enterprise Result in Lower Costs?" *American Economic Review,* May 1948 (Supplement); Federal Trade Commission, *The Divergence between Plant and Company Concentration,* 1947 (1950); William L. Crum, *Corporate Size and Earning Power* (1939);

National Association of Manufacturers, *Business Size and the Public Interest* (1949); Richards C. Osborn, *Effects of Corporate Size on Efficiency and Profitability* (1950); National Association of Manufacturers, *Comments on "The Divergence between Plant and Company Concentration, 1947"* (1951).

19. Richards C. Osborn, "Efficiency and Profitability in Relation to Size," *Harvard Business Review,* March 1951, p. 92.

20. See Monopoly Subcommittee, House Judiciary Committee, Hearings, Part 2-B, 81st Cong., 1st Sess., pp. 1311–39, 1600–25 (1949).

21. Ibid., pp. 1601–04. The purpose in listing and defining specific types of structural organization, which are to be forbidden under this law, is to lend clarity and precision to the general prohibitions of the Sherman Act. Thus coercive integration—of the horizontal, vertical, and conglomerate variety—is specified as an economically objectionable and, therefore, unlawful form of industrial organization. This does not mean that all integration *per se* is forbidden. Our bill would merely ban the kinds of integration which can be used—actually or potentially—for the coercion of competitors rather than for the achievement of competitively legitimate business objectives (as the enhancement of efficiency, for example).

22. Ibid., p. 1613. Critics of this proposal may argue that an extension of SEC's power into the industrial field is of debatable wisdom, feasibility, and public benefit. They may point out that the Commission's administrative procedure is cumbersome, time-consuming, and expensive; that the standards set forth in the proposed bill are not definite and precise enough to warrant what appears to be a delegation of legislative powers. Finally, these critics may contend that unless the standards set up in the law are more carefully spelled out, and unless the Commission and its staff take a less legalistic approach than at times has been employed in administering Section 11 of the Holding Company Act, business concerns might be unduly harassed by frequent investigations and information questionnaires. While these criticisms serve to underline some of the weaknesses in the proposed bill, they do not—we believe—vitiate the basic validity of the suggested approach.

23. In 1938, the editors of *Fortune* suggested that, in some sectors of American industry, a process of deconcentration or "unmerging" might not only be advantageous for the public but also profitable for the enterprises concerned. Said the editors: ". . . it is permissible to inquire whether business could conceivably profit by a transformation of itself. And the answer, of necessity perfunctory within the present limitations of space, would seem to be that some of it could. If the winding-up process of the last 70 years has been an extremely profitable process, there is not reason to suppose that an unwinding process could not be profitable too. Indeed, the greatest obstacle in visualizing the possibilities inherent in such a reversal of the economy would seem to lie chiefly in a habit of mind that has conditioned every businessman to think of mergers as inevitably more profitable than the sum of their constituent units." (Editorial, *Fortune,* March 1938.)

24. For a discussion of these standards as measures of business performance in the public interest, see Edward S. Mason, "The Current Status of the Monopoly Problem in the United States," *Harvard Law Review* (June 1949).

25. That this type of administrative procedure is not without precedent and has been followed without penalty to the respondent is shown by our experience with the "cost justification" clauses of the Robinson–Patman Act. See Albert E. Sawyer, "The Commission's Administration of Paragraph 2(a) of the Robinson–Patman Act: An Appraisal," *George Washington Law Review,* pp. 502–3 (1940).

26. There is some evidence that dissolution proceedings under a similar law (the Public Utility Holding Company Act of 1935) did not precipitate the fatal loss of efficiency which had been widely predicted prior to the law's passage. While the statistics are

by no means conclusive, it may even be argued that, in certain cases, efficiency after dissolution was increased and that this increase was reflected in the security values of those operating companies which were divorced from their parent organizations. As a spokesman for the Securities & Exchange Commission recently pointed out, "it has been the experience of the Commission that the liquidation of holding companies results in increasing the market value of the aggregate security interests affected. This appears also to be the consensus of financial opinion." Subcommittee on the Study of Monopoly Power, op. cit., p. 1469. For further documentation, see ibid., pp. 1460–69.

27. See n. 21, supra.
28. Ben H. Lewis, "How Bad is Bigness?" *The Oberlin Alumni Magazine,* May 1950.
29. Editorial, *Fortune,* March 1938.

10

The Case for Structural Tests

Almost two decades ago, in a landmark article, Edward S. Mason argued that a sound antimonopoly policy should aim at promoting not only workably competitive industrial structures but also effective business performance. The market structure and performance tests, he observed, "must be used to complement rather than exclude each other."[1]

In advocating a greater attention to performance considerations, Mason tentatively offered the following criteria for measuring business performance:

> 1. Progressiveness: are the firms in the industry actively and effectively engaged in product and process innovation?
> 2. Cost–price relationships: are reductions in cost, whether due to falling wages or material prices, technical improvements, discovery of new sources of supply, passed on promptly to buyers in the form of price reductions?
> 3. Capacity–output relationships: is investment excessive in relation to output?
> 4. The level of profits: are profits continually and substantially higher than in other industries exhibiting similar trends in sales, costs, innovations, etc.?
> 5. Selling expenditures: is competitive effort chiefly indicated by selling expenditures rather than by service and product improvements and price reductions?[2]

In suggesting an increased reliance on a performance standard, Mason was careful to point out that "although it is probably possible to arrive at informed judgments, it is extremely difficult to devise tests that can be administered by a court of law." Indeed, he recognized quite explicitly that of the possible applications of a performance standard—on the legislative level, the adjudicatory level, or the case selection level—it was probably most relevant in case selection. Mason was primarily concerned with combating the tendency of the enforcement agencies to ask "what cases can be won?" rather than "what difference does it make?" His suggestions were cautious, tentative, and exploratory.

Originally published in J. Fred Weston and Sam Peltzman, *Public Policy toward Mergers* (Goodyear Publishing, 1969).

Some three years later, S. Chesterfield Oppenheim published his famous guideposts for a revision of antitrust policy, based on the twin concepts of "workable competition" and the "rule of reason." Central to the suggested reformulation of the antitrust laws was the adoption of the following criteria for judging performance in the public interest:

> (1) Alternatives available to customers or sellers; (2) Volume of production or services; (3) Quality of the services or goods; (4) Number of people benefited; (5) Incentives to entrepreneurs; (6) Efficiency and economy in manufacturing or distribution; (7) The welfare of employees; (8) The tendency to progress in technical development; (9) Prices to customers; (10) Conditions favorable to the public interest in defending the country from aggression; (11) The tendency to conserve the country's natural resources; (12) Benefits to the public interest assuming the relief requested by the government in proceedings.[3]

One cannot help but note, in passing, the contrast between this vague articulation of performance standards and the precise, carefully circumscribed, and tentative language of the earlier Mason proposal.

It is significant that the Attorney General's National Committee to Study the Antitrust Laws, which was created in response to Oppenheim's suggestion and of which he became co-chairman, did not choose to endorse the adoption of a performance standard in the adjudication of the antitrust laws. The stony silence with which the Committee treated "performance" in its final report is perhaps the most remarkable aspect of its conclusions and recommendations.

In this paper, I propose to explore some of the reasons for rejecting performance as a workable antitrust criterion. The concrete examples cited in support of each major proposition are for illustrative purposes only, and not intended as definitive, conclusive empirical evidence.

In the absence of effective competition, there are no scientific yardsticks by which to measure an industry's performance. There are no operationally reliable criteria for determining whether an industry has done "well," or whether it could have done "better" in the light of the opportunities available to it. One can make impressionistic judgments concerning product quality, design, variety, and improvement, for example, but how are we to know that the industry's performance on that score reflects "the best attainable balance between buyer satisfaction and the cost of production"? How are we to establish whether the observed rate of technological progress is as rapid as it could have been? In a market structure characterized by monopoly or tight-knit oligopoly, the necessary yardsticks are either unavailable or difficult to implement operationally.

The automobile industry is a case in point. Despite its high degree of concentration, Mason argued that "it is possible from the record of the last two or three decades to determine that the performance of the automobile industry is relatively good." But how valid is that (admittedly impressionistic) judgment in the light of the following considerations:

1. Is the "mauve and cerise, air-conditioned, power-steered, and power-braked automobile" a good product? Is the complex and luxurious amalgam of super-engines, tailfins, quadruple headlights, and cornucopia of chrome a product which satisfies consumer wants, or a product which consumers are taught to accept by the industry's massive selling effort?

2. Does the estimated $5 billion spent by the industry on annual model changes constitute a "sound" contribution to welfare maximization?

3. Should the industry's "stylistic orgy" be replaced by a greater concern for safety, such as "the installation of superior braking systems, safer tires, fuel tanks that do not rupture and incinerate passengers in otherwise survivable accidents—collapsible steering columns, safer instrument panels, steering assemblies, seat structures and frame strengths"? Is 0.02 percent of its gross receipts enough for General Motors to spend on safety research and development? Should the industry have adopted a systematic and more effective program for recalling defective makes and models before being forced to do so by governmental pressure? What percentage of the more than 50,000 deaths and 4 million injuries attributable annually to automobile accidents would be avoidable if the industry were to follow a different product-safety policy?[4]

4. Has the industry performed "creditably" in trying to prevent and/or reduce air pollution, 60 percent of which has been attributed to the internal combustion engine? Would Los Angeles, for example, be a more livable city if the industry had been more aggressive in its efforts to eliminate this environmental hazard?[5]

5. Did the industry lag because of its failure so far to introduce a feasible electric automobile?[6]

6. Does an advertising outlay of $100 per car (in 1957) represent an "acceptable" level of selling costs?

7. Should the industry have introduced a "compact" car long before it was compelled to do so by the Volkswagen invasion of the late 1950's—i.e., before its domestic markets began to be eroded by import competition?

8. Is the dramatic deterioration of the industry's export position during the 1950's, and the concomitant transfer of its export efforts to its overseas plants, an element of good performance?

9. Is General Motors' target-rate-of-return pricing, which has yielded the industry (including American Motors) an average net profit of 17 percent on investment between 1954 and 1966, consistent with good performance?

10. Finally, how are we to evaluate the harassment and intimidation to which the industry subjects such critics as Ralph Nader who dare to challenge the adequacy of its performance?[7]

Obviously, as Mason points out, it is extremely difficult to devise meaningful performance tests that could be administered by a court of law: "no one familiar with the statistical and other material pertaining to the business performance of firms and industries would deny the extreme difficulty of constructing from this material a watertight case for or against particular firms in particular industries."[8]

Application of the performance standard, in a court of law or before an administrative tribunal, affords unusual opportunities for dilatory tactics and stratagems of confusion. It opens a Pandora's box of procedural obstructionism which is conducive neither to the scientific use of economic evidence nor to the expeditious determination of the issues in the light of such evidence. Given the inexactness of economic knowledge, even the more "objective" components of performance—such as profit levels—can be the subject of seemingly endless and inconclusive wrangling.

Indicative of the problem is the 1968 controversy over the proper interpretation of drug industry profits before the Senate Small Business Committee.[9] The facts were available, and there was no dispute over their measurement: (1) Between 1959 and 1965, the drug industry had an average rate of return of 17.5 percent, ranking fourth among 59 industries. (2) The median rate of return for all 59 industries was 10 percent. Only four of the 29 drug companies evaluated earned less than that during the period in question; of these, three were companies whose operations were only marginally involved in the development and production of ethical drugs. (3) Only 12 of the companies earned less than 10 percent in any one year during the period. Only two ever showed a loss—in both cases for but a single year. (4) Between 1950 and 1955 the eight largest drug companies showed a profit performance about equal to or slightly above that of the eight largest firms in 22 major manufacturing industries; but, starting in 1956, the leading drug companies ranked either first or second among all large manufacturing industries, sometimes exceeding the average profit rate by substantial margins. (5) In a comparison of *all* drug companies with *all* manufacturing firms for the period between 1956 and 1967, their profit performance ranked first in all years except two (when they ranked second). Again, they exceeded the average by rather comfortable margins.

While no one challenged the accuracy of these data, the Nelson Committee witnessed a lively (and heated) dispute over their interpretation. Representing the Pharmaceutical Manufacturers Association, Gordon R. Conrad and Irving H. Plotkin of Arthur D. Little, working in consultation with Professors Jesse W. Markham and P.J. Cootner, argued that the high level of drug profits was due primarily to the uniquely high risks incurred by large drug manufacturers. By econometric techniques, they attempted to show that the level of drug profits was positively correlated with the degree of risk assumed. They tried to quantify the risk factor by measuring the dispersion of individual companies' rates of return about their industry's average rate of return in a given year, and then computing a simple average of these values for the 1950–66 period. By this measure— which assumes that the greater the *variation* of company profit rates around the industry average, the *riskier* the industry—they found that the drug firms in their sample had an average profit of 17.5 percent over the period, with a standard deviation of 8.6 percent around this average. Put differently, this meant that roughly two-thirds of the companies in the industry fell in the range between 8.9 and 26.1 percent. By contrast the Conrad–Plotkin–Markham–Cootner group found that the average rate of return for aluminum companies was 7.8 percent, with a standard deviation of 1.3 percent. This meant that two-thirds of the time aluminum company profits fell in the range between 6.5 and 9.1 percent. On the basis of such comparisons, the PMA economists concluded that the drug industry was a high-risk industry, and aluminum a low-risk industry.

Willard Mueller, representing the Federal Trade Commission, disputed both the accuracy and propriety of the Conrad–Plotkin–Markham–Cootner risk measure. Its chief conceptual shortcoming, he said, was that it tells us nothing about the probability of losses. Indeed, using this measure, an industry might be defined as risky even though most firms earn excessively high profits, whereas an industry might be put in the low-risk category even though most firms earn little or no profits. Given the two-to-one chance that profits in the drug industry will fall in the 8.9–26.1 range, and that profits in aluminum will fall in the 6.5–9.1 range, how can it be argued that drugs are a risky investment but aluminum is not? After all, there is only one chance in six that drug companies will earn a profit below 9 percent (the high in the aluminum range), whereas there are four chances in six that drug companies will earn between 9 and 26 percent, and one chance in six that they will earn over 26 percent.

Moreover, comparing the Big Eight in the drug industry with their counterparts in 21 other major manufacturing industries, Mueller found that between 1954 and 1966 the range of profit rates for the latter was from 5 to 15 percent. If this range is considered a "norm," the eight largest drug manufacturers were in this "normal" range 25 percent of the time, and none ever fell below it; 75 percent of the time they earned profits exceeding 15 percent; and fully 17 percent of the time they earned profits of more than 25 percent.

Finally, citing the Fisher–Hall study done for the RAND Corporation, Mueller concluded that risk accounts for a very small portion of the high profits of drug companies. On the contrary, he advanced the hypothesis that such profits are due primarily to the entry barriers created by patents, high advertising outlays, and other promotional efforts. He pointed out that intraindustry profit variance measures the height of an industry's entry barriers, and not—as Conrad–Plotkin–Markham–Cootner contended—the industry's investment risks.

Whether Mueller was right or wrong may be debatable, but Plotkin was certainly wide of the mark when he tried to assure Senator Nelson that "If economics has made any progress in the last 20 years, it is our ability to take things out of the field of judgment, out of the field of authority and whose textbook you read, and into objective, verifiable, repeatable experiments."[10]

The performance standard, because it focuses only on market results rather than market structure, contains no mechanism for assuring that performance will systematically and predictably be "good." Unlike the structure standard, it only permits good results; it does not compel them. It is devoid of any built-in, inherent safeguards to insure that the "good" results of today will not be the "bad" results of tomorrow. It provides no reward-and-punishment system to discipline delinquent firms or industries. In the absence of exogenous competitive pressures, or direct government interference to control particular performance variables, it lacks the necessary compulsions which militate toward the reform of market conduct with a view to achieving market results that are in the public interest.

An outstanding example, of course, is the steel industry, to which I have devoted not inconsiderable attention elsewhere.[11] In this industry, after World War II, the oligopoly "planning" which Galbraith so glowingly extolled in *The New Industrial State* resulted in truly shabby performance. There was an almost unbroken climb in steel prices, in good times and bad, in the face of rising or falling demand, increasing or declining unit costs. Prices rose even when only 50 percent of the industry's capacity was utilized. Price policy was based on a break-even point to be reached at 30 percent utilization of capacity. The typical operating rate seemed to decline steadily from the 82.2 percent of capacity worked in 1957. Domestic markets were eroded by substitute materials and burgeoning imports. Steel's export-import balance deteriorated in both absolute and relative terms: whereas the industry once exported about five times as much as it imported, the ratio today is almost exactly reversed, and steel exports are confined almost exclusively to AID-financed sales guaranteed by "Buy American" provisos.

Most remarkable was the technological somnolence of the giants in this highly concentrated industry. Spending only 0.7 percent of their sales revenue on research and development, the dominant firms in this industry consistently (and almost perversely) lagged behind their smaller domestic rivals as well as their smaller foreign competitors. Thus, the basic oxygen furnace—considered the "only major breakthrough at the ingot level since before the turn of the century" was invented in 1950 by a minuscule Austrian *firm* which was less than one-third the size of a single *plant* of the United States Steel Corporation. The innovation was introduced in the United States in 1954 by McLouth Steel, which at the time had about 1 percent of domestic steel capacity—followed some 10 years later by the steel giants: United States Steel in December 1963, Bethlehem in 1964, and Republic in 1965. Despite the fact that this revolutionary invention involved an average operating cost saving of $5 per ton and an investment cost saving of $20 per ton of installed capacity, the steel giants during the 1950's, according to *Business Week,* "bought 40 million tons of the wrong capacity—the open-hearth furnace," which was obsolete almost the moment it was put in place.

It is significant that only after they were subjected to actual and threatened competition from domestic and foreign steelmakers in the 1960's, did the steel giants decide to accommodate themselves to the oxygen revolution. Thus, it was the cold wind of competition, and not the catatonia induced by industrial concentration, which proved conducive to innovation and technological progress, i.e., improved performance. In this industry, at least, better performance had to await the appearance of structural changes in the market which compelled the reforms in market conduct thus belatedly and grudgingly adopted.

Antitrust regulation is basically a "prohibitory" mechanism designed to preserve competitive market structures, militate toward competitive market conduct and indirectly compel "good" industrial performance. Its prohibitory approach is designed to avoid precisely the type of direct interference with business decisions and pervasive controls over market conduct which application of a performance standard would necessitate. Indeed, a performance standard can be applied intelligently only within an explicit regulatory framework, where an industry is subjected to the comprehensive and continuing surveillance of an administrative board or "independent" regulatory commission. And this, I submit, would be neither wise nor prudent—in the light of our disastrous experience with this form of economic statecraft.

As I have shown elsewhere, regulation by independent regulatory commissions has not turned out to be the new, flexible, creative control instrument envisaged by the New Deal philosophers of the administrative process.[12] On the contrary, regulation has been static, negative, and protective. Even in the absence of venality and corruption, regulation has come to suffer from deep-seated institutional infirmities which militate against the competitive entrepreneur and dynamic innovator. The cost and delay of proceedings; the harassment by powerful protestants; the slavish adherence to technicalities; the pharisaical devotion to a case-by-case approach; the sacrifice of substance for form; the use of differential, inconsistent, and often discriminatory standards; the adoption of restrictive and protective policies; the undue identification with established interests; the petulant defense of the status quo; the sensitivity to organized pressures; the pervasive distrust of large numbers—these have become the hallmark of the regulatory process. Lacking boldness of vision, and beset by an anticompetitive bias, a bureaucratic rigidity, and an annoyance with the forces of change, the commissions have generally been hostile to the newcomer, the challenger, the innovator.

Experience has shown that what starts as regulation almost invariably winds up as protection. The power to license becomes the power to exclude; the regulation of rates, a system of price supports; the surveillance of mergers, an instrument of concentration; and the supervision of business practices, a pretext for harassing the weak, unorganized, and politically underprivileged. Typically, the commissions have used their power to dispense and protect privilege—to shield their regulatees from competition rather than to protect the public from exploitation. Indeed, in those areas where performance can be said to approximate what might be called "good," such performance has been achieved as a result of "institutional" competition (e.g., the yardstick provided by TVA) or by the marginal competition of unregulated interlopers—the truckers carrying agricultural commodities, the nonscheduled airlines, private operators without common-carrier status, FM radio and UHF television, etc. It is this form of very limited yardstick competition that has modified the conservative, unexperimental, unprogressive, and restrictionist conduct of regulated firms, whose performance languished under the protective umbrella of public regulation.

This experience is hardly worthy of emulation and proliferation under the guise of promoting better performance in the public interest.

The performance standard, if used to replace the structure standard or allowed to supersede it in importance, is subject to serious erosion by giant firms in a concentrated industry. Economic power, after all, is more than a decorative status symbol. It is there to be used when needed—benignly if possible, antisocially if necessary. Thus, a powerful oligopoly will attempt to shield itself from the Schumpeterian gales of creative destruction, and use all its economic and political power to do so. Willy-nilly, it will build storm shelters against those gales, either by private action or by manipulation of the state. Where necessary, and by whatever means, it will try to shield its questionable performance from public criticism or against reform by public authority. And, in the absence of the structural constraints and discipline of a competitive market structure, its efforts may well succeed.

Again the steel industry provides a dramatic illustration. It could luxuriate in its persistently poor performance as long as it commanded a large, protected market, undisturbed by competition-minded rivals or outside interlopers. A high degree of concentration, seemingly immune from antitrust attack, seemed to sanction its monopolistic price policy and technological catatonia. But, starting in 1959, accelerating imports convinced the industry that free international trade may be an effective antimonopoly policy, and that barriers were needed to insulate itself from this subversive force. Instead of meeting import competition in the market place, the industry proceeded to use its political power to preserve the *status quo ante*. Successively, it filed "peril point" proceedings before the Tariff Commission, followed by antidumping action under a 1921 statute, followed by demands to Congress for "temporary" tariff protection, and followed finally by a request for legislatively fixed import quotas. In pursuing what *Barron's* calls the "protection racket," the industry seemed intent on neutralizing the one exogenous force that could compel it to reform its laggard ways—competition. Roger Blough, congenitally unable to resist the ludicrous, opined that

> . . . obviously there are many things in life that should and must be protected. For example, millions of our people—and a number of government agencies—are laudably striving to protect certain vanishing forms of wildlife that are threatened with extinction; and one may reasonably wonder, I suppose, how far down the road to oblivion some of our major industries must go before they are deemed to merit similar concern.

To this, the President of the American Iron and Steel Institute added the ominous warning that "a first-class power with global responsibilities cannot afford to rely for any important part of its needs on overseas source of steel thousands of miles away, lying in the shadow of Communist China and the Soviet Union." Finally the United Steel Workers of America, upon whom Galbraith once relied as a source of countervailing power, not to be outdone in their concern for the public interest and national security, lent their voice and not inconsiderable political influence to the fight for a quota law to limit steel imports.[13]

What is at stake, of course, is the steel industry's right to preserve its administered price structure, to remain the catalyst of seller's inflation, to impose periodic price squeezes on independent fabricators, to price itself out of world export markets, to encourage the growth of substitute materials, and to persist in its technological lethargy. Given the concentrated economic power of the industry, its concomitant political power, and its "vertical integration" with the power of the United Steelworkers, this effort to perpetuate the industry's discretion over "performance"—its right to determine what performance the public must accept as "adequate," "reasonable," or "good"—may well be legitimized by congressional sanction.

General Motors affords a different illustration of how concentrated power can be employed, in the "private sector," to insulate entrenched positions—not from outside competition, or potential competition, but mere verbal criticisms of "performance." When Ralph Nader's *Unsafe at Any Speed* was published, and after he appeared before a congressional committee investigating traffic safety, General Motors hired a private detective agency to investigate Nader's "background" —his professional clients, his education, his friends, his sex habits, his alleged anti-Semitism, etc. Only after exposure by the press did General Motors revoke its orders to the detective agency; only then did a contrite General Motors president apologize to the committee for a decision made by his subordinates without his knowledge. Apparently no challenge, large or small, in the market place or the forum of public opinion, is too insignificant to escape the ubiquitous attention of the octopus. The task of attaining and maintaining power brooks no interference.[14]

Such examples can no doubt be multiplied, even though some are buried without spectacular (temporary) publicity. They underscore the fact that economic concentration is not a neutral phenomenon. Indeed, where it is free from the structural checks and balances of competition, economic power tends to be self-perpetuating—almost irrespective of "good" or "bad" performance.

The foregoing propositions aside, we may note, in conclusion, that no affirmative showing has yet been made of the need for a performance standard (except in the selection of antitrust cases). No one has yet demonstrated, validly or convincingly, that reliance on the structure standard has resulted in *bad* performance, and that far-reaching modification of current antitrust criteria is necessary to assure *good* performance. No one has yet proved that such policy goals as efficiency and progress are incompatible with the preservation of effectively competitive market structures. I suspect that the failure to make such a case is best explained by the lack of evidence to support it.

In the last 20 years enough empirical data have become available to dispel the naive belief, so fashionable in our age of innocence, that firms are big because they are efficient; that firms are big because they are progressive; that firms are big because they are good; that firms are big because consumers have made them big. By now, we should have learned that industrial concentration in some sectors of the economy is not the result of natural law, or the outgrowth of inexorable technological imperatives, but rather the product of unwise, man-made, discriminatory, privilege-creating action of Big Government—the result of governmentally sanctioned privilege, protection, and subsidy.[15]

If this be so, a comprehensive antimonopoly policy, going beyond mere enforcement of the antitrust laws, could result in substantially more competitive industries and markets—and without demonstrable damage to "performance." Thus, the withdrawal of tariff protection from concentrated industries; the refusal to grant patents on publicly financed research and development; a greater reliance on advertised-bid, competitive defense procurement; the termination of government sanction for private cartels (as in petroleum and transportation); the circumscription of the patent, agency, and franchise privileges; the toleration, if not encouragement, of more competition in the regulated industries; the removal of government protection from product-differentiation devices (as in drugs) which serve few other functions than to raise entry barriers—these are only illustrative of the measures which would liberate the natural forces of competition from the heavy hand of a protectionist state. Their implementation, I believe, would not only promote a more competitive industrial structure in many industries, but do so without detracting from good performance.

Notes

1. Mason, "The Current Status of the Monopoly Problem in the United States," *Harvard Law Review*, p. 1280 (1949).

2. Ibid., pp. 1281–1282.

3. S. Chesterfield Oppenheim, "Federal Antitrust Legislation: Guideposts to a Revised National Antitrust Policy," *Michigan Law Review*, p. 1188 (1952). [Quoting Blackwell Smith, "Effective Competition: Hypothesis for Modernizing the Antitrust Laws," *New York University Law Review*, p. 405 (1951).] See also riposte by Walter Adams, "The 'Rule of Reason': Workable Competition or Workable Monopoly?" *Yale Law Journal*, pp. 348–370 (1954).

4. *Federal Role in Traffic Safety, Hearings before the Subcommittee on Executive Reorganization, Senate Committee on Government Operations*, Part 3, pp. 1263 ff (1966).

5. *The Automobile and Air Pollution: A Program for Progress*, U.S. Department of Commerce, Part I, p. 10 (October 1967).

6. Ibid., Part II, pp. 83 ff.

7. *Federal Role in Traffic Safety*, op. cit., Part 4, pp. 1379 ff.

8. Mason, op. cit., p. 1282.

9. *Competitive Problems in the Drug Industry, Hearings before the Subcommittee on Monopoly, Senate Small Business Committee*, Part 5, pp. 1618–89, 1807–61 (Dec.–Jan., 1967–68).

10. Ibid., p. 1652.

11. Walter Adams and Joel B. Dirlam, "Steel Imports and Vertical Oligopoly Power," *American Economic Review*, pp. 626–656 (Sept. 1964); also Adams and Dirlam, "Big Steel, Invention, and Innovation," *Quarterly Journal of Economics*, pp. 167–189 (May 1966).

12. Walter Adams, "The Role of Competition in the Regulated Industries," *American Economic Review*, pp. 527–543 (May 1958).

13. Walter Adams, "The Military–Industrial Complex and the New Industrial State," *American Economic Review*, pp. 663–64 (May 1968).

14. *Federal Role in Traffic Safety*, op. cit., Part 4, pp. 1379 ff.

15. Walter Adams and Horace M. Gray, *Monopoly in America: The Government as Promoter*, p. 221 (1955).

11

Dissolution, Divorcement, Divestiture: The Pyrrhic Victories of Antitrust

"The hard core of the monopoly problem is the concentration of economic power, specifically, the ownership and control of a large proportion of the industrial economy by a small number of giant corporations. Within the framework of the antitrust laws, the problem can be met in only one way, namely through dissolution—trust-busting in the literal sense."[1] Dissolution can be achieved under present law through vigorous enforcement of Section 2 of the Sherman Act[2] which makes it unlawful to "monopolize, or attempt to monopolize, or combine or conspire with any other person or persons, to monopolize any part of the trade or commerce among the several states, or with foreign nations."[3] Section 4 of the Act authorizes proceedings in equity to eliminate unlawful monopolies and to restore competition.[4]

Prior to World War I, no substantial progress was made in breaking up great industrial combinations. The two outstanding dissolution cases during the period —*United States* v. *Standard Oil Co. of New Jersey*[5] and *United States* v. *American Tobacco Co.*[6]—failed to produce momentous results and can hardly be cited as good examples of what a dissolution policy can accomplish. The Standard Oil decree had the fatal flaw of leaving economic control over the successor companies with the same interests that had exercised control over the parent company prior to dissolution. The American Tobacco decree was even weaker, for here:

> The Court adopted the celebrated "three way" principle whereby monopoly was conceived to be eliminated and competition restored by the simple means of dividing a trust into three roughly equal parts. The reason for selecting the

Originally published in *Indiana Law Journal,* vol. 27 (Fall 1951); reprinted with permission.

magic figure "3" and not 7, 11, 60 (as was proposed), 100, or any other number was based, as might be expected, on legal rather than economic considerations. The Court felt that the firms created by a "three-way" division would be too small to be subject to prosecutions as "monopolies" under the Sherman Act. The possibility that the firms might be so large that they could readily follow uniform price policies and in other ways adopt monopolistic practices—as they have recently been convicted of doing[7]—was given no weight by the Court.[8]

The period between the great wars was marked by two major defeats for the Government. In the United States Steel case[9] of 1920, the Supreme Court announced its famous ruling that "the law does not make mere size an offense, or the existence of unexerted power an offense."[10] This doctrine was given added vitality by the International Harvester decision[11] of 1927. Needless to say, these two opinions constituted a virtual cease fire order on the dissolution front.[12]

Then, starting in the late 1930's, the nation became alarmed over the high degree of concentration in the economy. Even greater concern was expressed over the growing centralization of control that occurred during World War II and the post-war merger movement.[13] As a result, and in an effort to check this trend, the Department of Justice has in recent years attempted to revitalize the long dormant Section 2 of the Sherman Act by filing an increasing number of dissolution, divorcement and divestiture cases.[14]

The obvious purpose behind this recent emphasis on dissolution, divorcement and divestiture is to reduce the degree of concentration in highly concentrated industries[15]; to deprive monopolistic firms or groups of firms of their power over price and their ability to exclude competitors; in short, to promote competition by creating a larger number of bona fide independent competitors in certain lines of commerce.[16]

Unfortunately, however, the Department's dissolution program has not, on the whole, produced the desired results. In sharp contrast to the many legal triumphs, economic relief has generally been unimpressive. Remedial action approved by the courts has, in most instances, failed to lessen concentration and restore effective competition.[17] As the following case studies indicate, firms found guilty of possessing and exercising monopoly power have—with the notable exception of the motion picture companies[18]—escaped dissolution, divorcement, and divestiture.

Aluminum

United States v. *Aluminum Co. of America*[19] is a prize example to demonstrate how ready the courts are to denounce iniquity while steadfastly refusing to correct it. It is a case in which the Government, after a battle of thirteen years, won a resounding legal victory only to suffer a crushing economic defeat.

The proceedings were initiated on April 23, 1937 with a complaint against

Alcoa, 25 of its subsidiary and affiliated companies, and 37 of its directors, officers and stockholders. The complaint charged Alcoa with monopolizing the manufacture of virgin aluminum and the sale of aluminum sheets, alloys, cables, bars, etc, in the United States. It alleged that this monopoly was preserved and protected by the purchase of plants abroad and by cartel agreements with foreign producers. It claimed that the monopoly was acquired by restrictive contracts and oppressive tactics, including discriminatory prices and the squeezing of price spreads between virgin ingot and aluminum sheet for the purpose of eliminating new competitors. In order to obtain effective relief—in order to re-establish competition in the aluminum industry—the Government requested Alcoa's dissolution.

After a lengthy trial, the district court on June 23, 1942 entered an opinion holding the defendants not guilty and ordering the petition dismissed.[20] This decision was reversed, however, by the circuit court of appeals[21] on March 12, 1945 in one of the most celebrated judicial opinions of our time. Judge Learned Hand ruled that Alcoa was an illegal monopoly at the time of trial; that the company had monopolized the aluminum sheet market and squeezed independents out of the fabricating business; and that Alted (Alcoa's Canadian subsidiary) had entered into agreements with European aluminum producers which affected imports into the United States.

From a legal point of view the Hand decision was a milestone, for it finally interred and reversed the old dictum that mere size is no offense under the Sherman Act. As one writer observed:

> Size [to Judge Hand] was not only evidence of violation, or of potential offense . . . it was the essence of the offense. Size, meaning market control, was what competition and monopoly were about. All other aspects of the case were subordinated to the central and decisive fact that the Aluminum Company of America, many years after its patents had expired, made, and then fabricated, or sold, over 90 percent of the virgin aluminum used in the United States. Its arrangements with foreign companies for dividing world markets were further evidence of monopolizing. That it had engaged in deplorable tactics to prevent other companies from entering the field helped compound the offense. But the case was proved, in Judge Hand's view, by showing the company's market power. It made over 90 percent of the virgin aluminum, and therefore had monopoly power.[22]

In sharp contrast to the court's willingness to pronounce Alcoa a monopoly, stands the court's refusal to alleviate the situation. On the problem of relief the court merely recommended that remedial measures be withheld until such time as the district court could evaluate the effects of the Government's program for the disposal of surplus aluminum plants. Only if this disposal failed to create substantial competition in the industry was the trial court authorized to consider dissolution. In other words, the task of creating competition in the aluminum industry was shunned by the court and "assigned" to the disposal agency of the Government.

Perhaps, on the face of it, this solution of the relief problem seems plausible, especially since the objectives of the Surplus Property Act of 1944[23] coincided in many respects with those of the antitrust laws. Under that Act preference was to be given to smaller purchasers to an extent consistent with "the usual and customary commercial practice."[24] Above all, no disposal agency was even to begin negotiations for selling a plant valued in excess of $1,000,000 without first being advised by the Attorney General whether the proposed disposition would violate the antitrust laws.[25] Impressed with these provisions of the Surplus Property Act, the court thought that the prospects for competition in aluminum were bright and that the disposal of Government plants might make the dissolution of Alcoa unnecessary.

The court was mistaken—if not naive—however, to think that a disposal of surplus aluminum plants could stimulate competition sufficiently to obviate the necessity of dissolving Alcoa. The court failed to recognize that its refusal to deal with the specifics of relief confined the disposal agency to a limited and narrow course of action. Faced with an Alcoa of colossal dimensions, the disposal agency was forced to adopt a program which would create new producers of substantial enough size and integration to compete effectively with the undiminished monopolist. The disposal agency had no power to reorganize the facilities owned by Alcoa. It could hardly dispose of the Government plants to a large number of independent concerns incapable of coping with Alcoa's position of dominance and entrenchment. The agency chose the only feasible alternative: it brought into being two new integrated producers and created them in the image of Alcoa. It elected a course of action made inevitable by the court's refusal to deal with the problem of Alcoa's size.

Had the circuit court seriously attacked the problem of relief, it would have appreciated the importance of reorganizing Alcoa's structure; it would have recognized that such reorganization was an essential prerequisite to stimulating greater competition in the aluminum industry and placing that industry on a broad base of independent competing producers. As things turned out, the structure of the aluminum industry was reshaped after 1945, but this was due almost entirely to the actions of the War Assets Administration rather than to the relief granted by the circuit court.

The 1945 decision was not the end of this case, however, for both Alcoa and the Government were permitted to seek further relief. Accordingly, when the disposal program of the War Assets Administration was completed, Alcoa petitioned the court (March 1947) to declare that it no longer had a monopoly of the ingot market. In September 1948, the Government also filed a petition alleging that competitive conditions had not been re-established in the aluminum industry; that Alcoa had continued to dominate and control the aluminum ingot market; and that, only through divestiture by Alcoa of plants and other properties, could competitive conditions be established. The Government's petition attempted to show that divestiture of Alcoa was practicable; that at least one new domestic integrated producer could be established as part of a program to create competitive conditions; and that following divestiture Alcoa would continue to be a fully integrated producer, under no competitive disadvantage, and with such facilities, production, sales volume, and ability to expand so as to permit and encourage it to grow with the rest of the industry. The petition attempted to demonstrate that a fourth producer could be established without disintegrating Alcoa; that the structure of Alcoa was not that of an inseparable entity, but of duplicate facilities which fulfill the needs of market control rather than integrated efficiency.[26]

These issues were tried before Judge Knox in 1949, and the court's opinion was handed down on June 2, 1950.[27] The court, in denying both petitions, found that competitive conditions had not been restored in the aluminum industry and that the Government was entitled to further relief. The relief granted by the court included the finding that certain provisions in the patent licenses issued by Alcoa were unenforceable; and that persons who held stock in both Alcoa and Alted (the Canadian subsidiary) be required to divest themselves of the stock in either of the two corporations. Jurisdiction over the case was retained for another five years during which time both parties, if conditions so warrant, can petition the court for further and more complete relief.

The court's opinion is disturbing for a number of reasons. First, the relief granted is inadequate and the prospects for further relief are dim. Judge Knox seemed satisfied with the industry's present structure and expressed little concern over the small number of firms in the field. Disregarding almost entirely the implications of the three-producer oligopoly, the court focused its primary attention on the ability of Reynolds and Kaiser to survive and expand. It is likely, therefore, that no reorganization of the aluminum industry by judicial action will take place in the next five years; that at the end of this period—if Reynolds and Kaiser hold their own—the court will pronounce competitive conditions in aluminum to have been re-established: the court will then terminate its jurisdiction in the case.

Needless to say, Kaiser and Reynolds *will* survive and the status quo in the industry *will* be maintained during the next five years. This outcome seems certain because Alcoa—in order to forestall any future relief action by the court —will refrain from expanding its share of the market. By exercising self-restraint, Alcoa will demonstrate that Kaiser and Reynolds can maintain their market position, and possibly, improve it. By judiciously avoiding any aggressive or expansive activity, Alcoa can thus effectively bar the Government from showing the need for further relief in the crucial five-year period. By pursuing a "live and let live" policy, which has proved so effective in other industries, Alcoa can then insure the termination of the court's jurisdiction by 1955. Given the present high level of business activity, such a conservative course of action need by no means be unprofitable.

The second cause for concern is the precedent which the Knox opinion establishes with respect to future antitrust cases involving oligopolistic industries. The Government brief dwelt at considerable length on the fact that failure to grant divestiture relief in this case would be tantamount to judicial approval of a three-producer industry. The court's refusal to divest Alcoa and, thus, create at least one additional domestic producer might, therefore, be construed as a judicial sanction for the type of structural organization now prevailing in the aluminum industry. Furthermore, the court's refusal to concede that in an industrial structure of this sort, Alcoa, as the dominant firm, exercises control over its competitors seems ominous. The monopolistic significance of price leadership and the zone system of pricing enforced by Alcoa was ignored. The court failed to appreciate the fear engendered among fabricators that Alcoa, because of its dominant position, could ruin them by a simple refusal to sell (or, as it is euphemistically called, maintaining the right to "select its customers"). Thus, some of the more basic elements of the "parallel action" theory, which is essential in proving an oligopoly case, were disregarded. This opinion may, therefore, become a substantial obstacle in the future prosecution of cases involving companies in highly concentrated industries.

A third cause for concern is the court's effort to establish a foreign producer as the fourth competitor in a highly concentrated domestic industry. This objective was sought to be accomplished by separating the control of the Canadian company from Alcoa. Realistically viewed, however, such action is unlikely to promote a more competitive market in the United States for a number of reasons: first, despite the change in stock control, the Canadian company will not become an active competitor, either in the domestic ingot or the fabricated aluminum market, since the largest customers of ingot in the United States are the three primary producers (Alcoa, Reynolds, and Kaiser) and since Alted does not have the facilities for expanded participation in the American fabricated aluminum market. Furthermore, Alted is Canada's sole producer and therefore enjoys an undisputed monopoly position in its own country. In addition, Alted has long been the motivating force in the cartelization of the world aluminum industry and will probably continue its efforts in that direction in the future. Finally, if the Canadian company should ever initiate an aggressively competitive policy in the United States market, tariff barriers could always be raised sufficiently to "protect" our vital domestic industry. Keeping these facts in mind, it is difficult to conceive how a corporation so traditionally opposed to the competitive philosophy as Alted, can take the place of a fourth producer in the American aluminum industry.[28]

There is one final aspect of the court's opinion which is disturbing, especially since it relates to national security. As has been noted above, the opinion places great emphasis on the maintenance of the status quo in the industry. This fact is bound to discourage, therefore, any expansion of Alcoa's productive facilities (such as the company had contemplated in Alaska, for example).[29] At the same time, the potential threat of Canadian competition may inhibit expansion by Reynolds and Kaiser, at least until such time as the nature of that competition has been determined. The Canadian company, by contrast, is free to expand without restraint and is currently doing so by adding substantially to its facilities in British Columbia.[30]

The result is anomalous: Canadian facilities during the next five years will tend to expand while our own aluminum capacity may remain static. Thus, we may well become more dependent on a foreign producer for an increasing part of our national aluminum requirements.[31]

In summarizing the results of thirteen years of litigation in the Alcoa case, one is impressed with the insignificance of the relief obtained by the Government. A company which had monopolized the aluminum industry for fifty years was permitted to remain intact. An economically mild—probably excessively mild—proposal for divestiture was refused. Once again, the court chose the easy solution. Judge Hand passed the task of stimulating competition in this basic industry to the War Assets Administration. Judge Knox attempted to introduce a new competitor in the domestic market by severing the *formal* ties between Alcoa and Alted. Both refused to undertake the kind of physical reorganization of the industry necessary to bring about a competitive structure consistent with the objectives of the Sherman Act.[32]

As a result, aluminum today is a three-producer industry; Alcoa, instead of being a single-firm monopoly, now exercises residual monopoly power through price leadership and other means; the concerted action typical of oligopoly has replaced the unilateral action characteristic of monopoly. A ringing judicial denunciation of monopoly has produced little in the way of affirmative relief. Vigorous and effective competition has not been re-established in this basic and vital industry.

Titanium

Another illustration of some of the problems which confront the Antitrust Division in obtaining adequate relief from the courts is the case of *United States* v. *National Lead Co.*[33] The decision shows that while the Division is extremely successful in establishing liability, i.e. proving a violation of the antitrust laws, it seems ineffective in securing meaningful relief.

The case involved three corporations charged with the creation of a world-wide cartel in titanium compounds and conspiracy with substantially all of the important chemical companies of the world. At the conclusion of the trial, the court upheld the Government's charges. It ruled that the defendants had violated the antitrust laws through participation in an international cartel, and that their agreements creating a world-wide patent pool and dividing the world into exclusive territories, for the purpose and with the effect of suppressing imports into and exports from the United States, had violated the Sherman Act. In spite of this finding, however, the district court refused to grant the Government's requests for royalty-free licensing and divestiture. The Supreme Court, in upholding the decision, rejected the Government's plea that each duopolist be required to divest one of its two principal titanium pigments plants:

> There is no showing that four major competing units would be preferable to two, or, including Zirconium and Virginia Chemical, that six would be better than four. Likewise, there is no showing of the necessity for this divestiture of plants or of its practicality and fairness. The findings of fact have shown vigorous and effective competition between National Lead and du Pont in this field. . . . Such competition suggests that the District Court would do well to remove unlawful handicaps from it but demonstrates no sufficient basis for weakening its force by divesting each of the two largest competitors of one of its principal plants. It is not for the courts to realign and redirect effective and lawful competition where it already exists and needs only to be released from restraints that violate the antitrust laws. To separate the operating units of going concerns without more supporting evidence than has been presented here to establish either the need for, or the feasibility of, such separation would amount to an abuse of discretion.[34]

The Court's reluctance to resolve this basic issue in favor of the Government was perhaps due in large part to the Government's failure to prove the need for, or practicability and feasibility of, divestiture relief. The Government never made an overwhelming case for, or presented preponderant evidence in favor of, the type of relief requested. It did not allay the fears of the Court concerning the effect of a divestiture decree on the efficiency of the successor companies, nor was the probative benefit of divestiture for the re-establishment of competition in the industry shown. It neither demonstrated that the principal titanium plants of the defendants were adapted to separate ownership and independent operation, nor did it establish the compelling need for the particular remedy requested in any scheme to free this growing industry from the fetters of the dominant defendant firms.[35] The failure to show that the "tough" competition which allegedly existed in this industry, in fact, merely took the form of sales rivalry between two nominally independent firms was unfortunate. The impression seems inescapable that had the Government devoted as much energy toward establishing the appropriateness of the relief requested as it did to proving a violation of the law, the Court might have granted a more drastic, yet more effective, remedy.[36]

Had the Government done so, the Court might have appreciated more fully the need for structural reorganization—a mild one, at that—of a highly concentrated industry. The statement by one of du Pont's general managers that competition in titanium pigments was "tough" and "plenty tough"[37] might not have been so readily accepted. The Court might not have shuddered at the idea of cutting "living tissue" or of disturbing a delicately adjusted oligopolistic machine. Convinced of the necessity, fairness, practicability and feasibility of divestiture the Court might have been more willing to accept the Government's proposal for an effective remedy.

Even if it is granted, however, that the Government did not present the strongest possible evidence to support its demand for divestiture, it is still doubtful whether the Court used valid (and economically meaningful) criteria for choosing an appropriate remedy. As Justice Douglas, in a vigorous dissenting opinion, pointed out:

> The task of putting an end to monopolistic practices and restoring competition is one of magnitude and complexity; Congress has authorized use of the broadest powers of equity to cope with it. . . . The [court's] powers under the antitrust laws, though not specifically enumerated, are ample to thwart the plans of those who would build illegal empires, no matter how imaginative their undertakings or subtle their techniques. The power of the court is not limited to the restraint of future transgressions. The impairment of property rights is no barrier to the fashioning of a decree which will grant effective relief. . . . Divestiture or dissolution may be ordered in spite of hardship, inconvenience, or loss. . . . Devices or instrumentalities which may be used for legitimate ends may nevertheless be outlawed entirely where they have been employed to build the monopoly or to create the restraint of trade. . . .[38]

This view was nevertheless rejected, with the result that the decree approved by the Court stopped short of granting effective relief. Divestiture was refused and, while compulsory licensing was ordered, it was put on a "reasonable royalty" instead of a royalty-free basis. Moreover, any company which applied for a license from the defendants had to be prepared reciprocally to license its own patents to the defendants. In both these respects, the Court increased the odds against the restoration of competition in this industry. It forced independents and potential newcomers to pay royalties on misused patents and to surrender one of their few competitive advantages—the exclusive right to use such patents as they might possess. It is hardly surprising, therefore, that the *National Lead* decision did little to stimulate the entry of newcomers into the titanium pigment industry.[39]

Anti-Friction Bearings

The case of *United States* v. *Timken Roller Bearing Co.*[40] which, in many respects, is a "sequel" to the National Lead case, is significant because it indicates a growing trend against the liberal granting of divestiture by the Supreme Court. Moreover, the case is important because it demonstrates the rather dubious grounds on which the Court can refuse—and, in the foreseeable future, is likely to refuse—divestiture relief in any manner or form.

The amended complaint was filed December 15, 1947, and charged Timken and two foreign corporations (which were named co-conspirators but not defendants) with engaging in an unlawful conspiracy and combination to restrain foreign commerce by entering into agreements to eliminate competition in the manufacture and sale of anti-friction bearings in all markets of the world.

On March 3, 1949, the district court filed an opinion,[41] which it thereafter adopted as its findings of facts and conclusions of law, declaring the defendant guilty of having violated Sections 1 and 3 of the Sherman Act. After considering and rejecting all of the various defenses raised by Timken in the course of the trial, Judge Freed held that the defendant, together with British Timken and French Timken (its co-conspirators), had unlawfully combined and conspired to restrain foreign commerce by: (1) dividing the world among themselves into exclusive sales and production territories[42]; (2) fixing prices on all sales made into territories assigned to another member of the conspiracy[43]; (3) cooperating to protect each others' markets and to eliminate competition from outsiders[44]; and (4) participating in foreign cartels which restricted exports from and imports into the United States.[45] Judge Freed concluded that the restraints involved were not only illegal *per se*, but were entered into with the clear intent of controlling "commerce in the tapered bearing industry throughout the entire world."[46]

On the basis of these findings, the district court entered a final judgement[47] which enjoined, among others, the following practices: (1) exclusive exchange of know-how, patents, material and machinery between Timken and its co-conspirators; (2) agreement between defendant, British Timken, French Timken, or their subsidiaries, agents, sales representatives, or distributors to fix prices for the sale or resale of bearings in the United States; (3) defendant's refusal to sell bearings on the grounds that they are for resale or distribution in the territories allotted by the conspiracy to British Timken or French Timken; (4) the defendant's entry into agreements with its co-conspirators for the transfer of trade-mark rights upon restrictive conditions, such as allocation of territories and exclusive exchange of know-how and materials.[48] In addition, the district court ordered that the defendant divest itself of its 30.25 percent common stock interest in British Timken and its 50 percent common stock interest in French Timken.[49]

On appeal to the Supreme Court,[50] four major questions were presented for review,[51] namely: (1) whether defendant had in fact combined with British Timken and French Timken to restrain foreign commerce by allocating world markets, fixing prices, and restricting competition in the sale of anti-friction bearings; (2) whether the restraints were reasonable as ancillary to a "joint venture" or to the "licensing" of the trademark "Timken"; (3) whether the evidence at the trial and the findings of the district court supported the judgment; and (4) whether the divestiture and injunctive relief ordered by the lower court were appropriate and necessary. With the exception of divestiture, the Supreme Court, on June 4, 1951, resolved all of these issues in favor of the Government.[52] By a vote of 4 to 3, however, the Court refused divestiture and thus added another to the Government's long list of Pyrrhic victories in the enforcement of the antitrust laws.[53]

The Court's refusal to grant divestiture in this case was apparently motivated by two major considerations. One was a feeling that a more liberal rule of reason should be applied to international trade arrangements under the Sherman Act, even though similar arrangements under similar circumstances in domestic commerce might be deemed unreasonable. The second was that divestiture is a harsh remedy, that it should not be used to punish but to correct, and that it should not be employed if "effective" alternatives are available. How valid are these objections to divestiture relief when viewed in terms of the facts brought out during the trial and in terms of the precedents developed by the Court in similar cases?

First, as to the application of the rule of reason in international trade cases, defendant had contended—and Justices Jackson and Frankfurter apparently agreed—that the obstacles to foreign commerce created by tariff barriers, quota restrictions, governmental limitations on foreign exchange, etc., were such as to effectively foreclose any major invasion of foreign markets by Timken and of domestic markets by the co-conspirators. The defendant had further urged that, since a reciprocal invasion of market territories was impossible even if divestiture was granted, a divestiture decree by the Court would merely operate as a penalty against defendant rather than as a measure of relief against past and future violations of the law.[54]

Justice Jackson, in his dissenting opinion, accepted this view and concluded that "this decision will restrain more trade than it will make free."[55] In a separate dissenting opinion, Justice Frankfurter expressed a similar view. After stating that "even 'cartel' is not a talismanic word, so as to displace the rule of reason by which breaches of the Sherman Law are determined,"[56] he urged that the rule of reason be applied more liberally in the international trade field, and that arrangements which might be deemed unreasonable in domestic commerce be, under certain circumstances, considered reasonable when involving foreign commerce.[57]

While the Jackson and Frankfurter opinions, theoretically at least, seem plausible they are not supported by the facts of this case. As the district court, in an explicit and comprehensive finding, held, "all that the evidence discloses is an intent to form a smoothly operating combination to control commerce in the tapered bearing industry throughout the entire world."[58] The agreements and conspiracy into which the defendant had entered, in addition to being illegal *per se*, could not even be justified by "good business reasons," and could hardly be regarded as an attempt to compete under the difficult conditions confronting world trade.

The record reveals that, not only did the conspirators refrain from selling outside their allocated territory, but also prevented their customers from doing so. Sales of bearings for replacement purposes outside of allocated territories, though permitted by the contracts between the conspirators, were discouraged by a penalty or "commission" of 10 percent (later 5 percent) imposed on such sales.[59] Furthermore, even where this penalty was imposed, the prices charged were regularly fixed by agreement among the parties.[60] The record reveals that, by mutual understanding, each party to the conspiracy, when selling replacement parts for export into the other's territory, charged substantially higher prices (*i.e.* imposed a "protective" discount) than on similar sales within its own territory.[61] American Timken, although it was not actually a party to any cartel agreements, cooperated and consulted with British

Timken and French Timken in organizing them, and approved the agreements before they were executed, all as part of a plan to eliminate outside (including American) competition.[62] Finally, the record reveals that, as a result of its own restrictive covenants, the defendant could not, in many parts of the world, use the "Timken" trade-mark in competition with its British and French co-conspirators.[63]

From an examination of the record it would appear, therefore, that Timken was hardly the victim of the difficult circumstances surrounding world trade; that Timken, far from attempting to expand world trade, did everything in its power to contain and restrict it; that instead of being a silent and unwilling partner to a conspiracy imposed on it by external necessity, Timken was a prime mover in a division of the world into non-competitive spheres from which outsiders were excluded and in which the conspirators behaved in accordance with an "orderly" and "rational" mode of conduct characteristic of international cartels.

Perhaps the most telling answer to the Frankfurter–Jackson position was provided by the district court itself when it inquired why, if competition between Timken and its co-conspirators was impossible, did Timken need to enter into restrictive agreements in the first place, and why has it since then so vigorously defended its right to continue them.[64] Why, if divestiture was a vain and futile gesture in any attempt to restore competition, did Timken so vehemently oppose this form of relief?

It is unfortunate indeed that neither the defendant, nor Justices Jackson or Frankfurter, specifically demonstrated how the existence of tariffs and other trade barriers hampered Timken in its efforts to sell tapered bearings abroad. It is unfortunate that neither the defendant, nor the Justices who upheld its position, specifically indicated how the combination and contractual agreements into which Timken entered promoted world trade, in general, and exports from, or imports to, the United States, in particular. It is regrettable that Justice Frankfurter failed to explain the exact manner in which he would have applied his more "liberal" rule of reason to the specific facts of this case. Finally, it seems incongruous that Justice Frankfurter, while recognizing that "it is not for this Court to formulate economic policy as to foreign commerce," nevertheless chose to write an opinion which would make the foreign commerce provisions of the Sherman Act a dead letter and thus, institute a drastic change in the law which only Congress has the power to make.

The second major reason for the Court's refusal of divestiture relief was set forth in the Reed–Vinson concurring opinion which held that "[s]ince divestiture is a remedy to restore competition and not to punish those who restrain trade, it is not to be used indiscriminately, without regard to the type of violation or whether other effective methods, less harsh, are available."[65] In urging upon the Court the same judicial restraint that was followed in United States v. National Lead Co.,[66] Justice Reed argued that a divestiture order in this case was excessively severe, and that such an order was unnecessary since injunctive relief would prove adequate in terminating the illegal conspiracy and in restoring competition.[67] By thus relying on a series of injunctions, backed by the threat of civil and criminal contempt, Justice Reed thought that the purpose and functions of the Sherman Act would effectively be served.

That this view is rather naive should be self-evident. The paucity of cases dealing with contempt of Sherman Act injunctions is probably evidence, not of how carefully such decrees are obeyed, but rather of the ease with which they are evaded and the niggardly appropriations made available for their surveillance. Moreover, the past record of prison sentences and fines imposed on individual defendants for antitrust violations makes the threat of contempt against corporate officials an empty threat indeed. Finally, even if we assume that the injunctions in the present case will be observed with punctilious exactitude, it is questionable whether these injunctions—absent divestiture—would add much to what the Sherman Act already prohibits *per se*.

Unfortunately, the Reed–Vinson opinion not only fails to substantiate the adequacy of the injunctive relief, standing by itself, but also does violence to three important precedents developed by the Court in previous divestiture cases. Thus, the Reed-Vinson position seems to ignore a previous ruling by the Court that divestiture may be required not only where a stock acquisition, though lawful, was part of a conspiracy to suppress competition. As the Court stated in the Paramount[68] case:

> To the extent that these acquisitions were the fruits of monopolistic practices or restraints of trade, they should be divested. . . . Moreover, even if lawfully acquired, they may have been utilized as part of the conspiracy to eliminate or suppress competition in furtherance of the ends of the conspiracy. In that event divestiture would likewise be justified. . . .
>
> Furthermore, if the joint ownership is an alliance with one who is or would be an operator but for the joint ownership, divorce should be decreed even though the affiliation was innocently acquired. For that joint ownership would afford opportunity to perpetuate the effects of the restraints of trade which the . . . defendants have inflicted on the industry.[69]

The Reed–Vinson opinion also does violence to the ruling of the *Crescent*[70] case. There the Court held that the inducement to avoid competition, which was afforded by a conspiratorial stock affiliation between potential competitors, warranted effective assurance, through divestiture, that the opportunity therefore would be unavailable in the future. In explaining the necessity of divestiture in such cases, the Court had recognized that "the government should not be confined to an injunction against further violations," and that:

> [T]he relief need not, and under these facts should not, be so restricted. The fact that the companies were affiliated induced joint action and agreement. Common control was one of the instruments in bringing about unity of purpose and unity of action and in making the conspiracy effective. If that affiliation continues, there will be tempting opportunity for these [defendants] . . . to continue to act in combination against the independents. The proclivity in the past to use that affiliation for an unlawful end warrants effective assurance that no such opportunity will be available in the future. Hence we do not think the

District Court has abused its discretion in failing to limit the relief to an injunction against future violations. There is no reason why the protection of the public interest should depend solely on that somewhat cumbersome procedure when another effective one is available.[71]

The Reed–Vinson opinion further seems to ignore the previous rulings by the Court that those who violate the Sherman Act may "not avoid an undoing of their unlawful project on the plea of hardship or inconvenience"[72] and that "the policy of the antitrust laws is not qualified or conditioned by" the disadvantages or inconvenience which the judgment provisions may cause to those whose conduct is regulated.[73] On the basis of these precedents Justices Reed and Vinson could easily have rejected defendant's plea that hardship, inconvenience and loss of profit would result from the divestiture order of the lower court. They could have rejected this plea on the simple ground that the alleged hardship was immaterial as a matter of law.

Indeed, Justices Reed and Vinson could have gone beyond precedent and pointed out that the alleged hardship, even if material as a matter of law, was doubtful and speculative as a matter of fact. To be sure, defendant had urged that, under a divestiture judgment, the sale of its stock in British Timken and French Timken would be difficult; that serious financial losses would be involved in the sale; that defendant would be unable to realize in dollars on securities sold in Great Britain; and that it would suffer losses through the payment of taxes on gains from the sales.

While these contentions appear plausible, they are more speculative than real. In the first place, there is, as the record shows, a regular market for British Timken shares, since they are listed on the London Stock Exchange and also traded on the "switch-pound" market in New York. In addition, there is a market which can be tapped through privately negotiated sales or syndicate operations. Secondly, the price at which the shares were to have been sold need not have been artificially depressed by offering them all at one time or in large blocks. The district court decree proposed to allow a two-year period for the sale of the stock, thus providing adequate flexibility for advantageous disposition.[74] Thirdly, there would appear to be little danger that defendant could not realize American dollars from the sale of its British or French holdings. If the securities were sold in the United States, there would, of course, be no problem of currency conversion. But even if the securities were sold abroad, the National Lead experience indicates that the conversion problem is not insuperable. As the Government informed the Court, defendants in that case had used the proceeds from an enforced stock sale to purchase British Government bonds (which pay 3 to 4½ percent interest withdrawable immediately in dollars) the principal of which may be withdrawn in dollars upon maturity and, in some cases, before maturity.[75] In the light of the record and the testimony by some of defendant's own witnesses, it would appear that the hardship which would allegedly have ensued from divestiture was to say the least, doubtful and speculative.[76]

We may conclude, therefore, that Justices Reed and Vinson erred in their refusal to grant divestiture. Since they both concurred with the district court finding that defendant's investments in potentially competing companies were carried out as part of an illegal conspiracy to suppress competition; agreed with the finding that these investments served initially, and have continued to serve, as an inducement to defendant not to compete with British Timken and French Timken; must have had cognizance of previous Court rulings authorizing divestiture (a) where the acquisition of stock investments was itself illegal, or (b) where the investments—though lawfully acquired—were utilized as part of an unlawful conspiracy to restrain trade, or (c) where the investments served as an inducement to restrain competition; must have recalled that even in the National Lead case (which they quoted with approval)—to the extent that it involved an illegal division of world territories—defendant was ordered to divest itself of its foreign stock interests because "the stock acquisitions were part and parcel of the territorial allocation agreements"[77]; must have realized that the prospective hardship flowing from divestiture rested more upon allegations of defense counsel than upon evidence developed at the trial; should have recognized that the injunctive provisions of the decree did not go much beyond the *per se* prohibitions already existing under the Sherman Act; should have known that the threat of civil and criminal contempt does not by itself assure compliance with an injunctive decree; and finally, should have resolved doubts as to the efficacy of relief in favor of the Government and against the conspirators,[78]—for all these reasons, we believe that divestiture in this case should have been authorized.

In appraising the results of the Timken case one cannot help but wonder why the majority refused to allow divestiture; why they rejected the Black–Douglas–Minton view that "obviously the most effective way to suppress further Sherman Act violations is to end the intercorporate relationship which has been the core of the conspiracy."[79] Does the Court act unwittingly? Does the Court unconsciously condone what the antitrust laws were designed to prevent? In short, does the Court propose to stand idly by while America's foreign trade is recreated in the image of the Old World cartels?

Passenger Rail Cars

The manner in which the dissolution, divorcement and divestiture remedy is implemented is of crucial importance in attaining the antimonopoly objectives of the Sherman Act. This fact is demonstrated by the case of *United States* v. *Pullman Co.*[80] The complaint in that case was filed on July 12, 1940, charging Pullman, Inc., three subsidiaries thereof, and 31 individuals with violation of Sections 1 and 2 of the Sherman Act and Section 3 of the Clayton Act. The Government charged that the defendants had secured a monopoly in the *operation* and *servicing* of sleeping cars by buying out competitors and by making contracts with the railroads for exclusive operating and servicing rights. The

Government also charged that the defendants had conspired to monopolize the *manufacture* of sleeping cars.

Pullman, Inc. was a holding company controlling The Pullman Company, Pullman–Standard Car Manufacturing Company, and Pullman Car & Manufacturing Corporation of Alabama. Together, these companies exercised vertically integrated domination of the manufacture and operation of sleeping cars in the United States.

The Pullman Company (the operating subsidiary) was engaged in the business of operating sleeping, parlor, private and miscellaneous cars for railroads. By 1940 it had achieved a complete monopoly in the operating field by systematically acquiring competitors, coercing railroads into signing operating contracts, and forcing railroads to deal exclusively with Pullman.[81] The company thus exercised a stranglehold from which no important railroad could escape. The reason is obvious: a substantial part of all sleeping car travel involves the use of connecting carriers. Even if a railroad could operate its own sleeping car service, it could not send its sleeping cars over the lines of connecting carriers with which The Pullman Company had contracts, or—if these Pullman contracts were abrogated—without then entering into numerous complicated contracts for the exchange of cars.

The Pullman–Standard Car Manufacturing Company and Pullman Car & Manufacturing Corporation of Alabama were the manufacturing subsidiaries of Pullman, Inc. Together these companies exercised a virtual monopoly in the making of sleeping, parlor, dining, and similar cars. The monopoly in the manufacture of these cars was secured by The Pullman Company's refusal to *operate* any cars not *manufactured* by the Pullman organization. This refusal was, in turn, made effective by The Pullman Company's operating monopoly and its agreement to own and use only cars produced by Pullman–Standard. Since the railroads were dependent on Pullman service for carrying first-class passengers, the Pullman organization had the power to restrain these railroads from buying certain types of cars from other manufacturers. Thus, although there were a number of manufacturing companies in 1940 capable of producing sleeping car equipment,[82] they were not able to do so as long as Pullman exercised its vertically integrated control over the industry.

The economic effects of the integrated monopoly in the operation and manufacture of sleeping cars were clear: since the Pullman operating company had no competitive incentive to lower rates or to improve its equipment, it exacted excessive charges for its services and operated a fleet of obsolete cars.[83]

The railroads were exploited in many ways. They were required to guarantee Pullman a minimum profit on all cars used and could share only part of the profits earned in excess of such minimum.[84] (The railroads thus took all risks of loss, but were rewarded with only part of any accrued profits.) They were required to pay in some instances 75 percent and in others more than 100 percent of the total cost of air conditioning sleeping cars, in spite of the fact that the air conditioning equipment became a fixture of the Pullman car and the property of The Pullman Company.[85] Pullman also forced contracting railroads to pay for all improvements on "standard" equipment cars, in spite of the fact that such cars were built on a model more than 20 years old and in spite of the fact that the improvements became the property of The Pullman Company.[86] The company thus exacted non-competitive and excessive prices and terms for the operation of sleeping car services.

The consumers suffered not only from the arbitrary rates on sleeping car services, but also from the inadequate facilities provided. For two decades, prior to 1940, there was no important change in the type of car operated by Pullman and a substantial number of the sleeping cars owned by the company were more than 20 years old.[87] Because of Pullman's ability to restrain other car manufacturers from marketing their product, the consumer did not receive the benefit of improved equipment kept up to the standards of speed, comfort, and convenience made possible by advances in rolling stock construction.

The unreasonably high profits earned by Pullman over the years were another effect of monopoly. While the I.C.C. had the same regulatory power over the fares of The Pullman Company as over the fares of other common carriers, the Commission never chose to fix either maximum or minimum fares and charges. The Pullman rates in effect in 1940 were not fixed by the Commission but were initiated by The Pullman Company pursuant to its own monopolistic price policies. Since the manufacturing subsidiary of the Pullman organization was not subject to I.C.C. supervision, any regulation of the operating company's rates was incapable of preventing exploitation and the accumulation of excess profits.[88]

Finally, the Pullman monopoly resulted in the limitation and restriction of sleeping, parlor, and dining car production; in the suppression of developments in modern car construction; in discrimination between railroads in the terms for operating sleeping cars; and in the exclusion of companies eager to embark upon the manufacture of sleeping cars and similar equipment.

When the court's decision in the case was announced on April 20, 1943, the Government seemed to have won a complete victory. It was held there had been a violation of the Sherman Act in both manufacture and operation of sleeping cars. The court directed that the final decree provide for divorcement of the operating company from the manufacturing company; that The Pullman Company be required to operate and service sleeping cars of any manufacture tendered to it for operation; that any railroad be allowed to operate its own sleeping car business; that The Pullman Company be required to furnish through-line sleeping car service to any railroad; and that the company eliminate its exclusive dealing contracts with the railroads.[89]

The decision left one vital question unanswered, namely, whether Pullman, Inc. should dispose of its operating or manufacturing subsidiary. On January 22, 1944, this question was resolved by leaving the election between the two alternatives to Pullman, Inc.,[90] a step which foreshadowed the inadequate relief which the Government was eventually to obtain in this case.

Judge Biggs, in his dissent, recognized the drawbacks inherent in the court decision. He argued that the Pullman organization, rather than being allowed a choice in the matter, should be required to sell the *manufacturing* part of its business. Judge Biggs reasoned as follows: If permitted a choice, Pullman will almost certainly elect to retain the manufacturing subsidiary and sell the operating company. It would be extremely difficult to find a bona fide independent purchaser for the operating company, thus necessitating a sale of its facilities to the railroads.[91] Judge Biggs did not relish this prospect. Moreover, he thought it was a "striking anomaly that the tort-feasor, Pullman–Standard, should be left in a position where it can profit greatly by way of the monopoly from the sale of light-weight sleeping cars in the postwar market."[92]

However, Judge Biggs did not prevail. As he had predicted and in accordance with the court's judgment, Pullman elected to sell its operating business. After extensive negotiations, it accepted the purchase offer made jointly by railroads doing over 95 percent of the nation's passenger business. The court approved acceptance of this offer, and on March 31, 1947, the Supreme Court, being equally divided, affirmed without opinion.[93] This brought to an end seven years of litigation in the course of which divorcement was granted. Yet, instead of being used as a means to provide an open market, the separation of Pullman's operating and manufacturing subsidiaries came to be regarded as an end in itself.

The sale of Pullman's operating facilities to the railroads was unfortunate. It created the potential danger of: (1) vesting in the railroads monopoly control of a nationwide competing system of transportation; (2) perpetuating the Pullman manufacturing monopoly; and (3) resulting in discrimination against the smaller railroads.

As to the danger of monopoly control over competing transportation systems, the Government had argued that:

> [P]urchase of The Pullman Company by the railroads would reduce to common ownership and control an important part of the passenger transportation system of the United States. There is no qualitative difference between common ownership of Pullman cars and common ownership of all rail passenger cars. Common ownership of the sleeping car business would be unlike individual ownership by the railroads of all passengers coaches. In the passenger coach field the railroads compete for coach travel. They own all the coaches but ownership is individual, not common. Incentive to compete among themselves as to sleeping car service . . . as well as to make sleeping car service competitive with coach service will be lacking under common ownership. . . . Competition between coach and sleeping car service will be eliminated. As in all cases involving large investments the inevitable tendency, absent competition, is to use the existing equipment until it is completely worn out.
>
> There is the same objection to railroad ownership of sleeping cars as there would be if the railroads were to purchase all passenger busses, or all of the air lines or all of the water transportation. In any of these situations such a purchase would permit the railroads to monopolize an important means of public transportation and suppress or develop it as they chose, regardless of public needs. It would vest in the railroads monopoly control of a competing system of transportation. . . .[94]

As to the danger of perpetuating Pullman's manufacturing monopoly, the Government had argued that:

> [S]ale of The Pullman Company to the railroads may easily defeat the express order of the Court directing complete separation of the operating company from the manufacturing company. This is occasioned by the existence of inter-lacing relations among several large banks and insurance companies, Pullman Incorporated and the railroads. The Morgan, Vanderbilt, and Mellon interests have substantial representation on the present directorate of Pullman Incorpo-rated which has elected to retain ownership of Pullman–Standard Car Manu-facturing Company. These financial interests likewise dominate a large number of the great railroads of the country, both through ownership, and more importantly, through the financial syndicates which float the securities of such railroads. Equally important in the financial operations of the railroads and Pullman Incorporated are several of the largest insurance companies which invest in railway securities.[95]

From the evidence at hand, the Government had concluded that through the:

> . . . banker and insurance nexus the railroads are affiliated with Pullman Incor-porated which owns, and will continue to own, Pullman–Standard Car Manu-facturing Company. If they purchase the operating company the railroads might still purchase substantially all of their sleeping car requirements from the Pullman–Standard Car Manufacturing Company. If the Court's decree is to become effective and competition restored in the sleeping car operating and the sleeping car manufacturing fields, such affiliations must be avoided.[96]

Pointing to the danger of discrimination against the smaller railroads, the Gov-ernment had warned that:

> [S]ale of the sleeping car business to the railroads might cause a marked deterioration in the service on small roads. Under the plan submitted by the railroads the stock would be distributed in accordance with the percentage of sleeping cars operated by the several railroads. This means that the twenty railroads making the offer would own 81 percent of the stock and would effec-tively control the policies of the new company. The smaller roads would get only such types of equipment and services that the controlling roads did not want, thus lessening the smaller road's ability to compete for traffic. The small roads would become captives of the large roads. The public traveling on small roads would be required to use inferior accommodations or shift their patronage to the larger roads supplying more desirable accommodations.[97]

In spite of these objections, the sale of the Pullman operating subsidiary to the railroads was given judicial sanction. Similar approval was granted by the I.C.C. on May 6, 1947, after a finding that "the proposed pooling will be in the interest of better service to the public and of economy in operation," and that such pooling "will not unduly restrain competition."[98] With this opinion, litigation in the Pullman case came to an end.

What did the seven years of litigation accomplish? What affirmative relief was obtained? How effective was that relief in destroying monopoly power and restoring vigorous competition? To be sure, Pullman's manufacturing and operating business were divorced. The new railroad-owned servicing company was required to purchase new cars on the basis of competitive bidding. The railroads promised that, after an interim three-year period, the jointly owned servicing company would be sold to a purchaser not connected with either the railroads or Pullman, Inc.[99] Finally, the new operating company was required to provide, upon request, service for cars not owned by it. The suit has thus succeeded in removing some of Pullman's monopolistic restraints which previously prevented the railroads from purchasing and owning sleeping cars operated over their lines. The decree made possible, to some extent, the entry of newcomers into the manufacture of sleeping cars and similar equipment. It put an end to the exploitation of the railroads by the Pullman organization.

On the other side of the ledger, however, must be entered the failure to provide for the *financial* as well as physical divorcement of Pullman's subsidiaries. The number and strength of interlocking directorships between Pullman, Inc. and the railroads (or companies which are the source of railroad financing) were left untouched. The Pullman operating company was sold without requiring the would-be purchaser to demonstrate its complete independence of all connections, direct or indirect, with Pullman, Inc. In view of the financial ties between Pullman–Standard and the railroad-owned operating company, and in spite of the "competitive bidding" provision, a potential newcomer in the manufacturing field was thus made to face considerable odds against his successful entry.

Here a great opportunity was muffed. The courts could have created three independent groups in the industry: (1) two or more car manufacturers, (2) an independent operating company, and (3) the railroads. This could have been done preferably by ordering the sale of the Pullman manufacturing subsidiary to a bona fide independent or by forcing the sale of the operating company to a bidder other than the railroads. There would thus have come into being three separate groups whose economic self-interest was such as to promote development of better equipment and service, competition between rival modes of transportation, and freedom from monopolistic domination or influence over the manufacture of sleeping cars. Without punishing Pullman for past offenses, provision could have been made for more effective competition in the future.

As it turned out, the concentration of economic power was not substantially lessened. The seat of monopoly power was merely transferred from a giant firm to a highly concentrated industry. Divorcement was obtained, but it was carried out in a manner which largely ignored the economic realities of intercorporate relationships.

Conclusions and Recommendations

To the extent that the above case studies are representative—and an examination of the record would seem to indicate that they are[100]—we may conclude that the relief obtained by the Government in Section 2 cases under the Sherman Act has generally been inadequate; that the Government, while successful in establishing the defendants' violation, has not been able to secure the kind of remedy which would dissipate the effects of monopoly and encourage the restoration of a more competitive industrial structure; that the Government, therefore, has won many a law suit but lost many a cause.[101]

There are many factors which explain the Government's failure, except in a handful of cases, to get meaningful dissolution, divorcement and divestiture relief. The most important factor is the attitude of the courts to this problem. The courts have exhibited a disinclination to undertake drastic economic reorganization of a monopolized industry and have, therefore, often failed to establish the structural prerequisites for vigorous competition. They have generally refrained from breaking asunder what man has illegally joined together.

The "shyness" of the courts in this respect stems not only from the temperament of many judges but also from a lack of training in the economic problems involved in monopoly cases. Perhaps it is this lack of comprehension of intricate economic forces rather than an unwillingness to grant drastic relief which is responsible for the *ad hoc*, uncomplicated and readily implemented remedies traditionally embraced by the courts. Perhaps it is a lack of expertness in wielding the knife which has made the courts so reluctant to sanction the drastic economic surgery necessary to strike at the core of the monopoly cancer.

Another factor influencing the relief obtained in monopoly cases is the method of presenting such cases to the courts. Since relief cannot be obtained until the Government has proved a Section 2 violation, the evidence is presented for the primary purpose of showing the existence of monopoly. Usually the record contains little concerning the specifics of relief, and relief problems are not considered until the conclusion of the trial and the announcement of the court's opinion. In most cases, therefore, the court has no evidence before it as to the nature of the remedy necessary to neutralize the effects of the monopoly. It must frequently proceed on the basis of conjecture as to what the Government's ultimate relief problems will be.

In addition, the preoccupation of the trial staff with developing the kind of record which will substantiate its monopoly charges tends to deemphasize the importance of a well-organized and comprehensive plan for relief. The legal problem of "winning" the case is permitted to take precedence over the economic problem of obtaining adequate remedial action. There arises, therefore, a tendency to improvise relief measures when reality demands that a concrete relief program be spelled out. Often the trial attorneys "estimate" how much by way of relief the judge is likely to grant rather than considering what kind of relief is required to effectuate the purposes of the law. The result is that frequently the battle is won while the war is lost.

The analysis of the above cases demonstrates to the writer that the present system of presenting and deciding antitrust cases fails to achieve the results demanded by the Sherman Act. The inadequacies of present practices are mostly self-imposed by the courts and the Antitrust Division: the solution to the problem is within their domain. While it is unlikely that the judges can be schooled in the intricacies of economic theory or the complex pattern of economic reality, competent economic counsel can be made available to assist them in the analysis of monopoly cases, and to render assistance in the formulation of adequate relief programs. The courts could either employ full-time economic experts or call upon professional consultants from the ranks of industry, government, or the universities.[102] On the basis of comprehensive industry studies by experts in the field, the courts might then more readily invoke such "drastic" remedies as dissolution, divorcement and divestiture.[103]

While the Antitrust Division is aware of the difficult problems faced in securing adequate relief,[104] it is recommended that its requests for dissolution, divorcement and divestiture be based on more thorough-going studies of relief alternatives. Such studies should be made by an adequate staff of economists, industry specialists, and engineers (within the Antitrust Division) who possess the technical qualifications essential for the development of a practical, yet economically meaningful and effective relief program. A preponderance of evidence should be presented to demonstrate that the relief proposals are not only necessary but also practical and feasible. The Government should attempt to prove, with more convincing evidence than it has in the past, that dissolution, divorcement and divestiture is, in particular cases, the *only* remedy capable of neutralizing monopoly power and restoring competition in accordance with the mandate of the Sherman Act. To establish the case for its relief proposals, the Government might emphasize and effectively demonstrate that a company's size is not necessarily the guarantor of economic efficiency; that the company's favorable profit record is often the result of its coercive power in the market place rather than its efficiency of operation; that the dissolution of a giant might actually enhance rather than diminish the efficiency of its operating components; that dissolution in particular cases would not impair our ability effectively to mobilize the country's resources in times of national emergency. Most important of all, any remedy proposed must be specific; it must show why plant X has to be divested; how such a plant can operate as a functionally independent unit; why such divestiture is necessary for the dissipation of monopoly power; how such divestiture will in fact be instrumental in promoting greater competition, etc.

In requesting drastic relief, the Government should point to cases where such relief was granted and where as a consequence satisfactory results were achieved. Our experience under the Public Utility Holding Company Act of

1935,[105] for example, might be cited to show how industrial efficiency was increased in many instances through dissolution, divorcement and divestiture.[106] Similarly, innumerable cases could be cited where drastic relief was requested and denied and where, as a result, competition was not restored.

In making its case for a particular relief program, the Government should not rely entirely on the expert testimony of the Antitrust Division economists. Since the courts might consider such testimony as being of an *ex parte* nature, greater reliance should be placed on expert and disinterested witnesses drawn from industry, government, and the universities. In this connection, consideration might also be given to a more frequent use of Section 6(e) of the Federal Trade Commission Act which authorizes the Commission:

> Upon the application of the Attorney General to investigate and make recommendations for the readjustment of the business of any corporation alleged to be violating the antitrust Acts in order that the corporation may thereafter maintain its organization, management, and conduct of business in accordance with law.[107]

The powers here granted should be used very selectively, however, in order to minimize the problems connected with effective inter-agency cooperation; to minimize delay in the settlement of cases; and to conserve the Commission's energies for comprehensive investigations affecting the national economy.

During the trial and in the course of relief hearings the Government should impress upon the courts what effective competition means and what the prerequisites for such competition are. The courts should be shown that one price in one place at one time is not necessarily the manifestation of competition; that such price uniformity is often imposed arbitrarily from *outside* the market rather than being determined by the forces of supply and demand within the market. The Government should impress upon the courts that, in an oligopolistic market structure, administered prices, price leadership, price uniformity, and price inflexibility are often as valid a proof of monopoly power as the domination of an industry by a single firm. The distinction between active, vigorous competition in the economic sense and psychological competition which consists merely of a gentlemanly sales rivalry between competing producers should be stressed.[108] In short, the Government must emphasize and re-emphasize that competition from the viewpoint of the individual businessman does not necessarily meet the standards of competition from the viewpoint of the economy as a whole.[109]

If, after having been advised by the Antitrust Division of all the considerations and relief alternatives, the courts are still reluctant to undertake the kind of reorganization necessary to accomplish the purpose of the Sherman Act, it might be advisable for Congress to consider passage of a new antitrust act. By this suggestion, it is not implied that the relief powers under the Sherman Act are inadequate. We do believe, however, that judging by past performance, these powers have not been used to a sufficiently far reaching extent. The new law should be designed to supplement, not supersede, the Sherman Act. It should be modeled perhaps along the lines of the Public Utility Holding Company Act of 1935, which proved so successful an instrument in the dissolution of vast utility empires. The new law should clearly set forth the evils against which antitrust action is to be directed and specify some concrete and detailed, yet comprehensive, standards for the application of the dissolution, divorcement and divestiture remedy. It should constitute a clear mandate to the courts that any firm found to possess monopolistic power be dissolved into its component parts, unless such firm can prove its size to be necessary for the maintenance of efficiency.[110] By placing a new "charter of freedom" on the statute books, congressional intent to promote competition might be more readily effectuated.

Notes

1. Address by Dr. John M. Blair before the Economic Workshop at the University of Minnesota, July 12, 1949. As used in the subsequent discussion, "divestiture refers to situations where the defendants are required to divest themselves of property securities or other assets. Divorcement is . . . used to indicate the effect of a decree where certain types of divestiture are ordered. It is especially applicable to cases where the purpose of the proceeding is to secure relief against anti-trust abuses flowing from [vertically] integrated ownership and control. The term 'dissolution' is generally used to refer to any situation where the dissolving of an allegedly illegal combination or association is involved, including the use of divestiture and divorcement as methods of achieving that end. While the foregoing definitions differentiate three aspects of remedies, the terms are frequently used interchangeably without any technical distinctions in meaning." Oppenheim, *Cases on Federal Anti-Trust Laws,* p. 885 (1948).

2. 26 Stat. 209 (1890), as amended, 15 U.S.C. 1 *et seq.* (1946).

3. 15 U.S.C. 2 (1946).

4. While the Sherman Act contains no specific provisions for equitable relief to the public on account of violations of the Act, Section 4 does invest the courts with jurisdiction not only to *restrain* violations (by means of injunction), but also to *prevent* violations (by means of injunction "or otherwise"). The courts thus have the power to dissolve an unlawful combination and can use that power whenever necessary to give complete relief. *United States* v. *Great Lakes Towing Co.,* 217 Fed. 656 (N.D. Ohio 1914). As Oppenheim points out, it is essential to recognize "that the essence of equity jurisdiction is the power of the court to mould the decree to the necessities of the particular case. Invocation by the United States of the general authority of a court of equity under the Sherman Act enables the court to exercise a wide discretion in framing its decree so as to give effective and adequate relief. Since the public interest is directly involved, the court may go further in giving relief than it does when only private rights are involved. The Sherman Act vests the court with jurisdiction not only to 'restrain' but also to 'prevent' violations of the Act by injunctions 'or otherwise.' " Oppenheim, op. cit., pp. 885–6.

5. 221 U.S. 1 (1911).

6. 221 U.S. 106 (1911).

7. See 328 U.S. 781 (1946).

8. Blair, op. cit. for a further discussion of the *Tobacco* case and the dissolution decree of 1911, see Jones, *The Trust Problem in the United States,* pp. 123–63, 452–74 (1929);

Seager and Gulick, *Trust and Corporation Problems,* pp. 149–95 (1929); Stevens, *Industrial Combinations and Trusts,* pp. 440–61, 472–516 (1913); Cox, *Competition in the American Tobacco Industry* (1932); Hale, "Trust Dissolution: 'Atomizing' Business Units of Monopolistic Size," *Columbia Law Review,* pp. 617–20, 628–31 (1940).

9. *United States* v. *United States Steel Corp.,* 251 U.S. 417 (1920).

10. Ibid., p. 451.

11. *United States* v. *International Harvester Co.,* 274 U.S. 693 (1927): "[T]he law . . . does not make the mere size of a corporation, however impressive, or the existence of an unexerted power on its part, an offense, when unaccompanied by unlawful conduct in the exercise of its power." Ibid., p. 708.

12. In this connection it is interesting to observe that less than two months after the *Steel* opinion, the Supreme Court decided *United States* v. *Reading Co.,* 253 U.S. 26 (1920), and decreed that the defendant company be dissolved. The Court held that the company's "dominating power was not obtained by normal expansion to meet the demands of a business growing as a result of superior and enterprising management, but by deliberate, calculated purchase for control. That such a power, so obtained regardless of the use made of it, constitutes a menace to and an undue restraint upon interstate commerce within the meaning of the Anti-Trust Act has been frequently held by this court." Ibid., p. 57. The Court concluded, therefore, that "for flagrant violation of the first and second sections of the Anti-Trust Act, the relations between the Reading Company, the Reading Railway Company and the Reading Coal Company and between these companies and the Central Railroad of New Jersey must be so dissolved as to give to each of them a position in all respects independent and free from stock or other control of either of the other corporations." Ibid., pp. 59, 60.

Of special significance in this opinion is the Court's assertion that the existence of a combination and its inherent market power, *regardless of the use made of it,* constitutes a violation of the law. By making monopoly power, rather than its exercise, the crucial test of legality, the Court followed the ruling of *Northern Securities* v. *United States,* 193 U.S. 197 (1904) and *United States* v. *Union Pacific R.R.,* 226 U.S. 61 (1912) (as well as the dissent in the Steel case), and seemingly rejected the subsequent precedents of *United States* v. *United Shoe Machinery Co.,* 247 U.S. 32 (1918) and *United States* v. *United States Steel Corp.,* 251 U.S. 417 (1920). Of further significance is the fact that in the Reading case the Court deemed a 33 percent control over the market as constituting monopoly, whereas in the Shoe Machinery and Steel cases the same Court held that a 95 and 65 percent control over the market, respectively, did not come within the meaning of the statute. How, it may be asked, can such widely divergent opinions be issued by the same court in a period of three years?

The answer seems to be that only seven Justices participated in the Shoe Machinery and Steel cases, while the full Court heard and decided the Reading case. Both the Shoe Machinery and Steel cases were decided by a 4–3 vote—Justices White, McKenna, Holmes, and Van Devanter voting with the majority; Justices Pitney, Clarke, and Day with the minority; and Justices Brandeis and McReynolds abstaining. Had Brandeis and McReynolds cast their votes (as they did in the Reading case), the Shoe Machinery and Steel decisions would have gone down as 5–4 victories instead of 4–3 defeats for the Government.

One other question warrants explanation, *viz.* why the Reading case, since it was decided by a full court, never became the controlling precedent in subsequent litigation. The answer seems to lie in the drastic changes which occurred in the composition of the Court shortly after the Reading decision was announced. By 1922, four Justices had retired: White, Pitney, Clarke, and Day. Of these, Pitney, Clarke, and Day had voted with the minority in the Shoe Machinery and Steel cases, and with the majority in the Reading case. Chief Justice White, on the other hand, had voted against the Government in all three cases. Thus, of the retiring Justices, three could be classified as "antitrust minded" while one was not. By contrast, all of their successors had little if any sympathy for a vigorous anti-trust program: Taft (1921), Sutherland (1922), Butler (1922), and Sanford who wrote the majority opinion in the Harvester case (1923). By 1923, therefore, only Brandeis and McReynolds remained (to be joined by Stone in 1925) to raise their dissenting voice against judicial acquiescence in the combination and merger movement of the Harding–Coolidge–Hoover era.

13. *Smaller War Plants Corporation, Economic Concentration and World War II*, Senate Doc. No. 206, Part 1, 79th Cong., 2d Sess. (1946); United States Federal Trade Comm'n, *Report on the Present Trend of Corporate Mergers and Acquisitions* (1947); United States Federal Trade Comm'n, *The Concentration of Productive Facilities, 1947* (1949); National Resources Committee, *The Structure of the American Economy* (1947).

14. Among the more important dissolution, divorcement, and divestiture proceedings in this group are those filed against Aluminum Company of America (1937), Paramount Pictures, Inc. (1938), The Pullman Company (1940), General Electric (1941), National Lead Company (1944), Libby–Owens–Ford (1945), American Can Company (1946), Continental Can Company (1946), A.B. Dick Company (1946), American Society of Composers, Authors, and Publishers (1947), United Shoe Machinery Corp. (1947), Armour & Company (1948), Western Electric Company, Inc. (1949), E.I. du Pont de Nemours & Company (1949), The New York Great Atlantic & Pacific Tea Company, Inc. (1949), Celanese Corporation of America (1949), Lee Shubert (1950), Standard Oil Company of California (1950), and General Outdoor Advertising Corp. (1950).

15. Testifying before the Senate Subcommittee on Appropriations in 1946, Attorney General Clark (now Mr. Justice Clark of the Supreme Court) stated the need for restoring competition "by the seldom used processes of dissolution, divorcement, and divestiture." Similarly, in his Annual Report of June 30, 1947, he said: "In regard to monopolies, I have encouraged the application of the remedies of divestiture and divorcement in civil suits brought under Section 2 of the Sherman Act, as the most expeditious means of eradicating this economic evil. The ramifications of monopoly are myriad and, when allowed to develop unchecked, have an effect upon every aspect of the economic scene. Nowhere is this effect more apparent than in the fields of production and pricing and upon no one is the impact of monopolistic policies more severe than upon the small businessman." *Report of the Attorney General*, p. 8 (1947).

16. Needless to say, many of the recent Section 2 cases are not directed against the cruder forms of monopoly (as typified by the pre-1911 Standard Oil and American Tobacco companies). They are concerned, instead, with oligopoly—a type of market structure where a *few* sellers (the "Big Three" and the "Big Four") are dominant. Under this type of market organization, the entry of newcomers is effectively deterred—not so much by the threat of economic reprisals as by the size and entrenched power of existing firms. Under oligopoly, moreover, a seller no longer can afford to be independent in his choice of a price policy. He must, of necessity, take the reaction of his rivals into account. He must anticipate that price cutting will inevitably cause his large competitors to follow suit with the result that the market is shared as it was before—only at a lower level of prices and profits. It is this certainty that price cuts will eventually be met, it is this fear of retaliation, that leads to conservative and non-aggressive price policies in many of our oligopolistic industries.

The economic result of oligopoly pricing is substantially similar to that which would obtain if but a single firm dominated a given field. The result is collusion—not in the common sense meaning of the word, to be sure—but parallel action, nevertheless, as far as the effects of market behavior are concerned. As Fritz Machlup observed not long ago:

"A covenant signed with blood, an agreement signed with ink, an understanding without written words, concerted acts approved with a wink or a nod, a common course of action followed without physical communication—these may be different methods of collusion, but the differences are irrelevant if the effects are the same." Machlup, What's Best for the Competitive Enterprise System?, *Delivered Pricing and the Future of American Business,* p. 195 (1948).

17. In discussing the choice of a remedy in civil antitrust cases, Justice Jackson stressed the importance of granting such economic relief as will effectively prevent future violations and be adequate in restoring competition in the industry concerned: "The District Court is not obliged to assume, contrary to common experience, that a violator of the antitrust laws will relinquish the fruits of his violation more completely than the court requires him to do. . . . When the purpose to restrain trade appears from a clear violation of law, it is not necessary that all of the untraveled roads to that end be left open and that only the worn one be closed. The usual ways to the prohibited goal may be blocked against the proven transgressor. . . . In an equity suit, the end to be served is not punishment of past transgression, nor is it merely to end specific illegal practices. A public interest served by such civil suits is that they effectively pry open to competition a market that has been closed by defendant's illegal restraints. If this decree accomplishes less than that, the Government has won a lawsuit and lost a cause." *International Salt Co.* v. *United States,* 332 U.S. 392, 400, 401 (1947).

18. *United States* v. *Paramount Pictures, Inc.,* 334 U.S. 131 (1948). The motion picture cases represent what is probably the Government's greatest economic victory in the sixty year history of antitrust enforcement. For more than eleven years the Department of Justice battled through three court decisions, a war, and two intervening consent decrees in order finally to achieve the complete divorcement of the major motion picture producers from their affiliated exhibition outlets. Moreover, the Government obtained, in addition to vertical divorcement, a considerable measure of horizontal dissolution on the exhibition level.

Throughout, the major question in the motion picture cases was not the guilt or innocence of the defendants but rather the finding of a suitable remedy to prevent future violations. And on this question, the district court was adamant; it stated that, while vertical integration is not a *per se* violation of the Sherman Act, vertical integration does become illegal if conceived with a *specific intent* to control the market or if used to create a *power* to control the market. Furthermore, the court held that vertical integration in this industry was a definite means by which unlawful competitive methods were effectuated. Hence, the court concluded that there had been collective use of monopoly power and that "divorcement . . . appears to be the only adequate means of terminating the conspiracy and preventing any resurgence of monopoly power on the part of the . . . defendants." 85 F. Supp. 881, 896 (S.D. N.Y. 1949).

19. 148 F.2d 416 (2d Cir. 1945). The following discussion of the aluminum litigation is based on Adams, The Aluminum Case: Legal Victory—Economic Defeat, *American Economic Review,* p. 915 (1951).

20. 44 F. Supp. 97 (S.D. N.Y. 1941).

21. 148 F.2d 416 (2d Cir. 1945). The case was certified to the Circuit Court of Appeals for the Second Circuit on June 12, 1944 (322 U.S. 716 (1944)) because the Supreme Court was unable to obtain a quorum to sit on the appeal (320 U.S. 708 (1942)).

22. Rostow, *A National Policy for the Oil Industry,* p. 127 (1948).

23. 58 Stat. 765 (1944), 50 U.S.C. 1611 (1946). The express intention of Congress was, among others, to "give maximum aid in the re-establishment of a peacetime economy of free independent enterprise . . .; discourage monopolistic practices and to strengthen and preserve the competitive position of small business concerns in an econ-

198 SELECTED POLICY STUDIES

omy of free enterprise; . . . foster the development of new independent enterprise; . . . dispose of surplus property as promptly as feasible without fostering monopoly or restraint of trade. . . ." Ibid.

24. 50 U.S.C. 1627(b) (1946).

25. 50 U.S.C. 1629 (1946).

26. The Government relief petition was exceedingly mild. It merely requested a partial horizontal disintegration of Alcoa. What the Government should have demanded as a minimum additional requirement was that Alcoa be enjoined from any further *vertical* integration—especially in the fabrication field. Some such requirement—limited perhaps to a period of five years—was essential to deprive Alcoa of its power to squeeze independents in the future as it had done in the past. Moreover, as a House committee investigating the aluminum industry recently pointed out, "it is not price competition of ingot that worries any of the 'Big Three,' for that question seems to have been resolved by a price leadership pattern that suits all of them. While the courts may have their eye on the price of pig as an indication of monopoly pricing, it is in reality a vertical organization of each of the 'Big Three' from ingot production to finished products that is the hazard to the survival and growth of new independent producers. It is the same integrated organizational structure which prevents the widest possible use of aluminum for purposes which are not only possible but which would prove a great boon to the public." House Report No. 255, 82d Cong., 1st Sess., p. 24 (1951).

27. *United States* v. *Aluminum Company of America,* 91 F. Supp. 333 (S.D. N.Y. 1950).

28. After an extensive investigation of the aluminum industry, a House committee appraised the competitive potential of the Canadian company in the United States market as follows: "Thus far, there are only three primary aluminum producers in the United States. Alcan [Alted] does not constitute the fourth competitor in domestic markets as its pricing policy (despite its lower costs) is to follow Alcoa's price. . . . Competition would not be fostered if instead of increasing the number of American producers [in the wartime expansion program], this Government aided the further growth of Alcan. . . . Alcan lives and operates in a world of trade beyond the United States antitrust laws and often unfriendly to the United States philosophy of competition. Alcan for years was the leader of the European aluminum cartel. Although no longer a member, Alcan is subject to influences in world markets that restrain trade. Alcan and its various competitors in other countries jointly own aluminum companies in a number of countries including Norway, Australia, and China. Although the European cartel has formally ended after Alcoa's prosecution, Alcan's behavior in world markets, including the United States, necessarily departs from United States concepts of competition. Therefore, further expansion of Alcan in United States markets can hardly be regarded as a healthy gain for competition." *Committee Report,* op. cit., p. 32.

29. See 91 F. Supp. 333, 400 (S.D. N.Y. 1950).

30. Committee Report, op. cit., pp. 29, 30.

31. That this is not a desirable prospect was pointed out by the Monopoly Subcommittee of the House Judiciary Committee. As the Committee observed, "Canadian aluminum is subject to any regulations placed by the Canadian Government and any agreements entered into with the United Kingdom and other Commonwealth countries. In other words, British Empire countries have a preferential position. In October 1950, Alcan had to reduce its offer to this country of 1951 and 1952 deliveries because of increased obligations to the United Kingdom. In the 1939 and 1940 loan agreement between Alcan and the United Kingdom, Alcan agreed to give the British Government first call annually on 107,500 metric tons. In the 1950 agreement with the British Government, Alcan gave another first call of 200,000 metric tons annually for a long term. Perhaps the United

States Government also could obtain a first call on any additional capacity Alcan may build. However, that capacity will always be under the jurisdiction of another country, no matter how friendly, and that is not the same thing as being fully accessible to the United States at all times." *Committee Report,* op. cit., pp. 32–33.

32. In all fairness to Judge Knox, it is to be remembered that Learned Hand, sitting on a higher court, had refused dissolution and ordered that only if the Government's surplus disposal program failed to create substantial competition in the industry was the trial court authorized to consider dissolution. Judge Knox might have felt that this decision by Hand restricted his choice, since the appearance of Kaiser and Reynolds arguably had created "substantial" competition. Moreover, Judge Knox was probably aware of the possibility that a number of future developments could subvert the effort to end the common control exercised by Alcoa and Alted, when he decided to retain jurisdiction of the case for another five years. Declared Judge Knox: "Together, Limited and Alcoa are in a position at any time, to restrain effectively the growth of Reynolds and Kaiser. Accordingly inasmuch as irreparable harm can result from a delay in remedies, it is unwise for this court to relinquish jurisdiction of this action until it is assured that the aluminum industry has been oriented in a lawful direction." *United States* v. *Aluminum Company of America,* 91 F. Supp. 333, 418 (S.D. N.Y. 1950).

33. 63 F. Supp. 513 (S.D. N.Y. 1945), *aff'd,* 332 U.S. 319 (1947).

34. 332 U.S. 319, 352, 353 (1947).

35. Such proof is, of course, very difficult. But by making use of factual economic and technological data and by drawing from the experience and opinions of experts in the field, the Government could do much to alleviate the judicial reluctance to employ the more drastic but more effective remedies of dissolution, divorcement, and divestiture. See Dession, "The Trial of Economic and Technological Issues of Fact," *Yale Law Journal,* p. 1019 (1949), for a discussion of the judicial and legal techniques and considerations involved in such proceedings.

36. There has been judicial recognition that the Government cannot establish with certainty the economic effect a given course of action will have in the future. Hence, the rule arose that all doubts regarding remedies should be resolved in favor of the Government and against an adjudged monopolist. See *Hartford Empire Co.* v. *United States,* 323 U.S. 286, 409 (1945); *United States* v. *Bausch and Lomb Co.,* 321 U.S. 707, 726 (1944). Unfortunately, despite this rule, the Government has found it difficult to establish the propriety of an effective remedy.

37. 332 U.S. 319, 352 (1947).

38. Ibid., pp. 366, 367.

39. For a penetrating discussion of this case, see Zlinkoff and Barnard, "The Supreme Court and a Competitive Economy: 1946 Term," *Columbia Law Review,* pp. 933–948 (1947).

40. 83 F. Supp. 284 (N.D. Ohio 1949), *modified and aff'd,* 71 Sup.Ct. 971 (1951).

41. 83 F. Supp. 284 (N.D. Ohio 1949).

42. Ibid., pp. 306, 307.

43. Ibid., pp. 306, 308.

44. Ibid.

45. Ibid.

46. Ibid., p. 310.

47. The final judgment, as is so often the case, was not published.

48. The injunctions are contained in paragraphs V–IX of the district court's final judgment.

49. Paragraph VIII, final judgment.

50. The direct appeal of this case to the Supreme Court was allowed under Section 2

of the Expediting Act of 1903, 32 Stat. 823 (1903), 15 U.S.C. 29 (1946), as amended by Section 17 of the Act of June 25, 1948, 62 Stat. 869 (1948), 15 U.S.C. 29 (Supp. 1950).

51. Actually defendant attacked the district court decision in 206 assignments of error, including 69 alleged errors in the findings of fact, 26 in the conclusions of law, and 62 based on the court's refusal to make new and additional findings. In spite of the fact that the Supreme Court considered these assignments as unduly repetitious and—in part— frivolous, it nevertheless agreed to consider the appeal. Cf. *Local 167* v. *United States,* 291 U.S. 293, 296 (1934); *Phillips & Colby Constr. Co.* v. *Seymour,* 91 U.S. 646, 648 (1876).

52. 71 Sup.Ct. 971 (1951).

53. The court was strangely divided on this case. Justices Black, Douglas and Minton signed the majority opinion, Reed wrote a concurring opinion in which Vinson joined, Jackson and Frankfurter wrote separate dissenting opinions, while Burton and Clark did not participate. On the divestiture issue Black, Douglas and Minton voted to uphold the district court, while Reed, Vinson, Jackson and Frankfurter voted to reverse the lower court judgment.

54. *Brief for Appellants,* pp. 22–28, 196–198, *Timken Roller Bearing Co.* v. *United States,* 71 Sup.Ct. 971 (1951).

55. 71 Sup.Ct. 971, 979 (1951). ". . . not all agreements are conspiracies and not all restraints of trade are unlawful. In a world of tariffs, trade barriers, empire or domestic preferences, and various forms of parochialism from which we are by no means free, I think a rule that it is restraint of trade to enter a foreign market through a separate subsidiary of limited scope is virtually to foreclose foreign commerce of many kinds." Ibid.

56. 71 Supp.Ct. 971, 978 (1951).

57. "Of course, it is not for this Court to formulate economic policy as to foreign commerce. But the conditions controlling foreign commerce may be relevant here. When as a matter of cold fact the legal, financial, and government policies deny opportunities for exportation from this country and importation into it, arrangements that afford such opportunities to American enterprise may not fall under the ban of a fair construction of the Sherman Law because comparable arrangements regarding domestic commerce come within its condemnation." Ibid.

58. 83 F. Supp. 284, 310 (N.D. Ohio 1949).

59. Ibid., pp. 293, 294, 298.

60. Ibid., pp. 298, 301, 306.

61. Ibid., pp. 301, 306.

62. Ibid., pp. 304, 307.

63. Ibid., p. 314.

64. "If all the impediments to foreign trade existed ever since 1914, which became more and more pronounced to the present day, why were the contracting parties, defendant, British Timken and French Timken so concerned about airtight agreements to keep each one within its own commercial domain? The repeated and persistent provisions of the successive contracts, for territorial restriction, contradict any claim of lack of ability to compete." 83 F. Supp. 284, 317 (S.D. Ohio 1949).

65. 71 Sup.Ct. 971, 977 (1951).

66. See pp. 177–179.

67. "An injunction was entered by the District Court to prohibit the continuation of the objectionable contracts. Violation of that injunction would threaten the appellant and its officers with civil and criminal contempt. . . . The paucity of cases dealing with contempt of Sherman Act injunctions is, I think, an indication of how carefully the decrees are obeyed. . . . Prompt and full compliance with [this] decree should be anticipated." 71 Sup.Ct. 971, 978 (1951).

68. *United States* v. *Paramount Pictures, Inc.,* 334 U.S. 131 (1948).

69. Ibid., pp. 152–153.

70. *United States* v. *Crescent Amusement Co.*, 323 U.S. 173 (1944).

71. Ibid., pp. 189–190.

72. Ibid., p. 189.

73. *United States* v. *Paramount Pictures, Inc.*, 334 U.S. 131, 159 (1948).

74. Paragraph VIII(A), final judgment.

75. *Brief for the Government*, p. 12, *United States* v. *Timken Roller Bearing Co.*, 83 F. Supp. 284 (N.D. Ohio 1949).

76. "Defendant's argument that it will have heavy taxes to pay upon any gain from the sale of its foreign investments cannot be said to be a hardship argument, for it is flatly inconsistent with the position that defendant will suffer any loss from the sale. Taxes are due, on defendant's own assumption, only in the event of profit or capital gain resulting from the enforced sale." Ibid.

77. 332 U.S. 319, 363 (1947).

78. See *Local 167* v. *United States*, 291 U.S. 293, 299 (1934), where doubts concerning the *scope* of relief were thus resolved.

79. 71 Sup.Ct. 971, 976 (1951).

80. 50 F. Supp. 123 (E.D. Pa. 1943); 53 F. Supp. 908 (E.D. pa. 1944); 64 F. Supp. 108 (E.D. Pa. 1946).

81. 50 F. Supp. 123, 127 (E.D. Pa. 1943).

82. Ibid.

83. Ibid., pp. 131, 132.

84. Ibid., p. 132.

85. Ibid., pp. 131, 132.

86. Ibid., p. 132.

87. Ibid.

88. This situation is quite typical of vertically integrated public utilities, where the operating subsidiary is subject to public regulations, but the manufacturing subsidiary is not. Cf. Federal Communications Commission, *Report of the Investigation of the Telephone Industry in the United States,* 74th Cong., 1st Sess. (1939).

89. 50 F. Supp. 123, 137 (E.D. Pa. 1943).

90. 53 F. Supp. 908 (E.D. Pa. 1944).

91. Judge Biggs discussed the problems raised by railroad ownership of the Pullman operating company as follows: "Who will police the operations of the pool in order to make sure that those carriers who contribute to the purchase of Pullman Company stock . . . will treat their partners in the joint enterprises or the public without discrimination? I know of no power presently vested in the Interstate Commerce Commission or in any other government agency which would enable it to regulate such a pool operation." Ibid., p. 910.

92. Ibid.

93. 330 U.S. 806 (1947), *rehearing denied,* 331 U.S. 865 (1947).

94. *Brief for United States,* p. 3, *United States* v. *Pullman Co.,* 64 F. Supp. 108 (E.D. Pa. 1946).

95. Ibid., p. 6.

96. Ibid., p. 7.

97. Ibid., p. 8.

98. 268 I.C.C. 473, 492 (1947).

99. This sale has not as yet taken place and an extension of the "interim" period has recently been authorized by the I.C.C. See 276 I.C.C. 5 (1949).

100. As stated supra note 18, *United States* v. *Paramount Pictures, Inc.,* 334 U.S. 131 (1948), is the exception and not the rule.

101. In all fairness, however, it should be noted that the Antitrust Division has attempted to overcome the apparently insuperable obstacles to divestiture by making increasing use of the consent decree as a means of obtaining relief "just short" of divestiture. Between 1935 and 1950, for example, 134 of the civil cases filed were settled by the consent procedures whereas only 37 cases were tried. See Timberg, "Equitable Relief under the Sherman Act," *University of Illinois Law Forum,* pp. 629, 630 (1950). Under the policy now in force, consent decrees are negotiated in cases "where the Government feels that there is an advantage in taking a present settlement that will immediately alleviate the alleged restraints, instead of pursuing a protracted course of litigation that would permit those restraints to continue for an indefinite future [compare the 'time utility' of the economists]; and where there are good, but not assured, possibilities that the restraints will be removed by the operation of the judgment. Frequently, in these situations, the defendants present an economic justification for less far-reaching relief than the Department may have asked for in its complaint—a justification which the Government is willing to test (without acquiescence) in the light of operations under the judgment." Ibid., p. 657.

As Timberg aptly points out, the Government, under the consent procedure, has been able to secure certain forms of relief which had not generally been granted in litigated judgments. Thus a number of recent consent decrees have provided for the dedication or royalty-free licensing of patents in flat glass products, colored motion picture film, plastics, automotive air brakes, magnetos, cast iron pressure pipe, railway spring products, stainless steel, filters, glass bulbs, fiberglass, air conditioning equipment, disconnecting switches, and stencil duplicating machines and supplies. Ibid., pp. 640, 641. Some of these decrees have provided for the licensing of future patents, typically for a five year period, as well as for the extensive disclosure of know-how to any applicant either without payment or at actual cost. Many have included affirmative injunctive provisions designed to forestall not only the precise violations charged but also all similar violations. Finally, and perhaps most important, recent consent judgments have contained the "Damocles' Sword" provision under which jurisdiction is retained for from three to five years so that the Government may, at the end of the "probationary" period, petition for divestiture relief if competition has not been re-established in the industry. While these decrees have been the vehicle for solving many of the Government's difficult relief problems, their relatively recent origin makes it impossible to appraise and evaluate their economic effectiveness. Unless it can be demonstrated that competition has been successfully restored in industries where these decrees are now operative, the consent procedure can hardly be embraced as an efficacious substitute for dissolution, divorcement and divestiture.

102. In a recent discussion of the relief problem in dissolution, divorcement and divestiture cases, Professor Oppenheim makes the same recommendation. He points out that "[u]pon the judges fall the final responsibility for interpreting the antitrust laws and determining the appropriateness of the 'D.D.D.' remedies in concentration of economic power cases. It is most important, therefore, that consideration should be given to appropriate methods of providing judges with assistance in the form of sound and unbiased advice of economists. Such assistance would help the judges in appraising the relative merits of opposing economic facts and views as developed in the record of particular cases and upon which proof of antitrust violation and the applicability and scope of remedies depend." Oppenheim, "Divestiture as a Remedy under the Federal Antitrust Laws," *George Washington Law Review,* pp. 130–131 (1950).

103. As an alternative to the above suggestion, the courts could make use of Section 7 of the Federal Trade Commission Act, which provides that: "In any suit in equity brought by or under the direction of the Attorney General as provided in the antitrust Acts, the court may, upon the conclusion of the testimony therein, if it shall be then of opinion that

the complainant is entitled to relief, refer said suit to the commission, as a master in chancery, to ascertain and report an appropriate form of decree therein. The commission shall proceed upon such notice to the parties and under such rules of procedure as the court may prescribe, and upon the coming in of such report such exceptions may be filed and such proceedings had in relation thereto as upon the report of a master in other equity causes, but the court may adopt or reject such report, in whole or in part, and enter such decree as the nature of the case may in its judgment require." 38 Stat. 722 (1914), 15 U.S.C. 47 (1946). The former alternative, however, would be preferable, since the proceeding might lose its desired objective flavor if the investigation was conducted by a governmental body.

104. See Timberg, op. cit.

105. 49 Stat. 803 (1935), 15 U.S.C. 79 (1946).

106. See *Hearings before the Monopoly Subcommittee of the House Judiciary Committee*, 81st Cong., 1st Sess., pp. 1460–69 (1950).

107. 38 Stat. 721 (1914), 15 U.S.C. 46(e) (1946).

108. Cf. *American Tobacco Co.* v. *United States,* 328 U.S. 781 (1946).

109. The structural characteristics of workable competition in a particular market may be listed as follows: "1. There must be an appreciable number of sources of supply and an appreciable number of potential customers for substantially the same product or service. Suppliers and customers do not need to be so numerous that each trader is entirely without individual influence, but their number must be great enough that persons on the other side of the market may readily turn away from any particular trader and may find a variety of other alternatives. 2. No trader must be so powerful as to be able to coerce his rivals, nor so large that the remaining traders lack the capacity to take over at least a substantial portion of his trade. 3. Traders must be responsive to incentives of profit and loss; that is, they must not be so large, so diversified, so devoted to political rather than commercial purposes, so subsidized, or otherwise so unconcerned with results in a particular market that their policies are not affected by ordinary commercial incentives arising out of that market. 4. Matters of commercial policy must be decided by each trader separately without agreement with his rivals. 5. New traders must have opportunity to enter the market without handicap other than that which is automatically created by the fact that others are already well established there. 6. Access by traders on one side of the market to those on the other side of the market must be unimpaired except by obstacles not deliberately introduced, such as distance or ignorance of the available alternatives. 7. There must be no substantial preferential status within the market for any important trader or group of traders on the basis of law, politics, or commercial alliances." Corwin Edwards, *Maintaining Competition,* pp. 9–10 (1949).

110. For a proposed bill, drafted along these lines, see *Hearings,* supra note 106, at 1600–25.

12

Business Exemptions from the Antitrust Laws: Their Extent and Rationale

"The statesman, who should attempt to direct private people in what manner they ought to employ their capitals," Adam Smith wrote, "would not only load himself with a most unnecessary attention, but assume an authority which could safely be trusted to no council and senate whatever, and which would nowhere be so dangerous as in the hands of a man who had folly and presumption enough to fancy himself fit to exercise it."[1] Not the state, but the free play of market forces should determine the kinds of goods to be produced, the factors of production to be employed, and the division of distributive shares. Individual economic activity should be coordinated through an autonomous and impartial planning mechanism—one that is external to human control, manipulation, or perversion. Competition should serve the dual function of harnessing the individual to social ends, while depriving him of power so great that, if abused, it would result in harm to his fellows.

This is still the official credo of American free enterprise. It is the ideological facade of N.A.M. slogans—the ritual cant invoked on behalf of "rugged individualism," "rigorous competition," and "undiluted laissez-faire." It is the catechrestic catechism nurtured at home and the redemptive formula promoted abroad. It is, as Galbraith notes, the medicine which American businessmen would not think of taking themselves but which they unhesitatingly prescribe to others—especially to foreigners.[2]

Like other religious beliefs, the free enterprise dogma is no guarantee of behaviorial purity. The doctrine need not be translated into concrete action. Thus, American businessmen can embrace the official position articulated by spokesmen like Henry Ford II. They can proudly proclaim: "We believe that monopolies cause stagnation. We believe that our country could not prosper as it has without the benefit of sound antitrust legislation which has helped to keep us competitive over the past half-century. Though American businessmen may sometimes complain about the interpretation or administration of those laws, we know that—like spinach—they are good for us."[3] This is the official version of the creed. It accepts the regulatory mechanism of competition and the legal framework of antitrust. While tolerant of the government as umpire, it still holds that the government which governs least, governs best. It abhors socialistic interference and abjures the protection of the welfare state—at least, in theory.

The practice is quite different and, as the old proverb tells us, "it ain't what you pray for that counts, it's what you bet on." Despite its ideological precepts, American business seems to follow a course of compromise and pragmatism. It opposes governmental intervention only when such intervention is clearly for someone else's benefit. It seems to have no qualms about accepting "socialistic" favors, privileges, and subsidies. (Apparently, it has no fears that governmental largesse will weaken its moral fibre.) Indeed, American business actively seeks particular forms of government interference. Its richly endowed lobbies wage a constant battle to manipulate the rules of the competitive game, to gain special advantages and immunities, and to secure protective shelter from the impersonal cruelties of competition. There is no frontal attack on the citadel of competition. The strategy is simply one of erosion, attrition, and subversion.

If I am correct, the study of antitrust policy and enforcement represents an unduly restricted approach to the public control problem. Covering an ever-narrowing sector of American industry, it leaves out of account the proliferation of exemptions and exceptions which tend to undermine the core of competitive philosophy and policy. In our preoccupation with antitrust, we may well be straining at a gnat while swallowing the camel.

The extent to which we have forsaken competition as a national policy is most dramatically illustrated by the simple listing of the statutory exemptions from the antitrust laws which appears in the Appendix to this paper. Some of these exemptions are partial, others complete. Some apply to particular industries or organizations, others immunize specific activities and practices. Some were originally installed in periods of depression, others in periods of war or defense mobilization. *All* were secured by the political influence of special interest groups which succeeded in persuading Congress to accord them private commercial advantage—ostensibly to promote some legitimate public purpose.

Obviously, these exemptions are piecemeal responses to particular pressures and circumstances. They do not constitute integral parts of a master plan. Nor can they be easily reconciled or synthesized with the pattern of antitrust control. Their thrust, however, is unmistakable—reflecting a judgment by Congress that competition is not a paramount economic, social, or political objective. The pervasiveness of such exemptions, as Justice Frankfurter observed, indicates that competition is at best a coordinate, not paramount, goal of national policy. "That there is a national policy favoring competition cannot be maintained today without careful qualification. It is only in a blunt, undiscriminating sense that we speak of competition as an ultimate good. Certainly, even in those areas of economic activity where the play of private forces has been subjected only to the negative prohibitions of the Sherman Law, this Court has not held that competition is an absolute." In the exempt industries, this would be even more difficult. "To do so would disregard not only those areas of economic activity . . . in which active regulation has been found necessary to compensate for the inability of competition to provide adequate regulation. It would most strikingly disregard areas where policy has shifted from one of prohibiting restraints on competition to one of providing relief from the rigors of competition. . . ." Therefore, Justice Frankfurter concluded, "it is for us to recognize that encouragement of competition as such has not been considered the single or controlling reliance for safeguarding the public interest."[4]

In the pages which follow, I propose to discuss two major phenomena: exemption by regulation and exemption by administrative preemption.

Exemption by Regulation

The creation of independent regulatory commissions, exercising a potpourri of legislative, administrative, and judicial powers, and armed with the doctrine of primary jurisdiction, today constitutes the single most important explicit antitrust exemption. In creating this headless fourth branch of government, Congress did not intend to underwrite a total abandonment of competition. It did not make the antitrust laws wholly inapplicable to the regulated industries, nor did it authorize the commissions to ignore their policy. At the very least, Congress commanded the commissions, as an administrative matter, to take antitrust considerations into account. But the legislative mandate was so broad as to make commission discretion virtually unlimited.

Originally, Congress had hoped that the commissions would be staffed by men "bred to the facts" and imbued with a dispassionate professional expertise. The commissions, it was thought, would curb the power of the "economic royalists" by substituting rational planning, promotion, and policing for an ineffectual and anachronistic market mechanism. They would make the economic well-being of entire industries their bailiwick, and formulate policies directed "toward broad imaginative ends, conceived in terms of management rather than police."[5] This was the justification for extending the public utility concept from local, "natural" monopolies to nationwide industrial empires in transportation, communications, and energy. "This was the ultimate view that enthralled the New Dealer," says Professor Jaffe. "This was the torrid specter that terrified the world of private industry."[6]

In practice, neither the hopes nor the fears of the 1930's were realized. The independent regulatory commissions turned out to be a disastrous experiment in economic statecraft and an abomination of administrative law. They have been neither administratively independent nor politically responsible.[7] Their vaunted expertise has become a euphemism for red tape, ritualism, and harassment.[8] Canons of judicial ethics have been violated, and commission integrity shaken by periodic scandals.[9] Regulatory policy has been negative, unimaginative, wasteful, and restrictionist—characterized by undue limitation of entry, benign tolerance of mergers, sanction for anticompetitive rate and service agreements, erosion of inter-industry rivalry, and outright suppression of yardstick competition.[10] In short, the commissions turned out to be handmaidens of the regulatees rather than protectors of the public—using their quasi-legislative, quasi-administrative, and quasi-judicial powers to build a never-never land of quasi-solutions.[11]

Two aspects of commission regulation deserve particular emphasis: the proclivity to neo-mercantilist protectionism and the related tendency toward euthanasia of competitive interlopers. Both have been accomplished under the guise of regulating entry, rates, and such business practices as collusive agreements and mergers. In the motor carrier industry, for example, the I.C.C. has repeatedly held that where existing carriers "have expended their money and energy in developing facilities to handle all available traffic, they are entitled to protection against the establishment of what would be tantamount to a new service in competition with them."[12] As long as such carriers had the *physical* capacity to perform a given service, the Commission would deny the entry bid of newcomers who, in the opinion of shippers, could perform the service faster, better, and cheaper. In one, not atypical, case the Commission denied a small trucking company (operating 6 tractors, 9 semi-trailers, and 3 pick-up trucks) the right to expand into two towns with a combined population of 8,115 inhabitants—on the ground that this might injure competing colossi like the Southern Railroad.[13] In exercising its minimum rate powers, as the Brownell Committee found, the Commission apparently made it its duty "both to protect the railroads from motor carrier competition as well as to safeguard the motor carrier industry from 'destructive' competition in its own ranks. Indeed, from the inception of motor carrier regulation to the present day, the power to fix minimum rates has been more significant than the authority to fix maximum charges."[14]

Other commissions have shown a similar addiction to protecting the status quo. "In every instance," says a former C.A.B. chairman, "in which the Board has found that additional and competing passenger trunkline services on high density segments are required by the public convenience and necessity, it has concluded that the objectives of the act would be better served by the award of the route to a carrier already holding certificate authority than to a new company."[15] Thus, despite an increase in demand of truly fantastic proportions, amounting to more than 4,000 percent between 1938 and 1956 alone, the Board has not allowed a single new passenger trunkline carrier to enter the industry.

The Federal Maritime Board's administration of the operating differential subsidy and dual rate contracts has also resulted in undue entry limitation. So has the F.C.C.'s refusal to order A.T.&T. to interconnect Western Union's microwave system with its long-distance telephone lines.

Such protectionism sometimes manifests itself in regulatory apathy and nonfeasance. Thus, the Federal Power Commission has expended more energy in persuading the courts that it lacks the power to regulate field prices of natural gas than in protecting consumers against possible extortion. The C.A.B. and F.M.B. have shown little inclination to examine discriminatory practices or unfair competition in their respective industries. The F.C.C. has never investigated international telephone rates, nor exercised any direct control over television networks. Indeed, speaking through its former chairman, the commission has defended two-network domination of the industry: "Somebody has to be dominant," Mr. Doerfer told a Congressional Committee. "Somebody is big . . . [D]ominance is just the natural result of the ebb and flow of business relations from day to day . . . [W]hen you are talking about dominance, there is always somebody that is dominant."[16] The I.C.C. has shown the same tolerance for trucking concentration, proceeding on the assumption, candidly stated by former chairman Clark, that "there hasn't been enough concentration in the industry."[17] The Controller of the Currency, entrusted with enforcement of the Bank Merger Act, has eschewed interference with giant mergers—the recommendations of the Attorney General and the Federal Reserve Board to the contrary notwithstanding.[18] In so doing, the regulators have transmuted the meaning of regulation; not only was it to be an exemption from competition, but a protective device against meaningful surveillance.

The "undue shift of emphasis from public convenience and necessity to the seeking and protection of private carrier rights"[19] is perhaps best illustrated by the commissions' treatment of competitive "interlopers." So persistent and ruthless has been the attempt of some commissions to eliminate the fringes of unregulated competition, that the Albigensian crusades appear like missions of mercy by comparison. The suppression of the infidels has been executed with monolithic single-mindedness and unparalleled bureaucratic efficiency. In the airline industry, the "non-skeds," despite their innovative progressiveness and the value of their promotional competition, have been subjected to "strangulation by regulation." In trucking, the haulers of agricultural commodities and, to a lesser extent, private and contract carriers—have been victimized by systematic persecution, carried out with algorismic precision. In ocean shipping, such independents as Isbrandtsen have been forced, first by administrative harassment and eventually by legislative mandate, to submit to a government-sponsored, compulsory cartel. In industry after industry, regulatory rule-making and adjudication, operating within a broad delegation of discretion and reinforced by Congressional tolerance or support, have resulted in the elimination of both actual and potential competition.

In a sense, this was almost inevitable. Regulation breeds regulation. Competition, even at the margin, is a source of disturbance, annoyance, and embarrassment to the bureaucracy. By providing a yardstick for performance, an outlet for innovation, and a laboratory for experiment, competition subverts the orthodox conformity prescribed by the regulatory establishment. It undermines the static, conservative, and unimaginative scheme of bureaucratic controls, and erodes the artificial values created by protective restrictionism. From the regulator's point of view, therefore, competition must be suppressed wherever it may arise. What starts as regulation almost inevitably winds up as protection.[20] The power to license becomes the power to exclude; the regulation of rates, a system of price supports; the surveillance of mergers, an instrument of concentration; and the supervision of business practices, a pretext for harassing the weak, unorganized, and politically underprivileged. Given the power of the commissions to dispense and protect privilege, there is little hope for competition. To suggest that commissions follow a libertarian policy of entry control, rate regulation, and yardstick competition, is like asking East Germany to tear down the Berlin Wall.

Exemption by Administrative Preemption

Another instrument of privilege creation, more recent in vintage than regulation, but equally significant, insidious, and virulent, and operating without the benefit of explicit antitrust exemptions, is the unimaginative, short-sighted, discriminatory, or corrupt use of the government's executive power. It constitutes a (perhaps unwitting) promotion of monopoly by the government itself, and represents a major deviation from our national commitment to the preservation of competition.[21] For want of a better term, this phenomenon may be called "exemption through administrative preemption."

In an age of Big Government, born in response to the needs of a Garrison State, the "conjunction of an immense military establishment and a large arms industry" not only affects "the very structure of our society," but poses the very real danger "of unwarranted influence, whether sought or unsought, by the military–industrial complex."[22] In defense, space, and atomic energy, governmental creation of privilege can damage competition more seriously and more quickly than all other specifically authorized antitrust exemptions combined. It can create by administrative decision—by the stroke of a pen—what the antitrust laws are designed to prevent.

Patents on Government-Financed Research

The allocation of government research and development expenditures (R&D), and the patent policy governing the distribution of proprietary benefits therefrom, is a prime case in point. The importance of federal policy in this area derives from a number of characteristics of federally financed research[23]:

(1) Since World War II, the government has generally paid for roughly 65

Table 1

**Rank of Principal Contractors in Research
and Procurement for DOD, Fiscal 1962**

Company	Rank Among DOD Research Contractors	Rank Among DOD Prime Contractors	Rank Among Fortune's 500 Largest U.S. Industrial Corporations for 1962
General Dynamics	1	2	13
Lockheed	2	1	28
Boeing	3	3	19
North American	4	4	29
General Electric	5	5	4
Martin Marietta	6	6	32
Western Electric	7	8[a]	9[b]
Aerojet-General	8	12	55
Douglas	9	13	56
Sperry Rand	10	9	34

Source: Based on Hearings before the U.S. Senate Small Business Committee, *Economic Aspects of Government Patent Policies,* 88th Cong., 1st Sess. (1963), p. 57.

Notes:
[a] Included with American Telephone & Telegraph Co.
[b] Rank given is for Western Electric alone. Western Electric is a subsidiary of AT&T, the largest utility.

percent of the nation's research and development, but performed only about 15 percent of the work. Industry, by contrast, has paid for about 33 percent and performed 75 percent of the R&D activity. In other words, the government has financed over half of industry's R&D effort.

(2) Two agencies, the Department of Defense (DOD) and the National Aeronautics and Space Agency (NASA), account for about 80 percent of the government's R&D outlays. In fiscal year 1964, this will amount to almost $12 billion.

(3) The lion's share of these expenditures is concentrated in a few industries—notably the aircraft and parts industry and the electrical and communications industry. The former receives 85 percent, the latter 70 percent of its R&D financing from the government.

(4) The concentration of R&D contracts is even greater than that of procurement contracts. Thus, small business tends to get about 17 percent of the DOD's procurement business, but only about 3.5 percent of the military R&D. In fact, as Table 1 indicates, federal R&D bounties accentuate the concentration pattern in privately financed research and development work.

(5) There is a high correlation between companies receiving R&D contracts

and those receiving defense production orders. (See Table 1.) In fiscal year 1962, General Dynamics, Lockheed, and Boeing headed the list of DOD research contractors, and also captured the top three spots on the DOD list of prime procurement awards. Production orders seem to follow R&D contracts as night follows day.

(6) The benefits of military R&D tend to spill over into civilian markets. The development of nuclear power, blood plasma, drugs, new high-temperature alloys, and a variety of plastics during World War II, and the more recent development of Boeing's 707 jet and North American's Sabreliner are merely suggestions of the strong link between military research and civilian use. "More than 90 Sabreliners," says North American in a recent *Fortune* ad, "have already proved themselves in military service. Now this remarkable twin-jet aircraft is available for purchase."

In the light of this situation, it is not surprising that the Department of Justice has consistently attempted to countervail the anticompetitive effects of federal R&D policies. It has repeatedly recommended against granting private patents on inventions developed at public expense: "Where patentable inventions are made in the course of performing a Government-financed contract for research and development, the public interest requires that all rights to such inventions be assigned to the Government and not left to the private ownership of the contractor. Public control will assure free and equal availability of the inventions to American industry and science; will eliminate any competitive advantage to the contractor chosen to perform the research work; will avoid undue concentration in the hands of a few large corporations; will tend to increase and diversify available research facilities within the United States to the advantage of the Government and of the national economy; and will thus strengthen our American system of free, competitive enterprise."[24] Despite this policy pronouncement, however, some government departments—notably Defense—have made it a practice to grant patent rights along with their R&D contracts, as if an extra bonus were required to make a giant bonanza acceptable.

The typical R&D contract, it should be noted, is a riskless cost-plus-fixed-fee venture. It usually protects the contractor against increases in labor and materials costs; it provides him with working capital in the form of periodic progress payments; it allows him to use government plant and equipment; in addition, it guarantees him a fee up to 15 percent of the estimated cost. Nevertheless, some contractors demand additional incentives. With the arrogance characteristic of all privilege recipients, they want to extend and compound such privilege. "We recognize," says the Vice President of the Electronics Industries Association, a prime beneficiary of government-financed R&D, "that the ownership of a patent is a valuable property right entitled to protection against seizure by the Government without just compensation."[25] In this view, the patent is a right, not a privilege voluntarily bestowed by the government to effectuate a public purpose. Instead of being recognized for what it is—an alienation of the public domain—

the patent is assumed to be a vested right belonging to private interests, even where it is paid for with public funds. By a curious perversion of logic, it becomes a vested privilege to which the private recipient feels entitled and of which he is not supposed to be deprived without just compensation.

In the United States, patents have traditionally been held out as an incentive "to promote the progress of science and the useful arts"—an incentive to private persons, willing to assume the necessary risks to earn the stipulated reward. They were never conceived to be property rights inherently vested in private hands. Nor were they ever intended to reward persons who performed research at someone else's expense as part of a riskless venture. To allow contractors to retain patents on research financed by and performed for the government, therefore, "is no more reasonable or economically sound than to bestow on contractors, who build a road financed by public funds, the right to collect tolls from cars that will eventually use it"[26]—or the right to close down the road altogether. It would be tantamount to socializing the financial support for research, while permitting private monopolization of its benefits.

Yet this is the current practice of the Defense Department. If, as is proposed, NASA is allowed to adopt the same patent policy, the two agencies accounting for 80 percent of the government's R&D outlays, in effect, would be sanctioning the erection of private toll booths on public access routes to scientific and technical advance. The bulk of the government's R&D expenditures would forge a chain of privilege protection, and privilege subsidization. It would solidify an implicit (but crucial) antitrust exemption produced by simple administration fiat.

Procurement and Power

The DOD procurement of weapons systems further illustrates the anticompetitive effects of administrative discretion, wrought without explicit exemption from the antitrust laws. Here, too, the public grant becomes a "haven of refuge for all aspiring monopolists who [may find] it too difficult, too costly, or too precarious to secure and maintain monopoly by private action alone. Their future prosperity would be assured if only they could induce government to grant them monopoly power and protect them against interlopers, provided always of course, that government did not exact too high a price for its favors in the form of restrictive regulation."[27] The steps in the process are deceptively simple: government dismantles its facilities for serving a public need, and turns the job over to a chosen instrument; as the government's dependence increases, so does the arrogance of its instrument; the government becomes vulnerable to blackmail; to get the job done, it is forced to pay extortionate profits and subsidies; stripped of its bargaining power, and lacking competitive alternatives, it cannot break the self-imposed stranglehold. Thus, it winds up not as the master but the servant of its own chosen instrument. It becomes an accomplice in the stifling and suppression of competition.

The development of the NIKE missile illustrates the process. Early in 1945,

Table 2

Pyramiding Profits Through Top Three Tiers Nike Production (in millions)

	In-House Costs of Producer.	In-House Mark-up of Producer	Douglas Mark-up on Subcontracts & Purchases	Western Electric Mark-up on Subcontracts & Purchases
3d Tier				
Fruehauf Trailer Co.	$ 49.3	$ 4.5	$ 3.7	$ 3.3
Consolidated Western	146.2	9.3	10.4	9.9
Misc. 3d Tier Subcontractors to Douglas	286.6	*	23.2	16.3
2d Tier				
Douglas In-House Cost Including G & A	103.0	8.3		5.9
Misc. 2d Tier Subcontractors to Western Electric	428.8	*		42.0
1st Tier				
Western Electric In-House Cost Including G & A	359.3	35.2	—	—
Total				
Production Costs	$1373.2			
Total Mark-up by Producers		$57.3		
Total Douglas Mark-up on Subcontracts & Purchases			$37.3	
Total Western Electric Mark-up on Subcontracts & Purchases				$77.3
Total Cost to Army				$1,545.1

Source: Hearings before the U.S. Senate Permanent Subcommittee on Investigations, *Pyramiding of Profits and Costs in the Missile Procurement Program,* Part 2, 87th Cong., 2d Sess. (1962), p. 427.

Note:
*Undetermined Profits Included in Costs.

having dismantled its in-house R&D capability, the Army asked Western Electric to conduct a preliminary feasibility study on a guided missile system for defense against supersonic aircraft. A CPFF contract for $181,450 was signed on May 30, 1945, marking the kick-off of the NIKE program. In September 1945, Western got its first R&D contract, amounting to $4.9 million. By 1961, Western's R&D and service contracts for the NIKE totaled $956 million.[28]

In 1950, the first production contract on the new missile was let—and, to no one's surprise, it went to Western Electric. The eventual total of NIKE produc-

Table 3

1955 Profit Rates for Twelve Aircraft Companies

	Profit Rate on		
	Net Worth	Invested Capital	Sales
1. Boeing	51.6	102.7	7.3
2. Chance Vought	39.1	58.9	7.0
3. Convair[a]	29.9	70.9	4.7
4. Douglas	29.9	127.3	5.2
5. Fairchild	25.5	63.0	5.9
6. Grumman	47.5	120.7	10.0
7. Lockheed	44.8	151.9	6.5
8. Martin	40.5	74.1	7.8
9. McDonnell	52.3	316.1	7.4
10. North American Aviation	71.8	1,038.0	8.3
11. Northrop	92.0	386.7	9.1
12. Republic	71.0	198.9	5.7

Source: Committee on Armed Services, House, *Report on Aircraft Production Costs and Profits,* 84th Congress, 2d Sess., July 13, 1956, pp. 3105–3109. Reproduced in Frederick T. Moore, *Military Procurement and Contracting: An Economic Analysis*, Memorandum RM–2948-PR, The RAND Corporation (June 1962), p. 107.

Note:
[a] For 1953.

tion contracts was $1,545 million—with Western collecting a 31.3 percent mark-up on an in-house effort of $359.3 million. By using subcontractors for roughly three-quarters of the work and retaining responsibility for overall "system compatability," Western was able to play what Robert Lanzillotti has called the "game of piggy-back profits"—complete with piggy-back refills. Table 2 shows the profit pyramiding which took place.

Each subcontractor collected not only his in-house cost of production (including overhead costs for general and administrative expenses) plus a profit, but also a profit on the work done by other subcontractors further down the line. Thus Douglas Aircraft, a second-tier subcontractor, was allowed an $8.3 million mark-up on its in-house costs (including G&A) of $103 million, in addition to profits of $3.7 million on the work of Fruehauf, $10.4 million on the work of Consolidated Western, and $23.2 million on the work of other subcontractors for a total of $37.3 million. This represented a return of 44.3 percent on the total of work done in its own plants.[29] Similarly, Western Electric collected an in-house mark-up of $35.2 million, as well as $77.3 million profit on the work of all the subcontractors, giving it total profits of $112.6 million on an in-house effort of $359.3 million—or 31.3 percent.[30]

The McClellan Committee Hearings which unearthed these revealing statistics did not produce the far more interesting figures on profits as a percentage return on investment. Hence, we can only speculate about the astronomic proportions involved. Such speculation, however, is somewhat concretized by Table 3 which shows a comparison of profit rates as a percentage of net worth, invested capital, and sales for 12 aircraft companies during the year 1955. The staggering rates on invested capital, including 102.7 percent for Boeing, 127.3 for Douglas, 151.9 percent for Lockheed, and 1038.0 percent for North American, indicate that "modest" mark-ups on sales can be translated into fantastic returns on invested capital—especially by companies which typically receive sizable portions of their fixed and working capital from the government. Western Electric, for example, paid a rental of $3.075 million for the use of certain government plants; the company was then reimbursed in full for this expenditure and, in addition, allowed to charge the government a profit of $209,000 as a mark-up on this cost item.[31]

Why, then, does the government not procure certain items directly instead of assigning a procurement package to the prime contractor who employs several tiers of subcontractors and then pyramids the profits charged to the government? Why, in DOD parlance, does the government not "break out" certain parts of the procurement package for competitive bidding? The answer, as the NIKE history demonstrates, is the refusal of the prime contractor to permit such a breakout. Despite repeated efforts to effect cost-savings by buying parts of the NIKE directly from their manufacturer—efforts initiated by Redstone Arsenal, the New York Ordnance District, or G-4 of the Army—Western Electric was able to exercise a virtual veto. On one occasion the Army asked Western to screen a list of 13,000 items that might be procured directly and then give its approval for the break-out of some of these items. Western delayed long enough, so that the Army was forced to continue its sole-source procurement through Western.[32] On other occasions, Western refused to give the Army production drawings—developed at Government expense—so that certain replacement parts components could be broken out for competitive bidding.[33] In 1954, Redstone Arsenal wanted to break out the missile's thrust structure and miscellaneous parts of the booster, but Western replied that it could not concur in the purchase of these items from any other source than itself. This, despite the fact that the thrust structures were connected with the booster, which was government-furnished, and which was in a sense separate from the rocket itself.[34] On each occasion, Western Electric threatened to decline responsibility for system compatibility and to discontinue performance of the management function. Knowing that the Army had substantially dismantled its in-house engineering capability, and that the Army was in effect its captive, Western repeatedly and consistently refused to give its permission for direct procurement of NIKE components. With the exceptions of certain automotive components, as well as minor items, Western for 17 years (1945–1962) successfully resisted the break-out of the NIKE missile—until Senator McClellan started his investigation. Thereafter Western acted with dispatch. The investigation started in the middle of May 1961. Two weeks later, Western suggested to the Army that the NIKE be broken out for direct procurement.[35]

In his appearance before the McClellan Committee, Paul R. Ignatius, Assistant Secretary of the Army, stated: "I am convinced that only through competition can we be assured of receiving the maximum amount of defense for the dollars which we in the Army have to spend. I am well aware that in some instances sole-source procurement may be necessary. However, I am also convinced that in many instances . . . we have found ourselves in a sole-source position not as a result of a careful assessment of the situation leading to a deliberate decision, but by default. In these cases, we have had no alternative other than to buy from a single company."[36] The testimony—at least, in the case of the NIKE missile—showed that "the government was almost helpless in this case, that the government was almost a captive of Western Electric because every time they would want to break out Western Electric would say, 'We will not assume responsibility for the system.' "[37]

The moral is clear: The government favors a private corporation with an R&D contract. It makes no provision for protecting itself against future dependence on this corporation as a sole-source supplier. By getting in on the ground floor, the corporation is able to preempt the future—more so than through similar activity in the free market sector. Whether or not it receives patent rights on its inventions developed at government expense, the corporation has achieved preeminence without meeting any market test. It has been successful in obtaining government favor—perhaps through manipulation of administrative discretion—and this initial success then breeds further advantages. The production contract almost inevitably goes to it because of its R&D lead. It becomes the prime contractor for an entire weapons system—an entire procurement package. Not only can it pyramid profits—i.e., accumulate piggy-back rewards for work done by others—together with piggy-back refills on replacement orders—but also prevent the government from breaking out portions of the contract for competitive procurement. It thus is in the enviable position of benefitting from government subsidies, while insulating itself from competition. It becomes a chosen instrument which dictates to its master. Having reduced the government to a position of abject dependence, it can effectively blackmail the government out of any effort to terminate such dependence. And blackmail leads to extortion and further dependence. No explicit exemption from antitrust is necessary. Competition is foreclosed by administrative discretion. Concentration results not from technological or economic imperatives, but from governmental action. "Everything," as Jane Austen said, "nourishes what is strong already."[38]

Conclusion

Our concern here, of course, is not with the exploitation of the public purse by greedy courtiers. But when public subsidy for riskless ventures becomes the underpinning for a system of privilege creation and privilege protection—when the government promotes what the antitrust laws forbid—and when all this is accomplished without explicit exemptions from the national commitment to competition, then there is need for redefining the problem. We must recognize that both the dimensions and the context of the problem of promoting competition are no longer the same as in 1890. When Government is as big as it is today—when it dispenses favors and privilege on a gargantuan scale—"decisions will not be on the lofty and abstract grounds which are somewhat naively assumed by many economists who favor pervasive and far-reaching economic controls." Instead, as Senator Douglas so sagely observed, "the crucial decisions will commonly be made in an atmosphere of pressure, influence, favoritism, improper deals, and corruption."[39] To suppose that these decisions will promote competition by favoring the outsider, the newcomer, the unorganized, or the disadvantaged is to engage in catatonic self-deception. Concentrated power in the hands of government is not likely to be a source of countervailance but coalescence—not compensatory but reinforcing.

The real issue in preserving competition, therefore, is not so much a vigorous enforcement of the antitrust laws—important though that may be—but rather an end to explicit exemptions which erode the competitive sector of the economy, and a reversal of government policies which wittingly or otherwise undermine the competitive fabric of our society.

Policy toward that end should follow the central guideline of diffusing economic power to the maximum degree feasible and confining bureaucratic discretion within the narrowest practicable limits. This means *inter alia* the implementation of the following recommendations:

(1) Total deregulation of those industries where the regulatory scheme protects an industry from competition rather than the public from monopolistic extortion. In trucking, for example, where competition is both technically and economically workable, where entry in the absence of regulation would be easy, and where economies of scale are virtually nonexistent, why not let the market decide who shall transport what commodities over what routes at what rates? Why not consider the deregulation of the entire surface transportation industry—subjecting that industry to the general prohibitory restraints of antitrust, while maintaining a strict proscription against the erosion of intermode competition either by merger or internal expansion? There is no longer the same need for government regulation as in the days of the railroad monopoly.[40]

(2) In other regulated industries, where unrestricted competition is not workable for technical or economic reasons, and where total deregulation is therefore not feasible, Congress should specifically direct the regulatory agency "to promote competition to the maximum extent practicable," to deny entry to an applicant only where such entry can be shown to be inconsistent with the public convenience and necessity, and to permit structural or behavioral arrangements contrary to the antitrust laws only where "the regulatory need therefore is

clear."[41] Under such a mandate, in TV for example, there would be no reason to tolerate network ownership of television stations, multiple ownership of stations, erosion of intermedia competition, and such restrictive practices as "must buy" and "option time."

(3) In those industries where competition is not allowed to have full sway, yardstick competition should be encouraged from whatever source it may spring. This implies promotion (instead of the current harassment) of airline "non-skeds" and charters, educational and pay television, independents in ocean shipping, and federal, state, municipal, and cooperative organizations in electric or atomic power. In necessarily concentrated industries, institutional competition, even though it is only marginal, should be allowed to supplement regulation and thus serve as an antidote to bureaucratic conservatism and protectionism.

(4) The antitrust philosophy should be built into the decision-making structure of the federal government, so that government does not act as a creator and protector of privilege. There is no justification for protecting concentrated, administered price industries through tariffs or antidumping statutes. Nor is there a public purpose to be served by giving R&D contractors patent rights on inventions growing out of government-financed research. Nor is there sound reason for dismantling in-house capabilities of the Defense Department as a prelude to making the government a dependent vassal of industrial barons. In short, where the government, by force of circumstance must become a participant in the nation's economic life, it should participate to a sufficient extent to prevent concentration in the private sector resulting from a proliferation of restraints by its chosen instruments.

Above all, the government must not be captured by private interests and made subservient to them. If it is to play its proper role, it must intervene in the economy only as a public shield, never as a mask for privilege.

Enough has already been said to sketch the outlines of the work to be done. There are cases where words are superfluous. The government now knows what to do. As somebody once said, "The milk-wagon horse knows where to stop."[42]

Notes

The Editors wish it known that an appendix which originally appeared in this article has been deleted for this publication.

1. *The Wealth of Nations*, p. 423 (Modern Library ed., 1937).

2. *The East and West Must Meet: A Symposium*, p. 103 (1959).

3. Address by Henry Ford II to a group of German industrialists and government officials in Cologne, Germany, June 25, 1954.

4. *Federal Communications Commission* v. *RCA Communications, Inc.*, 346 U.S. 86, pp. 91–96 (1953).

5. James B. Landis, *The Administrative Process*, pp. 13, 16 ff (1938).

6. Louis L. Jaffe, "The Scandal in TV Licensing," *Harpers*, vol. 215, p. 77 (September, 1957).

7. Marver H. Bernstein, *Regulating Business by Independent Commission* (1955).

8. Louis B. Schwartz, "Legal Restriction of Competition in the Regulated Industries: An Abdication of Judicial Responsibility," *Harvard Law Review*, esp. pp. 471ff (1954). The low repute which commission expertise enjoys in some judicial quarters is illustrated by Judge Frank's review of an I.C.C. valuation decision:

> If, however, the Commission is sustained in this case, and, accordingly, behaves similarly in future cases, then its conduct will indeed be a mystery. Its so-called valuations will then be acceptable, no matter how contrived. In that event, it would be desirable to abandon the word "valuation"—since that word misleadingly connotes some moderately rational judgment—and to substitute some neutral term, devoid of misleading associations, such as "aluation," or, perhaps better still, "woosh-woosh." The pertinent doctrine would then be this: "When the ICC has ceremonially woosh-wooshed, judicial scrutiny is barred." It would then be desirable to dispense, too, with the Commission's present ritualistic formula, "Taking into consideration, etc." replacing it with patently meaningless words—perhaps the same words spelled backward, i.e., "Gnikat otni noitaredisnoc, etc.," Then no one would be foolish enough to believe that the figures in a Commission plan necessarily have anything to do with deliberation, but everyone would know that the figures might well have been the product of omphalic inspiration, or ornithomancy, or haruspication, or aleatory devices, and that the conclusions of the ICC might well be but the conjurations of mystagogues.—[*Old Colony Bondholders et al.* v. *New York, New Haven & Hartford R. R.*, 161 F. 2d 413 (1947).]

9. Bernard Schwartz, *The Professor and the Commissions* (1959).
10. Walter Adams, "The Role of Competition in the Regulated Industries," *American Economic Review, Papers and Proceedings*, pp. 527–43 (May 1958).
11. Address by Newton N. Minow, then chairman of the Federal Communications Commission, to the National Association of Broadcasters, Chicago, April 2, 1963.
12. See e.g. Willers, Inc.—Purchase (Portion)—Everson, 10 Fed. Carr. Cas. 222 (1953). See also Walter Adams and James B. Hendry, "Trucking Mergers, Concentration, and Small Business; An Analysis of Interstate Commerce Commission Policy, 1950–56," *Hearings before the Senate Small Business Committee, Trucking Mergers and Concentration*, 85th Cong., 1st Sess., pp. 213–384 (1957).
13. *Hearings before the Senate Small Business Committee, Administration of the Motor Carrier Act by the Interstate Commerce Commission as it Affects Small Truckers and Shippers*, 84th Cong., 1st Sess., pp. 93–94 (1955).
14. *Report of the Attorney General's National Committee to Study the Antitrust Laws*, p. 265 (1955).
15. Address by Judge Ross Rizley before the Chamber of Commerce, Enid, Oklahoma, November 18, 1955, quoted in *The Airlines*, H.R. Rep. No. 1328, 85th Cong., 1st Sess., pp. 102–103 (1958).
16. Quoted in Bernard Schwartz, "Antitrust and the FCC: The Problem of Network Dominance," *U. of Pennsylvania Law Review*, p. 763 (1959).
17. *Hearings before the Senate Small Business Committee*, op. cit., fn. 12, above, p. 111.
18. See e.g. *U.S.* v. *Philadelphia National Bank et al.*, 374 U.S. 321 (1963) and *U.S.* v. *Continental Illinois National Bank et al.*, Civil Action No. 61-C-1441, U.S. District Court, Northern District of Illinois, filed August 29, 1961. Between November 16, 1961 and April 19, 1963, the Comptroller approved 144 bank mergers, consolidations and purchases—39 of which the Attorney General considered to have substantially adverse effects on competition. For additional data, see *Annual Report of the Comptroller of the Currency* (1961), pp. 65 and 79ff and *Hearings before the House Committee on Banking and Currency, Conflict of Federal and State Banking Laws*, 88th Cong., 1st Sess., pp. 403, 482, and 500ff (1963).
19. Ross Rizley, op. cit., fn. 15, above.

20. For a discussion of the regulatory protectionism practiced by state and local governments under the aegis of their licensing power, see Walter Gellhorn, *Individual Freedom and Governmental Restraints*, pp. 106ff (1956).

21. Walter Adams and Horace M. Gray, *Monopoly in America: The Government as Promoter* (1955).

22. Farewell Address by President Dwight D. Eisenhower, January 1961.

23. The following data are based primarily on Robert F. Lanzillotti, *Hearings before the Senate Small Business Committee, Economic Aspects of Government Patent Policies*, 88th Cong., 1st Sess., pp. 117–143 (1963), hereafter cited as *Long Committee Patent Hearings*, and Richard J. Barber, *Long Committee Patent Hearings*, pp. 47–91, and *Hearings before the Joint Economic Committee, State of the Economy and Policies for Full Employment*, 87th Cong., 2d Sess., pp. 858–65 (1962). For a comprehensive examination of the impact of government patent policies, see the hearings and reports issued by Senator Russell B. Long's Monopoly Subcommittee of the Senate Small Business Committee, 1959–1963.

24. U.S. Department of Justice, *Investigation of Government Patent Practices and Policies, Final Report*, vol. 1, p. 4 (1947).

25. *Long Committee Patent Hearings*, p. 132.

26. Wassily W. Leontief, *Long Committee Patent Hearings*, p. 234.

27. Horace M. Gray, "The Passing of the Public Utility Concept," *Journal of Land and Public Utility Economics*, p. 11 (1940). Gray's observation, originally made with reference to public utility franchises, is equally applicable to all governmental grants of privilege.

28. *Hearings before the Senate Permanent Subcommittee on Investigations, Pyramiding of Profits and Costs in the Missile Procurement Program*, 87th Cong., 2d Sess., part 2, pp. 344–345, 416 (1962).

29. For other examples of profit pyramiding by Douglas, see ibid., part 1, pp. 207–228.

30. For similar examples of profit pyramiding by Boeing, see ibid., part 4, p. 706.

31. Ibid., part 2, p. 482.

32. Ibid., part 2, pp. 338–340.

33. Ibid., part 2, pp. 349–353.

34. Ibid., part 2, pp. 357–359.

35. Ibid., part 2, p. 405.

36. Ibid., part 2, pp. 509, 508.

37. Ibid., part 2, p. 359.

38. Long ago, Alfred Marshall warned of "the danger that in the trade which had got a bounty and in other trades which hoped to get one, people would divert their energies from managing their own businesses to managing those persons who control the bounties." *Principles*, p. 473. Not only does this warning apply to all forms of governmental privilege creation and protection, but *a fortiori* to an economy in which the state plays a preeminent role.

39. Paul H. Douglas, *Ethics in Government*, p. 33 (1954).

40. See Merton J. Peck, "Competitive Policy for Transportation," in Almarin Phillips, ed., *Perspectives on Antitrust Policy*, pp. 244–272 (1965).

41. See recommendations of the Attorney General's National Committee, op. cit., fn. 14, above, pp. 269–270.

42. Herbert Block, *Herblock's Special for Today*, p. 246 (1958).

13

Import Restraints and Industrial Performance: The Dilemma of Protectionism

With the internationalization of markets and the progressive liberalization of world trade, the threat of foreign competition has revived the age-old cry for protectionism: to protect the nation's balance of payments, to protect domestic labor from import-induced unemployment, and to protect domestic industry from the unfair competition of low wage countries. These arguments are particularly appealing in times of recession, and political office seekers are not loath to embrace them, especially in election years.

For an industry constrained to live in a free trade environment where it is striving for survival, profitability, and growth, foreign competition is a serious challenge. It is a disruptive force which undermines the market control of oligopolized industries and the cartel-like price maintenance schemes prevalent in many competitive industries. It causes instability by undermining "mutual dependence recognized," by promoting defection among cartel partners, and by encouraging entry. Foreign competition is the nemesis of orderly marketing and hence becomes a prime target for neomercantilist governments and the interest groups which manipulate them.

It is the thesis of this article that the remedies for the import problem—quotas, orderly marketing agreements, trigger price systems, and the like—do not provide adequate mechanisms for insuring acceptable industry performance or protecting the public interest. Instead of compelling—or even promoting—the kind of structural and behavioral changes which are imperative if an industry is to overcome its competitive infirmities, these protectionist devices, more often than not, are likely to have precisely the opposite effect, i.e., to perpetuate the very infir-

---

Originally published in *Michigan Yearbook of International Legal Studies,* vol. 1, 1979; reprinted with permission.

mities that caused the industry's plight to begin with. In short, an ailing organism is not prepared for the rigors of survival in nature by being privileged to live in the shelter of a hothouse.

The United States Steel Industry: A Case Study

The domestic steel industry has demanded protection from the steadily burgeoning import competition since the long steel strike of 1959, claiming at various times and in diverse forums that it has been victimized by dumping, unfair competition, and export subsidies.[1] A review of the industry's economic performance since World War II, and an assessment of the protection it has been accorded—first under the Voluntary Restraint Agreement (hereinafter VRA) of 1969 and later under the Trigger Price Mechanism (hereinafter TPM) of 1978—should underscore the difficulties of fashioning public policies designed to improve industrial performance through import restraints.

Performance: Price Escalation and Loss of Competitiveness

The persistent price escalation of steel prices during the 1950s was the primary cause of the industry's lackluster performance during the 1960s—resulting in the erosion of domestic markets by substitute materials and imports, the loss of export markets not tied to Agency for International Development (AID) control, and the decline in return on investment.

The facts on steel pricing are beyond question. According to the Council of Economic Advisers:

> Steel prices played an important role in the general price increases of the 1950s. Between 1947 and 1951, the average increase in the price of basic steel products was 9 percent per year, twice the average increase of all wholesale prices. The unique behavior of steel prices was most pronounced in the mid-1950s. While the wholesale price index was falling an average of 0.9 percent annually from 1951 to 1955, the price index for steel was rising an average of 4.8 percent per year. From 1955 to 1958, steel prices were increasing 7.1 percent annually, or almost three times as fast as wholesale prices generally. No other major sector shows a similar record.[2]

During the 1960s, steel prices entered a relatively quiescent stage. The major factor in dampening the industry's enthusiasm for marching in lockstep toward constantly higher price levels was the burgeoning of import competition. Thus, between January, 1960 and December, 1968, a period of nine years, the composite steel price index increased only 4.1 points, or 0.45 points per year. Starting in January, 1969, however, after the State Department had successfully persuaded the Europeans and Japanese to accept voluntary quotas on their sales to the United States (*i.e.*, to enter into an informal international steel cartel), imports were cut back drastically and the domestic steel prices resumed their pre-1960 climb.

The Nixon administration's price controls, in effect from August, 1971, to April, 1974, temporarily attenuated the steady climb of steel prices. But in 1974, spurred by a worldwide steel shortage, they resumed their long-run trend upward, rising 30 percent, as compared to 17 percent for all industrial commodities. In spite of its contention that it was living under a regime of *de facto* price controls, the record indicates the contrary. *The Wall Street Journal* reported:

> The base price of hot-rolled sheet steel has climbed about 63% to the present $283.50 a ton from its $173.50 a ton level when government wage and price controls ended in April, 1974. A few days after the controls ended, the price was boosted 10% to $191 a ton, and it was raised 15% to $220 a ton in July, 1974. The base quote climbed 6.3% to $234 a ton on Oct. 1, 1975.
> The hot-rolled sheet base price was raised twice in 1976. The quote went up 6.4% to $249 a ton on June 14 and was increased another 6.5% to $265 a ton on Dec. 1. The 7% boost that took effect June 19 of this year brought the base price to its present $283.50 a ton.[3]

The industry, it seemed, had once again returned to its traditional behavior model. The leaders again set prices "at full costs—fixed costs plus marginal costs—plus target rate of return, subject to certain limits."[4] The followers again did what was expected of them. Inevitably, prices were characterized by uniformity and upward rigidity.

Performance: Technological Backwardness

The United States steel industry's performance on the technology front—like its rigid, inflationary price policy—served to reduce its international cost competitiveness and to make it vulnerable to import competition. The facts of the case document this finding.

The major steel inventions in recent years, including the basic oxygen furnace, continuous casting, and vacuum degassing, came from abroad. They were not made by the American steel giants.

In innovation, as in invention, the American steel giants seem to lag, not lead their smaller domestic rivals and their foreign competitors. The oxygen furnace, for example, the only major technological breakthrough in basic steel making since the turn of the century, was invented and innovated by the minuscule Austrian steel industry in 1950. It was first installed in the United States in 1954 by a small company (McLouth) and not adopted by the steel giants until more than a decade later: United States Steel in December, 1963, Bethlehem in 1964, and Republic in 1965. As of September, 1963, the largest steel companies, operating more than 50 percent of basic steel capacity, had not installed a single basic oxygen furnace, whereas smaller companies, operating only 7 percent of the nation's steel capacity, accounted for almost half of the basic oxygen installations in the United States.[5] Despite the fact that the new oxygen process entailed substantial operating cost as well as capital cost savings, the United States steel industry during the 1950s "bought 40 million tons of the wrong kind of capacity—the open-hearth furnace."[6] As *Fortune* observed, much of this capacity "was obsolete when it was built," and the industry, by installing it, "prepared itself for dying."[7] Or, as *Forbes* put it more mildly, "In the Fifties, the steel industry poured hundreds of millions of dollars into equipment that was already obsolete technologically—open-hearth furnaces."[8] The technological blunder may have cost close to $1 billion in "white elephant" facilities.

The belated adoption of continuous casting by the steel giants is a further illustration of their technological lethargy. Again, it was a smaller company (Roanoke Electric), with an annual capacity of 100,000 tons, that pioneered in introducing this European invention in the United States in 1962. Other small steel companies followed, so that by 1968, firms with roughly 3 percent of the nation's steel capacity accounted for 90 percent of continuous production in the United States.[9]

Even defenders of the American steel giants concede that it was the cold winds of competition rather than the sheltered atmosphere of protectionism that ultimately forced the domestic majors to belatedly follow the path of technological progress. Thus, Alan McAdams admits that by "1962 it appeared that the costs to United States producers for *not* innovating were significantly raised by actual and threatened competition from both domestic and foreign oxygen steelmakers."[10] Competition, not protection, broke down the industry's habitual lethargy and resistance to change.

Even today, the United States steel industry seriously lags behind Japan in the adoption and use of the latest steel technology. Thus, according to the International Iron and Steel Institute, 81 percent of Japan's crude steel in 1976 was produced in efficient basic oxygen furnaces, compared with only 63 percent of United States output. By contrast, higher-cost open-hearth furnaces accounted for 18 percent of United States crude steel production, but for only 0.5 percent in Japan. Moreover, 35 percent of Japanese steel was produced by the labor-saving continuous casting method, more than triple the 11 percent in the United States.[11] Also, as *The Wall Street Journal* reports, the Japanese appear to benefit from economics of scale by using giant blast furnaces to an extent unparalleled in the American steel industry.[12]

Performance: Profits

It is a truism that steel industry profits are intimately linked, not only with price increases that outpace cost increases, but with its ability to maintain high rates of capacity utilization. The steel study by the Council on Wage and Price Stability underscores this point. It finds that profit rates from the end of World War II through 1957 were good because of rapidly increasing prices and a high rate of capacity utilization. Between 1958 and 1972, the Council says, profits were poor because foreign competition prevented the industry from raising prices substantially and because the industry's market strategy—its refusal to cut prices to meet import competition—resulted in suboptimal levels of production. Only with the restriction of imports after 1969, the termination of government price controls in 1973, and an abnormally strong worldwide demand for steel in 1974 was the industry able to operate at near full capacity and, hence, earn higher profits.[13]

Under the circumstances, one obvious (and, to the industry, painless) way of increasing profits and cash flow is to restrain the most potent competitive force in domestic steel markets, i.e., import competition, and thus prevent price erosion and maintain capacity utilization without a constant need to upgrade performance.

Import Restraints: Voluntary and Mandatory Quotas

The lesson was not lost on United States steel producers. Faced with what they viewed as a mounting flood of imports, and after filing unsuccessful countervailing duty and antidumping complaints, they shifted their protectionist efforts to the legislative and public relations front. This strategy eventually paid off with the signing of the Voluntary Restraint Agreement (hereinafter VRA) that went into effect on January 1, 1969.

Under the Agreement, annual steel imports from Japan and the European Community were limited to 5.8 million tons each, compared to their then current levels of 7.5 million and 7.3 million tons, respectively. The Agreement also provided for an annual growth of 5 percent in the allowable quotas. It was described approvingly by the Chairman of the powerful Ways and Means Committee of the United States House of Representatives as a "welcome and realistic step."

Within three years, the domestic industry found the VRA unsatisfactory; quotas had not been established, either for specific products or for individual exporting countries (other than Japan). Moreover, both the Japanese and Europeans claimed that fabricated structural steel and cold finished bars were not included in the VRA quotas, since the quotas were expressed in tonnage terms. Therefore, they rapidly expanded their shipments of stainless steel and other high-value products to the United States market—despite their promise to "try to maintain approximately the same product mix and pattern of distribution" as before the accord was signed. The effect of this upgrading in imports, combined with the inevitable increase in the price of imported steel, was that the total value of steel imports was as high in 1970 as in 1968 notwithstanding a 25 percent decline in the volume of imports during the same period.[14]

As a result, the three-year extension of the Agreement—announced by the White House on May 6, 1972—contained specific tonnage limitations on three categories of specialty steels (stainless, tool, and other alloys) and set the quotas at less than their 1971 import level. In addition, fabricated structural steel and cold-finished bars were specifically included in the Agreement. Also, the participants agreed to maintain their product mix and their customary geographic distribution pattern. Finally, a 2.5 percent (instead of the former 5 percent) annual increase in the allowable imports was to be applied to the global tonnage allocated to Japan and the EEC.

To enforce the extended VRA, the United States installed a monitoring system to be administered by Treasury and the Customs Service. The exporting countries not only had to agree among themselves to observe the VRA, but also had to set up machinery for the producers within each country to arrive at mutually satisfactory export quotas to the United States market. In other words, Japanese and European steel producers, under United States pressure, were obliged to set up cartels in order to arrange for their share of the United States market, and thus to engage in activity that is suspect, if not illegal, under the Treaty of Paris. More importantly, however, the connivance between the domestic industry, the State Department, and foreign steel producers to limit imports triggered an antitrust suit by Consumers Union which charged that the VRA constituted a *prima facie* conspiracy under the Sherman Act. While the Court eventually ruled only on the State Department's authority to insulate the agreement from the antitrust laws, it left little doubt that the foreign signatories to the pact could be held accountable for participation in any trade restraints. In any event, the decision was clear enough to persuade all concerned that the VRA should not be renewed when it expired in May, 1975.[15]

After the passage of the Trade Act of 1974, the industry's pressure for action by the government—reinforced this time by the political influence of organized labor—was crowned with success in the stainless and specialty steel sector. The International Trade Commission ruled that the domestic firms were indeed injured by rising imports, and recommended to the President the imposition of quotas on four categories of specialty steel products.[16]

Stating that quotas are an inflexible and relatively undesirable remedy for the supposed injury, the President gave Japan, the EEC, and Sweden ninety days to enter into voluntary "orderly marketing agreements" with United States negotiators before approving the Commission's recommendation. Under the threat, the Japanese gave in, signing a VRA on the final day of the ultimatum. The other countries, however, spurned the proposed arrangement. Quotas were imposed, as threatened, with the Japanese benefiting and the EEC losing, as compared to the original Commission recommendations.[17]

At every stage of the proceeding, the political power of the steel industry was brought to bear on the decision makers. Senator Schweiker of Pennsylvania, admitting that he was unfamiliar with the relevant economic data, testified as an industry witness for the Specialty Steel Committee. Mr. I.W. Abel, president of the United Steel Workers, also testified as an industry witness. While the petition was still under consideration, Senator Ribicoff took the floor in Congress[18] to excoriate the failure of the ITC, as evidenced in its negative decisions theretofore, to carry out the Congressional intent of the Trade Act of 1974. Moreover, after the ITC decision was announced, the president of Allegheny Ludlum Steel, the industry spokesman, "truculently" threatened to go to Congress to override the President if he did not approve the quotas recommended by the ITC,[19] only to have his threat echoed by Senator Ribicoff as he presided over the Senate Finance Committee's oversight hearings on United States foreign trade policy. The chain of events was an object lesson in political economy.

What, then, were the economic consequences of the steel industry's maneuverings on behalf of import quotas? First, the succession of antidumping complaints, countervailing duty charges, mandatory quota threats, the VRA, and the import injury case (followed by a separate proceeding for the so-called round stainless steel wire industry) must have had a chilling effect on the intensity of import competition. Import sales were probably reduced simply to avoid the appearance of an excessive inflow during the period when remedies were being considered.

Second, there is hard evidence that the VRA has increased steel prices and raised costs to American industry and consumers. Thus, according to one study, between January, 1960, and December, 1968, a period of nine years, the composite steel price index rose 4.1 points—or 0.45 points per year, indicating the moderating effects which surging imports had on domestic prices. In the four years between January, 1969, and December, 1972, while the VRA was in effect, the steel price index rose 26.7 points—or 6.67 per year. Put differently, steel prices increased at an annual rate fourteen times greater after the import quotas went into effect than in the nine years prior thereto.[20] Other studies have estimated the annual cost burden to the United States at between $386 million and $1 billion.[21]

Third, the use of quotas, or the threat of quotas, to moderate the intensity of competition from foreign steel has profound implications for the battle against inflation. While it may be difficult to specify the precise quantitative importance of steel in the wholesale price index, there can be little doubt that price increases in steel are used to justify concomitant price increases in a host of other products, particularly in the durable consumer goods industries.

Fourth, quotas are contagious, especially in times of weak demand, and are reminiscent of the "beggar-thy-neighbor" policies of the industrial nations during the Great Depression. Thus, while the United States imposed specialty steel quotas on the major exporting countries, the Europeans forced Japan to accept a "voluntary restraint" agreement on steel shipments into the EC. Japan "voluntarily" agreed to reduce steel exports to EC nations during 1976 by 23.8 percent from 1975 levels.[22]

Import Restraints: The Trigger Price System

The most recent import relief accorded the United States steel industry was an outgrowth of the Solomon Report. A trigger price system,[23] administered by the Treasury Department, was a thinly veiled scheme to put a floor under the price of imported steel,[24] freeing the domestic industry to resume its price escalation tactics. The consequences were predictable.

First, the trigger price system, as its authors intended, resulted in an increase in steel prices. Inevitably, it also fueled the cost-push inflation which bedevils the United States economy.

Since the trigger prices were set at a level close to domestic list prices, they precipitated a two-pronged upward pressure on the price level: (a) importers could now raise prices that formerly reflected world market conditions to the higher level dictated by trigger prices; and (b) domestic producers could and did raise actual prices to at least the list price, thus wiping out the discounts from list prices which market conditions formerly compelled them to grant to their customers. Furthermore, domestic producers, protected by the minimum prices established under the trigger price system, were now free to raise list prices so that they would be higher than import prices to at least the extent of the accustomed differential between domestic and foreign prices.

The quantitative impact was substantial. On December 7, 1977, one day after the concept of trigger pricing was announced by President Carter, a steel company executive stated that United States steel prices would be increased in the first quarter of 1978. Shortly thereafter, a 5.5 percent increase—reduced from an original 10.5 percent increase—in the domestic price of basic steel products was posted. This was followed by a further price rise of 1.1 percent in April, 1978.

On May 10, 1978, Treasury announced that it was raising trigger prices by 5.5 percent on sheet, plate, wire, and cold-finished bars; 13.9 percent on angles; 14 percent on reinforcing bars; and 14.5 percent on flat bars.[25] On August 2, Treasury raised the trigger prices by another 4.86 percent, effective October 1, 1978[26]; trigger price increases for calendar year 1978 totalled 10.6 percent.

While domestic steelmakers had raised their list prices by some 9.5 percent as of October 1, 1978, steel buyers report that the prices they actually had to pay increased by as much as 15 percent because, as The Wall Street Journal notes, "last fall's widespread discounting has evaporated."[27]

Foreign producers are not displeased with these developments. Thus, M. Jacques Ferry, head of the Common Market's steelmakers' group, Eurofer, states: "We don't have any problems [with the trigger price mechanism]. It has raised steel prices all around the world."[28] Similarly, Nippon Steel Corporation's president, Eishiro Saito, states that United States trigger prices—coupled with the EEC's minimum prices under the Davignon Plan—"have gone a long way in improving the world steel market, as these pricing measures helped steelmakers everywhere to achieve better results [by] eliminating sales below costs previously practiced for some steel products."[29]

The inflationary impact on the United States economy is, of course, quite another matter. Considering only the original trigger prices announced by Treasury in January, 1978, the Federal Trade Commission, for instance, estimated the direct cost increase to steel consumers at $1 billion.[30] An official of the Brookings Institute estimated that the direct price effect could be as much as $1.25 billion.[31] Kurt Orban, a steel importer and international expert on steel markets, found that the trigger price system had resulted in a veritable price explosion and estimated the increased steel costs to consumers at $4 billion.[32] Finally, if the domestic steel industry is to be believed in its claim that imports have caused transaction prices to be $60 per ton below list prices, then estimates of increased steel costs could range up to $6 billion. (Note that all these estimates are based on the trigger prices of January, 1978, and do not, therefore, take account of their 10.63 percent increase since then.)

Second, the long-run implications of trigger pricing are even more foreboding. The publication and elaborate enforcement, under the guise of monitoring, of minimum steel prices, is one of the most efficient techniques for insuring concerted action among oligopolists conscious of their interdependence. Thus, John Shenefield, Assistant Attorney General in charge of the Antitrust Division, is currently calling attention to the role of press conferences on price changes, widely-publicized price announcements, and other techniques for keeping one's fellow oligopolists informed of prevailing prices and proposed changes, to insure parallel action.[33]

The trigger pricing system carries this process one step further. It provides wholly reliable, government-certified, minimum price lists, subject to adjustment on a regular quarterly basis. Every domestic producer of wire rod, for example, will at all times know the minimum price at which this product can be imported and made available at every major port in the United States. Importers will be privy to the same information. To allow—or, in this case, virtually to compel—foreign steel producers to observe price floors on every major steel product carries *ad extremis* the very conduct which Mr. Shenefield finds in contravention of the antitrust laws. Through the intercession of government, interdependent oligopolists are therefore in a much better position to pursue a policy of price escalation than if they had to depend on private means to achieve that objective, and still remain within the strictures of the antitrust laws.

Third, most cartels break down because their members have a proclivity and incentive for cheating. A maverick cuts prices, expands his market share, and thus destroys the mutual trust on which the cartel, of necessity, is based. The trigger pricing system, especially when it is linked with a similar system enforced by the European Economic Community, achieves cartel goals without assigning market shares to its participants. By facilitating a framework of minimum import prices, it forecloses price competition as a means of winning new customers and hence insulates importer/customer relations from competition. Market shares will tend to change little, if at all. Most importantly, the bargaining and negotiating that in the past kept import prices flexible and forced the domestic firms to quote varying discounts below their list prices will have been effectively subverted. In brief, the trigger price mechanism, especially if it is to be supplemented by import quotas, is a long step toward the reconstitution of the old, interwar steel cartel.

Finally, we should note one further impact of the trigger price mechanism, *viz*, the impact on independent, nonintegrated wire drawers and fabricators. In the wire segment of the industry, for example, independent nonintegrated wire drawers are obliged to purchase wire rod (their raw material) at trigger price minima while facing competition in the sale of wire products at price levels prevailing in a free, unsupported market. Further, to the extent that foreign producers of wire products can purchase wire rod abroad at lower prices, they can produce and sell wire products in their home market and in the United States at a fair value that may be lower than profitable sales prices or cost of production of domestic wire producers. Thus, the independent, nonintegrated wire producers of the United States are inevitably caught in a squeeze imposed by the integrated mills at home and their rivals abroad.[34]

Treasury does not dispute the existence of the squeeze on independent nonintegrated wire drawers and fabricators resulting from its imposition of the trigger price mechanism. Indeed, it insists that the Antidumping Act—as administered under this mechanism—does

> not prevent a foreign producer of merchandise such as barbed wire from acquiring rod at low prices and fabricating that rod into wire that is sold at correspondingly low prices in both its home and export markets. In that situation, the producer is using savings in one factor of production no less proper than savings it may achieve in labor costs or energy expenses. The Antidumping Act is not aimed at preventing foreign producers from relying on savings in their production costs; it only seeks to prevent price discrimination in the sale of merchandise.[35]

Treasury further maintains that:

> [t]o the extent that the independent producers of wire products face competition from foreign and domestic rod suppliers who also use some of their rod to make wire products—and, thus, compete with their own customers—that problem is also beyond the reach of the Antidumping Act. No provision of that law prevents a supplier of a product, such as a rod, from setting high sales prices for that product, even though it also sells articles it makes therefrom, such as wire products, at relatively low prices to the disadvantage of its rod customers. To the extent such competition comes from domestic firms, the Antidumping Act cannot be applied at all; to the extent it comes from foreign companies,

only to the extent that the wire product prices are below their own "fair value" can the Act apply. But in that setting, the foreign wire maker's sales prices for rods are not relevant.[36]

Treasury admits that its administration of the trigger price mechanism will squeeze the nonintegrated fabricators—both by the domestic integrated mills and foreign wire and wire products producers. At the same time, Treasury disclaims responsibility for this result. It takes the position that there is no relief for the nonintegrated fabricators under the Antidumping Act, when in fact it is Treasury's administration of that Act through the trigger price mechanism which has caused the very injury to which the fabricators are subjected. Not only does Treasury's posture represent an abdication of responsibility for promoting the public interest, but it ignores the vital competitive role played by nonintegrated fabricators in what would otherwise be a rigid, vertically integrated oligopoly market.[37]

Import Restraints: Pending Proposals

Regulation breeds regulation; some protection leads to demands for more protection, and eventually ends up with demands for total protection. Steel imports are no exception to this rule.

Thus, Lewis Foy, chairman of the Bethlehem Steel Corp. and president of the American Iron and Steel Institute, is threatening to file a major antidumping complaint against European steelmakers, unless Treasury acts to curb imports (which in July, 1978, captured 19 percent of the United States market as compared to 18 percent in the same month a year earlier).[38] The industry, according to The Wall Street Journal, "just wants to keep the pressure on" in the hope of obtaining favorable revisions of the trigger price system from Treasury.[39] What the steel lobby wants is a new set of trigger prices based on European costs rather than on the lower Japanese costs.

Further, the United States industry, as might be expected from a study of cartel history, and judging by rumors current in industry circles, will almost inevitably have to demand an imposition of quantitative import restrictions to supplement the artificially high prices mandated by the trigger price mechanism. The reason is obvious. As the rising value of the yen pushes up the trigger prices based on Japanese costs, more and more steel exporters find sales in the American market increasingly remunerative which, in turn, induces them to raise their export volume to the United States market. Without more, high prices induce an increase in supply which must be restricted if the artificial price level is to be effectively maintained. Import quotas, therefore, become an indispensable supplement to trigger prices. And the higher the trigger prices, the greater the need for such quotas.

Even quotas, however, are not the final step in this evolving scenario. Import quotas may be "necessary to prevent severe continuing damage to the American steel industry,"[40] but they are no more than the first element of the industry's proposed, two-step "safeguard" system.[41] The second element is a permanent, worldwide, mandatory, multilateral orderly marketing agreement for steel products.[42] Stripped of euphemism, this means, as *The Wall Street Journal* noted, that the industry is really "angling for world-wide market rigging and price fixing along the lines of the international textile agreement."[43] It would mean comprehensive regulation of world steel markets by a cartel organized with the succor, and operated under the aegis of governmental authorities.

Summary

In light of the steel industry's performance since World War II, and the import relief it has been periodically accorded, the fundamental questions about the link between import restraints and improved performance remain. Are trigger prices, import quotas, or orderly marketing agreements likely to provide the necessary spur for technological progressiveness? Will they assure the badly needed modernization of the industry's anachronistic facilities? Will they provide the competitive discipline to curb the industry's proclivity for constant price escalation? Will they provide the government, in exchange for protection, the ability to exact "good performance" as a *quid pro quo* for the abandonment of competitive markets? In sum, as long as the industry can reasonably count on periodic government bailouts to avoid the consequences of its own conduct, does it have the incentive to perform at levels which, given the compulsions of competition, it would have to attain in order to survive? In light of the steel industry's record, these questions hardly survive the asking.

Some Public Policy Conclusions

Steel, of course, is not the only industry where deficient performance rather than imports is the basic explanation for "injury" or "probable injury," and where import restraints are not the appropriate remedy if improved economic performance is the goal.

In the automobile dumping case,[44] for example, the complaint filed by the United Automobile Workers charged that the increased market share of imported automobiles—up from 15.2 percent in 1970 to 15.9 percent in 1974 to 20.3 percent in the first half of 1975—was "at the expense of domestic sales"; that, discounting the effects of the United States recession, there was still a loss of domestic sales to imports; and that the pricing of imported cars caused the resulting injury to the American automobile industry and its workers. The union demanded the imposition of dumping penalties and simultaneously asked Congress for quota protection against the import of compacts and subcompacts from Europe and Japan.

The complaint was dismissed "provisionally," after extended and bizarre maneuvering by various instrumentalities of the administrative bureaucracy.[45] It was eventually settled when foreign producers, at the insistence of United States government authorities, agreed to raise their prices in the United States market.

To a disinterested observer it is apparent that such injury as the industry suffered was not caused by imports, but rather deficient performance. First, a primary factor explaining the industry's travails—one that requires no elaboration —was the national recession which drastically reduced the demand for virtually all consumer durables, including automobiles.

Second, the success of the imports was partly attributable to the delayed response by United States car manufacturers to a shift in consumer demand toward smaller, more fuel-efficient models. As of January, 1975, according to the Council on Wage and Price Stability, no domestic cars obtained twenty miles per gallon or more in the EPA city driving test, whereas fifteen of nineteen foreign compacts and subcompacts obtained twenty miles per gallon or better. In the highway driving test, no United States compact or subcompact car had a mileage rating of over thirty miles per gallon whereas fourteen of nineteen foreign makes did.[46]

Third, while foreign producers liquidated their large inventories of 1974 models at 1974 prices well into 1975, United States manufacturers posted price increases of roughly 12 percent on their 1975 models which went on sale in the autumn of 1974. This perverse pricing policy by United States producers in the face of a deepening recession, combined with the realistic market-oriented price policy of their foreign competitors, was an additional factor explaining the dramatic market penetration of the imports.

Fourth, the fact that imported compacts and subcompacts offered consumers a far wider range of price alternatives compared to their United States counterparts, may also have given imports a competitive edge over domestic models.

In any event, as the Council on Wage and Price Stability told the International Trade Commission (hereinafter the ITC), the most important factors explaining the increased market share of foreign automobiles "are the pricing policies of domestic producers and the inability of domestic manufacturers to respond rapidly to changing market conditions."[47] The Council warned the ITC that the imposition of special dumping penalties

> would likely result in an immediate increase in the price of automobiles to the American consumer. Moreover, such penalties, or even the threat of penalties, could substantially check what has been perhaps the single most effective spur to competition in this highly concentrated industry. This, in turn, could lead to less competitive prices and a reduced level of innovation.[48]

One can only speculate on what might have been, if either dumping penalties or import quotas had been ordered. Would this have intensified the sensitivity of the domestic industry to the vagaries of consumer tastes? Would it have given the lusty automobile oligopoly (which cast itself in the role of an infant industry) the needed respite to adjust to foreign competition without long-term protection? Would it have accelerated the introduction of revolutionary engines or the development of radically new body designs? Would it have spurred investments in United States plants by foreign manufacturers, or discouraged the expansion by United States multinationals in their foreign affiliates? What would have been the effect on X-efficiency and on the industry's traditional pricing policy? Neither a *savant-sans-culottes* nor an expert armed with computer models and multiple regressions would dare offer a definitive response.

Clearly, the problem of assessing quota–performance links is complex, if not insoluble. As United States experience with the so-called independent regulatory commissions demonstrates, an administrative agency, in the absence of competitive yardsticks, does not know what constitutes "good" performance; nor does it know how performance could be improved by changing an industry's structure. Most important, even if it did, the agency would lack the regulatory arsenal to exact "good" performance as a *quid pro quo* for protection from competition.

It is a truism that once competition has been abandoned, or significantly crippled—and this is a necessary consequence of import quotas—some surrogate for the competitive process must be devised to assure acceptable performance and to induce progressive performance. Otherwise, the restrictions imposed would not only be injurious to consumers and detract from the general welfare, but would also fail to accomplish their only justifiable goal, *i.e.*, to give temporary protection to an infant industry.

It would seem, and here again the United States experience with regulation is enlightening, that there are only two systems of industrial organization, each with inherent shortcomings, which might be effective substitutes for competitive controls. One alternative is pervasive, dictatorial regulation, with an elaborate mechanism of rewards and penalties, reaching down to the management level, utilizing the most advanced techniques of management science, and capable of simulating the crucial elements of competitive structure and behavior. The cost of such regulation, not only directly, but in terms of stifling entrepreneurial initiative, may suffice to condemn it. Another alternative is government ownership, again with the appropriate complement of efficiency-compelling and progress-inducing directives. In some circumstances, this solution appears to economize resources as compared to "effective" regulation. However, when the industry in question is not a natural monopoly, both regulation and nationalization (as Oscar Lange recognized long ago) almost inevitably tend to introduce bureaucratic rigidities and inefficiencies whose intensity will increase with the extent and detail of control.

One is driven to the conclusion, therefore, that import restrictions are to be embraced, if at all, only within a framework of comprehensive control, so that "good" performance is not jeopardized by the attenuation of competition and its disciplinary incentives.

Notes

1. Prior to 1958, annual steel imports remained below the 2-million-ton level (except in 1951, a Korean War year, when 2.18 million tons were brought in). From 1959 on, imports steadily increased, reaching a total of 6.4 million tons in 1964, 10.8 million tons in 1966, and a high of slightly less than 18 million tons in 1968—the last year before "voluntary" quotas went into effect.

2. U.S. Council of Economic Advisers, *Report to the President on Steel Prices*, pp. 8–9 (1965).

3. "Antitrust Unit Studies Possible Steel Price Fixing," *Wall Street Journal*, July 14, 1977, p. 3.

4. U.S. Council on Wage and Price Stability, Staff Report, *A Study of Steel Prices*, p. 1 (1975). In defense of the steel industry's pricing practices, it is sometimes argued that list prices may be characterized by upward rigidity, but that transaction prices fluctuate with the vagaries of market demand. Prior to the mid-1970s, there is little empirical evidence to support that claim. As George J. Stigler and J.K. Kindahl found in their comprehensive study, "the quoted and transaction prices of steel products move together so closely that a description of one is a description of the other. . . . This finding, it must be confessed, comes as a surprise to us. The steel industry is now unconcentrated as compared with the first decade of the century, or indeed as compared with many other industries in our sample. Import competition was growing fairly steadily during the period. With the exception of three steel products, however, we were not able to learn of any important and continuous departures from quoted prices. The exceptions were reinforcing bars (where we saw, but could not obtain, records of extensive short-run price fluctuations), pipe, and stainless steel products. One encounters minor incidents of price cutting such as quantity discounts granted on small orders and the supply of qualities somewhat better than minimum specifications. Nevertheless, the general picture was one of close adherence to quoted prices even for very large buyers of steel." G. Stigler & J. Kindahl, *The Behavior of Industrial Prices*, pp. 72–74 (1970).

5. Adams and Dirlam, "Big Steel, Invention, & Innovation," *Quarterly Journal of Economics*, pp. 167, 182–84 (1966).

6. "Why Steelmakers Raise the Ante," *Business Week*, Nov. 16, 1963, pp. 144, 144–46.

7. McDonald, "Steel is Rebuilding for a New Era," *Fortune*, October 1966, pp. 130, 135.

8. "Operation Catch-Up," *Forbes*, Mar. 1, 1967, p. 23.

9. W. Adams ed., *The Structure of American Industry*, p. 119 (5th ed. 1977).

10. McAdams, "Big Steel, Invention, and Innovation Reconsidered," *Quarterly Journal of Economics*, pp. 457, 472 (1967).

11. As reported in "Aging Mills," *Wall Street Journal*, Aug. 3, 1978, p. 1.

12. Ibid.

13. Council on Wage and Price Stability Report, op. cit., p. 17.

14. L. Weiss, *Case Studies in American Industry*, p. 193 (2d ed. 1971).

15. *Consumers Union of U.S. Inc.* v. *Rogers*, 352 F. Supp. 1319 (D.D.C. 1973), *aff'd sub nom. Consumers Union of U.S. Inc.* v. *Kissinger*, 506 F.2d 136 (D.C. Cir. 1974), *cert. denied*, 421 U.S. 1004 (1975).

16. *Stainless Steel and Alloy Tool Steel*, TA201–5, USITC Publ. 756 (1976).

17. See 41 Fed. Reg. 11,269,24,101 (1976).

18. 121 Cong. Rec. 538, 862 (1975).

19. At a press conference shortly after the ITC decision, a journalist asked Mr. Richard P. Simmons, president of Allegheny–Ludlum Steel, about prices: "If the President

imposes quotas to protect his industry from foreign competition, would Mr. Simmons support wage and price controls to protect consumers from his industry?" Mr. Simmons replied that he opposes wage and price controls, and that he puts his faith in the free market. But, as the *Washington Post* said in an editorial comment, "A country under import quotas is not everybody's idea of a free market." (Mar. 8, 1976, § A, p. 18.)

20. Cited in Comptroller General of the United States, *Economic and Foreign Policy Effects of Voluntary Restraint Agreements on Textiles and Steel,* Report B–179342, p. 23 (1974). See also, Richard Fanara, University of Rhode Island (unpublished study).

21. Magee, "The Welfare Effects of Restrictions on U.S. Trade," *Brookings Papers,* pp. 645–701 (1972) ($386 million); Comptroller General, op. cit., p. 23 (up to $1 billion).

22. A steel industry spokesman pointed out that Japan's steel exports during 1975 were approximately 1,600,000 tons; the agreement limited Japanese producers to 1,220,000 tons between them. *Oversight Hearings on U.S. Foreign Trade Policy before the Senate Comm. on Finance,* 94th Cong., 2d Sess., p. 171 (1976) (prepared statement of R. Heath Larry, vice chmn., Trade Committee, American Iron and Steel Institute).

23. 42 Fed. Reg. 65,214 (1977); 43 Fed. Reg. 1,964 (1978).

24. While Treasury claims that trigger prices are not minimum prices, it admits that "most foreign producers have raised their prices to the trigger price level to avoid an antidumping investigation which could result in antidumping duties equal to or greater than the difference between their export prices and the trigger prices." Treasury considers this a "voluntary decision" on the part of foreign producers and finds it "understandable" and "reasonable" (Treasury Findings, op. cit., p. 30). In other words, Treasury concedes that, irrespective of an exporter's legal rights to sell at lower prices, the trigger prices as a matter of practical reality are in fact minimum prices.

25. 43 Fed. Reg. 20,020 (1978).

26. 43 Fed. Reg. 33,993 (1978).

27. "Tarnished Shield: Steel Companies are Irked with Trigger-Price Plan," *Wall Street Journal,* Sept. 26, 1978, p. 1.

28. Quoted in "Treasury Official Says U.S. May Initiate an Inquiry Into Cut Rate Steel Imports," *Wall Street Journal,* Oct. 3, 1978, p. 2.

29. Ibid.

30. U.S. Federal Trade Commission, *The United States Steel Industry and Its International Rivals,* pp. 559–65 (1977).

31. *Wall Street Journal,* Sept. 26, 1978.

32. *American Metal Market,* Mar. 29, 1978. (Mr. Orban is one of the largest steel importers in the United States and is president of the American Institute for Imported Steel in New York City.)

33. Remarks before the Financial Analysts Federation, June 29, 1977 (mimeo); "Block the Press Conference," *Forbes,* Feb. 20, 1978, p. 31.

34. *Findings of the Department of Treasury with Regard to the Coverage of Wire Rod, Wire and Wire Products under the Trigger Price Mechanism,* p. 21 (April 13, 1978).

35. Ibid., p. 22.

36. Ibid., pp. 23–24.

37. See, e.g., Adams & Dirlam, "Steel Imports and Vertical Oligopoly Power," *American Economic Review,* p. 626 (1964).

38. *Wall Street Journal,* Sept. 26, 1978, p. 19.

39. Ibid.

40. Statement by Thomas C. Graham, quoted in "Steel Industry Trade Group Urges Quotas on U.S. Imports of Carbon Steel Products," *Wall Street Journal,* July 5, 1977, p. 8.

41. Petition of the Tool and Stainless Steel Industry Committee for Import Relief, Investigation No. TA–201–5, p. 36 (1975).

42. Ibid. The remedy section of this petition sets forth a detailed draft of the proposed "Multilateral Specialty Steel Arrangement" (pp. 42–70) which is reminiscent of the constitution of the pre–World War II international steel cartel. (E. Hexner, *The International Steel Cartels* (1943)).

43. "Steel's Trauma," *Wall Street Journal*, June 20, 1977, p. 14.

44. *New, On-the-Highway, Four-Wheeled, Passenger Automobiles from Belgium, Canada, France, Italy, Sweden, the United Kingdom, and West Germany.* AA1921-Inq.-1 USITC Publ. No. 739 (1975).

45. For a detailed discussion of the factors involved, see *Comments of the Staff of the Council on Wage and Price Stability,* submitted to the ITC during its investigation.

46. Ibid.

47. Ibid.

48. Ibid.

14

Competition, Monopoly, and Countervailing Power

I. Introduction

"Political liberty," a leading exponent of economic conservatism once remarked, "can survive only within an effective competitive economic system. *Thus, the enemy of democracy is monopoly in all its forms*: gigantic corporations, trade associations and other agencies for price control, trade unions or in general, organization and concentration of power within functional classes."[1] Failure to check the growth of concentrated economic power, he warned, would ultimately result either in giant pressure groups controlling the government or in the direct regulation of pressure groups by the government. In either event, he concluded, the result would be the triumph of collectivism over free enterprise and the destruction of a democratic society as we, in America, have known it.[2]

The implications of this analysis for public policy were clear: economic power had to be dispersed among many buyers and sellers competing actively in open markets. While scrupulously avoiding any direct interference with private enterprise, the government had to provide and enforce certain basic rules of the game, so as to keep the channels of trade free; prevent monopolistic pre-emption of opportunity; preserve the incentives for efficiency and progress; and forestall the growth of both economic feudalism and political tyranny. This was the philosophy of America's antitrust laws—the core of our traditional belief in competition and hatred of monopoly.

Somehow, in spite of the efforts to translate this blueprint into reality, economic power became progressively more concentrated[3] and the decline of competition a common phenomenon in many industries. To the neoclassical economist, this fact was a cause for alarm and a source of despair. To the

---

Originally published in the *Quarterly Journal of Economics,* vol. 67 (November 1953); reprinted with permission.

collectivist, it seemed but the manifestation of natural law—the operation of inexorable technological and economic forces which could not be reversed. To the defender of the status quo, however, it presented a unique challenge to explain the great transformation of the American economy—to demonstrate the compatibility of monopolistic and oligopolistic power aggregates with the stability and soundness of modern democratic capitalism.

In the advance guard of the "new enlightenment" was Professor J.M. Clark, who urged that the effectiveness of competition be judged in terms of its results, viz., the extent to which it promotes an efficient use of resources. It was Clark who suggested that the abstract theoretical model of "pure" competition be replaced by the more realistic concept of "workable" competition[4] as a gauge for judging the performance of specific industries in the public interest. Similarly, Professor E.S. Mason recommended that, in our public policy deliberations, we emphasize the constructive accomplishments and achievements of an industry rather than its market structure; that we accept an industry as workably competitive —regardless of its degree of concentration—if it evidenced, among other things, "a progressive technology, the passing on to consumers of the results of this progressiveness in the form of lower prices, larger output, improved products, etc."[5] And finally, Professor J.K. Galbraith—in an attempt to explain not just the workability of specific industries but of the whole economy—theorized that the American economy can perform quite brilliantly in spite of the widespread prevalence of industrial oligopoly. He tried to demonstrate that the American economy can provide better things for better living notwithstanding the fact that it operates in defiance of the rules laid down by "men of such Newtonian stature as Bentham, Ricardo and Adam Smith."[6]

In developing his theory, Galbraith credits Clark and Mason with a pragmatic concern for results—a recognition that "consequences, which in theory are deplorable, are often in real life quite agreeable." Yet Galbraith criticizes the exponents of workable competition for failing to make clear "why what is unworkable in principle becomes workable in practice," a failure which he attributes to their preoccupation with competition. He says[7]:

> In the competitive model the restraint on the power of any producer was provided by the competition of other producers—it came from the same side of the market. The tendency of any seller to exploit his customers was checked, not by the customers, but by another seller across the street and by many others in the same market. It was natural that in looking for restraints on the behavior of the large seller, who was one among few in the market, the search would be made in the same place. Competition, even though it might be different in kind from that of the competitive model, was still the object of the search. Indeed it was assumed that competition was the only possible restraint on private market power. This preoccupation with competition kept the investigators from seeing the actual restraints on market power—those that made not competition but the economy workable.

The actual or real restraints on a firm's market power are, according to Galbraith, vested not in its competitors but in its customers and suppliers; they are imposed not from the same side of the market, but from the opposite side. Thus "private economic power is held in check by the countervailing power of those who are subject to it. The first begets the second."[8] A monopoly on one side of the market offers an inducement to both suppliers and customers to develop the power with which they can defend themselves against exploitation. Thesis gives rise to antithesis, and there emerges a system of checks and balances which makes the economy as a whole workable, a *modus operandi* which lends stability to American capitalism. Most important of all, it relieves the government of its obligation—imposed by the now antiquated antitrust laws—to launch any frontal attack on concentrated economic power. No longer need there be concern about the decline of competition, the fewness of sellers in a particular market. Countervailing power (supported, where necessary, by government action) can be relied on to eliminate—through a process of creative destruction—the danger of any long-run exploitation by a private economic power bloc.

The following discussion will be concerned with an examination of the countervailing power thesis in terms of its practical as well as theoretical applicability.[9] Without attempting to discredit the fundamental plausibility and attractiveness of the thesis, we shall point to some of its limitations: (1) countervailing power is often undermined by vertical integration and top-level financial control; (2) bilateral monopolies created through the process of countervailance are not a happy solution of the economic power problem; (3) the countervailing influence of technological and inter-industry competition is not a meaningful substitute for competition in the neoclassical sense; (4) countervailance through government action is often subverted by unduly intimate affiliation between regulator and regulatee; and (5) the whole thesis rests on the dubious assumption that giant sized firms are the inevitable result of twentieth century technology and economics. These are the points which will now be discussed.

II. Top-Level Financial Control and Vertical Integration

According to Galbraith, the existence of concentrated power on one side of the market will eventually give rise to countervailing power on the other side of the market. Powerful sellers will cause the growth of powerful buyers and vice versa. As a result, the concentration of the steel barons will be offset by similar concentration among their automobile manufacturing customers, thus precluding, or at least reducing, the likelihood of monopolistic exploitation.

This argument leaves out of account the possibility of undermining and subverting the effectiveness of countervailing power as a regulatory mechanism. This objective can be accomplished by the co-ordination and centralization of both the buyer's and the seller's business policy within a single decision-making unit. It can be achieved through the common techniques of top-level financial control and vertical integration. Countervailing power can be exercised only so long as the forces on opposite sides of the market engage in arm's length bargaining, only so long as they are controlled by separate and financially independent decision-making units. Once we admit, however, the existence of economic interest groupings and giant vertical integrations, the opposing sides of the market are blended into one and any potential countervailance is automatically vitiated.

A fitting illustration of this process is Pullman Incorporated which, for many years, had a virtual monopoly over the manufacture and operation of sleeping car equipment.[10] Its customers were the nation's railroads, members of a highly concentrated industry. Here, then, was an almost perfect setting for the development of countervailing power—a monopolistic seller facing a number of economically powerful buyers. The expected countervailance, however, never materialized. Its potential development was frustrated by the existence of an intricate maze of interlacing relations among several large investment banking concerns, insurance companies, the railroads, and Pullman Incorporated. The Morgan, Vanderbilt, and Mellon interests had a substantial representation on the boards of directors of Pullman, while simultaneously dominating a large number of major railroads—both through ownership and, more importantly, through the financial syndicates floating the securities of such railroads. Equally significant were the connections between Pullman Incorporated and several of the largest insurance companies holding considerable investments in railroad securities.[11]

It was through such banker and insurance nexus that the railroads were affiliated with Pullman Incorporated. It was through such relationships on the top level of big business finance, that the railroads—far from countervailing the power of the Pullman monopoly—were made an integral part of it. It is an ominous and perhaps ironic reflection on the inability of countervailing power to function in accordance with theoretical expectations[12] that, as a result of this interlocking control, the competition of progressive sleeping car manufacturers was stifled, and that the public, as well as the railroads, were detrimentally affected by the technological backwardness of sleeping car service.

Outright vertical integration between powerful suppliers and powerful customers is merely a variation on the above theme. It is but another technique for subverting the arm's-length-bargaining and countervailing power which may otherwise operate under conditions of bilateral monopoly and/or oligopoly. A case in point is the recent merger between Paramount Pictures Corporation and the Du Mont television network.[13] Here was a combination of the largest motion picture producer and the nation's fourth largest TV network; here was a union of a giant maker and a giant exhibitor of films—in short, the very kind of vertical arrangement which the Supreme Court had found prejudicial to the public interest in the motion picture industry.[14] Once the Federal Communications Commission approved this merger, any countervailance which Paramount might have exercised against Du Mont, and vice versa, was of course destroyed. Once the vertical control over motion picture *production* and *exhibition* was approved (by a government agency presumably intent on fostering countervailing power), the previous efforts of the Supreme Court to divorce these functions were effectively vitiated and boldly undermined.[15]

III. Bilateral Monopoly and Countervailing Power

As was pointed out above, countervailing power operates primarily through the creation of bilateral monopoly and/or oligopoly situations. A monopoly on one side of the market finds its power neutralized by the appearance of a monopoly on the other side of the market. There thus develops a system of checks and balances, built on the foundation of bilateral power concentrations.

The labor market is cited as an area where this process can be observed with the greatest clarity,[16] for it is in the labor market that giant unions bargain on a national, industry-wide scale against groups of employers acting jointly either through a trade association or an informal *ad hoc* bargaining committee. The countervailing power advocates defend this type of arrangement in highly concentrated industries like steel, rubber, automobiles, etc. They point out that "not only has the strength of the corporations in these industries made it necessary for workers to develop the protection of countervailing power; it has provided unions with the opportunity for getting something more as well. If successful they could share in the fruits of the corporation's market power."[17] Bilateral monopoly in the labor market is thus justified on the grounds that it prevents unilateral exploitation, while simultaneously allowing one monopolist to share in whatever exorbitant gains may accrue to the other.

The fly in this ointment is self-evident, *viz.*, that unions and management—without necessarily conspiring—can jointly exploit the consumer. This is true especially in times of inflation[18] when employers may grant wage increases with relative impunity, and then pass their higher costs on to the consumer in the form of higher prices. These higher prices thereupon become the basis for new wage demands, and the inflationary spiral is sent on another merry spin. The bilateral monopoly of union and management fuels the engine for accelerating and perpetuating inflation.[19]

The inadequacy of bilateral monopoly in the labor market is rather pointedly illustrated by the recent wage dispute in the steel industry. After collective bargaining procedures had broken down, the case was referred to the Wage Stabilization Board. The Board promptly recommended a wage increase which would have raised production costs by approximately $6 per ton. To offset these higher costs, industry representatives demanded a price increase of $12 per ton, a demand which the OPS was compelled to refuse. The agency did agree, however, to permit a $3 per ton price increase in line with the provisions of the Capehart amendment to the Defense Production Act. This increase would have yielded the industry a return of more than 28 per cent on stockholders' investment—a return which was far higher than the 1947–49 profit rate of 18½ per cent, which in turn was higher than any the industry had enjoyed since 1918.[20] In spite of its apparently generous terms, this OPS offer was rejected by the industry—thus precipitating a strike, the seizure of steel plants by the government, and the invalidation of this seizure by the Supreme Court. The result was that eventually the government was compelled—in the interests of uninterrupted production during the emergency period—to authorize both the requested wage increase and the $12 per ton price increase. The irresistible force had met the immovable object. Bilateral monopoly, instead of providing countervailing checks and balances, was instrumental in wrecking price controls and supporting the inflationary forces which drove the economy into dizzy spirals of ever higher prices, wages, costs and prices.

Given the existence of power concentrations on both sides of the market, this result was perhaps inevitable. Indeed it was predicted by Robert Liefmann, the great exponent of industrial cartels, as long ago as 1927. In justifying cartels *ex visu* the workers, Liefmann pointed out that cartels were in a better position than competitive firms to grant wage increases, since they could more easily shift the resulting cost increases on to the consumer in the form of higher prices. Said Liefmann[21]:

> Where the firms are in a cartel, they are more inclined to concede the workers higher wages than in a state of free competition, because they find it easier to pass the increased costs on to their customers by charging higher prices. The workers will therefore, generally speaking, find it easier to impose higher wages upon organized firms, and it is in their power, at least if they can form strong trades unions, to demand wages increasing with the cartel's prices, *i.e.*, a "sliding wage-scale."

Here indeed were prophetic words, foreshadowing the kind of escalator arrangements recently popularized by General Motors and the United Automobile Workers (CIO). Here were the naked implications of bilateral monopoly as a technique for wage determination—resulting not in the countervailance of power between union and management but rather in a *combination* of the two against the consumer. That such labor–management "co-operation" rather than widespread industrial strife is likely to become more common in the future, and that it might even be formalized by structural reorganization of the decision-making unit in the economy, is indicated by the spread of co-determination schemes in Germany and other countries where industrial monopoly is unchallenged by national economic policy.[22] Whether or not such arrangements will prove of long-run advantage to capital and labor is problematical; whether or not they will redound to the benefit of unorganized consumers, however, is a question which can—unfortunately—be answered with greater certainty.

IV. Technological and Inter-Industry Competition

The advocates of the countervailing power thesis maintain that competition in the neoclassical sense, *i.e.*, competition among sellers and among buyers within a particular industry, is outmoded. Their argument runs somewhat as follows. Old-fashioned intra-industry competition tends to promote maximum output, minimum prices, and optimum utilization of capacity; in short, it stimulates efficiency. But this efficiency is static and unprogressive in character. It makes no allowance for the research, development, and innovation required for economic growth. While it prevents concentration, it stifles progress. To have progress, we need more, not less concentration. Only bigness can provide the sizable funds necessary for technological experimentation and innovation in the industrial milieu of the twentieth century. Only monopoly earnings can provide the bait that lures capital on to untried trails. While progress may thus require high power concentration in many industries, this need not be a source of concern to society at large. Technological development will serve as an offset against any short-run position of entrenchment which may be established. The monopoly of glass bottles will be countervailed by the introduction of the tin can; and the dominance of the latter will in turn be undermined by the introduction of the paper container. The consumer need not rely, therefore, on the static competition between large numbers of small firms as protection against exploitation. In the long run, he can find far greater safety—and better things for better living, to boot—in the technological competition of a small number of large firms, which through research and innovation eventually destroy any position of market control that may be established.[23]

There are two basic flaws in this argument. The first is that history seems to contradict it. "As a general rule monopolistic combinations and cartels have followed, not preceded, periods of extensive capital investment. For example, before the American trust movement from 1897 to 1903, the merger movement of the twenties, and the widespread resort to cartels during the thirties, industrial expansion was rapid and the volume of new capital commitments large. Moreover, the biggest single expansionary influence in twentieth century industrial development has been the automobile industry and in that field monopoly has been conspicuously absent."[24] It must always be remembered that neither Morgan's rationalization of the railroad industry in 1889, nor Morgan's organization of the U.S. Steel combine in 1901, nor Roosevelt's NRA in 1934 were conspicuous for stimulating technological innovation or increased capital investment. It must always be remembered that the phenomenal performance of American capitalism over the last hundred years may have been achieved not primarily because of the behavior of well entrenched large-scale firms, but "because there was still enough virility left in the competitive process to permit innovations and the breaking into established fields to go on."[25] Certainly we would be guilty of the *post hoc ergo propter hoc* fallacy were we to argue that since monopolization accompanied the long-run growth of output, it also was its cause. Certainly, the European experience with the restrictionism of monopoly capitalism should give us pause before society places exclusive reliance on the countervailing influence of technological competition as a protective device against exploitation, inefficiency, and monopolistic retrogression.

There is another flaw in the argument that inter-industry, product, or technological competition is an effective offset against entrenchment or market domination in any one industry. The facts are that when the paper container began to threaten the tin can duopoly, Continental Can entered the paper container industry; when magnesium threatened the aluminum monopoly, Alcoa started its participation in the magnesium cartel[26]; when aluminum began to be used as a substitute for copper, Anaconda embarked on its venture in the aluminum industry.[27] Today, newspapers control radio stations, and TV outlets are operated by the licensees of AM stations. But most significant of all, perhaps, is the recent merger between the United Paramount Theatres, the largest motion picture theatre chain, and the American Broadcasting Company, the third largest radio and television network.[28]

Here is a combination between giant firms in two separate industries which formerly competed with one another both with respect to audience (people's time and money) and with respect to product (films, talent, stories, etc.). It seems hardly in doubt that this merger tends toward the elimination of inter-industry competition between TV broadcasting, theatre TV, theatre exhibition of motion pictures, and subscription TV (when developed)—to the end of obtaining the largest possible monopolistic benefit for UPT-ABC's over-all operations. As FCC Commissioner Hennock pointed out[29]:

> In such a situation there is a substantial risk that the merged company, through the medium of . . . restrictive practices, may subordinate its television interests to its motion picture exhibition interests, particularly so when the company's greater investments in theatres may be in an especially vulnerable or precarious position. Given the opportunity for economic gain through such restrictive practices, and in the absence of adequate safeguards against them it cannot be assumed that the merged company will push its motion picture theatre and television interests fully and independently of each other, or to anywhere near the same extent that completely unfettered business competitors normally would. . . .

It would seem too much to expect full, vigorous and unrestricted competition between different parts of the same company when the obvious result of such activity would redound to the disadvantage and loss of the company's total operations.[30] Truly, the Brandeis maxim that "one cannot be expected to compete against one's self" is as applicable today as it was forty years ago. Inter-industry competition and technological innovation become a farce when public policy permits them to be subverted by merger and combination. Yet that is exactly what has been happening recently to an increasing extent. That is exactly why the argument of the countervailing power advocates is unconvincing if not outright erroneous.

V. The Role of Government

According to its exponents, countervailing power does not always arise autonomously. Indeed, in some cases, its development may require positive promotion by government action. Galbraith looks upon this promotive activity as the main peacetime function of the federal government and applauds, for example, the enactment of New Deal measures designed to give a group market power it did not previously possess. As a rule of thumb, Galbraith simply suggests that the government "attack positions of original market power in the economy if these are not effectively offset by countervailing power."[31] He regards such action as neither adventitious nor abnormal, since its purpose is merely to support a "natural" economic process. Given the existence of private market power, Galbraith considers governmental countervailance a desirable technique for strengthening the "capacity of the economy for autonomous self-regulation," and deems it an indirect method for lessening the "amount of over-all government control or planning that is (eventually) required or sought."[32] So, at least, the countervailing power doctrine would have us believe.

This thesis rests on the doubtful assumption that there is a sharp dichotomy between the economy, on the one hand, and government, on the other. It assumes that government is an autonomous, monolithic, and self-contained organism. This view is, unfortunately, an intellectual amusement of the past. It ignores the fact that economic interest groups are today largely politicized units, making their claims upon and through the institutions of the state. As V.O. Key observes[33]:

> The dilemma of the politics of economic control comes from the fact that governments must keep in check the pressures of particularism, yet at the same time governments derive their power in no small degree from the support of particularistic interests. Government—that is, political parties, public agencies, the bureaucracy—has a social strength within itself, but fundamentally its power comes from the support won for its policies among the organized and unorganized private interests of society. These are the groups whose activities the government must control in the general interest.

These are the groups against whom countervailing power must, at times, be brought into play. That this is a task of formidable proportions is indicated by an examination of governmental operations on the legislative, administrative, and quasi-judicial levels.

Legislation

In the legislative consideration of many economic measures, the absence of countervailing power is painfully apparent. In the enactment of tariff laws, for example, equal stakes rarely elicit equal pressures. Tariff duties are determined by a process of log-rolling and pressure politics, so that a few "control the process at the expense of the many. The inertia of the masses is so great that not even the strongest incitements of economic interest arouse them."[34] Since the majority is affected only indirectly and obliquely, it seems to acquiesce in the compromises and adjustments made to appease special interests. The result may be legislation devoid of public interest considerations, but the very forces which make such legislation bad economics, assure its political invincibility.

There is little doubt that particularistic, politically vocal, economic pressure groups can use the legislative process for their own advantage. They can demand, and often obtain, governmental aid in countervailing the power of entrenched interests. This does not mean, however, that the form of this countervailance will redound to the general welfare as it does to a narrowly-defined private welfare. Nor does it mean that the basic problems underlying the demand for governmental countervailance will thereby be solved. The NRA may have given businessmen what they wanted at the time; it did not, however, attack the basic causes of depression; nor did it stimulate economic recovery; and it certainly failed to promote the general welfare. The price support program for agriculture may have raised farm incomes, but it has hardly disposed of the farm surpluses rotting away in government warehouses.[35] The fiscal policy of the 80th Congress may have given tax relief to a variety of politically influential groups, but it did not counteract the postwar inflationary spiral nor effectuate a reduction in the national debt. The Capehart, Talle, and Herlong amendments to the Defense Production Act may have pleased the groups benefiting from their enactment, but the resultant emasculation of price controls was not what the majority wanted in a period of defense and inflation. In short, the countervailing action expected of government tends more often than not merely to be an appeasement of special interest pressures. Legislation designed to countervail the power of "economic royalists" is not the product of an independent governmental unit functioning in a vacuum, but the result of a log-rolling process involving compromise with, adjustment to, and appeasement of a variety of special interest claims. Everybody who is somebody seems to get what he wants; only the sum total of these wants is not always equivalent to the needs and desires of the community as a whole.

Administration

The administration of economic laws by various branches of the Executive Department reveals similar limitations on the effective exercise of governmental countervailance. One Congressional investigation, for example, indicated that early in 1941 the Arabian–American Oil Company (a joint subsidiary of Standard Oil of New Jersey, Standard Oil of California, Socony–Vacuum, and Texas Co.) induced our government to extend $99,000,000 in lend-lease aid to Saudi Arabia. In return, the company promised to supply oil to the U.S. Navy at $.40 a barrel. In spite of this commitment, however, Aramco later demanded a price of $1.05 per barrel on a take-it-or-leave-it basis—terms which, under wartime conditions, the Navy could hardly decline. As a result, the Government was over-charged between $30 million and $38 million on oil purchases from Aramco and its affiliates between January 1942 and June 1947. These overcharges—this failure of the most powerful purchaser in the world to exert countervailing power against a dominant supplier—were not unrelated to the fact that the Government was represented in this transaction by persons connected with Aramco, its affili-ates, and its parent companies.[36] As the Senate Committee investigating this matter was prompted to remark: "At times such personnel by reason of past association, training, and habit are susceptible of allowing their past background or thoughts of future benefits to color their official actions. In rare cases there have been a few who designedly sought key positions in Government service so that they could control situations for selfish interests."[37] The Committee which offered these findings and observations was the Brewster Committee of the 80th Congress—hardly a group of willful and habitual muckrakers.

The employment of industry men in government agencies—many on a dollar-a-year basis—seems to have become standard operating procedure in periods of war or defense emergency. As of September 1, 1951, for example, twelve de-fense agencies had on their rolls 876 WOC's (without compensation personnel), many of whom occupied vital policy-making positions.[38] In the Petroleum Ad-ministration for Defense WOC's were at the head of ten divisions having opera-tions service responsibility while only two such divisions had paid government personnel as their directors. WOC's were in positions of comparable responsibil-ity in the Defense Production Administration, the Defense Transport Administra-tion, and the National Production Authority. Many of these WOC's came from the country's largest industrial corporations. Thus, "as of April 20, 1951, 30 of the WOC's working in the National Production Authority were privately em-ployed by the 100 largest manufacturing companies in the United States. This number had increased to 47 by June 25, 1951, or more than one-fourth of all WOC's employed by the NPA."[39]

That the results of these arrangements were not always calculated to bring countervailing power into play is illustrated in the following not unrepresentative cases. In one instance a $68,000,000 contract on vertical turret lathes for the Air Force was awarded to a General Motors subsidiary at a price of $90,000 per lathe, although a smaller firm—the Bullard Company of Bridgeport, Conn.—had submitted a lower bid at $38,000 per lathe. The contract award went to General Motors, however, on the recommendation of H.R. Boyer, a GM official, who was then serving as chairman of the Government's Aircraft Production Board.[40] In another instance, it was found that the commandant of the Army Tank Arsenal in Detroit had permitted a manufacturer who sought contracts with the Arsenal to pay for his travel and hotel expenses, while his subordinates borrowed a total of $200,000 from a number of government contractors. That the Arsenal, during the same period was accumulating a 104 year supply of some jeep replacement parts; that "in many instances the Government was actually gouged in the price paid . . . in the form of what might be considered a disguised subsidy to certain segments of the automotive industry"[41]—these were perhaps mere coincidences in the demonstration of countervailing power in action.

Regulation

The independent regulatory commissions are a third example of how difficult it is to achieve countervailing power through governmental action. The Interstate Commerce Commission is a case in point. This Commission, created to protect the public from the abuses of a highly concentrated power group, today seems mainly to protect the railroads against effective regulation by the public.[42] While it defends the railroads from encroachment by rival means of transportation, the Commission also serves as an effective lobby on behalf of railroad interests. It is the main spokesman for the railroads in their recurrent demands for rate increases; it shields them against efforts by the Post Office Department (acting on behalf of the taxpayers) to induce a reduction in the charges for carrying the public's mail; etc.—phenomena which one careful student has explained as follows[43]:

> The railroads are alone among the interests surrounding the Commission in their constant and comprehensive support of that body. By their continuous praise of the Commission, by their defense of its independence and by their efforts to protect and extend its authority the railroads have made the Commission the beneficiary of what has been their not inconsiderable political power. But in the rough world of competitive politics nothing comes free. Political support must be purchased, and the price which the ICC has paid for its railroad support may be traced through almost all important phases of its policy and behavior.

The result is so close an affiliation between regulator and regulatee, that some observers have recommended the abolition of the ICC as an independent regulatory agency and its replacement by "other instrumentalities better able to act in the public interest."[44]

A similar pattern seems to apply to other independent regulatory bodies. In the case of the Civil Aeronautics Board, its chairman, James Landis, was denied reappointment for objecting to the merger of Pan American and American Overseas Airlines. When he was replaced by Delos W. Rentzel, a brilliant young man who had served the previous fifteen years with the country's largest airlines, doubts were raised concerning the CAB's future exercise of countervailing power in the public interest. Unfortunately, the Commission's recent actions— both with respect to the subsidy–mailpay controversy[45] and with respect to the nonscheduled airlines[46]—have done little to dispel those doubts.

The Federal Power Commission affords another example of how established interests have strengthened their position in the national economy by preventing the appointment of men they considered hostile to their interests. In this case, the target was Leland Olds who had spent a lifetime promoting natural gas conservation and resisting rate increases which influential producer groups and utility companies considered vital to their interests. When Olds was denied confirmation by the Senate, the way was clear for a Commission ruling that the FPC had no jurisdiction over the rates of nonintegrated natural gas producers[47]—a ruling that enacted by administrative fiat what the pressure groups had failed to obtain by legislation. Senator Kerr's Natural Gas Bill,[48] which Mr. Truman had previously vetoed, thus became—for practical intents and purposes—the law of the land. Countervailing power in the public interest had once again been frustrated by the action of an "independent" regulatory agency of the government. Perhaps it was this kind of experience which once prompted Senator Wheeler to remark sadly: "It seems to invariably happen, that when Congress attempts to regulate some group, the intended regulatees wind up doing the regulating."[49]

Senator Wheeler's remark is, of course, only one reaction to the ancient and universal problem: *quis custodiet ipsos custodies?* Painful experience would seem to indicate that governmental creation of countervailing power to curb the market entrenchment of "economic royalists" is more readily accomplished in theory than in practice. As Key points out[50]:

> The solution of the dilemma of controlling the controllers is not easy. Government can play one group against another. . . . Such deftness of political leadership, however, is not a dependable quality of government. The problem of organizing public power, adequate in strength yet responsibly exercised under public control, for the reconciliation of group conflict, and the imposition of programs promotive of the general welfare will doubtless remain for some time without a completely satisfactory solution.

VI. Size, Technology and Efficiency

The final limitation of the countervailing power thesis is inherent in its basic assumption, *viz.*, that the giant size of America's dominant enterprises is the inevitable result of twentieth century technology and economics. The theory assumes that "the process by which the typical industry passes from the hands of the many to the few has not been well understood"[51]; that the causes for this concentration are not to be found in the designs of individual empire builders; that, instead, these causes are deeply organic in the fabric of American industry. It contends that firms grow because they realize the technical economies of large-scale organization; the successful ones acquire the earnings, the reputation and the experience which permit them to expand further; and eventually, as a result of this process, there is no longer freedom of entry into industries where the scale of production is considerable. "At the same time that entry becomes difficult or impossible, the forces which tend to reduce the number already in the industry continue. Weaklings may still fail, and disappear, especially in bad times. Good times make it easy to finance consolidations and tempting for the strong company to expand and the weak to sell out. Thus . . . the combination of a low or zero birthrate and a continuing death rate must always be a declining population."[52] To the extent that this phenomenon is widespread in the American economy, it seems futile to counteract it by antitrust prosecution. "It is possible to prosecute a few evil-doers; it is evidently not so practical to indict a whole economy."[53]

This explanation of the concentration process is the cornerstone of the whole countervailing power theory. If it is valid, then antitrust litigation is obviously outmoded, and countervailing power becomes *one*—if not the—method of dealing with huge economic power aggregates. If the explanation is inadequate, however, other public policy alternatives may become more desirable. In any event, it is important to subject this basic assumption to empirical tests, for as Keynes once remarked, conclusions may be arrived at by clearness and consistency and by easy logic but be based on assumptions inappropriate to the facts.[54] We must examine, therefore, the crucial assumption of the Galbraith thesis, *viz.*, that firms are big because they are efficient; that the firms are big because consumers want them to be big; that bigness is little more than the natural result of modern technological and economic forces.

Elsewhere I have argued[55] that the data on the relation between size and efficiency are by no means conclusive; efficiency is not always the concomitant of giant size; in aluminum and steel, for example, the largest firms are neither great technical innovators nor the paragons of efficient operation; modern technology, far from giving industrial giantism its undivided blessings, may actually militate in favor of industrial deconcentration; and finally, in the one industry where the large-scale dissolution of giant enterprises has been attempted (under the Public Utility Holding Company Act), the result has been an increase rather than a decrease in the efficiency of the successor companies. There is additional evidence. Part of this evidence is submitted here merely to caution against accepting public policy changes on the basis of plausible, yet unsubstantiated, theories of industrial growth.

The record of antitrust prosecutions is replete with cases which demonstrate that industrial pre-eminence is often achieved as much by resort to coercive practices as by "natural" growth processes. In the Tobacco case,[56] for example, a unanimous Supreme Court found that the exorbitant profits of the Big Three in the early thirties attracted the entry of the "10¢ brands"; the appearance of these venturesome newcomers precipitated a devastating price cutting campaign by the majors (which went so far that Camels and Luckies were being sold at a loss, while Liggett curtailed its normal business activities and cut its advertising to the bone); upon elimination of the new competitors, the old price and profit equilibrium of the cigarette oligopoly was successfully restored. Here certainly was one instance where the Big Three held their position, not through a decisive victory in the arena of free consumer choice, but through an aggressive campaign of restricting the range from which the consumer could select a genuine favorite. The victors in this popularity contest were chosen by a process not unlike the "free elections" held in the "people's democracies" of Soviet satellite states.

The more recent case against the United Shoe Machinery Corporation is another illustration of how a firm can enjoy a virtual monopoly, not only on the basis of efficiency but also because of a systematic resort to coercive practices. United used the kind of leasing system, for example, which effectively deterred and prevented their customers from replacing any United machine with that of a competitor. In addition, United apparently engaged in the systematic infringement of patents held by small undiversified competitors, and then cut the bottom out of the specialized market for the machines covered by these patents. So brazen and contemptuous was this practice that, in one of the resulting infringement suits (by N.W. Mathey against United), "the United States District Court for the District of Massachusetts found that United had *intentionally* infringed Mathey's patent, and that United 'knew or must have known' that the effects of the terms established by it on its heel flap trimming machine 'would ruin the plaintiff as its only competitor in a distinctive field.' "[57] This patent infringement, far from being an isolated occurrence, seemed to be just part of a comprehensive program to eliminate competition. It was the kind of competitive tactic which should have proved unnecessary for a company whose pre-eminence rested on technological superiority and/or consumer popularity.

Many cases could be cited to show that competition often dies from other than natural causes, while those responsible for its euthanasia advertise themselves as victors in an unfettered Darwinian struggle. There is evidence that at times the survival of the fittest is promoted, not alone through a process of natural selection, but with the helping hand of a benevolent authority. Government supported research activity is a case in point. Of the nearly 2,000 industrial organizations receiving government research contracts for the fiscal years 1940–44, the 10 largest corporations received 37 per cent of the funds; the 20 largest, 50 per cent; the 40 largest, 60 per cent; and the 60 largest, 65 per cent.[58] Yet in spite of the fact that government funds were expended, the patent rights and know-how on the commercial application of this research were not made freely available to industry in general but became the exclusive property of a handful of large corporations working under contract with the government.[59]

Similarly, during the period 1940–44, the 100 largest corporations received two-thirds of the prime contracts awarded, with more than 51 per cent of such contracts accruing to the top 33 corporations, and a major portion of the subcontracts also going to larger companies. The government permitted this concentration of war contracts despite the fact that smaller plants had a considerable amount of idle, but usable, capacity—despite the fact that "nearly one-third of these plants reported that they could increase their production by 50 per cent or more over January 1943 levels without adding new machinery or construction."[60] According to a report by the Senate Small Business Committee, the concentration of defense contracts as of July 19, 1951 was even greater than during World War II: "10 large manufacturing companies have been handed 40 per cent of the total dollar volume of defense contracts since Korea; 50 companies command almost two-thirds of the dollar volume of defense contracts."[61] Again, existing facilities of smaller manufacturers seem to be ignored, both in the award of prime and subcontracts. As a matter of fact, there are many instances where giant companies are subsidized in their expansion of plant facilities, while the plants of their smaller brethren languish in idleness.

An examination of the allocations and priority system,[62] the accelerated amortization program,[63] the disposal of war surplus establishments,[64] the structure of business taxes[65] reveals the same pattern of promoting concentration—at times through unconscious, at times through deliberate action by the most powerful economic unit in the world. The net effect is that established giants remain dominant while the competition of newcomers is effectively handicapped. As Galbraith rightly points out, "in this race the horse with the poorest record, or no record, must carry the greatest weight."[66] In the present institutional framework this is practically inevitable, but—as Galbraith fails to point out—there is nothing inevitable about the framework itself. It might be well to remember that, given the status quo, horses are assigned their jockeys not by a system of natural law, but by the rules of men. A different weight distribution may result in different racing returns. A racing commission which is not loaded against the long-shot; a punctilious supervision of the track while the race is in progress— these changes may not alter the composition of the winner's circle; they will, however, shorten the odds. My point is simply this: the nature of the man-made handicaps has a more decisive influence than we are willing to concede. Until we know more about the correlation between handicaps and derby winners, it ill behooves us to consider racing results under current rules as inexorable, inevitable and unavoidable.

VII. Conclusion

In conclusion, we can say that the countervailing power thesis is not without merit; that it rightly calls attention to the existence of potential checks and balances which, in our economy, supplement competition as a device for counteracting concentrated economic power. This does not mean, however, that countervailing power is a suitable substitute for competition; or that it can long survive in the absence of competition; or that it affords any clear and administratively feasible guidelines for public policy.

Some measure of countervailing power is obviously ubiquitous. It exists in a socialist state where the steel monopoly countervails the aluminum monopoly and where the trades union congress offsets the power of the central industry planning board. It is present, to some degree, in a fascist corporate state as well as in a sovietized society. This hardly affords any assurance, however, that the people will be protected against actual or potential abuse of concentrated economic power.

Before we discard competition as the cornerstone of national economic policy, we might well recall that even our socialist critics regard competition as the oldest and strongest defense of private capitalism and enterprise. As Herbert Morrison once observed[67]:

> Free competition, the intelligent anti-socialist used to argue, is the only way of bringing prices down to the level of costs and seeing that production is not unnecessarily restricted and the public overcharged. There was great force in this argument—but it is now dead, killed by events. When Lord McGowen defends the cartel, with often cogent arguments drawn from the benefits of large-scale organization, research, etc., he is publicly consigning to the scrap heap the one powerful argument against socialism that ever existed.

It is to be hoped that we will not consign the most powerful defense of our economic system to what may prove to be a totalitarian scrap heap before a careful examination of all existing alternatives.

Notes

1. H.C. Simons, *Economic Policy for a Free Society,* pp. 43–44 (1948). Italics in original.

2. Mutual Security Administrator Harold Stassen supported this contention when he said: "World economic history has shown that nationalization and socialization have come when there has been complete consolidation and combination of industry, not when enterprise is manifold and small in its units. . . . We must not permit major political power to be added to the other great powers that are accumulated by big business units. Excessive concentration of power is a threat to the individual freedoms and liberties of men, whether that excessive power is in the hands of government or of capital or of labor." (Address reprinted in *Congressional Record,* February 12, 1947, p. A545.)

3. For conflicting views on the extent of concentration in the American economy, see M.A. Adelman, "The Measurement of Industrial Concentration," *Review of Economics and Statistics* (Nov. 1951); and J.M. Blair, "The Measurement of Industrial Concentration: A Reply," *Review of Economics and Statistics* (Nov. 1952).

4. J.M. Clark, "Toward a Concept of Workable Competition," *American Economic Review* (June 1940). It should be noted that the first significant and sophisticated departure from the use of pure competition as an "ideal" was made earlier than this. E.H. Chamberlin in his *Theory of Monopolistic Competition* (1933) had indicated (pp. 94 and 104) that the "ideal" was not to be identified with pure competition, and had developed the matter further in "Monopolistic Competition or Imperfect Competition," *Quarterly Journal of Economics,* Aug. 1937, see esp. pp. 576 ff (reproduced as chap. 9 of the 5th ed. of *Monopolistic Competition,* esp. pp. 213–15). See also his "Product Heterogeneity and Public Policy," *American Economic Review* (May 1950), pp. 85–92. Clark's references to Chamberlin would indicate an attempt to define within the area of monopolistic competition the conditions which would be "workably satisfactory"—to apply to this field the pragmatic criterion, a criterion, by the way, which leaves much to be desired.

5. E.S. Mason, "The Antitrust Laws: A Symposium," *American Economic Review,* p. 713 (June 1949). See also C.E. Griffin, *An Economic Approach to Antitrust Problems* (1951).

6. J.K. Galbraith, *American Capitalism: The Concept of Countervailing Power,* p. 1 (1952). For a less sophisticated version of the Galbraith thesis, see D.E. Lilienthal, *Big Business: A New Era* (1953).

7. Galbraith, op. cit., pp. 61–62.

8. Ibid., p. 118.

9. It is of interest that the author served as economic counsel to the Senate Small Business Committee, 82d Congress.—Ed.

10. *U.S.* v. *The Pullman Company,* 50 F. Supp. 123 (1943).

11. As of 1945, fourteen major railroads had directors who also served on the directorate of one or more of seven investment banking houses; nine of the roads had directors who were also on the directorate of one or more of five big insurance companies; and four roads had directors who were also on the directorate of Pullman Incorporated. See *Brief for the United States in Opposition to Offer of the Railroads to Purchase the Sleeping Car Business, U.S.* v. *The Pullman Company et al.,* pp. 6–7 (1945).

12. For other examples of how top-level financial control can actually or potentially subvert the operation of countervailing power, see L.D. Brandeis, *Other People's Money and How the Investment Bankers Use It,* pp. 52ff (1932); Smaller War Plants Corporation, *Economic Concentration and World War II,* 79th Congress, 2d Session, Senate Document No. 206, pp. 354–56 (1946); *Federal Trade Commission Report on Interlocking Directorates* (1951); Complaint in *U.S.* v. *E.I. du Pont de Nemours et. al.,* Civil Action No. 49C–1071, filed June 30, 1949.

13. See Federal Communications Commission, *In the Matter of Allen B. Du Mont Laboratories, Inc., and Paramount Pictures, Inc.,* Docket No. 10032 (1953) (mimeographed edition).

14. *U.S.* v. *Paramount Pictures, Inc.,* 334 U.S. 131 (1948).

15. It is debatable whether from the consumer's point of view vertical integration is less desirable than bilateral monopoly (and the countervailing power situation inherent therein). In this connection, one careful student of the food industry has suggested that "(1) two successive monopolists, one above the other, would tend always to raise prices and limit supplies more than a single monopolist combining both their functions"; "(2) as the number of points of successive monopoly increases in the marketing system, the situation so far as the public is concerned becomes progressively worse"; and "(3) paradoxical as it seems at first thought, the public would probably be helped rather than injured by a conspiring between the successive monopolists to increase the amount of their combined profits." A.C. Hoffman, *Large-Scale Organization in the Food Industries,* T.N.E.C. Monograph No. 35, p. 85 (1940). In defending the integration activities of A & P, Adelman has argued along somewhat similar lines. See M.A. Adelman, "The A & P Case: A Study in Applied Economic Theory," *Quarterly Journal of Economics,* pp. 244–47 (May 1949).

16. Oliver W. Holmes was perhaps the first judge to apply the theory of countervailing power to a case involving a labor dispute. Said Justice Holmes: "I have seen the suggestion made that the conflict between employers and employed is not competition. But I venture to assume that none of my brethren would rely on that suggestion. If the policy on which our law is founded is too narrowly expressed in the term free competition, we may substitute free struggle for life. Certainly the policy is not limited to struggles between persons of the same class competing for the same end. It applies to all conflicts of temporal interests. . . . One of the eternal conflicts out of which life is made up is that between the effort of every man to get the most he can for his services, and that of

society, disguised under the name of capital, to get his services for the least possible return. Combination on the one side is patent and powerful. Combination on the other is the necessary and desirable counterpart, if the battle is to be carried on in a fair and equal way." 167 Mass. 92, 107–8 (1896).

17. Galbraith, op. cit., p. 122.

18. In fairness to Galbraith, it must be pointed out that he recognizes inflationary periods as a special situation under which countervailing power tends to become inoperative. Galbraith, op. cit., pp. 195–208.

19. For a further discussion of this problem, see W. Fellner, "Prices and Wages under Bilateral Monopoly," *Quarterly Journal of Economics* (Aug. 1947).

20. For the economic facts of this dispute, see E. Arnall, *Statement on Steel before the Senate Committee on Labor and Public Welfare,* Senate Document No. 118, 82d Cong., 2d Sess. (April, 1952).

21. R. Liefmann, *Cartels, Concerns, and Trusts,* p. 80 (1938).

22. For an incisive report on the implications of this new form of syndicalism, see National Association of Manufacturers, *Co-Determination,* Economic Policy Division Series No. 42 (1951).

23. Galbraith, op. cit., pp. 91–99. This argument is based largely on Schumpeter, *Capitalism, Socialism and Democracy,* pp. 79 ff (1942).

24. G.W. Stocking and M.W. Watkins, *Cartels or Competition?,* p. 236 (1948).

25. G.H. Hildebrand, "Monopolization and the Decline of Investment Opportunity," *American Economic Review,* p. 595 (Sept. 1943).

26. See the indictment in *U.S.* v. *Aluminum Company of America,* Criminal 109–89. The defendants pleaded nolo contendere and were fined $104,993 (April 15, 1942).

27. Joint Committee on Defense Production, *Aluminum Expansion Program and Competition,* House Report No. 1, 83d Cong., 1st Sess., p. 12 (1953).

28. In 1952, ABC operated 4½ AM, 5 FM and 5 TV outlets, all in key cities; in addition, ABC had 298 AM affiliates, 113 FM affiliates, and 64 TV affiliates, and achieved a total net sales of $53 million for the first eleven months of 1951.

29. Federal Communications Commission, *In the Matter of American Broadcasting Company, Inc. and United Paramount Theatres, Inc.,* Docket No. 10046, Dissenting Opinion, p. 13 (1953) (mimeographed edition).

30. "Thus it seems clear that the merged company would be less likely to push the fullest development of television service (by station construction or the finest programming) in a city in which its theatre investments were substantial and/or on a comparatively unsound financial basis than it would in a city in which its theatre interests were nonexistent, small or had already repaid investments and yielded large returns. Similarly, its presentations of theatre TV programs and the extent to which it promotes them by advertising, etc., would also quite naturally be affected by the existence and precise nature of its television interests in a particular city. Even the merged company's promotion of television service might in this same manner be aimed at accomplishing only personal gain to the company at the expense of overall TV service in general. Thus, in a city where the merged company has both television affiliates and its own theatres, it is only to be expected that it will arrange its special theatre events (either of feature films or theatre TV) on those particular nights when least likely to interfere with its own television programs and more likely to interfere with those of its broadcasting competitors, and vice versa. Such restrictive practices ad infinitum could be pursued by the merged company on a local as well as a national level and no theatre or station manager could be expected to manage his own particular operation in any way but to cause as great benefit and as little possible harm to the company as a whole." Federal Communications Commission, op. cit., p. 14.

31. Op. cit., p. 144.
32. Ibid., p. 155.
33. Key, *Politics, Parties and Pressure Groups,* p. 204 (1945).
34. E.E. Schattschneider, *Politics, Pressures and the Tariff,* p. 287 (1935).
35. The government now holds 342 million bushels of wheat, 100 million bushels of corn, 464 million pounds of tobacco, 1.4 million bales of cotton, 6.8 million dozens of eggs, 42.5 million pounds of butter, 48.4 million pounds of turkey, etc.—an investment valued at $1.25 billion. The prospects are that the size of these agricultural surpluses will increase, rather than diminish, in the foreseeable future. See *U.S. News & World Report,* February 6, 1953, p. 21.
36. The Director of the Foreign Division of the Petroleum Administration for Defense was a former Vice President of Aramco; the naval officer who wrote the purchase justification for Aramco oil at $1.05 per barrel was a former official of a Socony–Vacuum subsidiary; the admiral serving as executive officer of the Army–Navy Petroleum Board was a former president of a Texas–Socal subsidiary; and the Deputy Petroleum Administrator for War was a former officer of Standard Oil of California. See Special Committee Investigating the National Defense Program, *Navy Purchases of Middle East Oil,* 80th Cong., 2d Sess., Report No. 440, Part 5, p. 26 (1948).
37. Ibid., p. 26.
38. Subcommittee on the Study of Monopoly Power of the Committee on the Judiciary, *The Mobilization Program,* 82d Cong., 1st Sess., House Report No. 1217, p. 79 (1951).
39. Ibid., p. 81.
40. House Committee on Armed Services, *Hearings on Military Waste,* 82d Cong., 2d Sess., 1952; quoted in the *Detroit Free Press,* January 21, 1953, p. 6.
41. Committee on Expenditures in the Executive Departments, *Inquiry into the Procurement of Automotive Spare Parts by the United States Government,* 82d Cong., 2d Sess., House Report, No. 1811, p. 7 (1952).
42. This state of affairs was foreseen as long ago as 1892 by Richard Olney, the Attorney General during the Cleveland administration. In reply to his friend Charles E. Perkins, President of the Burlington and Quincy Railroad, who had recommended that Olney press for the abolition of the Interstate Commerce Commission, Olney wrote as follows: "My impression would be that looking at the matter from a railroad point of view exclusively it would not be a wise thing to undertake. . . . The attempt would not be likely to succeed; if it did not succeed, and were made on the ground of inefficiency and uselessness of the Commission, the result would very probably be giving it the power it now lacks. The Commission, as its functions have now been limited by the courts, is, or can be made, of great use to the railroads, at the same time that that supervision is almost entirely nominal. Further, the older such a commission gets to be, the more inclined it will be found to take the business and railroad view of things. It thus becomes a sort of barrier between the railroad corporations and the people and a sort of protection against hasty and crude legislation hostile to railroad interests. . . . The part of wisdom is not to destroy the Commission, but to utilize it." Quoted in M. Josephson, *The Politicos,* p. 526 (1938).
43. S.P. Huntington, "The Marasmus of the I.C.C.," *Yale Law Journal,* p. 481 (April 1952).
44. Ibid., p. 509.
45. House Committee on Interstate and Foreign Commerce, *Hearings on Air Mail Subsidies,* 82d Cong., 2d Sess., 1952; L.P. Marvin, Jr., "Air Mail Subsidy Separation," *Georgetown Law Journal,* pp. 161–240 (January 1952).
46. Senate Small Business Committee, *Report on Role of Irregular Airlines in United States Air Transportation Industry,* 82d Cong., 1st Sess., Report No. 540 (1951).

47. Federal Power Commission, *In the Matter of the Phillips Petroleum Company,* Opinion No. 217, Docket No. G–1148, August 16, 1951.

48. S. 1498, 81st Congress, 1st Session, introduced April 4, 1949.

49. Quoted in B. Bolles, *How to Get Rich in Washington,* p. 23 (1952).

50. Op. cit., p. 204.

51. Galbraith, op. cit., p. 36.

52. Ibid., p. 38.

53. Ibid., p. 55.

54. Keynes, *General Theory,* p. 371.

55. See W. Adams, "The Dilemma of Antitrust Aims: A Reply," *American Economic Review,* pp. 895–900 (Dec. 1952).

56. *U.S.* v. *American Tobacco Company et al.,* 328 U.S. 781 (1946).

57. Complaint in *U.S.* v. *United Shoe Machinery Corporation,* Civil Action No. 7198, p. 27 (filed December 15, 1947).

58. See Smaller War Plants Corporation, *Economic Concentration and World War II,* 79th Cong., 2d Sess., Senate Document No. 206, p. 52 (1946).

59. To correct this situation, the Attorney General has recommended that "Where patentable inventions are made in the course of performing a Government-financed contract for research and development, the public interest requires that all rights to such inventions be assigned to the Government and not left to the private ownership of the contractor. Public control will assure free and equal availability of the inventions to American industry and science; will eliminate any competitive advantage to the contractor chosen to perform the research work; will avoid undue concentration of economic power in the hands of a few large corporations; will tend to increase and diversify available research facilities within the United States to the advantage of the Government and of the national economy; and will thus strengthen our American system of free, competitive enterprise." U.S. Department of Justice, *Investigation of Government Patent Practices and Policies,* vol. I, p. 4 (1947).

60. Attorney General, *Report Prepared Pursuant to Section 708(e) of the Defense Production Act of 1950,* p. 14 (December 1950). See also H.R. Bowen, "Impact of the War upon Smaller Manufacturing Plants," *Survey of Current Business,* July 1943.

61. Senate Small Business Committee, *Concentration of Defense Contracts,* 82d Cong., 1st Sess., Report No. 551, p. 1 (1951).

62. House Small Business Committee, *Hearings on the Problems of Small Business under the Controlled Materials Plan,* 82d Cong., 2d Sess., Parts 1–4 (1952).

63. Joint Committee on Defense Production, *Hearings on Tax Amortization,* 82d Cong., 1st Sess. (1951).

64. *Report of the Attorney General under Section 205 of the War Mobilization and Reconversion Act of 1944,* Reports 1–5 (1945).

65. Senate Small Business Committee, *Hearings on the Tax Problems of Small Business,* 82d Cong., 2d Sess. (1952).

66. Op. cit., p. 37.

67. H. Morrison, *Government and Industry,* p. 11 (1944).

IV

A Public Philosophy

15

Interview: Economic Power and the Constitution

Q. When I picked up *The Bigness Complex*, I saw immediately that it was about economic power, its exercise and control. What advice would you give to the President of the United States based upon the most important information to be learned from your book?

A. To the extent that the President is inclined to read more than a two-page memo now and then, I would recommend that he first read *The Federalist Papers*, the manifesto of this nation's Founding Fathers, and then turn to Adam Smith's *The Wealth of Nations*.

Q. But why would you ask a leader at the end of the 20th century to consult 18th-century savants?

A. Simply because their insights into the political economy of power and the difficulties of controlling it in the public interest are as relevant today as they were 200 years ago. That is why we included a discussion of the two great revolutions of 1776—one in America, one in Great Britain.

As we celebrate the 200th anniversary of the U.S. Constitution, the President should be reminded that the Founding Fathers, colonists living under the absolute power of the British Crown, made us heirs to a political blueprint providing for a decentralized power structure, replete with checks and balances and overlapping safeguards against potential abuses by an all-powerful state. They understood that the state had to be strong enough to secure the rights of its citizens and to prevent one group from oppressing another. At the same time, they recognized that a government strong enough to protect its citizens might be powerful enough to enslave them.

The Founding Fathers knew that the paramount danger of the powerful state (and its enormous capacity for influence) was its susceptibility to capture by

Originally published in *Challenge*, July/August 1987.

special interests, or by coalitions of special interests, intent on perverting government to their private ends. They understood that once the state intervenes on behalf of one special interest group, an "orderly routine of democratic corruption" is set into motion as other organized interests seek counteracting state interference in their private behalf, too. The outcome is what Henry Simons later called "the moral disintegration of representative government in the endless contest of innumerable pressure groups for special political favors."

As the Founding Fathers were pondering these problems, Adam Smith, an ocean away, was writing his economic manifesto, *The Wealth of Nations*. He, too, wrestled with the question of the proper role of the state in a free society. But he framed the problem in an explicit context of political economy. Smith saw in the mercantilist state of his day a perfect example of the "orderly corruption" of (monarchical) government by special interests. In his polemical tract, Smith traced the nature, means, and consequences of the oppression of the public when the state is perverted into a handmaiden for private interest groups—that is, when government is subverted to the end of dispensing private privilege and preferment.

Q. What is the most important idea you would communicate to United States Senators and Congressmen today?

A. The Congress seems bedeviled by the tyranny of small decisions. It is preoccupied with a search for makeshift, ad hoc, quick-fix palliatives. It is constantly compelled to deal with "immediate" problems: first inflation, then recession; nagging unemployment; burgeoning imports, escalating trade deficits, and the threat of "Japan, Inc."; transformation of the industrial heartland into an obsolescent rustbelt; lagging R & D and lethargic innovation; a defunct nuclear power industry drowning in red ink; massive cost overruns in military procurement; overregulation and deregulation. The list seems endless.

Yet Congress seems incapable of dealing with these essentially structural problems in a structural context. It too, like the President, might profitably take time out from interest-group politics and contemplate how best to harmonize individual freedom with the public interest—how to reconcile free-enterprise economics with a political democracy.

Q. For the third part of the same question: What message would you convey to U.S. corporate leaders today, let us say, members of the Business Roundtable, for example?

A. I would recommend that they not emulate the Soviet model by trying to organize the American economy around ever larger Brobdingnagian bureaucracies. That is not the road to efficiency, creativity, technological progress, or international competitiveness.

The corporate welfare state may be an alluring attraction. Economic planning under the tripartite aegis of Big Business, Big Labor, and Big Government, may hold out the promise of the "quiet life." But, in the long run, this is the road to the demise of capitalism.

The concentration of power, when it runs its course, inevitably invites direct government supervision or, in the worst case, government ownership. Therefore, sophisticated conservatives, intent on saving the capitalist system, have to recognize that they confront an inevitable trade-off: either submit to regulation by a free competitive system or take the risk of eventual, direct government control.

Q. Do you think that U.S. capitalism is threatened? You used the phrase, to save capitalism.

A. Let me put it this way. It may not be threatened today, but if tomorrow we have a major recession and the system breaks down, the tendency will be— judging by past experience—to embrace radical solutions which really are no solutions at all.

Those of us who grew up during the Great Depression, when the unemployment rate hovered around 20 percent, and when one-third of the nation was "ill-fed, ill-clad, and ill-housed," remember that a surprising number of Americans flirted with the totalitarian solutions being implemented at the time in Italy, Germany, and the Soviet Union.

In those days, it was difficult to persuade people that the totalitarian state, which presumes to act in the best interest of the people, is as capable of economic exploitation, abuse of power, and oppression of the individual as a system of private monopoly or monopoly capitalism.

To me, capitalism means competitive free enterprise, with the emphasis on competitive. Competition has to be an essential component of a free-enterprise system. Its centerpiece has to be a decentralized power structure.

Q. But corporate executives, lawmakers, and the President himself, both conservatives and liberals all talk about competitiveness in an entrepreneurial society. They all want fair, equitable competition in our international trade. Yet, they don't necessarily give competition the same meaning as you do.

A. Well, let me cite Ross Perot, a true entrepreneur. When his company, Electronic Data Systems (EDS) was acquired by General Motors, he made some incisive analytical remarks about the American automobile industry. As he observed it, the industry didn't really know how to compete. It engaged in intramural sports for too long: General Motors played the competitive game as if it owned bat, ball, gloves, both teams, the stadium, and the lights. Under those conditions it could hardly lose. Things even got so bad that they tried to get divisions to compete with one another—Chevrolet with Pontiac, Oldsmobile with Buick, etc. This was rivalry, but it was oligopolistic rivalry, not genuine competition among independent decision-making units.

Eventually, when foreign competition reared its ugly head, the U.S. auto giants did not try to beat their foreign competitors in the marketplace, but instead ran to the government and asked for a bail-out in the form of protectionism. They obtained the so-called voluntary import quotas that now govern the auto trade. This is a brand of free-enterprise economics strangely inconsistent with the official rhetoric of the President and the Business Roundtable.

Q. How did they use the "breathing space" they enjoyed under the import quotas?

A. First of all, they entered into joint ventures with their foreign adversaries: GM/Toyota, GM/Daewoo, GM/Isuzu, GM/Suzuki, GM/Lotus; and there was also Ford/Mazda, Ford/Mazda/Kia; and Chrysler/Mitsubishi, Chrysler/Mitsubishi/Hyundai, Chrysler/Samsung, Chrysler/Maserati, and so on. The Big Three didn't use their breathing space to fight foreign competition; they merely ran up the white flag and joined their foreign competitors.

Second of all, the auto giants embarked on a strategy of diversifying out of the automobile industry. GM acquired Electronic Data Systems for $2.5 billion, and Hughes Aircraft for a cool $5 billion.

Q. What was the great attraction of Hughes Aircraft?

A. GM was entering an industry in which it anticipated it would not have to face foreign competition. GM obviously thought that its Hughes subsidiary was unlikely to encounter the Koreans, Japanese, and Taiwanese in selling to the Pentagon.

Finally the Big Three used their breathing space to relocate production offshore, exporting jobs to facilities abroad.

These decisions indicate tremendous discretionary power. These corporations possess power that has an impact not only on the welfare of individual companies but power to make broad-gauged planning decisions that have serious consequences for the economic system as a whole. In effect, they have usurped the planning function which in a free-enterprise economy is supposed to be performed by the "invisible hand" of the competitive market. They are *imperia in imperio*—governments in the guise of merchants.

This brings me back to the fundamental questions we have to ask over and over again in our efforts to construct a free, democratic economic system: who makes what decisions, on whose behalf, for whose benefit, and at what cost? To whom are these decisionmakers accountable? If they make mistakes, what are the possibilities for correcting the mistakes? What is the structural mechanism we choose for making the corrections? Does that mechanism militate toward good decisions and tend to prevent bad decisions with antisocial consequences?

Q. You argue that the Bigness Complex poses essentially structural problems. As you see it, they are rooted in economic giantism, and economic institutions of disproportionate size. How do you propose we attack and solve those problems?

A. First of all, we have to recognize that economic and political power is a fact of life. It has its origins in the Bigness Complex and is wielded by it. We have to recognize also that such power and its use have profound social consequences. Yet neither the neoliberals on the left, nor the neoconservatives on the right seem willing to tackle this problem. Neither camp provides a mechanism for disciplining or controlling the power of the Bigness Complex.

Q. But they do offer solutions, don't they?

A. Yes, the neoliberals would trust in a coalition of Big Business, Big Labor, and Big Government. In my view, this would merely result in a coalescence of power. It would institutionalize and legitimize economic planning by powerful special-interest groups. It would delegate decision-making to politically potent power blocs wedded to the status quo. It would not provide for an effective accountability mechanism or adequate safeguards to protect the public interest.

At the other end of the spectrum, the neoconservatives would place their faith in leaders who emerge victorious from the no-holds-barred struggle in the Darwinian jungle. This vision is, at best, naive. It ignores the fact that untrammeled market freedom—laissez-faire in the literal sense—includes the freedom to subvert the market. Contrary to neo-Darwinist ideology, the competitive market is not a gift of nature. It is a man-made institution that, in the absence of public supervision and nurturing, can be eroded by powerful private interests unwilling to submit to its disciplining constraint.

Moreover, as a man-made device, the competitive market cannot solve all economic problems. In "natural monopoly" sectors of the economy, competition is technologically infeasible and unworkable. Consumers are not omniscient and information is not perfect. Nor can a laissez-faire market resolve such "externality" problems as unclean air and water and lethal toxic wastes. To maintain otherwise is, as Dr. Johnson observed of second marriages, a triumph of hope over experience.

Q. We have always had the experience in this country and abroad, now and in earlier centuries, that private interests struggle to gain control over markets, or to gain power over the governing authorities who then could change the rules to their own private advantage.

A. For that very reason the Founding Fathers, in their wisdom, designed a government structure with limited powers—with checks and balances over the use of power, and decentralization of the sources of power. They created a governance structure which—they hoped—would be difficult to capture by special interests. As we celebrate the 200th anniversary of the U.S. Constitution, with all its remarkable features, it is well to remember that this governance system was not designed to function efficiently. Quite the contrary. The founders created—by design—a system with a decentralized power structure with built-in checks and balances, a tripartite division of power between executive, legislative, and judicial branches. Within the legislative branch, we have a Senate and a

House, with different constituencies. Just to get a bill passed is a major achievement, and once a bill is passed, it can be vetoed by the President. The process is designed to move slowly, to avoid haste. It is basically distrustful of ruling majorities, because of the suspicion that ruling majorities may become instruments of oppression. The Constitution makes it difficult to capture control of the state. Any such attempt would have to capture all three branches of government simultaneously. That is no easy task.

Q. Even though the framers of the Constitution knew well the tyranny emerging from within the government, and therefore created a government structure to prevent that, the Founding Fathers didn't anticipate concentrations of power outside the government or the tyranny that might potentially emerge from it.

A. I would not say "tyranny." That's too flamboyant. But it is true that the corporate sector can generate private fiefdoms of control, dominance, and unaccountable discretionary power. And I don't mean just the power of monopolies, oligopolies, or cartels in particular industries or in narrowly defined "relevant" markets.

I mean the ability of industrial giants to manipulate the state—to insulate themselves and their clients from the discipline of the competitive market, as well as from the social control of government.

I mean the ability of corporate giants, almost irrespective of efficient performance, to survive as federal protectorates in a cozy world of cost-plus, safely protected from the specter of competition, efficiency, and innovation.

I mean the power to thwart and sabotage broad social policies—for example, with respect to auto safety, fuel conservation, clean air, pure water, safe drugs, and so on.

As Louis D. Brandeis recognized long ago, the "evils of bigness are something different from and additional to the evils of monopoly."

Q. Can't the government provide a countervailing force against private-sector power?

A. American experience since World War II doesn't make me optimistic about that. In the 1950s, John Kenneth Galbraith argued in *American Capitalism: The Theory of Countervailing Power* that economic power on one side of the market, say among sellers, is not a social evil when that private economic power is held in check by some countervailing power from the other side of the market. Galbraith claimed, although I don't think he would do so today, that countervailing power, not classical competition, is the instrument for keeping concentrated power in check.

But experience shows that countervailing power is not a suitable substitute for antitrust policy, because it tends to be subverted by vertical collusion, whether tacit or overt, between the opposing power blocs. It tends to be transmuted into coalescing power, and this makes it even more difficult to control market power in noncompetitive industries.

The virulence with which management and labor in recent years have fought for protectionism, notably in steel and automobiles, affords a striking illustration of tacit vertical collusion and coalescing power in action. It reflects the common perception by both management and labor that immunity from competition confers private benefits on both groups—that, therefore, government protection from competition is in their rational, albeit short-run, mutual self-interest. In the longer run, to be sure, the exercise of such coalescing power may be tantamount to a mutual suicide pact between Big Business and Big Labor which exacerbates and perpetuates delinquent industrial performance. And government, by legitimatizing the exercise of coalescing power, becomes an accomplice in this game of counterproductive special-interest politics.

Q. Let me come back to the Constitution; while it created a structure of government that decentralized power and protected against political tyranny, did it really protect against tyranny based on concentrated economic power in the private sector?

A. Certainly the Founding Fathers did not foresee how a society might generate concentrations of private power that would constitute as potent a threat as government to individual freedom and equality. They did not anticipate the profound economic transformations that occurred after the Civil War and ushered in an era of private economic feudalism. They did not face up to the fact that a government that is too weak to oppress the individual by the abuse of public power is also too weak to protect us from the depredations of concentrated private power. Or conversely, as Hans Morgenthau pointed out, a government that is strong enough to keep the new feudalism in check in order to protect the freedom of the many is also strong enough to destroy the freedom of all.

This poses a major contemporary dilemma. Given the size of Big Government today, the incentives to capture control of the state have substantially increased. More than ever, Big Government can dispense monopoly, preferment, privilege, subsidies, and protection. Government can be used as an instrument to insulate and immunize private power from any mechanism of public control.

This danger has not suddenly come upon us. There are obvious historical precedents. But one of the great changes that has taken place since the days of the robber barons is the growth in the power and the role of government. The problem today, as compared with the turn of the last century, isn't simply a Standard Oil trust imposing taxation without representation on the consumers of its product. Today we have coalitions of power groups that can subvert the public interest.

Take, for example, the Big Three in the automobile industry and their relationship to the United Auto Workers. This labor–industrial complex can jointly exercise sufficient influence over government so that government will become an instrument for protecting and immunizing the labor–industrial complex from the kind of competition that would serve the public interest. "Voluntary import quotas" are only one case in point. The import problem, of course, was triggered by the industry's delinquent performance in its heyday of unchallenged oligopoly dominance. It was a self-inflicted injury resulting from a continuous price–wage–price spiral and a serious deterioration in the quality of its products that was bound eventually to bring new entrants into the U.S. market. Entry came in the form of foreign imports. When the labor–industrial complex persuaded a compliant government to protect them from this competitive threat, the power complex acquired a new dimension—it became the labor–management–government complex.

Q. Hasn't the government been forced to become a partner in the Bigness Complex because some industrial corporations and banks have become so large that the social cost of failure is simply too large?

A. That was the rationale used to intervene in the collapse of Penn–Central, Lockheed, Chrysler, and Continental Illinois Bank. But I don't share your belief that Big Government has no alternative other than to join the labor–industrial complex in organizing rescue missions for giant companies that have fallen victim to managerial incompetence, technological lethargy, or insensitivity to changing market conditions. If corporate behemoths can confidently expect government bail-outs from the adverse consequences of their own ineptitude, what are the effects on the incentive structure of a free-enterprise economy? To what extent do such bail-outs compromise a system that is supposed to reward successful firms with profits and punish poor performers with losses? If giant corporations are protected from the risks of failure, doesn't this encourage inefficiency and result in a misallocation of resources?

Q. What alternatives do you propose?

A. Clearly, chapter 11 bankruptcy is a feasible alternative to a bail-out policy. Insolvency, in the accounting sense, does not mean that the physical and human assets of an ailing corporation are condemned to disappear. Chapter 11 doesn't mean the physical shutdown of an enterprise—a closing of factories and firing of workers. It merely means that an ailing but economically viable corporation is made subject to drastic reorganization. Its deficient management may be ousted and replaced by a court-appointed trustee or a team designated by senior creditors. Its owners may suffer losses in the form of reduced equity values. But the corporation as a going concern would not disappear. It would be reorganized in order to enhance its prospects for long-run survival.

Q. Should banks, as creators of the money supply, be treated differently than large industrial enterprises?

A. In the Continental Illinois case, you may remember how the comptroller of the currency responded to a congressional committee when asked if he would bail out a local bank if it happened to fail. He answered, "No, we probably would bail out only the ten largest banks in the country." So I ask you, is it sound economic policy to permit corporations or banks to grow to such size of power that they have to be bailed out, even when their difficulties constitute self-inflicted injury?

I would say no. It is inevitable in a free enterprise economy that mistakes will be made—that some firms will miscalculate costs or product demands, that some will find themselves in uneconomic locations or product fields due to shifting economic circumstances, that efforts aimed at innovation in product and manufacturing technique will fail, that some will be unable to obtain loanable funds when they need them, and that they will suffer other unforeseen circumstances and events. So long as firms are relatively small in size, these private failures are prevented from becoming social disasters, and society is able to absorb mistakes. But once corporations are permitted to attain Brobdingnagian proportions, this is no longer the case. Then society confronts what Walter Lippman saw as "the problems and the tragedies of semi-obsolete corporate leviathans that are unable to live and unable to die." Then disproportionate size converts private mistakes into social catastrophes, the community's capacity to absorb private error is corroded, and society is rendered less stable and more vulnerable as a result.

Q. How can we work out better solutions to failures in the Bigness Complex? What policy guidelines would you establish?

A. Here again, the key is an economic architecture in which power is dispersed as much as possible, subject only to the constraints imposed by technological and economic imperatives. In social policy, as in private portfolio management, it is wise not to put all of one's eggs in one basket. It is prudent to diversify risk, so that the failure of an individual corporation does not become a social calamity.

The moral is clear. Where society tolerates the creation of great power concentrations, it may eventually confront an intractable dilemma: to be a bail-out agency of last resort for the malfunctioning of these power aggregates—thereby undermining the essence of market discipline for mismanagement—or to let them pay the price of self-inflicted injury—thereby ignoring the suffering of hundreds of thousands of people adversely affected by private miscalculation or incompetence.

In short, society may finesse the power problem, or ignore it altogether, but it cannot avoid the cost of doing so.

Q. What would you do about the current merger mania?

A. Megamergers are clearly out of control. We are witnessing a spectacle of mass "corpocide," the large-scale assassination of independent, functioning corporations. Billion-dollar megacorporations are rampaging through the Darwinian jungle, devouring acquisitions and merging with one another into giant conglomerates. Between 1980 and 1986, the number of acquisitions climbed from 1,565 to 4,022, up by a factor of more than two and a half. The total reported value of those acquisitions increased from roughly $33 billion in 1980 to $190 billion in 1986, by more than a factor of five. This doesn't even count the number of joint ventures, only mergers and acquisitions.

Many of these consolidations make no economic sense; they are unproductive at best, and counterproductive at worst. On the whole, they don't promote efficiency. Nor do they sharpen our international competitiveness, or give birth to technological breakthroughs. They don't build new factories, develop new products or processes, or create new jobs. These are ventures in paper entrepreneurialism that typically reshuffle existing assets and profit the Wall Street merger midwives.

Q. So you would limit them?
A. Yes. I have urged Congress to limit drastically megamergers. Consolidations involving the Fortune 500, or, say, the 1,000 largest industrial corporations in the United States, should be prohibited per se unless their proponents could demonstrate that the merger 1) would enhance operating efficiency; 2) would promote technological progress; 3) would enhance international competitiveness; and 4) that these objectives cannot be achieved by other, less anticompetitive means. The burden of proof would rest on the proponents of such consolidations to demonstrate—with evidence, not public relations slogans—that a merger would achieve the desired objectives benefiting the public interest.

The government could also bring a quick end to the takeover game by controlling the "junk bond" financing of acquisitions, as Federal Reserve Chairman Paul Volcker has suggested. That would prevent corporate raiders from financing takeovers by using the stock of companies being acquired as collateral for loans. The Federal Reserve could also restrict the banks in financing mergers with bank credit.

My own preference would still be to amend Section 7 of the Clayton Act along the lines I have just outlined. Please note that this would not restrict corporations from expanding by internal growth; that is, by building new business, new production from new factories, and expanding trade. The restraints I am talking about would only limit growth by acquisition. It would impose limits only on megamergers involving the nation's very largest corporations.

Q. In other words you want to see growth through investment, as the economist uses that word to mean productive capital formation.
A. Precisely. Contemplate, if you will, the perverse effects of merger mania and the high opportunity cost it imposes on the American economy. In 1985 American corporations spent $179.8 billion on mergers and acquisitions, but only $53.2 billion on research and development, and only $117.2 billion on nonresidential private domestic investment. In other words, the total spent on mergers and acquisitions—$179.8 billion—exceeded the $170.4 billion spent on industry-financed R & D and net nonresidential private domestic investment combined.

There is clearly an opportunity cost to playing the merger game: it diverts managerial, intellectual, psychological, and spiritual resources, not just the money resources alone, from doing the things that management ought to be doing to beef up the productive capacity of American industry and to enhance its competitiveness in world markets.

Q. You really do see danger in bigness per se, don't you? In contrast, officials in the Reagan Administration see nothing wrong with bigness. Has the merger mania in Wall Street, the illegal insider trading, the junk bond excesses changed the views from the executive branch or created sufficient outcry from the public to alter official views?

A. Giantism, bigness per se does pose a danger. I say this not as a matter of ideological conviction, but because it is based on incontrovertible evidence. By most objective standards, America's corporate giants have not performed very well over the last fifteen years.

Q. By what standards? Whose standards?

A. These mergers have proved to be counterproductive as measured by conventional economic standards for efficiency, technological progress, and international competitiveness. The U.S. giants have lost market shares to the Japanese and the newly industrializing countries. They have lagged in innovation and technological change. The quality of their products is often inferior and unreliable. In terms of employment, America's 500 largest industrial corporations as a group have failed to generate a single new job since 1970. Indeed, Donald Lambro, a conservative economist with the Cato Institute, has calculated that the 500 largest U.S. corporations have lost between four and five million jobs in the last fifteen years. Taken together this is a terrible indictment of bigness. Yet the mergers go on.

Q. What about the argument that bigness is better, more efficient as a result of economies of scale?

A. This, of course, is the quintessential myth of our times, propagated by Big Business and its apologists. In examining their claims, three caveats are in order.

First, the presumed links between size and efficiency are no more than an assertion. They are not supported by credible empirical evidence.

Second, we must guard against oversimplification. Efficiency is a multifaceted concept. There is operating efficiency. Here the question is whether giant corporations are producing mousetraps at the lowest possible cost. Then there is innovation efficiency. Are corporate giants in constant quest for a better mousetrap? Finally, there is social efficiency. Perhaps mousetraps should not be produced at all. Perhaps rodent control should be effectuated through superior pesticides or a greater investment in feline capital.

Third, if efficiency is the goal, it is not enough to say that giant firms will automatically be most productive. The optimum size of firms varies from industry to industry, and optimum size changes over time with the evolution of technology. The limit of efficient size is exceeded when the disadvantages attendant upon size outweigh the advantages.

E.A.G. Robinson has made the point in *The Structure of Competitive Industry* with a military analogy: "A platoon may drill very well as a platoon, but it may not always cover itself with equal glory in battalion drill. A battalion requires officers to coordinate the actions of its companies and platoons over and above the platoon commanders. The battalion has to be fitted into larger organizations, the brigade, the division, and the army. The problem of commanding an army is not simply the sum of the problems of commanding the platoons in it. All sorts of problems of organization and coordination arise because the unit to be controlled is now large instead of small, is out of earshot, takes time, space, and forethought to manage. A mistake made by a platoon commander demands only an instantaneous 'As you were!' A mistake by an army commander may require days of labor to set right. In just the same way the problem of organizing a large firm grows in complication as the firm grows."

Q. Doesn't the management of conglomerates pose just such problems?
A. The efficiency argument is particularly weak with respect to conglomerates. Conglomerate bigness doesn't confer any operating economies by virtue of a firm's horizontal size—that is, the ability to mass-produce a given article and reduce per-unit costs. Nor does it yield economies because of a firm's vertical size—the ability to gain cost savings by integrating successive, functionally related stages of production and distribution. The very nature of conglomerates rules out any efficiency rationale. Their organization cuts across industry and product lines; so there is no advantage in production derived from horizontal or vertical increase in the firm's size.

Q. What is the rationale then?
A. You may recall that in the 1960s conglomerate mergers were justified on the grounds that they provided a new and much needed synergism. That was explained in terms of two plus two equals five—the whole is bigger and better than the sum of its parts. The revolution in management science, it was said, would lead to super-managers and corresponding leaps in management efficiency.

Management failures over the past ten to fifteen years belie that rationale. Now it is increasingly recognized—something many of us recognized in the 1960s before the conglomerate merger craze really caught fire—that quite the opposite may be true. Two plus two may equal only three—the constituent parts separately may be worth more than the whole.

The current divestiture movement, the "lean and mean" trend in the restructuring of corporate giants, is eloquent testimony that mere size is not the guarantor of efficiency, technological progress, or international competitiveness. Nowadays corporate leaders like Martin S. Davis, president of Gulf & Western, one of the most trumpeted conglomerates of the sixties and seventies, are saying, and I quote: "Bigness is not a sign of strength; in fact, just the opposite is true." That is recognition of the fact that Gulf & Western strategy has been wrong for some twenty years. How much better would the economic performance of Gulf & Western and ITT have been—how much greater their contribution to the American economy—if they had not played the acquisition game that they did in fact play during the 1960s and 1970s.

There are also some interesting revelations in the business press: *Business Week*, for example, not long ago ran a cover story entitled, "Small is Beautiful in Manufacturing." *Forbes* magazine has published case studies to document what would seem to be an obvious fact—that "soap and pastrami don't mix"—and the *London Economist* has featured articles entitled "Big Won't Work" and "Big Goes Bust."

Q. So why do they take place?

A. Because they're promoted and propelled by the Wall Street marriage brokers who make huge profits from the commissions they earn both from the corporate marriages and the subsequent divorces over which they preside. According to some estimates, for example, the three leading M & A houses on Wall Street (Goldman Sachs, First Boston, Morgan Stanley) each generated more than $200 million in merger commissions in 1985. In Pantry Pride's takeover of Revlon alone, the banking commissions exceeded $100 million. These fees, says *Forbes,* "may do more to explain current merger mania than all the blather about synergy and diversification."

Q. Where does this leave us today in facing the concentration of political and economic power?

A. We need to design an economic architecture where societal planning is done by an autonomous mechanism not subject to private control; where the market is allowed to exert its discipline through competition; where special interests are not in a position to dominate the state; where private advantage cannot be achieved at social expense.

Q. But that implies that somewhere in the government people will be making decisions about deregulation, and enforcing the antitrust and antimerger laws.

A. I have a 19th-century liberal faith that individuals and society do learn from experience. I believe that we shall come to recognize that the current merger frenzy is unproductive and counterproductive; that it imposes inordinate opportunity costs on the U.S. economy; that, contrary to the claims of its apologists, megamergers are not conducive to enhanced efficiency, technological progress, and international competitiveness; that, therefore, the policy of the

Reagan Administration to emasculate and eviscerate the antimerger laws is wrong-headed; and that structural antitrust is indispensable for maintaining a competitive free-enterprise economy.

The recent victory in the battle to deregulate trucking and airlines shows that we are capable of learning from experience. When Horace Gray and I published *Monopoly in America: The Government as Promoter* in 1955, our recommendation to deregulate inherently competitive industries seemed to fall on deaf ears. Yet some 25 years later, Congress decided that competition in these industries was preferable to a government-created and government-protected cartel. Eventually —after a 25-year lag, to be sure—Congress saw fit to deregulate airlines in 1978 and trucking in 1980.

Q. But, weren't the benefits of that deregulation quickly eroded? Are we really better off today?

A. Deregulation by itself is not enough. Once you liberate an industry from direct government regulation, you must subject it to control by the competitive market. And that means strict antitrust enforcement in the deregulated industries to prevent mergers from eroding competition and restructuring the deregulated industry into a tight, noncompetitive oligopoly.

Unfortunately, the Reagan Administration has ignored this truism. In airlines, for example, it has tolerated anticompetitive mergers on a massive scale— Northwest/Republic, Delta/Western, TWA/Ozark, Texas Air/Continental/New York Air/People Express/Eastern, etc. Today, the six largest carriers dominate some 85 percent of the market. By 1990, if present trends continue, we shall have a tight airline oligopoly with a market share of more than 90 percent. That isn't competition. It is deregulation subverted by government failure to enforce the antitrust laws.

Q. This 200th anniversary year of the Constitution, then, seems to have special significance for this problem of coalescing of political and economic power.

A. That brings me full circle to the constitutional issue I raised at the outset. Advanced industrial societies today face a basic structural challenge if they want to preserve democratic institutions together with a free-market capitalist economy. The problem is how to prevent private concentrations of economic power, organized into powerful political pressure groups, from dominating the economy and eventually the political system.

The checks against private economic power have to be achieved without creating an omnipotent government, strong enough not only to control private oligarchies, but also to become an instrument of oppression beyond public control. There are no simple solutions to this problem. The Constitution provides a remarkable blueprint for decentralized political power that has worked exceedingly well with its checks and balances for 200 years. We need to create a similar economic architecture for checking the concentration of power in the economy.

The Founding Fathers didn't anticipate that problem. They tried to guard against undue power in the hands of government. Madison, writing in *The Federalist No. 51*, warned that government had to be administered by men, not angels, and that restraints on their discretion was therefore necessary. In this same vein, Jefferson advised that the structure of the system was more important than the personal integrity of the leaders who exercised power within it. The system, he wrote, has to be able to survive the shortcomings of its leaders.

Policymakers today still have to confront the reality that the private sector may generate concentrations of private power that create as potent a threat to individual freedom and equality as the unchecked power of government itself. And economists, in their analytical endeavors as well as their policy prescriptions, cannot continue to evade the problem of power, or economics itself will become irrelevant to the central issues of the day.

16

Creative Capitalism

> . . . Come my friends,
> 'Tis not too late to seek a newer world. . . .
> To strive, to seek, to find, and not to yield.
>
> —Tennyson, "Odysseus"

"Greed is good," said Gordon Gekko (Michael Douglas), the wheeler-dealer wizard in *Wall Street*. "Greed is right. Greed works. Greed clarifies, cuts through, and captures the essence of the evolutionary spirit. Greed in all its forms—greed for life, for money, for love, for knowledge—has marked the upward surge of mankind. And greed will not only save [our company], but that other malfunctioning corporation called the U.S.A."

"Greed is all right," Ivan Boesky told the graduating class of the University of California School of Business Administration in 1985. "Greed is healthy. You can be greedy and still feel good about yourself."

"Greed really turns me off," says Henry Kravis, the king of Wall Street's leveraged-buyout strategists. Who is right? What is the role of greed, the lust for profit, the penchant for self-enrichment—call it what you will—in a free enterprise economy?

In 1776, Adam Smith wrote that self-interest serves a vital function in economic life: "It is not from the benevolence of the butcher, the brewer, or the baker that we expect our dinner, but from their regard for their self-interest. We address ourselves not to their humanity, but to their self-love, and never talk to them of our necessities, but of their advantages." If left free to pursue their animal spirits, Smith counseled, they would automatically—as if guided by an "unseen hand"—not only enrich themselves but, at the same time, increase the wealth of the nation.[1] Private vice would result in public virtue.

Originally published as chapter 14 in Walter Adams and James W. Brock, *Dangerous Pursuits: Mergers and Acquisitions in the Age of Wall Street* (Pantheon Books, 1989); reprinted with permission.

However, Smith and his followers also believed that the pursuit of private gain had to be constrained within a framework of rules, so as to harness it to social ends. To them, laissez-faire was not the same as anarchy. They recognized, with Thomas Hobbes, that a state of nature is fraught with "fear and violent death" and that man's life in nature is "poor, nasty, brutish, and short"[2]; that good order does not arise from a universal perception of a harmony of interests; that government is not a purely voluntary association; that, on the contrary, good order requires an irreducible element of governmental force, coercion, and intervention to maintain the framework in which freedom can flourish. Harmony and mutuality of interests being neither automatic nor inevitable, it is necessary "to provide and enforce a framework of rules for securing freedom, and the conditions necessary for effective freedom, in economic life."[3] Laissez-faire was a policy prescription not so much for individual freedom as for a free economic system.

To ensure that individual freedom and the private profit motive perform their assigned social task, there must be a rule-maker and an umpire. As (Lord) Lionel Robbins put it: "The invisible hand which guides men to promote ends which were no part of their intention, is not the hand of some god or some natural agency independent of human effort; it is the hand of the lawgiver, the hand which withdraws from the sphere of the pursuit of self-interest those possibilities which do not harmonize with the public good."[4] In the lexicon of the Classicists, the harmony between the pursuit of self-interest and the maximization of general welfare was neither natural, nor spontaneous, nor self-generating.[5] Economists have long recognized that not all private activity in search of profit is necessarily "productive" from a social point of view. Some 150 years after the publication of *The Wealth of Nations*, John Maynard Keynes elaborated on the distinction between socially productive and unproductive economic activities. He was particularly concerned with the difference between speculation and enterprise, between emphasis on short-term value of securities and the underlying long-term value of investment. Speculators, he wrote, "are concerned, not with what an investment is really worth to a man who buys it 'for keeps,' but with what the market will value it, under the influence of mass psychology, three months or a year hence."[6] Their private objective is to beat the gun, to outwit the crowd, and "to pass the bad, or depreciating half-crown to the other fellow."[7] For speculators, investment is "a game of Snap, of Old Maid, of Musical Chairs—a pastime in which he is victor who says *Snap* neither too soon nor too late, who passes the Old Maid to his neighbor before the game is over, who secures a chair for himself when the music stops."[8]

Experience shows, Keynes argued, that investment which yields private profit is not necessarily socially advantageous. Indeed, when speculation becomes pervasive, it may inflict serious damage on an economy. It becomes a bane to industrial (that is, socially productive) enterprise: "When the capital development of a country becomes a by-product of the activities of a casino, the job is likely to be ill-done. The measure of success attained by Wall Street, regarded as an institution of which the proper social purpose is to direct new investment into the most profitable channels in terms of future yield, cannot be claimed as one of the outstanding triumphs of *laissez-faire* capitalism—which is not surprising, if I am right in thinking that the best brains of Wall Street have in fact been directed towards a different object."[9]

Clearly there is a need for rules—implemented by carrot or by stick—to channel business activity away from speculation and into productive investment.

The distinction between creative capitalism and speculative capitalism is fundamental. One generates wealth; the other merely redistributes it. One builds factories; the other merely trades their ownership. One gives birth to new goods, services, and techniques; the other merely rearranges control over them. One contributes to economic growth; the other is nothing more than a zero-sum game.

Henry Ford is the personification of creative capitalism. The quintessential industrial entrepreneur and innovator, he had the ability (in Schumpeter's famous phrase) "to see beyond the reach of familiar beacons." In the eyes of the public (and the money interests on Wall Street), he was cantankerous, eccentric, unconventional, and rash. A born maverick, he passionately pursued an idea, a dream, a vision: to make the automobile an article of mass consumption. He had the abiding faith that "every time I reduce the charge for our car by one dollar, I get a thousand new buyers"; that "every time the company cut prices it tapped a new layer of demand; that the number of these successive layers was greater than men supposed; and that as they went lower the layers grew bigger. Further price reductions meant new enlargements of the market, and acceleration of mass production's larger economies, and greater aggregate profits."[10] Its firm grasp of this principle was the company's unique strength.

Ford viewed price reduction and plant expansion as the key to the long-term growth of the company (which he called "the institution"). The institution did not exist to make money, but to create jobs and produce goods. The idea of hoarding money was abhorrent to him. People should use it; they should "invest wisely, to begin getting things that make their lives more productive of real values." His personal profits were tremendous—but they were nearly all reserved for plant expansion, "to build more and more factories, to give as many people as I can a chance to be prosperous."[11] To Ford, money was just "part of the conveyor line." It was just "what we use to keep tally."

Ford was a hands-on industrial entrepreneur par excellence. His office, reported *Detroit Saturday Night* in 1910, "would never remind one of those elegantly furnished headquarters generally ascribed to men of his position. You will find it on the other side of a little obscure door in a corner of the second floor of the factory. He has a little four by six flat desk, and no arm chair. In addition, there is a mammoth blackboard, a drafting table, a turret lathe, and several hundred patterns, castings, and samples. It is a workshop, not an office, and is typical of the busy life of the man who has revolutionized automobile conditions the world over. It opens into the tool room, and one is more apt to find him outside busy on some special tool than inside."[12]

The bankers came from a different world. They saw things differently. Sitting in their Wall Street offices, they dealt not in tangible wealth, but in slips of paper symbolizing wealth. They controlled wheat they had not sown, cotton they had not picked, ore they had not mined, steel plants they had not built. They were in the business of producing companies, not goods and services. The dominant financiers of the time saw little promise in the nascent automobile industry, and refused to provide it with capital. At the turn of the century, the eminent financier Chauncey M. Depew, president of the N.Y. Central & Harlem R.R. Co., counseled his nephew against investing $5,000 in the business of an unknown mechanic named Henry Ford. "The horseless carriage," he said, "will never supplant the horse." In 1908, when one of the automobile pioneers told George W. Perkins of J.P. Morgan and Company that "the time will come when five hundred thousand automobiles will be manufactured and sold in this country every year," the banker, incensed by what he took to be Durant's effrontery and stupidity, left the room. He could not foresee the day when Americans would not only want cars, but would virtually mortgage their lives to get one.[13]

No wonder Ford (who financed the growth of his company with capital provided by far-sighted investors in Detroit and later with retained earnings) had a jaundiced view of Wall Street. Bankers, he said, try to shape company policy to pay quick dividends at the cost of future growth, so as to unload stock issues on the public at excessive prices. Bankers "think solely in terms of money. They think of a factory as making money, not goods. They watch the money, not the efficiency of production."[14] They may be successful money-makers, but they "have never added one penny-worth to the wealth of the world." "Does a card player add to the wealth of the world?" Ford asked. His answer was unambiguous: "Speculation in things already produced—that is not business. It is just more or less respectable graft."[15]

Ford was undeterred by the rebuffs of the financial community. He began "with almost nothing." What he earned, he earned "by unremitting labor and faith in a principle." He took what was considered a luxury and turned it into a necessity, and did so "without trick or subterfuge." He built his car (and his company) at a time when the conventional wisdom viewed the automobile as "at the best a rich man's toy."[16] Above all, he never deviated from his conviction that a manufacturer is "an instrument of society and he can serve society only as he manages his enterprises so as to turn over to the public an increasingly better product at an ever-decreasing price, and at the same time to pay to all those who have a hand in his business an ever-increasing wage, based upon the work they do. In this way and in this way alone can a manufacturer or any one in business justify his existence."[17]

Ford expanded by building, not buying. (His only acquisition was the Lincoln Motor Co.) He exemplified what creative capitalism is all about.

Looking back on the entrepreneurial achievements of a Henry Ford, an Andrew Carnegie, a Thomas Alva Edison, or an Alexander Graham Bell, we might be tempted to agree with Emerson's dictum that "once we had golden priests and wooden chalices. Now we have wooden priests and golden chalices." That would be an exaggeration. America is not devoid of innovators and entrepreneurs. Nor does Japan, despite its remarkable achievements, have a monopoly of such talent.

Take, for example, the remarkable exploit of Howard Head, father of the Head ski and the Prince tennis racket, who built a multimillion-dollar business on the basis of a "simple" invention. *Sports Illustrated* tells the story:

> In 1946 Head went off to Stowe, Vt., for his first attempt at skiing. "I was humiliated and disgusted by how badly I skied," he recalls, "and, characteristically, I was inclined to blame it on the equipment, those long, clumsy hickory skis. On my way home I heard myself boasting to an Army officer beside me that I could make a better ski out of aircraft materials than could be made from wood."
>
> Back at Martin [Aircraft], the cryptic doodles that began appearing on Head's drawing board inspired him to scavenge some aluminum from the plant scrap pile. In his off-hours he set up shop on the second floor of a converted stable in an alley near his one-room basement flat. His idea was to make a "metal sandwich" ski consisting of two layers of aluminum with plywood sidewalls and a center filling of honeycombed plastic.
>
> Needing pressure and heat to fuse the materials together, Head concocted a process that would have made Rube Goldberg proud. To achieve the necessary pressure of 15 pounds per square inch, he put the ski mold into a huge rubber bag and then pumped the air out through a tube attached to an old refrigerator compressor that was hooked up backward to produce suction. For heat, he welded together an iron, coffin-like tank, filled it with motor oil drained from automobile crankcases and, using two Sears, Roebuck camp burners, cooked up a smelly 350 degree brew. Then he dumped the rubber bag with the ski mold inside into the tank of boiling oil and sat back like Julia Child waiting for her potato puffs to brown.
>
> Six weeks later, out of the stench and smoke, Head produced his first six pairs of skis and raced off to Stowe to have them tested by the pros. To gauge the ski's camber, an instructor stuck the end of one into the snow and flexed it. It broke. So, eventually, did all six pairs. "Each time one of them broke," says Head, "something inside me snapped with it."
>
> Instead of hanging up his rubber bag, Head quit Martin the day after New Year's 1948, took $6,000 in poker winnings he had stashed under his bed, and went to work in earnest. Each week he would send a new and improved pair of skis to Neil Robinson, a ski instructor in Bromley, Vt., for testing, and each week Robinson would send them back broken. "If I had known then that it would take 40 versions before the ski was any good, I might have given it up," says Head. "But fortunately, you get trapped into thinking the next design will be it."
>
> Head wrestled with his obsession through three agonizing winters. The

refinements were several: Steel edges for necessary bite, a plywood core for added strength, a plastic running service for smoother, ice-free runs. One crisp day in 1950, Head stood in the bowl of Tuckerman's Ravine in New Hampshire and watched ski instructor Clif Taylor come skimming over the lip of the headwall, do a fishtail on the fall line and sweep into a long, graceful curve, swooshing to stop in front of the beaming inventor.

"They're great, Mr. Head, just great," Taylor exclaimed. At that moment, Head says, "I knew deep inside I had it."[18]

Howard Head's credo? "You have to believe in the impossible."

Howard Head is not alone. There is Chester Carlson, inventor of xerography and founder of the Xerox Corporation, which now ranks No. 34 in the Fortune 500.

There is Edwin Land, inventor of the instant camera and founder of the Polaroid Corporation—No. 208 on the *Fortune* list.

There is Kenneth Iverson, president of Nucor, and Gordon Forward, president of Chaparral, innovators of the minimills that have revolutionized a somnolent, lethargic American steel industry.

There is Steve Jobs, the science wizard who in 1976 revolutionized the computer industry with the Apple Macintosh and in 1985 followed that triumph with the equally pathbreaking Next computer.

And then there is the legendary H. Ross Perot, the jug-eared, belt-and-suspenders former naval officer, who left IBM in 1962, founded Electronic Data Systems (EDS) with savings of $1,000, and later sold the company to General Motors for $2.5 *billion*. Although this made him the largest stockholder in General Motors (and a member of its board of directors), Perot found GM's corporate culture unpalatable. He was turned off by the committees, consultants, and MBAs, the corporate dining room, the chauffeured limousines, the hefty bonuses in hard times. At GM, he felt, the order of the day was "ready, aim, aim, aim . . . ." At EDS, the order had been "ready, aim, fire, fire, fire . . . ." He wanted to get back in the trenches with his troops. And so he accepted a "buyout" of his GM stake for $750 million and promptly set up Perot Systems Corp. A can-do entrepreneur, he would start all over again with a dedicated corporal's guard of 75 employees.[19]

These innovator-entrepreneurs illustrate Peter Drucker's observation on creativity in business: "Whenever anything is being accomplished, it is being done . . . by a monomaniac with a mission."[20]

When the priorities are properly ordered, the objective to be attained made clear, and the game to be played specified, latent entrepreneurial talent can be mobilized in even very large, bureaucratic organizations. World War II, when American industry was the arsenal of democracy, provides endless illustrations. Chrysler's contract for army tanks is a case in point: "In June 1940, Chrysler sent a research team to the Rock Island Arsenal to examine tanks and tank blueprints, as Chrysler had never made modern tanks before. Returning to Detroit with 186 pounds of blueprints Chrysler broke ground for the new plant in September, 1940, and regular production began the following April. Only 10 months had

282 A PUBLIC PHILOSOPHY

elapsed since Chrysler undertook the project, only 7 months since the plant was actually begun."[21]

Another case of spectacular achievement in a totally foreign field was General Motors' "production of .30 caliber machine guns at their Saginaw Steering Gear Division. A site was selected for the new plant in November, 1940, and the plant was dedicated and began producing on April 22, 1941, a period of six months. By March, 1942, the Saginaw plant had delivered over 28,000 guns on a contract calling for 280 by that date; the price per unit had dropped from $667.00 to $141.44."[22]

These were truly heroic achievements in industrial entrepreneurship—or, more precisely, intrapreneurship. They were feats of creative capitalism.

As a society, we must decide which game we want the business community to play. We must decide between enterprise and speculation; between creating wealth and trading it; between building factories and shuffling corporate paper; between investing in the future or playing an unproductive zero-sum game. Given the right signals, American business can rise to the challenge.

Notes

1. Adam Smith, *The Wealth of Nations,* pp. 14, 423 (Modern Library ed.).
2. Thomas Hobbes, *Leviathan,* p. 186.
3. Frank H. Knight, *Freedom and Reform,* p. 205 (1947).
4. Lionel Robbins, *The Theory of Economic Policy in English Political Economy,* p. 56 (1952).
5. Smith, op. cit., pp. 314–315.
6. John M. Keynes, *The General Theory of Employment, Interest and Money,* pp. 154–155 (1936).
7. Ibid.
8. Ibid., p. 156.
9. Ibid., p. 159.
10. Allan Nevins, *Ford: The Times, The Man, The Company,* pp. 492–493 (1954).
11. Ibid., pp. 575–576.
12. January 8, 1910; quoted in Nevins, op. cit., p. 496.
13. David L. Cohn, *Combustion on Wheels,* p. 114 (1944).
14. Henry Ford, *My Life and Work,* p. 176 (1926).
15. Ibid., p. 7.
16. Ibid., p. 272.
17. Ibid., p. 135.
18. Quoted in Thomas J. Peters and Robert H. Waterman, Jr., *In Search of Excellence,* pp. 202–203 (1982).
19. "The Hottest Entrepreneur in America," *Inc.,* January 1989. For an incisive examination of the Perot-GM affair, see Doron P. Levin, *Irreconcilable Differences: Ross Perot versus General Motors* (1989).
20. Quoted in Peters, op. cit., p. 225.
21. John B. Rae, *The American Automobile: A Brief History,* p. 146 (1965).
22. Donald Nelson, *Arsenal of Democracy,* p. 226 (19).

Publications of Walter Adams

Books

Readings in Economics (ed. with L.E. Traywick). New York: Macmillan, 1948.

The Structure of American Industry (ed.). New York: Macmillan, 1950; rev. ed., 1954; translated into Spanish and Japanese, 3d ed., 1961; 4th ed., 1971; 5th ed., 1977; 6th ed., 1982 (translated into Japanese); 7th ed., 1986 (translated into Japanese); 8th ed., 1989.

Monopoly in America: The Government as Promoter (with H.M. Gray). New York: Macmillan, 1955; translated into Japanese.

Trucking Mergers, Concentration and Small Business (with J.B. Hendry). Washington, DC: U.S. Government Printing Office, 1957.

From Mainstreet to the Left Bank (with J.A. Garraty). East Lansing: Michigan State University Press, 1959.

Is the World Our Campus? (with J.A. Garraty). East Lansing: Michigan State University Press, 1960.

A Guide to Study Abroad (with J.A. Garraty). New York: Channel Press, 1962; subsequent editions published by Harper & Row, 1969, 1971.

The Brain Drain (ed.). New York: Macmillan, 1968 (preface by Senator Paul Douglas); translated into Spanish, French, and Japanese.

The Test. New York: Macmillan, 1971.

The Bigness Complex (with James W. Brock). New York: Pantheon Books, 1986; German edition published by Bonn Aktuell, 1988.

Dangerous Pursuits: Mergers and Acquisitions in the Age of Wall Street (with James W. Brock). New York: Pantheon Books, 1989.

Antitrust Economics on Trial: A Dialogue on the New Laissez-Faire (with James W. Brock). Princeton: Princeton University Press, 1991.

Articles and Pamphlets

"Accounting Practices and the Business Cycle," *Journal of Business,* April 1949.

"Dissolution, Divorcement, Divestiture," *Indiana Law Journal,* Fall 1951.

"Is Bigness a Crime?" *Land Economics*, November 1951.

"The Schwegmann Case," *Detroit Law Journal*, November 1951; reprinted in *Congressional Record*.

"The Aluminum Case," *American Economic Review*, December 1951; reprinted in *Congressional Record*.

"The Dilemma of Antitrust Aims: A Reply," *American Economic Review*, December 1952.

"The Dilemma of Antitrust Aims: A Further Reply," *American Economic Review*, December 1952.

"The Sherman Act and Its Enforcement," *Pittsburgh Law Review*, Spring 1953.

"Competition, Monopoly, and Countervailing Power," *Quarterly Journal of Economics*, November 1953; reprinted in *Congressional Record*.

"The Rule of Reason," *Yale Law Journal*, January 1954.

"Technical Progress and Economic Institutions," *American Economic Review Proceedings*, May 1954 (comment).

"Atomic Energy," *Columbia Law Review*, February 1955.

"Comment," *American Economic Review Proceedings*, May 1955.

"Resale Price Maintenance," *Yale Law Review*, June 1955.

"The 'Fair Trade' Question," *National Industrial Conference Board*, June 1955.

"From Big to Bigger," *New Republic*, June 1955; reprinted in *Congressional Record*.

"Fair Trade and the Art of Prestidigitation," *Yale Law Journal*, December 1955.

"Merger Activity Sets Record Pace," *Detroit Free Press*, January 22, 1956.

"The Regulatory Commissions," *N.Y. Herald Tribune* (Paris ed.), May 13 & 15, 1958.

"La Reglementation de l'Industrie Americaine," *Diogene*, No. 24, October 1958; also appeared in Spanish, German, Arabic, and English.

"The Role of Competition in the Regulated Industries," *American Economic Review Proceedings*, May 1958; reprinted in *Congressional Record*.

"The Regulatory Commissions and Small Business," *Law & Contemporary Problems*, Winter 1959.

"Changing Structure of the American Economy: Comment," *Journal of Farm Economics Proceedings*, May 1959.

"A che servono i giganti dell 'industria?" *Mercurio*, January 1960.

"Economie, Ideologie et Politique aux Etats-Unis," *Diogene*, No. 36, October 1961; also appeared in Spanish, Arabic, and English; also printed in *Minervas* (Oslo).

"Parlez-vous on the Beach at Cannes" (with John A. Garraty), *Overseas*, March 1962.

Overseasmanship and the New Frontier," *AAUP Bulletin*, March 1962; reprinted in *The National Observer*, April 29, 1962 and *Congressional Record*.

"Consumer Needs and Consumer Sovereignty in the American Economy," *Journal of Business,* July 1962.

"Corporate Giantism, Ethics, and the Public Interest," *Review of Social Economy,* March 1963 (paper presented at annual convention of Catholic Economic Association, Pittsburgh, December 1962).

"The Reality of Administered Prices" (with R.F. Lanzillotti), *Administered Prices: A Compendium on Public Policy,* Subcommittee on Antitrust & Monopoly, U.S. Senate, 1963.

"Brown Shoe: In Step with Antitrust" (with J.B. Dirlam), *Washington University Law Quarterly,* April 1963.

"Statement before the Joint Economic Committee," *Antitrust Bulletin,* March–April 1963.

"What Should We Do about Big Business?" *Yale Political,* Summer 1964.

"On the Strategic Importance of Western Europe," *House Document No. 367,* 88th Congress, 2d Session, Washington, DC, 1964.

"Steel Imports and Vertical Oligopoly Power" (with J.B. Dirlam), *American Economic Review,* September 1964.

"Vertical Power, Dual Distribution, and the Squeeze: A Case Study in Steel," *Antitrust Bulletin,* May–June 1964.

"Exemptions from Antitrust: Their Extent and Rationale." In Almarin Phillips (ed.), *Perspectives on Antitrust Policy* (Princeton, NJ: Princeton University Press, 1965).

"Corporate Size: II," *Business Topics,* Spring 1965.

"Steel Imports and Vertical Oligopoly Power: Reply" (with J.B. Dirlam), *American Economic Review,* March 1966.

"Big Steel, Invention, and Innovation" (with J.B. Dirlam), *Quarterly Journal of Economics,* May 1966; reprinted in *Congressional Record.*

"Dumping, Antitrust Policy, and Economic Power" (with J.B. Dirlam), *Business Topics,* Spring 1966; reprinted in *Congressional Record.*

"Government, The Universities and International Affairs; A Crisis in Identity" (with Adrian Jaffee), House Document No. 120, 90th Cong., 1st sess., 1967; also published in Elizabeth N. Shiver (ed.), *Higher Education and the Public International Service* (Washington, DC: American Council on Education, 1967); abridged version published as "Government and the Universities," *The Progressive,* January 1968.

"Antitrust and Its Critics," *Nebraska Law Review,* May 1967.

"Big Steel, Invention and Innovation: Reply" (with J.B. Dirlam), *Quarterly Journal Economics,* August 1967.

"Steel Imports and Vertical Oligopoly Power: Reply" (with J.B. Dirlam), *American Economic Review,* September 1967.

"Market Structure, Regulation, and Dynamic Change" (with J.B. Dirlam). In Harry M. Trebing (ed.), *Performance under Regulation* (East Lansing: Michigan State University Public Utility Studies, 1968).

"The Military–Industrial Complex and the New Industrial State," *American Economic Review Proceedings*, May 1968; reprinted in several books of readings.

"Gigantisme et Progres Technique: Un Mythe?" *Revue d'Economie Politique*, 1968.

"Oxygen Steelmaking—The Phantasmagoria of Innovative Giantism" (with J.B. Dirlam), *Iron and Steel Engineer*, July 1968.

"How to Stop the Brain Drain," *NATO letter*, May 1968; also published in French, German, Italian, and Dutch.

"The Case for Structural Tests." In J.F. Weston & S. Peltzman (eds.), *Public Policy Toward Mergers* (Pacific Palisades, CA: Goodyear, 1969).

"The Military–Industrial Complex and the New Industrial State." In Omer L. Carey (ed.), *The Military–Industrial Complex and U.S. Foreign Policy* (Pullman: Washington State University Press, 1969).

"The 'Brain Drain': Fact or Fiction?" *Population Reference Bureau Bulletin #3*, June 1969.

"Economic Science, Public Policy, and Public Understanding," *Diogenes*, Fall 1969; also parallel editions in French and Spanish.

"The Problem of Concentrated Power," *Review of Social Economy*, March 1970.

"The Case for a Vigorous and Comprehensive Antitrust Policy." In Werner Sichel (ed.), *Antitrust Policy and Economic Welfare* (Ann Arbor: Michigan Business Papers No. 56, 1970).

"Financial Razzle Dazzle Powers Conglomerates," *Washington Post*, February 27, 1972.

"The Military–Industrial Complex: A Market Structure Analysis" (with William James Adams), *American Economic Review Proceedings*, May 1972.

"Competitive Measures and Competitive Facts as They Affect Economic Standards," in *Antitrust Problems and National Priorities* (Eleventh Conference on Antitrust Issues in Today's Economy), New York: The Conference Board, 1972.

"The Antitrust Alternative." In Ralph Nader and Mark Green (eds.), *Corporate Power in America* (New York: Grossman, 1973).

"The New Protectionism," *Challenge*, May–June 1973; also appeared as "Il Nuovo Protezionismo," *Mondo Economico*, no. 32/33, August–September 1973.

"Combatting Role Prejudice and Sex Discrimination: Findings of the AEA Committee on the Status of Women in the Economics Profession" (with C.S. Bell, M.O. Blaxall, K. Boulding, J.K. Galbraith, C. Moser, M. Strober, P.A. Wallace, and K.J. Arrow), *American Economic Review*, December 1973.

"Corporate Power and Economic Apologetics: A Public Policy Perspective." In Harvey Goldschmid, H. Michael Mann & J. Fred Weston (eds.), *Industrial Concentration: The New Learning* (Boston: Little, Brown, 1974).

"Collective Bargaining and Higher Education," *Proceedings of the 30th Annual Meeting of the American Conference of Academic Deans*. Ann Arbor, MI: University Microfilms, 1974.

"Can Regulation Curb Corporate Power?" In Werner Sichel and Thomas G. Gies (eds.),

Public Utility Regulation: Change and Scope (Lexington, MA: Lexington, D.C. Heath, 1975).

"Potere e Protezionismo nel settore 'moderno' dell'economia americana." In Roberto Artioli (ed.), *Il Dualismo Nelle Economie Industriali* (Torino: Editoriale Valentino, 1975).

"Comment on Market Structure in the Petroleum Industry," *Journal of Economic Issues*, June 1975.

"Antitrust, Laissez-Faire, and Economic Power." In Neumark, Thalheim, and Holzer (eds.), *Wettbewerb, Konzentration und Wirtschaftliche Macht* (Berlin: Duncker and Humblot, 1976).

"Colleges and Money," *Change Magazine*, 1976. Pamphlet written in collaboration with G.W. Bonham, H.R. Bowen, H. Champion, E.F. Cheit, J.D. Millett, and G.B. Weathersby.

"Private Planning and Social Efficiency" (with Joel B. Dirlam). In A.P. Jacquemin and H.W. de Jong (eds.), *Markets, Corporate Behavior and the State* (The Hague: Martinus Nijhoff, 1976).

"Der Militarisch–industrieller Komplex und die Privilegierung von Grossindustrien." In Lucian Kern (ed.), *Probleme der postindustriellen Gesellschaft* (Cologne: Kiepenheuer und Witsch, 1976).

"Import Quotas and Industrial Performance" (with J.B. Dirlam). In A.P. Jacquemin and H.W. de Jong (eds.), *Welfare Aspects of Industrial Markets* (Leiden: Martinus Nijhoff, 1977).

"Horizontal Divestiture in the Petroleum Industry." In W.S. Moore (ed.), *Horizontal Divestiture* (Washington, DC: American Enterprise Institute, 1977).

"Financing Public Higher Education," *American Economic Review*, February 1977.

"Le Protectionisme et l'Industrie Siderurgique des Etats-Unis" (with J.B. Dirlam), *Revue d'Economic Industrielle*, October 1977.

"Import Competition and the Trade Act of 1974: A Case Study of Section 201 and Its Interpretation by the International Trade Commission" (with J.B. Dirlam), *Indiana Law Journal*, Spring 1977.

"Vertical Divestiture of the Petroleum Majors: An Affirmative Case," *Vanderbilt Law Review*, November 1977.

"The Contribution of Economics to Public Policy Formulation." In M. Yinger and S. Cutler (eds.), *Major Social Issues* (New York: The Free Press, 1978).

"Antitrust and a Free Economy," *Antitrust Law Journal*, Fall 1977.

"Import Restraints and Industrial Performance: The Dilemma of Protectionism," *Antidumping Law*, Michigan Yearbook of International Legal Studies, vol. 1 (Ann Arbor: University of Michigan Press, 1979).

"No-Fault Monopoly," *Across the Board* (The Conference Board Magazine), November 1979.

"Business," *World Book Encyclopedia*, 1980.

"Mega-Mergers Spell Danger," *Challenge*, March/April 1982; reprinted in Richard D. Bartel (ed.), *The Challenge of Economics* (Armonk, NY & London: M.E. Sharpe, 1984).

"Integrated Monopoly and Market Power: System Selling, Compatibility Standards, and Market Power" (with James W. Brock), *Quarterly Review of Economics and Business*, Winter 1982.

"Economic Science and Economic Policy," *Review of Social Economy*, April 1982.

"Tacit Vertical Collusion and the Labor–Industrial Complex" (with James W. Brock), *University of Nebraska Law Review*, Fall 1983.

"Deregulation or Divestiture: The Case of Petroleum Pipelines" (with James W. Brock), *Wake Forest Law Review*, October 1983.

"The Trade Laws and their Enforcement by the International Trade Commission" (with J.B. Dirlam). In R.E. Baldwin (ed.), *Recent Issues and Initiatives in U.S. Trade Policy* (National Bureau of Economic Research, 1984).

"Echolalia Monopolistica: The Regulatory Disease" (with James W. Brock), *Challenge*, May/June 1984.

" 'Laissez-Faire', Import Restraints, and Industry Performance: A Case Study of Automobiles." In G. Ranis, R. West, M. Leiserson, and C. Morris (eds.), *Comparative Development Perspectives* (Boulder, CO: Westview Press, 1984).

"Industrial Policy and Trade Unions" (with James W. Brock), *Journal of Economic Issues*, June 1985.

"La politica industriale statunitense negli anni ottanta," *L'Industria*, January–March 1986.

"The Proposed Emasculation of Section 7 of the Clayton Act" (with James W. Brock), *Nebraska Law Review*, August 1986.

"The 'New Learning' and the Euthanasia of Antitrust" (with James W. Brock), *California Law Review*, October 1986.

"Corporate Power and Economic Sabotage" (with James W. Brock), *Journal of Economic Issues*, December 1986.

"Countervailing Power." In *The New Palgrave: A Dictionary of Economics*, London: Macmillan, 1987.

"Corporate Size and the Bailout Factor" (with James W. Brock), *Journal of Economic Issues*, March 1987.

"Giantism Doesn't Equal Competitiveness" (with James W. Brock), *New York Times*.

"Bigness and Social Efficiency" (with James W. Brock). In Warren J. Samuels and Arthur S. Miller (eds.), *Corporations and Society* (Westport, CT: Greenwood Press, 1987).

"Global Competition and the Alleged Redundancy of Antitrust" (with James W. Brock). In Robert L. Wills, Julie A. Caswell, and John D. Culbertson (eds.), *Issues after a Century of Federal Competition Policy* (Lexingtom, MA: Lexington Books, 1987).

"The Hidden Costs of Failed Mergers" (with James W. Brock), *New York Times*, June 21, 1987.

"Economic Power and the Constitution," *Challenge,* July/August 1987.

"Why Flying Is Unpleasant" (with James W. Brock), *New York Times,* August 6, 1987.

"Antitrust and Efficiency: A Comment" (with James W. Brock), *New York University Law Review,* November 1987.

"Hollywood Independents Start to Feel the Squeeze" (with James W. Brock), *Los Angeles Times,* November 22, 1987.

"Does Michigan Need an Anti-Takeover Law?" (with James W. Brock), *Detroit News,* February 7, 1988.

"Mr. Reagan and Antitrust" (with James W. Brock), in A.A. Heggestad (ed.), *Public Policy toward Corporations* (Gainsville: University of Florida Press, 1988).

"The 'Opportunity Cost' of Merger Mania" (with James W. Brock), *Forum for Applied Research and Public Policy,* Spring 1988.

"Exploding the Myth: Bigger Isn't Necessarily Better" (with James W. Brock), *Leaders Magazine,* April 1988.

"Interview," *Corporate Crime Reporter,* April 18, 1988.

"Wall Street—Not Main—Benefits from Buyouts" (with James W. Brock), *Los Angeles Times,* May 1, 1988.

"The Bigness Mystique and the Merger Policy Debate: An International Perspective" (with James W. Brock), *Northwestern Journal of International Law & Business,* Spring 1988.

"Reaganomics and the Transmogrification of Merger Policy" (with James W. Brock), *Antitrust Bulletin,* Summer 1988.

"Economic Organization and Entrepreneurship" (with James W. Brock), (United Nations) *Journal of Development Planning,* No. 18, 1988.

"Innovazione e complesso di grandezza delle imprese americane" (with James W. Brock), *L'Industria,* July–September, 1988.

"Corporate Concentration and Power." In R.S. Khemani, D.M. Shapiro, and W.T. Stanbury (eds.), *Mergers, Corporate Concentration and Power in Canada* (Halifax, Nova Scotia: Institute for Research on Public Policy, 1988).

"Do Leveraged Buyouts Really Help the Economy?" (with James W. Brock), *Detroit News,* December 11, 1988.

"Kleiner Ist Meist Besser" (with James W. Brock), *Wirtschaftswoche,* April 1989.

"Government and Competitive Free Enterprise." In Warren J. Samuels (ed.), *Fundamentals of the Economic Role of Government* (Westport, CT: Greenwood Press, 1989).

"Merger-Mania: An Empirical Critique" (with James W. Brock). In D.L. McKee (ed.), *Hostile Takeovers: Issues in Public and Corporate Policy* (New York: Praeger, 1989).

"The Evidence and Public Policy" (with James W. Brock). In D.L. McKee (ed.), *Hostile Takeovers: Issues in Public and Corporate Policy* (New York: Praeger, 1989).

"Power, Planning, Public Purpose" (with James W. Brock). In W.G. Shepherd (ed.),

Unconventional Wisdom: Essays in Honor of John Kenneth Galbraith (Boston: Houghton-Mifflin, 1989).

"Vertical Integration, Monopoly Power and Antitrust Policy: A Case Study in Video Entertainment" (with James W. Brock), *Wayne Law Review*, Fall 1989.

"I Processi di Concentrazione Industriale in una Prospettiva Storica" (with James W. Brock), *Economia Marche*, December 1989.

"Dangerous Pursuits: The Decade of the Corporate Deal" (with James W. Brock), *MSU Alumni Magazine*, Winter 1990.

"Merger Mania Isn't Helping U.S. Economy" (with James W. Brock), *The Cincinnati Enquirer*, January 1, 1990.

"Dealing into Debt: Takeover Frenzy Poses Long-term Threats to the Economy" (with James W. Brock), *Detroit Free Press*, January 29, 1990; reprinted in *Congressional Record*.

"Mergeritis: Another American Addiction" (with James W. Brock), *Challenge*, March/April 1990.

"Oil Industry's Grip on Markets" (with James W. Brock), *Cincinnati Enquirer*, August 17, 1990.

"Efficiency, Corporate Power and the Bigness Complex" (with James W. Brock), *Journal of Economic Education*, Winter 1990.

"The Sherman Act and the Economic Power Problem" (with James W. Brock), *Antitrust Bulletin*, Spring 1990.

"Speculative Capitalism Just A Shell Game" (with James W. Brock), *Denver Post*, April 9, 1990.

"The Political Economy of Antitrust Exemptions" (with James W. Brock), *Washburn Law Journal*, Winter 1990.

"Mergers and Economic Performance: The Experience Abroad" (with James W. Brock), *Review of Industrial Organization*, Summer 1990.

"Joint Ventures, Antitrust, and Transnational Cartelization" (with James W. Brock), *Northwestern Journal of International Law & Business*, Winter 1991.

"Do We Need a Global-Style Airline Monopoly?" (with James W. Brock), *Atlanta Journal & Constitution*, January 16, 1991.

"Pareto Optimality and Antitrust Policy: The Old Chicago and the New Learning" (with James W. Brock), *Southern Economic Journal*, July 1991.

"The Antitrust Vision and Its Revisionists Critics" (with James W. Brock), *New York Law Review*, Fall 1991.

"*Dangerous Pursuits* v. Dr. Pangloss and Associates" (with James W. Brock), *New York Law Review*, Fall 1991.

Index

JAMES W. BROCK is Bill R. Moeckel Professor of Economics and Business at Miami University in Oxford, Ohio. He is coauthor (with Walter Adams) of *The Bigness Complex, Dangerous Pursuits: Mergers and Acquisitions in the Age of Wall Street,* and *Antitrust Economics on Trial: A Dialogue on the New Laissez-Faire.* His Ph.D. is from Michigan State University.

KENNETH G. ELZINGA is Professor of Economics at the University of Virginia, where he has received the Alumni Association Distinguished Professor Award and the Z Society Outstanding Teacher Award. A former Special Economic Assistant to the head of the Antitrust Division and president of the Southern Economic Association, most recently he was Thomas Jefferson Visiting Scholar, Downing College, Cambridge University. He is the coauthor (with William Breit) of *The Antitrust Penalties,* and *The Fatal Equilibrium.* His Ph.D. is from Michigan State University.